990点を取るた

JN037038

TOEIC® L&R TEST 990点徹底 スピードマスター

山内　勇樹
Yamauchi Yuki

Jリサーチ出版

はじめに

TOEIC 990点満点は、実用的価値というよりは一つの「ステータス」と私は捉えています。英語力や努力できることをわかりやすく示す指標になり、TOEIC受験者や英語教育の関連事業に携わる人の中でも一目置かれるようになります。そして英語教育者にとっては、特にTOEICを教える上で必須であると言えるでしょう。

TOEICを教える私自身もそのスコアを保有していますし、生徒さんをこのスコア取得に導いてきました。また満点保有者に何人もお会いしましたが、実は彼ら・彼女らの実際の英語力はバラバラです。スピーキングについていえば、ネイティブ級に話せる人もいますが、全く話せない人もいます。語彙レベルも（TOEICレベルでは皆ありますが）それ以上、それ以外の範囲においてはネイティブを超えるレベルの人もいれば、制限がある人もいます。仕事はどうかというと、TOEIC 990点を持っている人が絶対に英語でバリバリ仕事ができるかというと、そうとは言い切れず、満点を持っていなくても、英語でバリバリ仕事ができる人はいます。つまりTOEIC 990点といってもその人の英語力には幅があるわけです。

TOEICは、900点を超えたあたりから人によってはいわば「余興」となり、950点を超えたあたりからは「こだわり」になります。満点へのこだわりです。取る必要もないが、ここまで来たら取りたい、取ってみせる、頂上への旅路のようなものです。

この書籍は、満点へのこだわりを持ち、TOEIC の頂上を目指す方のための本です。頂点に達したならば、あなたも満点達成者の「ステータスホルダー」の仲間入りです。そこまでお連れするのがこの書籍の唯一の目的です。

　この書籍では、頂きに達するために、通常よりも負荷が高いエキセサイズ、難易度が高い問題がたくさん用意されています。「こんなに難しい、ひねった、いじわるな問題は TOEIC ではでないでしょ！」という問題を、高地トレーニングの意味をこめて、あえてたくさん入れています。通り抜けることであなたの実力は確実に上がります。また、時間はかかるかもしれませんが、努力を続ける限り、いつか頂点に達することを保証します。

Let's get the journey started!

山内 勇樹

目 次

第3章

990点満点を取るためだけの **正答ハイテクレッスン！** ········ 239

第4章

990点満点を取るためだけの **ハイレベル完全模試！** ·········· 263

別　冊

990点満点を取るためだけの **ハイレベル完全模試！**
問題冊子

本書の使い方

第1章 990点満点を取るためだけの 英語脳徹底トレーニング

Point
英語の全てを知る必要はありませんが、TOEICで満点を取るに足りる英語力は存在します。基盤となる英語力が弱ければ990点を取ることはできません。高得点になればなるほど、英語力の向上に時間をかける必要があります。

英語脳徹底トレーニング

part別に特別トレーニングを行うことで、990点を取るために必要な高い英語力を身につけることができます。

Part1 写真描写問題

英語脳 徹底 トレーニング法①
正解例を自分で作る

Goal 》 写真の隅々まで英語で言えるようになる

Part1では、写真のどの部分が説明されても正解できるスキルが必要です。一切の聞き漏らしを防ぐことが、Part1全問題正解につながります。

例題
写真を見て、正解となる英文を例に倣って3個挙げよ。

例題

「英語脳徹底トレーニング」の例題を先に確認し、トレーニングの概要を理解しましょう。

1. The man is using a calculator.
2. Some documents are placed on the desk.
3. Some files are pushed against glass windows.

Point
電卓を使用している男性や、テーブルの上にある物以外についても、描写できるようにしよう！

トレーニングを実践！

「例題」でトレーニング方法を理解したら、早速実践に入ります。指示を確認し、音声やキーワードなどを参考にしながらトレーニングします。

トレーニングを実践！

練習問題 1

写真を見て、正解となる英文を例に倣って3個挙げよ。

- 例 A mug is placed next to an electronic device.
- 例 The glass windows are striped.
- 例 The man is pointing at the screen.

1. _____
2. _____
3. _____

Keywords
□ **glasses** めがね　□ **documents** 文書　□ **graphs** グラフ　□ **next to** となりに　□ **striped** しま模様の

解答例 / 正解と解説

トレーニングした問題の解答例や正解・解答を確認し、改善点を把握しましょう。解けなかった部分を理解し、繰り返し解くことが上達の秘訣です。

練習問題の解答例　写真を描写している英文の解答例を掲載しています。

練習問題 1

① One of the men is wearing glasses.
　男性の1人は眼鏡をかけている。

② Some documents are placed on the desk.
　幾つかの書類が机の上に置かれている。

③ Some graphs are shown on the report.
　グラフが幾つかレポートに載っている。

④ Some charts are included in the report.
　チャートが幾つかレポートに含まれている。

⑤ Three people are sitting next to each other.
　3人が隣同士に座っている。

⑥ They are facing the same direction.
　彼ら・彼女らは同じ方向を見ている。

⑦ The glass wall encloses the space.
　ガラスの壁が部屋を仕切っている。

⑧ They are discussing something.
　彼ら・彼女らは何かを協議している。

第2章 990点満点を取るためだけの 高難度問題の徹底攻略

Point

「英語力が上がる＝満点が取れる」というわけではありません。難しい問題に対しても正解が重ねる力を身につけるために、part別に実戦形式で高難易度の問題に取り組んでいきます。第一章で増強した英語力をスコアに転換するための具体的な練習の場となります。

絶対に押さえたい満点ポイント

part別で高得点者が落としやすい「高難度問題」や身につけるべきポイントを学ぶことができます。

Part1 写真描写問題

絶対に押さえたい満点ポイント①
受け身の英文を瞬時に理解する

Part 1 で特に気をつけたい問題は、「現在進行形受け身」と「現在完了形受け身」が使われている英文です。このような Part 1 に独特な文法を徹底的にマスターしましょう。

◆ 現在進行形受け身・現在完了形受け身の問題

TOEIC Part 1 では、「現在進行形受け身」や「現在完了形受け身」が使われている選択肢もあります。こうした表現には TOEIC 独特なものもあり、日常生活でよく使う表現・文ではないものもあるのですが、実際にテストで出る表現なので、理解した上で慣れておかなければいけません。

例えば、この写真では、以下のような選択肢も正解として扱われています。

例題 (12) 🇨🇦 w

例題

「絶対に押さえたい満点ポイント」で出てきた問題の具体例が出題されます。イメージをつかんで、実際の試験でもパターンを見抜けるようになりましょう。

高難度問題にトライ！
各partの「高難度問題」ばかりを集めた練習問題にチャレンジしましょう。

高難度問題にトライ！

本番と同じ問題数、6問を用意しました。全問正解してください！

 M

練習問題1

Ⓐ Ⓑ Ⓒ Ⓓ

正解と解説
「高難度問題」の正解を確認し、改善点を把握しましょう。「解説」も読み込むことで、解けなかった部分を理解し、繰り返し解きましょう。

練習問題2 **正解** C

(A) The man is putting away a microscope.
(B) The man has separated the specimen.
(C) Some stones have been placed on the scale.
(D) A microscope is being displayed for examination.

(A) 男性は顕微鏡を片付けている。
(B) 男性は標本を分けた。
(C) 幾つかの石がはかりに載せられている。
(D) 顕微鏡は検査のために展示されている。

解説 写真右手に、2つの石がはかりに乗せられているため(C)が正解。写真の全体の中ではマイナーな箇所ではありますが、一瞬でくまなく写真を捉えて反応できるようにしておくことが肝要。

練習問題3 **正解** C

(A) The woman is clearing up dishes.
(B) The woman has is holding a dish above some bread.
(C) Some glasses are positioned next to each other.
(D) The silverware is being washed by the woman.

第3章 990点満点を取るためだけの 正答ハイテクレッスン

Point

英語力、解答力に加え、技術的な要素でスコアを上げることも微量ながら可能です。第3章では、テクニック的な面で、より多くの正解を重ねていく方法を紹介します。

正答ハイテクレッスン
1問も落とさないための、試験テクニックを5つ学ぶことができます。

正答ハイテクレッスン①
写真に大きく写っているものが英文で流れたら、選択肢から外せ

対象 》Part 1

> 英文がうまく聞き取れなかったとき、写真にあからさまに写っているもの・人に関する英単語を含んだ選択肢を選んでしまいがちですが、その選択肢は選ばないようにしましょう。

◆ わかりやすい英単語を含んだ選択肢は ひっかけ問題の可能性が高い

例えばドアの前に人が立っている、以下のような写真があったとします。

例題

例題
試験テクニックを実践できる問題を例題として用意。解説も読み込み、テクニックの使い方を学びましょう。

テクニックの注意点！
テクニックを正しく使用し、得点につなげるための注意事項も紹介！

テクニックの注意点！

・Part 1で、写真があからさまに大きく表示されているものはひっかけが多い、と心得ておこう！
・聞き取れれば中身を検討して答えるべき！

Point

特に難易度が高い問題で構成されている模試です。過去の統計上、正解率が低い問題や、難易度が高い問題が多めに盛り込まれています。テストで難しい問題が来てもテンポよく解き進められる力を養っていきましょう。

2.

ハイレベル完全模試

高難度問題ばかりを集めた、完全模試1回分に挑戦！ 英語力・解答力をさらに高め、990点満点への総まとめができます。

GO ON TO THENEXT PAGE →

3

Part 1 写真描写問題

1 正解 A

(000) 🇨🇦 W

(A) Vehicles are coming out of a tunnel.

(B) The traffic goes in one direction.

(C) The tunnels are blocked by the trees.

(D) The trees are being trimmed.

(A) 車両がトンネルから出てきています。

(B) 交通が同一方向に向かっています

(C) トンネルは木々で塞がれています。

(D) 木々は刈り込まれています。

(A) 00.0%

(B) 00.0%

(C) 00.0%

(D) 00.0%

解説 トンネルから出てきている場合は coming out of、入っていっている場合には going into が使われます。ここでは車両が出てきていることを表す (A) が正解。

Vocabulary
□ **trim** 刈り取る

正解と解説

全問題に正答までの解説と TOEIC 学習者の平均回答率も併せて収録。正答率も繰り返し解くことで、実力も大幅に UP！

音声内容・音声ダウンロードについて

◆音声内容

第1章 英語脳徹底トレーニング！　Part 1 〜 4
第2章 高難度問題の徹底攻略！　Part 1 〜 4
第3章 正答ハイテクレッスン　①〜④
第4章 ハイレベル完全模試1回分　全PartのDirections+Part 1 〜 4の問題文

◆音声ダウンロードについて

上記の音声が無料でダウンロードできます。ダウンロードの方法は、以下のとおりです。

STEP 1 商品ページにアクセス！　方法は次の3通り！

❶ QRコードを読み取ってアクセス。

ダイレクトにアクセス

❷ https://www.jresearch.co.jp/book/b597368.html を入力してアクセス。

ダイレクトにアクセス

❸ Jリサーチ出版のホームページ（https://www.jresearch.co.jp/）にアクセスして、「キーワード」に書籍名を入れて検索。

ホームページから商品ページへ

STEP 2 ページ内にある「音声ダウンロード」ボタンをクリック！

STEP 3 ユーザー名「1001」、パスワード「25458」を入力！

STEP 4 音声の利用方法は2通り！　学習スタイルに合わせた方法でお聴きください！

❶ 「音声ファイル一括ダウンロード」より、ファイルをダウンロードして聴く。

❷ ▶ボタンを押して、その場で再生して聴く。

※ダウンロードした音声ファイルは、パソコン・スマートフォンなどでお聴きいただくことができます。
　一括ダウンロードの音声ファイルは.zip 形式で圧縮してあります。解凍してご利用ください。ファイルの解凍が上手く出来ない場合は、直接の音声再生も可能です。

音声ダウンロードについてのお問合せ先
toiawase@jresearch.co.jp（受付時間：平日9時〜18時）

序章

990点満点を取るためだけの 心 得

990点満点を取るためには、いったいどの程度の能力が求められるのでしょうか。

本章では990点満点を取るために必要なスキルやマインド、また本書の990点満点へのアプローチをご紹介します。

◆ TOEIC 満点取得のために必要な条件とは？

そもそもTOEIC990点を取るとは、どういうことでしょうか。満点というのは、理論上は誰にでも可能です。ランダムに回答しても、$1 / (4^{175} \times 3^{25})$ の確率で満点が取れます。ばかげた数字ですね。実質不可能です。私たち上級者の場合は、多くの問題で確信を持って答えを選べる一方、スピードについていけない、理解が不十分、集中力の欠如などで、予想で回答する状況が発生すれば、確率の話が適用されることになります。

仮に3問失点しても満点を取れるテスト回だとします。4つの問題を予想で答えると、あなたが満点を取れる確率は7割弱となります。予想で答える問題が5つ、6つ、7つと増えるにつれ、満点が取れる確率が急激に下がっていきます。

このレベルでは、満点への実現性は極めて低いと言えます。ここで、「満点を取るための前提条件」が見えてきます。990点満点を取るための前提条件はこれです。

予想(guess)で答える問題を4問以内に抑える

あなたはTOEIC受験の際、何問予想で答えていますか。「これが正解だ」と自信を持って選べている問題以外は、すべて予想扱いとします。予想で答えている問題が5～10個以内であれば、現実的に半年程度で満点は狙えるでしょう。10～15個程度あるのであれば、半年から1年といったところでしょう。それ以上予想解答があるのであればスタートラインに立っているとは言えません。スタートラインに立っている人は早速スタートしましょう!

◆ TOEIC満点を取るのに求められる要素

TOEIC満点達成に必要な要素は以下の通りです。

スキル編：○英語力(語彙、文法)

　　　　　○TOEICの問題傾向への慣れ

　　　　　○速読するスキル

姿勢・マインド編：●テスト中の雑念を捨てること

　　　　　　　●自分は上級者なんだという自負を捨てること

上の3要素は「スキル」で、下の黒マルの2要素は心理的な要因です。

　最初の英語力は、詳細は割愛しますが、abilities measured において語彙と文法のバーができれば両方100ほしいです。

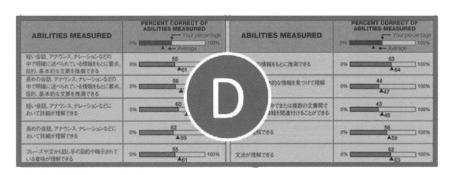

※一般社団法人　国際ビジネスコミュニケーション協会　TOEIC公式ページより」

　TOEIC問題への慣れ、についてですが、TOEICの独特な特徴があるので、その特徴を理解し、その上で練習しておくことが大事です。例えば

Part 2 で、問いかけに対して直接回答ではなく間接回答が多く見られますが、このパターンを把握していくのは有益です。

速読できるかどうか、ここが最後のワンプッシュの明暗を分けるでしょう。Part 3, 4 においては先読みできると正解は重ねやすくなります。Part 6, 7 で読む文章の量は多いので、素早く読み進めていかなければ時間切れになります。特に、表面的に読む速読ではなく、意味をちゃんと取りながら読むスピードを速めていくことが求められます。

雑念についてですが、集中力の重要性には誰も反対はないでしょう。一瞬違うこと考えていて何単語か聞き逃した、ということがあれば、どんなエキスパートでも正解できなくなってしまいます。前述の運ゲーになってしまいます。上級者になってくると、リスニング力がないから間違えた、というよりは、注意して聞いていなかったから失点した、という割合が増えてきます。満点を取るならこの手の失点は No です。

最後に自負の放棄についてです。中途半端な自負は真摯に取り組む姿勢への弊害になります。勘違いなきよう。自信を持つなということではありません。自分に自信は持ちつつ、自分の成長を妨げる自負は捨てましょうということです。

以上の5つを理解することで、最速で走れる挑戦者になれると私は考えます。これであなたも990点を達成する準備ができました。一緒に本書で990点を取れるようになりましょう。

リスニングの音声を聞くときは、
ヘッドフォンを使わない

　リスニング練習で音声を聞くときは、ヘッドフォンやイヤフォンで聞かずに、スピーカーから音声を聞くようにしましょう。

　TOEICの試験本番では、必ずスピーカーから音声が流れます。ヘッドフォン、イヤフォンでは、音は途中の空気での音質劣化なくそのまま耳に入るので聞きやすいのですが、スピーカーからの音質は劣化します。質だけではなく、音の強度の低下もありますし、壁・床からの反響音（diffraction）もあります。結果として、音がぼやけた印象になり、聞き取りづらくなります。

　これが本番の音声の特徴です。更には、部屋の中で聞こえる環境ノイズは本来あるものです。テスト中もあります。ヘッドフォンやイヤフォンでは、こうしたノイズの悪影響が最小化されてしまいます。より有利にリスニングできるヘッドフォンやイヤフォンではなく、スピーカーから音声を聞くようにしましょう！

英語力と集中力が
満点取得のカギを握る

　990点満点に必要なのは究極的には英語力と集中力です。もちろん問題への慣れ、パターン理解なども重要な要素ですが、いかにそれらが優れていたとしても、英語力と集中力がなければ満点にはたどり着きません。

　TOEICの超上級者でも、「今日は集中できなかった問題がいくつかあって取りこぼした」、という体験はしばしば起こります。これは実は、「集中できなかった」というよりも、「聞こえるはずと思っている音が聞きにくく感じる」ことを、「集中力が足りていないためだ」と考えてしまいがちなのではないかと私は考えています。

　同じ音源なら、離れた場所にあるスピーカーからの音声の方が数段聞き取りづらいものです。現実に沿った、現実的なリスニング練習をしていきましょう！

学びとは、自分で考え、
自分で調べるものだ

　本書は読み手を選びます。まず、タイトルどおり990点満点を目指す人へ向けた本です。990点を「本気で」目指していないという場合であれば、本書はあまり推奨できません。

　次に、テクニックだけで990点は取れないことも断言しておきます。そのため、自分の英語力のトレーニングは行わず、小手先でどうにか満点を出したいという人には、本書は合わないでしょう。

　何より重要なこととして、能動的学習について具体的な話をします。本書の構成や特長を考えた末、日本語訳をつけることにしました。成長を促す教育的目的でつけたのではなく、あれば心理的に安心できるだろうという、心理的理由でつけたものになります。これは多くの990点のための書籍執筆者や、実際の達成者にも共感してもらえることだと思いますが、「英語のテストで990点取りたいのに日本語訳がないと解決ができない」という受験者がいれば、その受験者は990点を目指せるステージにはいない、と言わざるを得ません。

　答えの解説も同様です。解説というのは、本来は990点満点を目指す方々には必要のないものだと考えています。なぜそれが正解なのか、なぜこれは誤答なのか、懇切丁寧な説明を与えられなくても、自分で聞き・読み直して、自分で考えて、自分で調べて、そうして解決できるはずです。

　990点を目指す私たち上級者には、自ら考え、自ら調べ、自ら学ぶという姿勢が最も重要です。本書は990点満点を目指す人のために本気で作った本です。効率よく、しかし甘えず、成長に楽しみを感じつつ、しかし自分に厳しく、990点達成のために一緒に進んで行きましょう。

第1章

990点満点を取るためだけの
英語脳徹底トレーニング

990点満点を取るために必ず必要な英語力は、確かに存在します。基盤となる英語力が弱ければ990点を取ることはできません。目標値が高得点になればなるほど、英語力の向上に時間をかける必要があります。

各Partのトレーニング方法について

まず第1章では、TOEICの問題を解くうえでベースとなる英語力（瞬時に英語の意味を把握する力）を強化していきます。読者の方は、既に英語上級者だと思いますので、初中級レベルの内容は省き、核心の部分のみで構成し、効率よく進めていきます。以下の順番で進めます。

Part 1 専用トレーニング

写真描写の例文を自分で作る

Part 1では、写真に写っているどの部分が出題されても正解できるスキルが必要です。ひっかけ選択肢に惑わされず、正解が選べるようトレーニングを積みます。

Part 2 専用トレーニング

シャドーイング

Part 2では、上級者であれば、質問に対して素直に返答する「ストレート」な問題は難なく正解を重ねられますので、間接的な応答を、状況把握しながら選べるかというのがポイントになります。間接的な応答を攻略するために、1単語も聞き漏らさない高い集中力と英語力を身につけることが不可欠です。そのためにはシャドーイングの練習は効果的でしょう。

Part 3&4専用トレーニング

問題文の先読み＆音声を聴きながら答える

Part 3&4 では、問題文を先に読み、流れる音声から即座に正解を選ぶことが求められます。問題を先に読むスキルの徹底強化と、聞く力そのものを上げる練習をします。

Part 5&6専用トレーニング

正答数無制限の６択問題

Part 5&6で出題される文法や単語は限られています。上級者でも間違いやすい文法項目や語いを攻略するため、通常のTOEICより難しい条件で、取りこぼしがないようにトレーニングを行います。

Part 7専用トレーニング

読解力養成

Part 7 が分かれ目です。Readingセクションはここで最終的な勝負がつきます。一定の速さと理解度で読み進めていける読解力をここで向上させます。テスト本番では、長文問題の配点が大きいため、ここで満点が出る・出ないの決定的な部分が分かれます。

Part1 写真描写問題

英語脳 徹底 トレーニング法①
正解例を自分で作る

Goal 》写真の隅々まで英語で言えるようになる

> Part1では、写真のどの部分が説明されても正解できるスキルが必要です。一切の聞き漏らしを防ぐことが、Part1全問題正解につながります。

例 題

写真を見て、正解となる英文を
例に倣って3個挙げよ。

1. The man is using a calculator.

2. Some documents are placed on the desk.

3. Some files are pushed against glass windows.

Point
電卓を使用している男性や、テーブルの上にある物以外についても、
描写できるようにしよう！

トレーニングを実践！

練習問題1

写真を見て、正解となる英文を例に
倣って3個挙げよ。

例 A mug is placed next to an
electronic device.

例 The glass windows are striped.

例 The man is pointing at the screen.

1. _____

2. _____

3. _____

Keywords
□ **glasses** めがね　□ **documents** 文書　□ **graphs** グラフ　□ **next to** となりに　□ **striped** しま模様の

練習問題2

写真を見て、正解となる英文を例に
倣って3個挙げよ。

例 Each person is working individually.

例 People are seated on the chairs.

例 The screens are reflecting some
images.

1. _____

2. _____

3. _____

Keywords
□ **cabinets** キャビネット　□ **window** 窓　□ **computers** コンピューター
□ **office supplies** オフィス用品　□ **under** 下に

練習問題3 写真を見て、正解となる英文を5個挙げよ。

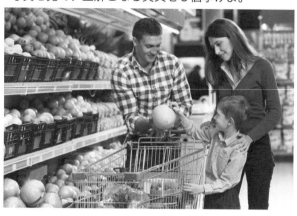

1. _____

2. _____

3. _____

4. _____

5. _____

Keywords
☐ **shopping cart** 買い物カート　☐ **hold** 持つ　☐ **shoulders** 肩　☐ **fruit** 果物　☐ **display** 陳列する

練習問題4 写真を見て、正解となる英文を5個挙げよ。

1. _____
2. _____
3. _____
4. _____
5. _____

Keywords
☐ **install** 設置する　☐ **protective gear** 防護具　☐ **reach for** 〜 〜に手を伸ばす
☐ **attach** 取り付ける　☐ **ceiling** 天井

練習問題5　写真を見て、正解となる英文を5個挙げよ。

1. _____
2. _____
3. _____
4. _____
5. _____

Keywords
☐ **attendees** 参加者　☐ **reflect** 反射する　☐ **glasses** コップ　☐ **point at** 〜 〜を指差す
☐ **enclosed** 囲まれている

第1章 英語脳徹底トレーニング

第2章 高難度問題の徹底攻略

第3章 正答ハイテクレッスン

第4章 ハイレベル完全模試

練習問題6 写真を見て、正解となる英文を5個挙げよ。

1. _____
2. _____
3. _____
4. _____
5. _____

Keywords
☐ **blinds** ブラインド ☐ **flowers** 花 ☐ **long-sleeved** 長袖 ☐ **folder** フォルダー
☐ **empty space** 空いているスペース

練習問題7 写真を見て、正解となる英文を5個挙げよ。

1. _____

2. _____

3. _____

4. _____

5. _____

Keywords
☐ **fabrics** 布　☐ **cloth** 布地　☐ **textile** 織物、布地　☐ **warehouse** 倉庫　☐ **commodity** 商品

練習問題8　写真を見て、正解となる英文を5個挙げよ。

1. _____

2. _____

3. _____

4. _____

5. _____

Keywords
☐ **railing** 手すり　☐ **water** 湖、海　☐ **leaning against** 〜 〜に寄りかかっている
☐ **in the distance** 遠くに

第1章　英語脳徹底トレーニング

第2章　高難度問題の徹底攻略

第3章　正答ハイテクレッスン

第4章　ハイレベル完全模試

練習問題の解答例 写真を描写している英文の解答例を掲載しています。

練習問題1

① One of the men is wearing glasses.
男性の1人は眼鏡をかけている。

② Some documents are placed on the desk.
幾つかの書類が机の上に置かれている。

③ Some graphs are shown on the report.
グラフが幾つかレポートに載っている。

④ Some charts are included in the report.
チャートが幾つかレポートに含まれている。

⑤ Three people are sitting next to each other.
3人が隣同士に座っている。

⑥ They are facing the same direction.
彼ら・彼女らは同じ方向を見ている。

⑦ The glass wall encloses the space.
ガラスの壁が部屋を仕切っている。

⑧ They are discussing something.
彼ら・彼女らは何かを協議している。

⑨ The room is occupied by three people.
部屋は3人によって占有されている。

⑩ Two of them are holding pens.
彼ら・彼女らのうち2人はペンを持っている。

⑪ People are resting their elbows on the desk.
皆ひじを机についている。

⑫ The woman is wearing a jacket.
女性はジャケットを着ている。

⑬ Two of them are wearing a striped tie.
2人はしまのネクタイをしている。

練習問題2

① The room is filled with many people.
部屋には多くの人がいる。

② Cabinets are placed between workers.
働いている人たちの間にキャビネットが置かれている。

③ A bag is put under the desk.
カバンが机の下に置かれている。

④ One of the windows is open.
窓の1つが開いている。

⑤ Some office supplies are placed on the desk.
オフィス器具が机の上に置かれている。

⑥ They are sitting in front of computers.
人々はパソコンの前に座っている。

練習問題3

① Food items are being displayed.
食料品が陳列されている。

② Some items have been put into a shopping cart.
一部の商品はショッピングカートに入れられている。

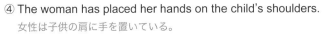

③ The cart is filled with some products.
カートは幾つかの商品で埋められている。

④ The woman has placed her hands on the child's shoulders.
女性は子供の肩に手を置いている。

⑤ Fruit is in baskets.
果物はバスケットに入れられている。

Point
fruit（果物）は不可算名詞で用いるため、some fruits ではなく some fruit となります（量ではなく、種類がたくさんあるときのみ many fruits が可能）。一方で野菜（vegetable）は可算名詞で通常 some vegetables とします。

⑥ The man is handing produce to the child.
　男性は子供に農作物を手渡している。

⑦ A few rows of shelves hold many vegetables.
　数列の棚にはたくさんの野菜が入っている。

⑧ Some fruit is piled on top of one another.
　幾つかの果物はお互いの上に置かれている。

⑨ The boxes on the shelves contain a lot of fruits.
　棚の箱にはたくさんの果物が入っている。

⑩ Some produce is being examined.
　農作物は検品されている。

練習問題4

① A camera is being installed on the ceiling.
　天井にカメラが設置されている。

② The man is wearing a helmet.
　男性はヘルメットをかぶっている。

③ The man is wearing protective gear.
　男性は保護具を身に着けている。

④ A camera has been attached to the ceiling.
　天井にはカメラが取り付けられている。

⑤ The man is reaching for a camera.
　男性はカメラに手を伸ばしている。

⑥ The man is holding a tool in his right hand.
　男性は右手に道具を持っている。

⑦ The man is reaching for the device on the ceiling.
　男性は天井の装置に手を伸ばしている。

⑧ The sleeves of his shirt have been rolled up.
　彼のシャツの袖はまくり上げられている。

⑨ The camera is overlooking the space.
　カメラはスペースを見下ろしている。

⑩ The door of the space is closed.
　そのスペースのドアは閉まっている。

練習問題5

① A presentation is being given.
プレゼンテーションが行われている。

② A graph is being used for a talk.
グラフが会話のために使われている。

③ All the attendees are facing the same direction.
全ての参加者は同じ方向を向いている。

④ Attendees are listening to the presentation.
参加者はプレゼンテーションを聞いている。

⑤ Some glasses are on the desk.
幾つかのグラスが机の上にある。

⑥ A man is speaking in front of an audience.
男が聴衆の前で話している。

⑦ The glass desk is reflecting some objects.
ガラスの机は幾つかの物を反映している。

⑧ There is a building in the distance.
遠くに建物がある。

⑨ The room is enclosed by glass walls.
部屋はガラスの壁で囲まれている。

⑩ The man is pointing at some data.
男性は幾つかのデータを指している。

練習問題6

① The woman is answering a call.
女性が電話に出ている。

② Documents are scattered on the desk.
書類は机の上に散らばっている。

③ Lots of papers are organized in the folders.
たくさんの書類がフォルダにまとめられている。

④ Some flowers are placed near the windows.
幾つかの花は窓の近くに置かれている。

⑤ The blind is completely closed.
ブラインドは完全に閉じている。

⑥ The woman is resting her left elbow on the desk.
女性は左ひじを机の上に置いている。

⑦ She is looking down at some documents.
彼女は幾つかの文書を見下ろしている。

⑧ The woman is wearing a long-sleeved dress shirt.
女性は長袖のシャツを着ている。

⑨ A cord is connected to the telephone receiver.
コードは受話器に接続されている。

⑩ There is little empty space on the desk.
机の上にはほとんど空きスペースがない。

練習問題7

① Some fabrics are on display.
幾つかの布が展示されている。

② One of the women is touching the cloth.
女性の1人が布に触れている。

③ One of the women is pointing at the textile.
女性の1人が繊維製品を指している。

④ The woman is wearing a watch.
女性は時計を着けている。

⑤ The rack holds several fabrics.
ラックには幾つかの布がある。

⑥ There are rows of racks in the warehouse.
倉庫にはラックの列がある。

⑦ Some textiles are being displayed.
幾つかの生地が展示されている。

⑧ They are studying the textiles.
彼らは繊維製品を調べている。

⑨ They are standing next to a commodity.
彼らは商品の隣に立っている。

⑩ Some fabric sheets are overlapping.
幾つかの布シートは互いに重なり合っている。

練習問題8

① They are leaning on the railing.
   彼らは手すりに寄りかかっている。

② The bicycles are locked to the railings.
   自転車は手すりに固定されている。

③ They are standing by the water.
   彼らは水辺に立っている。

④ A wooden deck runs alongside the water.
   木製の通路は水辺に設置されている。

⑤ There is a mountain in the distance.
   遠くに山がある。

⑥ No boats are floating on the lake.
   湖にはボートが浮かんでいない。

⑦ Two people are standing side by side.
   2人が並んで立っている。

⑧ The bicycles are leaning against the handrail.
   自転車は手すりに寄りかかっている。

⑨ They are looking out toward the lake.
   彼らは湖に目を向けている。

⑩ A path runs along the water.
   道は水に沿ってある。

Part2　応答問題

英語脳 徹底 トレーニング法②
シャドーイング

Goal 》1単語も聞き逃さない集中力を身につける

> Part 2では1単語も聞き漏らさず聞くための集中力と高い英語力が求められます。この観点から有効なリスニング練習法は「シャドーイング」です。

シャドーイングとは？

　シャドーイングとは、流れた音声を1秒程度あとすぐに、流れた音声どおりに自分も話す練習法です。

　TOEIC上級者でも、一瞬の聞き逃し、気の緩みで試験中「あれっ、今なんて言ったの？」と問題文を聞き逃してしまうことはありえます。

　一字一句素早くリピートしていくシャドーイングを行うことで、正答につながるヒントを聞き逃すこともなくなります。

例 題

※初めは文を見ながらシャドーイングしましょう。

Could you print out 50 copies of this chart by 4 P.M.?
午後4時までにこのチャートを50部印刷してもらえますか？

(A) Yes, I think I can fix the device.
(A) はい、その機器を修理できると思います。

(B) Isn't that way more than we need?
(B) 必要な枚数よりかなり多くないですか。

(C) I will call the manager at around 7 P.M.
(C) 午後7時くらいにマネージャーに電話します。

Point
シャドーイングは単語単語に注意が向きすぎると、文章や会話全体が見えなくなってしまいます。全体の大意を理解しつつ、単語レベルでもついていく、というスタンスで練習しましょう。

トレーニングを実践！

SET1

 W M

次の音声（10問分）を聞いて、その場で即座にシャドーイングせよ。完璧にできなかった場合は完璧になるまで繰り返し練習すること。

① ※1つの問題文と3つの選択肢の音声が流れます。
② ※1つの問題文と3つの選択肢の音声が流れます。
③ ※1つの問題文と3つの選択肢の音声が流れます。
④ ※1つの問題文と3つの選択肢の音声が流れます。
⑤ ※1つの問題文と3つの選択肢の音声が流れます。
⑥ ※1つの問題文と3つの選択肢の音声が流れます。
⑦ ※1つの問題文と3つの選択肢の音声が流れます。
⑧ ※1つの問題文と3つの選択肢の音声が流れます。
⑨ ※1つの問題文と3つの選択肢の音声が流れます。
⑩ ※1つの問題文と3つの選択肢の音声が流れます。

SET 1解答

① Do you know his e-mail address?
彼のEメールアドレスを知っていますか。

(A) I think I have it on his business card.

(B) I prefer postal mail.

(C) I admire him.

(A) 彼の名刺に書いてあったと思うよ。

(B) 郵送がいいな。

(C) 彼を尊敬しています。

発音に注意！
□ **have it on** は「ハヴィロン」と音が繋がります。

② Do you prefer a window seat or an aisle seat?

席は窓側と通路側のどちらがいいですか。

(A) Yes, I would like to.	(A) はい、そうしたいです。
(B) Whichever is fine.	**(B) どちらでもいいです。**
(C) I'll take that.	(C) それにします。

発音に注意！
□ **an aisle seat** は「アナイ **L**」と音が繋がります。**L** は舌先を上の前歯の歯茎に当てて止めます。

③ When is the next meeting?

次の会議はいつですか。

(A) It's in room 211.	(A) 211号室です。
(B) Mike and Susan will attend the meeting.	(B) マイクとスーザンが会議に出席します。
(C) Oh, wasn't it canceled?	**(C) それは中止になりませんでしたか。**

発音に注意！
□ **When is** は「ウェニズ」と音が繋がります。**wasn't** の **t** は発音されない場合があります。

④ Who opened this parcel?

誰がこの小包を開けましたか。

(A) It was sealed.	(A) それは封がされていました。
(B) My boss did.	**(B) 私の上司が開けました。**
(C) Not now.	(C) 今ではありません。

発音に注意！
□ **It was**，**Not now** の **t** はかすかに聞こえるくらいです。聞こえないこともあります。

⑤ Why was he absent from the meeting this evening?

なぜ彼は今日の夕方の会議にいなかったのですか。

(A) Thank you very much for your information.	(A) 教えてくださりありがとうございます。
(B) I don't think he is absent.	(B) 彼がいないとは思いません。
(C) Keiko suddenly gave him an urgent task.	**(C) ケイコが彼に突然緊急の仕事を与えました。**

発音に注意！
□ **gave him** は「ゲイヴィ **m**」と **him** の **h** が弱音化することがあります。

⑥ How many entries have you received so far for the opening?

そのポジションには何通応募がこれまで来ていますか。

(A) **Quite a few, I would say.**

(B) I entered the room because it was open.

(C) We are recruiting three marketers.

(A) とても多いです。

(B) その部屋は開いていたので入りました。

(C) 私たちはマーケッターを3人募集しています。

発音に注意！
□ **Quite a few** は **few** を少し強めにアクセントを置くと自然です。

⑦ I thought he had already retired.

彼は既に退職したと思っていました。

(A) I'm OK. I'm not tired.

(B) **I guess this week is his last week.**

(C) Will we hold a farewell party?

(A) 私は大丈夫です。私は疲れていません。

(B) **今週が彼の最終週だと思いますよ。**

(C) 私たちは送別会を行いますか。

発音に注意！
□ **hold a** は「ホーＬダ」と音が繋がります。

⑧ Aren't we going to the store to buy some office supplies?

事務用品を買うためにお店に行きませんか。

(A) **Yes, we are.**

(B) Where is your office?

(C) Do you like shopping?

(A) はい、行きますよ。

(B) あなたの事務所はどこですか。

(C) あなたは買い物が好きですか。

発音に注意！
□ **Aren't we** の **t** は発音されないこともあり、その場合「アーン ウィ」と聞こえます。

⑨ Who's responsible for the telephone calls from customers?

お客様からの電話は誰が担当ですか。

(A) That's mine.

(B) No, that's not true.

(C) **Anyone who is available.**

(A) それは私のものです。

(B) いいえ、それは真実ではありません。

(C) 対応可能なら誰でも。

発音に注意！
□ 文の形、意味から **who's** を **whose** と反応しないように注意。練習もしましょう。

⑩ Aren't you supposed to be in Chicago now?

あなたは今シカゴにいるはずではありませんでしたか。

(A) The convention was postponed.　(A) その会議は延期されました。

(B) You want to come with me?　(B) 私と一緒に来たいですか。

(C) He has already come back from Chicago.　(C) 彼は既にシカゴから帰ってきました。

発音に注意！

□ **supposed to** の **d** は次の **to** とくっついて「サポーＳトゥー」とします。

SET 2

次の音声（10問分）を聞いて、その場で即座にシャドーイングせよ。完璧にできなかった場合は完璧になるまで繰り返し練習すること。

① ※1つの問題文と3つの選択肢の音声が流れます。
② ※1つの問題文と3つの選択肢の音声が流れます。
③ ※1つの問題文と3つの選択肢の音声が流れます。
④ ※1つの問題文と3つの選択肢の音声が流れます。
⑤ ※1つの問題文と3つの選択肢の音声が流れます。
⑥ ※1つの問題文と3つの選択肢の音声が流れます。
⑦ ※1つの問題文と3つの選択肢の音声が流れます。
⑧ ※1つの問題文と3つの選択肢の音声が流れます。
⑨ ※1つの問題文と3つの選択肢の音声が流れます。
⑩ ※1つの問題文と3つの選択肢の音声が流れます。

SET 2解答

① Have you entered your password?
パスワードを入力しましたか。

(A) I'm already in the room.
(B) I forgot to bring my passport.
(C) Where can I find it?

(A) 私はすでに部屋にいます。
(B) パスポートを持ってくるのを忘れました。
(C) どこでわかりますか。

発音に注意！
□ **entered your** は「エンタージョア」と発音する場合もあります。**find it** はつなげて発音し、最後の **t** は聞こえるか聞こえないかくらいの弱い音になります。

② Why didn't you hire Mr. Carter?
なぜカーター氏を雇わなかったのですか。

(A) I'm not tired yet.
(B) He has not catered the service yet.
(C) He was not qualified.

(A) 私はまだ疲れていません。
(B) 彼はまだサービスを届けていません。
(C) 彼にはその資格がありませんでした。

発音に注意！
□ **not tired** は **t-t** が1つにくっつきます。**t** をはっきり2個分けて発音しないように。

③ Can I have a cup of coffee, please?

コーヒーを一杯いただけませんか。

(A) Yes, here's a copy of the document.　(A) はい、こちらがその書面のコピーになります。

(B) That'll be three dollars.　**(B) 3ドルになります。**

(C) She said she prefers the other one.　(C) 彼女は別の方が好きだそうです。

発音に注意！
□ **That'll be** に慣れましょう。聞こえるがままに発音しましょう。

④ Am I supposed to turn off the light?

私が電気を消すのでしょうか。

(A) I guess the battery is dead.　(A) 電池が切れていると思います。

(B) No, it's on your left-hand side.　(B) いいえ、それはあなたの左側にあります。

(C) I believe Marco is still here.　**(C) マルコがまだここにいると思いますよ。**

発音に注意！
□ アメリカ英語では **battery** の **tt** が **R** っぽくなりのようになり「バレリー」というように発音する場合が多いです。アクセントは頭に置きます。日本語ではバッテリーと末尾にアクセントを置くので注意です。

⑤ When will your team finish the report?

あなたのチームはいつレポートが終わりますか。

(A) We are doing our very best.　**(A) 私たちは最善を尽くしています。**

(B) Sure, let us do that for you.　(B) 勿論、あなたに代わってやりますよ。

(C) Since last Friday, I believe.　(C) 先週の金曜日からだと思います。

発音に注意！
□ **let us** は「レタ s」「レラ s」と音が繋がります。

⑥ Where can I attend the guest lecture?

ゲスト講演にはどこで参加できますか。

(A) My supervisor will make a speech.　(A) 私の上司がスピーチします。

(B) Welcome and be my guest!　(B) どうぞくつろいでください！

(C) You are talking to the wrong person.　**(C) 話しかける人を間違っていますよ。**

発音に注意！
□ **You are talking to** の **You are** は弱く速くさっと発音されることがあります。

⑦ Whom were you talking to on the phone?

誰と電話で話していたのですか。

(A) I don't think she is the right candidate.

(B) It's my brother's cell phone.

(C) It was just a voice message.

(A) 私は彼女が正しい候補だとは思いません。

(B) それは私の兄の携帯電話です。

(C) ただの留守番メッセージです。

発音に注意!
□ talking to on the phone の to on は完全につなげて発音しましょう。

⑧ I haven't watched the movie yet.

私はまだその映画を見ていません。

(A) It's not worth watching.

(B) Yes, I've watched the movie, too.

(C) I cannot agree more.

(A) 見る価値がないですよ。

(B) はい、私もその映画を見ました。

(C) 同感です。

発音に注意!
□ worth は 「ウォ」ではなく「ワ」です。また th は濁りません。worthy の場合は濁ります。

⑨ Weren't there any car part stores around here?

この辺りに自動車部品店はありませんか。

(A) I don't remember seeing one.

(B) I didn't need a carpet.

(C) Please check the drawer.

(A) 見た覚えがありません。

(B) 私はカーペットが必要ありませんでした。

(C) 引き出しを確認してください。

発音に注意!
□ car、part ともに 口が縦に開く R の発音です。口が閉じたままだと cur pert (生意気なのら犬) という音に近くなってしまいます。

⑩ Where is the telephone directory?

電話帳はどこですか。

(A) Our director is out of the office.

(B) It's on the bookshelf, I believe.

(C) Please drop me a line.

(A) 私たちの管理者は外出中です。

(B) それは本棚にあると思います。

(C) ご一報ください。

発音に注意!
□ directory は米英とも「ディ」で始め、direction, direct は米は「ディ」英は「ダイ」で始めることが多いです(地域、個人差あり)。

SET 3

次の音声（10問分）を聞いて、その場で即座にシャドーイングせよ。完璧にできなかった場合は完璧になるまで繰り返し練習すること。

① ※1つの問題文と3つの選択肢の音声が流れます。
② ※1つの問題文と3つの選択肢の音声が流れます。
③ ※1つの問題文と3つの選択肢の音声が流れます。
④ ※1つの問題文と3つの選択肢の音声が流れます。
⑤ ※1つの問題文と3つの選択肢の音声が流れます。
⑥ ※1つの問題文と3つの選択肢の音声が流れます。
⑦ ※1つの問題文と3つの選択肢の音声が流れます。
⑧ ※1つの問題文と3つの選択肢の音声が流れます。
⑨ ※1つの問題文と3つの選択肢の音声が流れます。
⑩ ※1つの問題文と3つの選択肢の音声が流れます。

SET 3解答

① Would you like to join us for dinner?
　私たちと一緒に夕食を食べませんか。

(A) Well, why not?　　　　　　　　　　**(A) 行きましょう。**
(B) The dining room is messed up.　　　(B) ダイニングルームはめちゃくちゃです。
(C) Oh, I didn't know that.　　　　　　　(C) 知りませんでした。

発音に注意！
□ join us は「ジョイナs」と音がつながります。

② Haven't you received the fax from the sales team?
　販売チームからファックスを受け取りませんでしたか。

(A) She knows nothing about that.　　　(A) 彼女はそれに関して何も知りません。
(B) Actually, we will send it today.　　(B) 実は、今日それを送ります。
(C) I'll go check it.　　　　　　　　　**(C) 確認してきます。**

発音に注意！
□ Haven't you は「チュー」と音が繋がります。

③ Why are you moving out of your current apartment?
　なぜ今のアパートから引っ越すのですか。

(A) I am expecting a ceremony for that.   (A) そのために式があると思います。

(B) I found a new job in Toronto.   **(B) トロントで新しい仕事を見つけました。**

(C) We belong to different departments.   (C) 私たちは違う部署に属しています。

発音に注意！
□ **out of your** は「アウトヴォア」「アウロヴォア」と聞こえます。

④ When is the conference supposed to start?

カンファレンスはいつ開始されるのですか。

(A) At the main conference center.   (A) メインカンファレンスセンターで。

(B) Yes, it will be held as planned.   (B) はい、それは計画通り行われます。

(C) I know it's about time, isn't it?   **(C) そろそろ時間ですよね？**

発音に注意！
□ **When is** は「ウェニズ」と音がつながります。冒頭でさりげなく速く発音されることが多いのでさりげなく速く発音する練習をしましょう。

⑤ How often do you see the vice manager?

どのくらいの頻度で副部長と会いますか。

(A) I frequently visit this district.   (A) 私はこの地区によく訪れます。

(B) This is out of the ordinary.   (B) これは普通ではありません。

(C) At least every other week.   **(C) 少なくとも隔週で。**

発音に注意！
□ **At least** の **least** は伸ばしましょう。伸ばさず発音すると **list** に近い音になります。

⑥ Can I make a to-go order?

持ち帰りの注文はできますか。

(A) Do you have a menu with you?   **(A) メニューはお持ちですか。**

(B) And I need two pairs of chopsticks.   (B) あと、箸が2膳必要です。

(C) That'll do for now.   (C) とりあえずそのくらいで。

発音に注意！
□ **That'll do for now** はよく使われる表現なのでそのまま音をまねしましょう。

⑦ How am I supposed to summarize the sales in the first quarter?

どのように第1四半期の売り上げを総括すべきですか。

(A) Yes, that's actually a marvelous idea.

(A) ええ、それは素晴らしい考えですね。

(B) You can make some graphs and tables.

(B) グラフと表を作るといいですよ。

(C) One-fourth of the data could have been lost.

(C) データの4分の1が失われたかもしれません。

発音に注意！
□ **could have been** は「クダ v ビー n」と音がつながります。

⑧ Should I talk to Mr. Smith or Mrs. Jones to discuss this problem?

この問題について話し合うためにスミス氏かジョーンズ氏どちらに話すべきですか。

(A) Either of them will be of help.

(A) どちらでも助けになるでしょう。

(B) It won't be too late.

(B) 遅すぎることはないでしょう。

(C) No, he is not familiar with it.

(C) いいえ、彼はそれに精通していません。

発音に注意！
□ **be of** ＋名詞の形に即座に反応できない人は多いようです。口で慣らしましょう。

⑨ Are you finding everything OK?

何かお探しでしょうか。

(A) Possibly now.

(A) おそらく今。

(B) Sorry, I don't have any.

(B) すみません、どれも持っていません。

(C) Where is the new arrival?

(C) 新商品はどこにありますか。

発音に注意！
□ **I don't have any** は「アイドンハヴェニー」と聞こえます。

⑩ We can cancel our booking, can't we?

私たちは予約をキャンセルできますよね。

(A) Please have the book closed.

(A) 本を閉じてください。

(B) I'm sorry, I cannot stop reading.

(B) すみません、読むのをやめられません。

(C) Yes, but an extra fee will apply.

(C) はい、ですが追加料金が適用されます。

発音に注意！
□ **but an** は「バタン」「バラン」と音がつながります。

Part3 会話問題　Part4 説明文問題

英語脳 徹底 トレーニング法③
問題文と選択肢の先読み練習

> Part 3 と Part 4 では、問題文と選択肢を先読みするスピード、そしてその内容を理解する瞬間読解力が求められます。

例 題

次の問題文と選択肢を、9割以上の理解度は保ちながら、20秒で全て読め。

▶制限タイム20秒

1. What are the two men discussing?
(A) Traveling abroad
(B) A work schedule
(C) Getting a roommate
(D) A sales training seminar

2. What will happen next Friday?
(A) There will be a sales training seminar.
(B) Visitors will come from the head office.
(C) Visitors will come from overseas.
(D) The friend's college roommate will visit.

3. What does the second man offer to do?

(A) Pick up the dealers at the airport

(B) Work late on Tuesday

(C) Come to work early on Tuesday

(D) Come to work on Sunday

》9割以上理解できているか、訳で確認！

1. What are the two men discussing?
   2人の男性は何について話していますか。

(A) Traveling abroad	(A) 海外旅行
(B) A work schedule	(B) 仕事の予定
(C) Getting a roommate	(C) ルームメイトを見つけること
(D) A sales training seminar	(D) セールストレーニングセミナー

2. What will happen next Friday?
   次の金曜日に何がありますか。

(A) There will be a sales training seminar.	(A) セールストレーニングセミナーがある。
(B) Visitors will come from the head office.	(B) 本社から訪問者が来る。
(C) Visitors will come from overseas.	(C) 海外から訪問者が来る。
(D) The friend's college roommate will visit.	(D) 友達の大学のルームメイトが訪問する。

3. What does the second man offer to do?
   2番目の男性は何をすると言っていますか。

(A) Pick up the dealers at the airport	(A) 取引相手を空港に迎えに行く
(B) Work late on Tuesday	(B) 火曜日遅く働く
(C) Come to work early on Tuesday	(C) 火曜日早く仕事しに来る
(D) Come to work on Sunday	(D) 日曜日仕事しに来る

1 次の問題文と選択肢を、9割以上の理解度は保ちながら、1分で全て読め。
　　（各セット20秒のペース×3セット）

▶制限タイム60秒

32. Why is the man talking to the woman?

(A) To report a result

(B) To ask for help

(C) To cancel an order

(D) To confirm a contract

33. What was ordered by the man?

(A) A mug

(B) A monitor

(C) A power cord

(D) A watch

34. According to the man, what was the store's mistake?

(A) They shipped a wrong order.

(B) They sent a direct mail.

(C) They delivered an item late.

(D) They processed a purchase order.

----

35. Where does this conversation take place?

(A) In a pharmacy

(B) In a gym

(C) In a restaurant

(D) In a doctor's room

36. What does the man recommend?

(A) Doing aerobics

(B) Swimming

(C) Both swimming and doing aerobics

(D) Neither swimming nor aerobics

37. When will the woman probably come back?

(A) In 5 days

(B) Sometime next month

(C) After she receives a call

(D) Tomorrow morning

----

38. What issue are the speakers talking about?

(A) There is a stain on the shirt.

(B) A store's style is outdated.

(C) There are few customers.

(D) The item is not attractive.

39. What does the woman propose?

(A) Trying the shirt on

(B) Removing the stain by herself

(C) Purchasing some other items

(D) Asking a staff member about the issue

40. What will the speakers do next?

(A) Go back home

(B) Call customer service

(C) Organize the interior

(D) Shop around for a shirt

》訳で確認！　―9割以上の理解度があるか確認しよう

32. Why is the man talking to the woman?
なぜ男性は女性に話しかけているのですか。

(A) To report a result　　　　　(A) 結果を報告するため
(B) To ask for help　　　　　　(B) 助けを借りるため
(C) To cancel an order　　　　　(C) 注文をキャンセルするため
(D) To confirm a contract　　　　(D) 契約を確認するため

33. What was ordered by the man?
男性は何を注文しましたか。

(A) A mug　　　　　　(A) マグカップ
(B) A monitor　　　　 (B) モニター
(C) A power cord　　　(C) 電源コード
(D) A watch　　　　　(D) 腕時計

34. According to the man, what was the store's mistake?
男性によると、その店の失敗は何でしたか。

(A) They shipped a wrong order.　　　(A) 間違った商品を送った。
(B) They sent a direct mail.　　　　 (B) ダイレクトメールを送った。
(C) They delivered an item late.　　　(C) 商品の配送が遅かった。
(D) They processed a purchase order.　(D) 購入依頼を処理した。

----

35. Where does this conversation take place?
この会話はどこでされていますか。

(A) In a pharmacy　　　　(A) 薬局で
(B) In a gym　　　　　　(B) ジムで
(C) In a restaurant　　　　(C) レストランで
(D) In a doctor's room　　(D) 診察室で

36. What does the man recommend?

男性は何を勧めていますか。

(A) Doing aerobics

(B) Swimming

(C) Both swimming and doing aerobics

(D) Neither swimming nor aerobics

(A) エアロビクス

(B) 水泳

(C) 水泳とエアロビクスどちらも

(D) 水泳とエアロビクスのどちらでもない

37. When will the woman probably come back?

いつその女性は帰ってきそうですか。

(A) In 5 days

(B) Sometime next month

(C) After she receives a call

(D) Tomorrow morning

(A) 5日以内に

(B) 来月のどこかで

(C) 電話が来たら

(D) 明日の朝

----

38. What issue are the speakers talking about?

何の問題について話者は話していますか。

(A) There is a stain on the shirt.

(B) A store's style is outdated.

(C) There are few customers.

(D) The item is not attractive.

(A) シャツにシミがある。

(B) 店のやり方が古い。

(C) 客がほとんどいない。

(D) 商品が魅力的でない。

39. What does the woman propose?

女性は何を提案していますか。

(A) Trying the shirt on

(B) Removing the stain by herself

(C) Purchasing some other items

(D) Asking a staff member about the issue

(A) シャツを試着すること

(B) 彼女自身がシミを取ること

(C) 違う商品を購入すること

(D) スタッフに問題について尋ねること

40. What will the speakers do next?

話者は次に何をするでしょう。

(A) Go back home

(B) Call the customer service

(C) Organize the interior

(D) Shop around for a shirt

(A) 家に帰る

(B) カスタマーサービスに電話する

(C) 内装を管理する

(D) シャツを買いに行く

2 次の問題文と選択肢を、9割以上の理解度は保ちながら、1分で全て読め。
（各セット20秒のペース×3セット）

▶制限タイム60秒

71. What is the purpose of the announcement?

(A) To inform people of the next event

(B) To stake out a seat

(C) To do some warm-ups

(D) To call off the show

72. According to the announcement, what will happen soon?

(A) Kids will run.

(B) A race will begin.

(C) It will become warmer and warmer.

(D) The event will end.

73. What were listeners urged to do?

(A) Secure a seat

(B) Warm up their body

(C) Give their kids a piggyback

(D) Make a road

- -

74. What is the purpose of the talk?

(A) To condemn the team

(B) To welcome a new member

(C) To collect a budget

(D) To recognize workers' contributions

75. What was limited in the previous project?

(A) Allotted time

(B) Product samples

(C) The number of workers

(D) Financial resources

76. What does the man mention about the next project?

(A) Many customers have already placed an order.

(B) They will have a larger property.

(C) It will be a pivotal achievement.

(D) They can overcome the problem.

----

77. Why is the speaker calling?

(A) To make an appointment

(B) To cancel a meeting

(C) To decline an offer

(D) To ask some questions

78. What is the primary concern of the woman?

(A) She has a time conflict.

(B) Some members cannot arrive on time.

(C) Some equipment is not ready.

(D) She does not have sufficient knowledge.

79. What will the speaker probably do tomorrow?

(A) Reschedule her appointment

(B) Talk to her friends

(C) Call her supervisor

(D) Find other suitable services

》**訳で確認！** ―9割以上の理解度があるか確認しよう

71. What is the purpose of the announcement?
    その告知の目的は何ですか。

    (A) To inform people of the next event　(A) 次のイベントについて人々に知らせるため

    (B) To stake out a seat　(B) 席を確保するため

    (C) To do some warm-ups　(C) ウォームアップをするため

    (D) To call off the show　(D) ショーの中止を知らせるため

72. According to the announcement, what will happen soon?
    その告知によると、もうすぐ何が起きますか。

    (A) Kids will run.　(A) 子どもたちが走る。

    (B) A race will begin.　(B) レースが始まる。

    (C) It will become warmer and warmer.　(C) どんどん暖かくなる。

    (D) The event will end.　(D) イベントが終わる。

73. What were listeners urged to do?
    聴者は何をするよう促されましたか。

    (A) Secure a seat　(A) 席を確保する

    (B) Warm up their body　(B) 体を温める

    (C) Give their kids piggyback　(C) 子どもを背中でおんぶする

    (D) Make a road　(D) 道を造る

- -

74. What is the purpose of the talk?
    話の目的は何ですか。

    (A) To condemn the team　(A) チームを非難するため

    (B) To welcome a new member　(B) 新メンバーを歓迎するため

    (C) To collect a budget　(C) 予算を集めるため

    (D) To recognize workers' contributions　(D) 労働者の貢献を称賛するため

75. What was limited in the previous project?
    前のプロジェクトでは何が制限されていましたか。

(A) Allotted time
(A) 割り当てられた時間

(B) Product samples
(B) 商品サンプル

(C) The number of workers
(C) 労働者の数

(D) Financial resources
(D) 財源

76. What does the man mention about the next project?
男性は次のプロジェクトについて何と言っていますか。

(A) Many customers have already placed an order.
(A) 多くのお客様が既に注文している。

(B) They will have a larger property.
(B) より大きな施設を使える。

(C) It will be a pivotal achievement.
(C) 大きな成果になるだろう。

(D) They can overcome the problem.
(D) 彼らは問題を克服できる。

----

77. Why is the speaker calling?
なぜ話者は電話していますか。

(A) To make an appointment
(A) 約束を取り付けるため

(B) To cancel a meeting
(B) 会議をキャンセルするため

(C) To decline an offer
(C) 申し出を断るため

(D) To ask some questions
(D) いくつか質問をするため

78. What is the primary concern of the woman?
女性の主な心配事は何ですか。

(A) She has a time conflict.
(A) 彼女は時間のバッティングがある。

(B) Some members cannot arrive on time.
(B) メンバーの何人かの到着が間に合わない。

(C) Some equipment is not ready.
(C) いくつかの部品が用意できていない。

(D) She does not have sufficient knowledge.
(D) 彼女には十分な知識がない。

79. What will the speaker probably do tomorrow?
話者は明日何をするでしょうか。

(A) Reschedule her appointment
(A) 予約をリスケジュールする。

(B) Talk to her friends
(B) 彼女の友達に話す。

(C) Call her supervisor
(C) 彼女の上司に電話する。

(D) Find other suitable services
(D) 他の適したサービスを見つける。

英語脳 徹底 トレーニング法④

音声を聴きながら問題を解く

> 長文リスニングをしながら問題に答えていく。これができなければ、次の問題文と選択肢を先読みするための十分な時間を確保することができません。理想は、長文が流れ終わったときには、3問全て答え終わっていることです。

例 題

次の問題セットを、音声を聞きながら答える形式で解け。常に問題文と選択肢は一通り「先読み」で速読を行うこと。また、音声が流れ終わったときには、全ての問題に答えていること。

※長文が流れ終わったときにスクリプトのリスニングが完了する必要があるため、選択肢の音声は収録されていません。

▶制限タイム55秒

Where are the speakers most likely working?

(A) At a clothes shop

(B) At a shoe store

(C) At a natural park

(D) At a stock market

What does the man propose?

(A) Sending some products to the woman

(B) Searching missing items online

(C) Contacting a different location for help

(D) Selling products as much as possible

What will the woman probably do?

(A) Call the largest branch in the region

(B) Recommend different sizes

(C) Call back the man later

(D) Recommend similar products

正解と解説

F: It's Noa Chapman from the Lakewood Mall. One of our customers is asking for size 11.0 for the product code 2178, the one without a shoelace, but the biggest one we have is 10.5. He is saying he doesn't mind waiting, and I was wondering if your store happens to have some of those.

M: It is fortunate that things are selling well there and also here as well, actually. But unfortunately, most of the business shoes are out of stock. Maybe you should call the store in Cerritos and see if they can help you. It's the biggest one around here, and they should be able to help you.

F: Thanks for the suggestion, but actually, I've called them just now. And they said I should call you. Well, it seems the best I can do is to recommend some similar ones.

女性：レイクウッド・モールのノア・チャップマンです。あるお客様が、商品コード2178のサイズ11.0、靴ひものないものをお求めなのですが、当店にある最大のものは10.5です。お客様は待ってもいいとおっしゃっているので、そちらのショップにその商品はあったりしますでしょうか。

男性：そちらでも、こちらでも商品がどんどん売れているのは幸いなことですね。ただ残念ながらビジネスシューズはほとんど在庫がありません。セリトスにある店舗に電話してみてはどうでしょうか。このあたりでは一番大きなお店ですから、きっと対応してくれるはずです。

女性：ご提案ありがとうございます、でも実はさっき電話してみたのです。そして、こちらに電話したほうがいいと言われていました。そうですね、私にできることは、似たようなものをいくつか薦めることくらいのようです。

Where are the speakers most likely working?

話者たちはどこで働いている可能性が高いですか。

(A) At a clothes shop

(B) At a shoe store

(C) At a natural park

(D) At a stock market

(A) 洋服屋さんで

(B) 靴屋さんで

(C) 自然公園で

(D) 株式市場で

What does the man propose?

男性は何を提案していますか。

(A) Sending some products to the woman

(B) Searching missing items online

(C) Contacting a different location for help

(D) Selling products as much as possible

(A) 女性に商品を送る

(B) 見つからない商品をネットで探す

(C) 別の場所に連絡して助けてもらう

(D) できるだけ商品を売る

What will the woman probably do?

女性はおそらく何をするでしょうか。

(A) Call the largest branch in the region

(B) Recommend different sizes

(C) Call back the man later

(D) Recommend similar products

(A) その地域で一番大きな支店に電話する

(B) サイズ違いを勧める

(C) 後ほど男性に再度電話する

(D) 似たような商品を薦める

解説　買い物に行くとよくある、サイズがないので他店に取り寄せ可能か確認してみます、という流れの会話です。最初のセリフで、shoelace（靴ひも）がないサイズ11.0のもの、と言っているので、ここが聞き取れれば靴屋さんということが分かります。ここでわからなくても、次の男性のセリフでビジネスシューズというヒントは出てきますが、最初の段階でキャッチできれば次の問題に後を引かずベストです。(C)の自然公園は、lake, woodなどの単語に、(D)株式市場は、stockという単語レベルでの誤反応を意図している選択肢で、引っかからないようにしましょう。2つ目の問題は、この地域で一番大きなセリトス店に問い合わせをしていることから、(C)が正解となります。3つ目の問題では、(B)の選択し、違うサイズ、に飛びつかないように注意です。違う似たような商品を薦めるのであって、違うサイズのものを薦めるわけではありませんので、(D)が正解です。

1

次の問題セットを、音声を聞きながら答える形式で解け。常に問題文と選択肢は一通り「先読み」で速読を行うこと。また、音声が流れ終わったときには、全ての問題に答えていること。

▶制限タイム90秒

41. What does the man need for his work?

(A) A fax machine

(B) Sales personnel

(C) A new job

(D) An invoice

42. Until what time can the man receive the fax?

(A) Until 19:00

(B) Until 20:00

(C) Until 21:00

(D) Until 22:00

43. What is the man asked to do after he receives the fax?

(A) E-mail the telephone operator

(B) E-mail John

(C) Fax the invoice

(D) Visit Chicago

正解と解説

M: **I just checked my mailbox, but I have not received the invoice from your office yet.** I would highly appreciate it if you could send it to me as soon as possible. **Without it, I cannot move on to the next step in my work.**

W: I understand your situation, but who did you talk to this matter? We have many salespeople, so I don't know who contacted your company.

M: Oh, I talked about this matter with John, but he may have forgotten about it. **I will be in my office until 9 P.M., so please send me the invoice by then.**

W: John is out of the office at the moment. He's in the Chicago branch today, so

I will have him fax you from there. **Please let me know by e-mail after you receive the fax.**

M：メールボックスをチェックしたばかりですが、まだ貴社から請求書を受け取っていません。お早めにお送りいただくようお願いします。それがないと、私は仕事の次のステップに進むことができません。

W：あなたの状況はわかりましたが、この件について誰とお話しされましたか。弊社には営業担当者がたくさんいますので、誰があなたの会社と連絡したのかわかりません。

M：ああ、ジョンとこの件について話しましたが、彼はそれを忘れていたのでしょう。私は午後9時までオフィスにいますので、それまでに請求書を送ってください。

W：ジョンは今出張中です。彼は今日シカゴ支部にいますから、そこからファックスしてもらいます。ファックスを受け取ったら、メールで私にお知らせください。

41. What does the man need for his work?
    男性は彼の仕事に何が必要ですか。

    (A) A fax machine　　　　　　　(A) ファックス機
    (B) Sales personnel　　　　　　(B) 営業担当者
    (C) A new job　　　　　　　　　(C) 新しい仕事
    (D) An invoice　　　　　　　**(D) 請求書**

    解説　I just checked my mailbox, but I have not received the invoice from your office yet「メールボックスをチェックしたばかりですが、まだ貴社から請求書を受け取っていません」から、送られたはずの請求書が来ていないことがわかります。その後、Without it, I cannot move on to the next step in my work「それがなければ、私は仕事の次のステップに進むことができません」と言っていることから、正解は(D)となります。Without it のit がinvoice を指していることがポイントです。

42. Until what time can the man receive the fax?
    男性は何時までファックスを受け取ることができますか。

    (A) Until 19:00　　　　　　　　(A) 19:00まで
    (B) Until 20:00　　　　　　　　(B) 20:00まで
    (C) Until 21:00　　　　　　　**(C) 21:00まで**
    (D) Until 22:00　　　　　　　　(D) 22:00まで

解説 Until what time ～「何時までに」という問いですので、時刻に言及する部分に注意しながら聞きましょう。I will be in my office until 9 P.M., so please send me the invoice by then「私は午後9時までオフィスにいますので、それまでに請求書を送ってください」から、午後9時までなら請求書を受け取れることがわかります。よって、正解は(C)となります。なお、by thenのthenはその前に出てきた9 P.M.を言い換えています。thenは「それから」など順序を表す意味も持っていますが、期限や過去のある時点を指す際にも使用されることに注意しましょう。

43. What is the man asked to do after he receives the fax?

ファックスを受け取った後、男性は何をするように求められていますか。

(A) E-mail the telephone operator   **(A) オペレーターにメールを送信する**

(B) E-mail John   (B) ジョンにメールを送る

(C) Fax the invoice   (C) 請求書をファックスする

(D) Visit Chicago   (D) シカゴを訪問する

解説 この問題では男性が依頼したことではなく、依頼されたことについて問われていることから、女性の発言に注意を払いましょう。女性がPlease let me know by e-mail after you receive the fax「ファックスを受け取ったら、メールで私にお知らせください」と発言していることから、答えは(A)となります。なお、女性がtelephone operatorと言い換えられている点に注意しましょう。

2

次の問題セットを、音声を聞きながら答える形式で解け。常に問題文と選択肢は一通り「先読み」で速読を行うこと。また、音声が流れ終わったときには、全ての問題に答えていること。

▶制限タイム70秒

44. What are the two men discussing?

(A) Traveling abroad

(B) A work schedule

(C) Getting a roommate

(D) A sales training seminar

45. What will happen next Friday?

(A) There will be a sales training seminar.

(B) Visitors will come from the head office.

(C) Visitors will come from overseas.

(D) The friend's college roommate will visit.

46. What does the second man offer to do?

(A) Pick up the dealers at the airport

(B) Work late on Tuesday

(C) Come to work early on Tuesday

(D) Come to work on Sunday

正解と解説

M1: **Do you think I can take the day off on Monday?** My college roommate is coming for a visit on Saturday, and he isn't leaving until Monday.

M2: **OK, you can have the day off**. We don't have a busy schedule next week except for the sales training seminar on Wednesday. **By the way, we're looking for volunteers to work late on Friday. We have important dealers coming from abroad, and we need someone to pick them up at the international airport. Are you interested?**

第1章 英語脳徹底トレーニング

第2章 高難度問題の徹底攻略

第3章 正答ハイテクレッスン

第4章 ハイレベル完全模試

M1: **Sure, I'll be happy to volunteer for that.**

M1：月曜日は休みが取れるでしょうか。私の大学のルームメイトが土曜日に来ます。そして
彼は月曜日までいます。

M2：はい、休めます。水曜日のセールストレーニングセミナー以外、来週は忙しいスケジュ
ールはありません。ちなみに、金曜日に遅くまで稼働できる志願者を探しています。海
外からの重要なディーラーが来るので、国際空港で迎えてくれる人が必要です。興味が
ありますか。

M1：もちろん、喜んで志願いたします。

Vocabulary

□ **volunteer** 志願者（必ずしも無給とは限らない）

44. What are the two men discussing?

2人の男性は何を話し合っていますか。

(A) Traveling abroad	(A) 海外旅行
(B) A work schedule	**(B) 仕事のスケジュール**
(C) Getting a roommate	(C) ルームメイトの取得
(D) A sales training seminar	(D) セールストレーニングセミナー

> 解説　会話文の主題を問う問題です。選択肢には会話内で使用された単語が含まれていますが、
> 中心的な話題が何かを意識し、派生的な話題に惑わされないようにしましょう。冒頭の
> Do you think I can take the day off on Monday?「月曜日は休みが取れるでしょうか」
> の問いに対し、OK, you can have the day off「はい、休めます」と返答していることから、
> 仕事のスケジュールについて話していることがわかります。したがって、答えは(B)です。
> なお、会話内でsales training seminarへの言及がありますが、1人の男性が述べたのみ
> でそのことについて話し合いは行われていない点に注意しましょう。

45. What will happen next Friday?

来週の金曜日は何がありますか。

(A) There will be a sales training seminar.	(A) セールストレーニングセミナーがあります。
(B) Visitors will come from the head office.	(B) 訪問者が本社から来ます。
(C) Visitors will come from overseas.	**(C) 訪問者が海外から来ます。**
(D) The friend's college roommate will visit.	(D) 友人の大学のルームメイトが訪問します。

解説　来週の金曜日に予定されていることを問う問題です。曜日を指す単語が含まれている文が
ポイントとなります。By the way, we're looking for volunteers to work late on
Friday. We have important dealers coming from abroad, and we need someone to
pick them up at the international airport「ちなみに、金曜日に遅くまで稼働できる志願
者を探しています。海外からの重要なディーラーが来るので、国際空港で迎えてくれる人
が必要です」とあることから、(C)が正解です。なお、(A)と(D)はそれぞれ、水曜日と土
曜日に予定されていることです。また、(B)は言及されていないため誤りです。

46. What does the second man offer to do?

2番目の男性は何をすることをお願いしていますか。

(A) **Pick up the dealers at the airport**

(B) Work late on Tuesday

(C) Come to work early on Tuesday

(D) Come to work on Sunday

(A) **空港にディーラーを迎えに行く**

(B) 火曜日に遅くに働く

(C) 火曜日に早く仕事に来る

(D) 日曜日に仕事に来る

解説　We have important dealers coming from abroad, and we need someone to pick
them up at the international airport. Are you interested?「海外からの重要なディーラ
ーが来るので、国際空港で迎えてくれる人が必要です。興味がありますか」の問いに対し、
Sure, I'll be happy to volunteer for that「もちろん、喜んで志願いたします」と返答し
ていることから、(A)が正解となります。それ以外の選択肢は会話内で言及されていない
ため、消去法でも答えは導くことができるでしょう。

3

次の問題セットを、音声を聞きながら答える形式で解け。常に問題文と選択肢は一通り「先読み」で速読を行うこと。また、音声が流れ終わったときには、全ての問題に答えていること。

▶制限タイム65秒

47. What are the two speakers discussing?

(A) A letter from John Reimers

(B) A talk by John Reimers

(C) Staff reading their e-mail

(D) A staff meeting

48. When will the event take place?

(A) Tomorrow

(B) Today

(C) Next Wednesday

(D) This Wednesday

49. How does the man think the staff should be informed of the event?

(A) By sending an e-mail

(B) At a meeting

(C) By posting notices

(D) By writing a letter

正解と解説

M: **I'm so excited that John Reimers is scheduled to give a lecture at our head office next Wednesday.**

W: Me, too! How do you think we can get the word out?

M: **Why don't we send all the staff e-mail about the event?**

W: That's not a good idea. The staff gets too much e-mail, so they don't read all their e-mail. Let's put notices up on the bulletin boards in the employee cafeteria and lounge.

M：ジョン・ライマーズが来週の水曜日に本社で講演する予定にとても興奮しています。

W：私も！　どうすればみんなに知らせることができると思いますか。

M：スタッフ全員にイベントについてのメールを送るのはどうでしょう。

W：それは良い考えとは言えません。スタッフはメールを受け取りすぎるため、すべてのメールを読むことはできません。社員食堂やラウンジの掲示板に掲示しましょう。

Vocabulary

☐ **set the word out** お知らせする

47. What are the two speakers discussing?

2人の話者は何について話し合っていますか。

(A) A letter from John Reimers	(A) ジョン・ライマーズからの手紙
(B) A talk by John Reimers	**(B) ジョン・ライマーズによる講演**
(C) Staff reading their e-mail	(C) メールを読んでいるスタッフ
(D) A staff meeting	(D) スタッフ会議

解説　話されている内容を問う問題です。(A)、(D)は言及されていないので不適切です。また、staffやe-mailへの言及はあるものの、The staff gets too much e-mail, so they don't read all their e-mail「スタッフはメールを受け取りすぎるため、すべてのメールを読むことはできません」から、(C)も誤りです。したがって、(B)が正解となります。なお、冒頭にI'm so excited that John Reimers is scheduled to give a lecture at our head office next Wednesday「ジョン・ライマーズが来週の水曜日に本社で講演する予定であることにとても興奮しています」とあることから、講演が中心的な話題であることがわかります。

48. When will the event take place?

イベントはいつ行われますか。

(A) Tomorrow	(A) 明日
(B) Today	(B) 今日
(C) Next Wednesday	**(C) 来週の水曜日**
(D) This Wednesday	(D) 今週の水曜日

解説　When ～「いつ」という問いですので、曜日や日時がポイントとなります。I'm so excited that John Reimers is scheduled to give a lecture at our head office next Wednesday「ジョン・ライマーズが来週の水曜日に本社で講演する予定にとても興奮しています」から(C)が正解です。なお、lectureをeventと言い換えている点に注意しましょう。会話内で言及されているイベントはlectureのみなので、推測できるはずです。

49. How does the man think the staff should be informed of the event?

男性は、スタッフにイベントについてどのように通知する必要があると思っていますか。

(A) By sending e-mail	**(A) メールを送信することで**
(B) At a meeting	(B) 会議にて
(C) By posting notices	(C) 通知を投稿することで
(D) By writing a letter	(D) 手紙を書くことで

解説　男性の意見を問う問題です。男性が Why don't we send all the staff e-mail about the event?「スタッフ全員にイベントについてのメールを送るのはどうでしょう」と提案していることから、(A)が正解です。(B)、(D)は言及されていないため誤りです。また、(C)は女性の提案なので不適切です。なお、be informed of ～は「～の知らせを受ける」という意味の熟語です。

4

次の問題セットを、音声を聞きながら答える形式で解け。<u>常に問題文と選択肢は一通り「先読み」で速読を行うこと。また、音声が流れ終わったときには、全ての問題に答えていること。</u>

▶制限タイム80秒

80. When in the day was the radio news broadcasted?

(A) In the morning

(B) At noon

(C) In the evening

(D) At night

81. What is the cause of the traffic jam on 147?

(A) A traffic accident

(B) Construction

(C) Heavy rain

(D) Shooting a movie

82. What does the speaker recommend listeners do?

(A) Use public transportation

(B) Wait in a line

(C) Report to the company about the traffic

(D) Take different routes

正解と解説

Good morning, everyone. This is WC Network broadcasting from Pasadena Radio Station. We would like to start today's news with the traffic on freeways in the Western areas. **Route 147 has been quite slow this morning because of maintenance work on the road.** Two lanes out of four are completely closed, and it's causing heavy traffic congestion. **If you are heading north, you can take a detour by taking Route 305. If you are heading south, get off at Atlantic Avenue, drive down the street, and you will be able to take Route 401 to avoid the traffic jam.** This news was brought to you by WC Network.

皆さん、おはようございます。パサデナラジオ局から放送されているWCネットワークです。今日のニュースは、西部地域の高速道路の交通量から始めます。ルート147は、道路の整備作業のため、今朝はかなり遅くなっています。4車線のうち2車線が完全に閉鎖されており、渋滞が発生しています。北に向かう場合は、国道305号線を利用して迂回できます。南に向かう場合は、アトランティックアベニューで降りて、通りを進むと、渋滞を回避するために国道401号線に乗ることができます。WCネットワークがニュースをお送りしました。

Vocabulary
☐ **head north** 北に向かう　☐ **head south** 南に向かう

80. When in the day was the radio news broadcasted?
その日のラジオニュースはいつ放送されましたか。

(A) In the morning	**(A) 朝**
(B) At noon	(B) 正午
(C) In the evening	(C) 夕方
(D) At night	(D) 夜

解説　冒頭のGood morning, everyone「皆さん、おはようございます」から、正解は（A）です。また、Route 147 has been quite slow this morning because of maintenance work on the road「ルート147は、道路の整備作業のため、今朝はかなり遅くなっています」より、朝方に放送されたことが推測できるでしょう。問題と選択肢を先読みすることにより、比較的容易に答えを導き出せるはずです。

81. What is the cause of the traffic jam on 147?
ルート147の渋滞の原因は何ですか。

(A) A traffic accident	(A) 交通事故
(B) Construction	**(B) 工事**
(C) Heavy rain	(C) 大雨
(D) Shooting a movie	(D) 映画撮影

解説　こちらも問題を事前に読み、Route 147を意識しながら音声を聞くことで能動的に必要な情報をピックアップすることができるでしょう。Route 147 has been quite slow this morning due to maintenance work on the road「ルート147は、道路の整備作業のため、今朝はかなり遅くなっています」と言っているので、正解は（B）です。なお、選択肢では、maintenance workがconstructionと言い換えられています。

82. What does the speaker recommend listeners do?

スピーカーはリスナーに何を勧めていますか。

(A) Use public transportation

(B) Wait in a line

(C) Report to the company about the traffic

(D) Take different routes

(A) 公共交通機関を利用する

(B) 並んで待つ

(C) 交通状況について会社に報告する

(D) 別のルートで行く

解説　If you are heading north, you can take a detour by taking Route 305. If you are heading south, get off at Atlantic Avenue, drive down the street, and you will be able to take Route 401 to avoid the traffic jam「北に向かう場合は、国道305号線を利用して迂回できます。南に向かう場合は、アトランティックアベニューで降りて、通りを進むと、渋滞を回避するために国道401号線に乗ることができます」より、いずれの場合も異なるルートを推奨しています。よって、正解は(D)です。take a detour「迂回する」という表現が分かれば比較的容易に正解にたどり着けるでしょう。そうでない場合も、(A)、(B)、(C)はいずれも言及されていないことから、消去法で正解を推測することができます。

5

次の問題セットを、音声を聞きながら答える形式で解け。常に問題文と選択肢は一通り「先読み」で速読を行うこと。また、音声が流れ終わったときには、全ての問題に答えていること。

▶制限タイム85秒

83. What is the main topic of the speech?

(A) Characteristics of diseases

(B) Advantages of eating fruit

(C) The use of vitamins

(D) The advancement of health sciences

84. What is mentioned about the effect of multi-vitamins?

(A) It accompanies severe side effects.

(B) It contains 300 types of vitamins.

(C) It is banned in some countries.

(D) It may lower the risk of terminal illnesses.

85. What is the benefit of the tablet form of multi-vitamins?

(A) It tastes better.

(B) It is cost-efficient.

(C) It also contains other nutrients.

(D) It is easy to drink.

正解と解説

The Association of Nutrition Sciences released today a study on the physiological effects of multi-vitamin tablets. The result of the study is quite astonishing. **The group that had a habit of regular intake of multi-vitamins showed a significantly lower prevalence of having serious illnesses such as cancer, metabolic diseases, heart disease, and so on compared to the group that did not have such a habit.** Some scientists insist, however, that natural forms of vitamins, such as the ones in fruit, are more desirable. **But since the**

tablet form contains a 300 times greater amount of vitamins than natural food per dollar, an increasing number of people are relying on tablets these days.

栄養科学協会は、マルチビタミン錠剤の生理学的効果に関する研究を本日発表しました。研究の結果は非常に驚くべきものです。マルチビタミンの定期的な摂取を習慣にしているグループは、そのような習慣がないグループと比較して、癌、代謝性疾患、心臓病などの重篤な病気の有病率が著しく低いものでした。しかし、一部の科学者は、果物に含まれるような天然の形のビタミンの方が望ましいと主張しています。しかし、錠剤でも1ドル当たり、天然食品の300倍の量のビタミンが含まれているため、最近では錠剤に依存する人の数が増加しています。

Vocabulary
□ **physiological** 生理学的な　　□ **prevalence** 流行、広がっていること

83. What is the main topic of the speech?
スピーチの主なトピックは何ですか。

(A) Characteristics of diseases
(B) Advantages of eating fruit
(C) The use of vitamins
(D) The advancement of health sciences

(A) 病気の特徴
(B) 果物を食べることの利点
(C) ビタミンの使用
(D) 健康科学の進歩

解説　(A)、(D)は言及されていないため不適切です。(B)は、Some scientists insist, however, that natural forms of vitamins, such as the ones in fruit, are more desirable「しかし、一部の科学者は、果物に含まれるものなど、天然の形のビタミンの方が望ましいと主張しています」の部分で言及されてはいるものの、ビタミン錠剤との比較の目的で述べられているのみで、中心的な話題とは言えないため不適切です。よって、正解は(C)です。The Association of Nutrition Sciences released today a study on the physiological effects of multi-vitamin tablets「栄養科学協会は、マルチビタミン錠剤の生理学的効果に関する研究を本日発表しました」からも、スピーチの主題はビタミンであることが推測できます。

84. What is mentioned about the effect of multi-vitamins?
マルチビタミンの効果について何が言及されていますか。

(A) It accompanies severe side effects.
(B) It contains 300 types of vitamins.
(C) It is banned in some countries.
(D) It may lower the risk of serious illnesses.

(A) それは重篤な副作用を伴う。
(B) 300種類のビタミンが含まれている。
(C) 一部の国では禁止されている。
(D) 深刻な病気にかかるリスクを下げる可能性がある。

解説　The group that had a habit of regular intake of multi-vitamins showed a significantly lower prevalence of having serious illnesses such as cancer, metabolic diseases, heart disease, and so on compared to the group that did not have such a habit「マルチビタミンの定期的な摂取を習慣にしているグループは、そのような習慣がないグループと比較して、癌、代謝性疾患、心臓病などの重篤な病気の有病率が著しく低いものでした」より、正解は(D)です。選択肢では、prevalenceがriskと言い換えられている点に注意しましょう。

85. What is the benefit of the tablet form of multi-vitamins?
    マルチビタミンの錠剤の利点は何ですか。

(A) It tastes better.	(A) 味がいい。
(B) It is cost-efficient.	**(B) 費用対効果が高い。**
(C) It also contains other nutrients.	(C) 他の栄養素も含まれている。
(D) It is easy to drink.	(D) 飲みやすい。

解説　But since the tablet form contains a 300 times greater amount of vitamins than natural food per dollar, an increasing number of people are relying on tablets these days「しかし、錠剤でも1ドル当たり、天然食品の300倍の量のビタミンが含まれているため、最近では錠剤に依存する人の数が増加しています」より、マルチビタミン錠剤は天然食品に比べ費用面で優れていることがわかります。よって、正解は(B)です。

6

次の問題セットを、音声を聞きながら答える形式で解け。常に問題文と選択肢は一通り「先読み」で速読を行うこと。また、音声が流れ終わったときには、全ての問題に答えていること。

▶制限タイム80秒

86. Where does this announcement probably take place?

(A) At a train station

(B) At an airport

(C) On a ship

(D) At an office

87. According to the talk, why did the cancellation occur?

(A) Bad weather in Boston

(B) Mechanical problems

(C) Bad weather in Chicago

(D) Heavy wind conditions

88. What should passengers do next?

(A) Go to a hotel

(B) Eat dinner

(C) Talk with another airline

(D) Go to the ticket counter

正解と解説

Attention, all passengers on flight 799 to Chicago. **Because of a heavy snowfall in Chicago, flight 799 has been canceled. The airplane for flight 799 has been unable to leave Chicago.** We apologize for the great inconvenience, but it would be unsafe to fly under present weather conditions. **Please come to the ticket counter to make arrangements for flights leaving tomorrow.** We will provide you with hotel and food vouchers in Boston. Again, flight 799 to Chicago has been canceled.

シカゴ行きの799便のすべての乗客の方にお知らせいたします。シカゴの大雪のため、799便は欠航となりました。799便の飛行機はシカゴを出発することができませんでした。ご不便をおかけして申し訳ございませんが、現在の気象条件での運航は安全ではありません。明日の出発便の手配は、チケットカウンターにお越しください。ボストンのホテルと食事の引換券を提供します。繰り返しますが、シカゴ行きの799便はキャンセルされました。

Vocabulary
□ **unsafe** 安全ではない　　□ **arrangement** 手はず、取り決め

86. Where does this announcement probably take place?

この発表はおそらくどこで行われていますか。

(A) At a train station	(A) 駅で
(B) At an airport	**(B) 空港で**
(C) On a ship	(C) 船上で
(D) At an office	(D) オフィスで

解説　The airplane for flight 799 has been unable to leave Chicago 「799便の飛行機はシカゴを出発することができませんでした」、およびPlease come to the ticket counter to make arrangements for flights leaving tomorrow 「明日出発便の手配は、チケットカウンターにお越しください」より、空港で放送されていることが推測できます。よって、正解は(B)です。

87. According to the talk, why did the cancellation occur?

話によると、キャンセルはなぜ発生しましたか。

(A) Bad weather in Boston	(A) ボストンの悪天候
(B) Mechanical problems	(B) 機械的な問題
(C) Bad weather in Chicago	**(C) シカゴの悪天候**
(D) Heavy wind conditions	(D) 強風の具合

解説　Due to a heavy snowfall in Chicago, flight 799 has been canceled 「シカゴの大雪のため、799便は欠航となりました」より、シカゴでの悪天候が欠航の原因であることがわかります。よって、正解は(C)です。選択肢(A)、(B)、(D)はいずれも本文中で言及されていないため不適切です。due to ～は「～に起因して」という意味の熟語で、因果関係を述べる際に使用される比較的フォーマルな表現です[厳密にはdue toは形容詞扱いですが、TOEICではこの形も使われています]。

第1章　英語脳徹底トレーニング

第2章　高難度問題の徹底攻略

第3章　正答ハイテクレッスン

第4章　ハイレベル完全模試

88. What should passengers do next?

乗客は次に何をすべきですか。

(A) Go to a hotel

(B) Eat dinner

(C) Talk with another airline

(D) Go to the ticket counter

(A) ホテルに行く

(B) 夕食を食べる

(C) 他の航空会社と話す

(D) チケットカウンターに行く

解説　乗客が取るべき行動を予想する問題です。Please come to the ticket counter to make arrangements for flights leaving tomorrow「明日の出発便の手配は、チケットカウンターにお越しください」と乗客に呼び掛けていることから、正解は(D)です。なお、本文内でhotel、およびvoucherに言及されているものの、乗客が何をするべきかが問われているため(A)、(B)は不適切です。また、(C)は全く言及されていないため誤りです。

Part5 短文穴埋め問題

英語脳 徹底 トレーニング法⑤

正答数無制限の６択問題

Goal 》語彙力・文法力の漏れをなくす

> Part 5の短文穴埋め問題に求められるのは、単語・文法の面で隙間なく準備していくことです。本番では４択の中から正解を１つ選ぶだけですが、990点を取るには「残りの３択が不正解な理由」もきちんと把握しておく必要があります。

例 題

次の穴埋め問題を解け。ただし、複数回答は可能で、正解の数は0個から6個の範囲で可能とする。（正解がない場合もあるし、1個だけ、2個だけ…6個全部のいずれもありえる）

When introducing a new curriculum that has been proven effective, the school carefully assessed risks ------- .

(A) too

(B) available

(C) hidden

(D) as well

(E) involved

(F) objectively

正解と解説

When introducing a new curriculum that has been proven effective, the school carefully assessed risks ------- .

効果的と示された新カリキュラムを導入する際、学校は注意深くリスク ------- 査定しました。

正解 A, D, E, F

(A) too

(B) available

(C) hidden

(D) as well

(E) involved

(F) objectively

(A) 〜も

(B) 可能な

(C) 隠れた

(D) 〜も

(E) 潜んだ

(F) 客観的に

解説 文法的に、意味的に、語順的にこの選択肢が可能かと考えます。(A)「リスクも査定した」で可能です。tooの前にカンマを打つ場合も打たない場合もあります。(B)availableは形容詞でrooms availableのように後置修飾は可能ですが、この文では「使用可能なリスク」という意味になり不自然で正解扱いにはできません。(C)hiddenは単独では後置修飾の用法は一般的ではありません。(D)はtooと同じく「リスクも査定した」で可能です。(E)のinvolvedは形容詞で単独で後置修飾が可能です。「潜んだリスク」と意味的にも可能となり正解です。(F)は「リスクを客観的に査定した」という意味で可能です。文法的に、意味的に、語順的に可能かと常に複数の観点から英文を分析する力を養うことで、根本的かつ飛躍的な英語力アップを実現できます。

トレーニングを実践！

SET1

次の穴埋め問題を解け。ただし、複数回答は可能で、正解の数は0個から6個の範囲で可能とする。（正解がない場合もあるし、1個だけ、2個だけ…6個全部のいずれもありえる）

101. The regional sales manager ------- the expected revenue of the quarter before the discussion on the main agenda.

    (A) shares

    (B) shared

    (C) sharing

    (D) has shared

    (E) had shared

    (F) is sharing

102. Professor McMaster at St. Paul University is conducting ------- on plants and substances that are potentially effective for diabetes.

    (A) study

    (B) analysis

    (C) research

    (D) survey

    (E) fieldwork

    (F) questionnaire

103. It was a great surprise that Susana successfully managed to lead the project, which was initially anticipated to -------.

    (A) progress

    (B) fail

    (C) change

    (D) initiate

    (E) succeed

(F) stagnate

104. Our subsidiaries in Southeast Asia have to make ------- proposals for expanding our regional business relations.

(A) adding

(B) addition

(C) additive

(D) added

(E) additionally

(F) to add

105. ------- employees requested a relocation to the main office because of the extremely bad and unhealthy working conditions at the local factory.

(A) Many

(B) Much

(C) Almost

(D) Most

(E) Few

(F) Little

106. The number of applicants won't increase ------- at least some of the requirements are removed from the list.

(A) if

(B) although

(C) should

(D) while

(E) unless

(F) even if

正解と解説

101. The regional sales manager ------- the expected revenue of the quarter before the discussion on the main agenda.

地域のセールスマネージャーは、主要な議題について話し合う前に、四半期の予想収益を共有します。

正解 A, B, E, F

(A) shares | **(A) 共有する**
(B) shared | **(B) 共有した**
(C) sharing | (C) 共有している
(D) has shared | (D) (今までに)共有した
(E) had shared | **(E) (そのときまでに)共有していた**
(F) is sharing | **(F) 共有しているところだ**

解説　主語である the regional sales manager に対応する動詞を選ぶ必要があります。まず、the regional sales manager は三人称単数なので、(A)、(F)が選択可能です。また、主語の人称・単数/複数を問わず使用できる過去形と過去完了形である(B)、(E)も可となります。しかし、(C)は動詞ではないので不適切です。また、文後半に before the discussion on the main agenda とあることから、(D)も不適切です。現在完了形の文で before が使用できるのは before が単独である場合のみです。before A のように before の後に名詞や SV がある場合は使用不可となります。

102. Professor McMaster at St. Paul University is conducting ------- on plants and substances that are potentially effective for diabetes.

セントポール大学のマクマスター教授は、糖尿病に効果がある可能性のある植物や物質の研究を行っています。

正解 C, E

(A) study | (A) 学習
(B) analysis | (B) 分析
(C) research | **(C) 研究**
(D) survey | (D) 調査
(E) fieldwork | **(E) 実地調査**
(F) questionnaire | (F) アンケート

解説　適切な名詞を選択する問題です。(A)、(B)、(D)は可算名詞ですので、使用するには conduct a/an ～ のように冠詞の a/an が必要になります。(F)は可算名詞ですが、questionnaire は「質問集、質問一覧」が本質的な意味となり、conduct a questionnaire だと「質問一覧を実施する」と不自然な意味になってしまいます。conduct とともに使用するには、conduct a questionnaire survey のように survey を補う必要があります。一方、

(C)、(E)はともに不可算名詞ですので冠詞を用いず conduct research/fieldwork のように使用することができます。(A) ～ (F)全単語が試験の頻出語です。他にこの形で可算名詞となるのは investigation, inquiry, inspection, scrutiny などがあります。

103. It was a great surprise that Susana successfully managed to lead the project, which was initially anticipated to -------.

当初は失敗すると予想されていたプロジェクトを、スサーナがうまく指揮できたことは大きな驚きでした。

正解 B, F

(A) progress	(A) 発展する
(B) fail	**(B) 失敗する**
(C) change	(C) 変化する
(D) initiate	(D) 開始する
(E) succeed	(E) 成功する
(F) stagnate	**(F) 停滞する**

解説 プロジェクトが成功したことに驚いていることから、当初はそのプロジェクトがうまくいっていないと思われていたことが推測できます。したがって、空欄には「うまくいかない」というニュアンスの単語が入るでしょう。選択肢の中でこれに該当するのは(B)、(F)となります。なお、stagnate は「低迷する、停滞する」という意味の動詞で、売り上げや経済、何らかの進捗状況を描写する際によく使用されます。

104. Our subsidiaries in Southeast Asia have to make ------- proposals for expanding our regional business relations.

当社の東南アジアの子会社は、地域のビジネス関係を拡大するために[追加の]提案を行う必要があります。

正解 なし

(A) adding	(A) 追加している
(B) addition	(B) 追加
(C) additive	(C) 添加物／足し算の
(D) added	(D) 追加された
(E) additionally	(E) 追加で
(F) to add	(F) 追加するために

解説 この中に正解はありません。proposals を修飾する適切な形容詞を選ぶ問題です。(A)追加している、(B)追加、(E)追加で、(F)追加するために、は品詞が適合せず不正解です。(C)は「添加物」という名詞とともに「付加的な」「加算の」という形容詞もありますが、make additive proposals では自然な意味を成しません。(D)も形容詞ですが同様に

make added proposals とは言いません。品詞が合えばどんな単語でも常に自然な英語になる、使用される英語になる、ということにはなりません。今回は、make additional proposals と、additional が正解となり得る単語です。

---

105. ------- employees requested a relocation to the main office because of the extremely bad and unhealthy working conditions at the local factory.

現地の工場の労働条件が非常に悪く、不健全だったため、多くの従業員が本社への移動を要求しました。

正解 A, D

(A) Many	**(A) 多くの**
(B) Much	(B) たくさんの
(C) Almost	(C) ほぼ、ほとんど
(D) Most	**(D) ほとんどの**
(E) Few	(E) ごく少数の
(F) Little	(F) ごく少量の

解説 employeesを修飾する適切な形容詞を選択する問題です。employeeは可算名詞ですので、不可算名詞とともに使用される(B)、(F)は使用することができません。また、(C)は「ほぼ」という意味の副詞ですので、こちらも不適切です。(E)は「ほとんどない」という意味の形容詞で、後に可算名詞を伴いますが、「多くの従業員」と反対の意味になってしまうため、文の意味を考えると不適切です。一方、(A)、(D)はそれぞれ「多くの」、「ほとんどの」という意味の形容詞で、可算名詞とともに使用されます。したがって、文法的にも意味的にも適切な選択肢となります。

---

106. The number of applicants won't increase ------- at least some of the requirements are removed from the list.

少なくとも必要事項の一部がリストから削除されない限り、応募者の数は増えません。

正解 E

(A) if	(A) もし〜なら
(B) although	(B) 〜であるが
(C) should	(C) 万が一〜でも
(D) while	(D) 〜の間、〜の一方で
(E) unless	**(E) 〜でない限り**
(F) even if	(F) たとえ〜でも

解説 「〜しない限り」という意味の接続詞を選択する必要があります。これを満たすのは(E)のunlessのみです。(A)を使用すると、「少なくとも必要事項の一部がリストから削除されれば」という意味になってしまうので不適切です。(B)は「〜だけれども」という意味の接続

詞で、空欄に使用すると「少なくとも必要事項の一部がリストから削除されるけれども」という意味になり不適切です。(C)のshouldは、仮定法の倒置に用いられ「万が一」という意味を持っています。空欄に使用すると(A)を使用した際の意味に近くなるため不適切です。(D)のwhileには「〜の間、〜にもかかわらず」という意味がありますが、こちらも空欄に使用すると意味的に不自然な文になります。最後に、(F)は「たとえ〜だとしても」という意味で仮定の話をする際に使用されますが、空欄に使用すると「たとえ少なくとも必要事項の一部がリストから削除されても」となり意味的に不適切です。

SET 2

次の穴埋め問題を解け。ただし、複数回答は可能で、正解の数は0個から6個の範囲で可能とする。（正解がない場合もあるし、1個だけ、2個だけ…6個全部のいずれもありえる）

107. Everyone agrees that this ------- milder and more comfortable climate on the west coast attracts a lot of visitors, especially during the winter season.

(A) noticed

(B) noticing

(C) noticeable

(D) noticeably

(E) to notice

(F) noticeability

108. Anyone who fails to turn in the assigned paperwork ------- the end of tomorrow will be required to work overtime.

(A) by

(B) when

(C) while

(D) before

(E) during

(F) prior

109. The application produced by Prop Tech is ------- more user-friendly than any other products, which accounts for its skyrocketing sales.

(A) even

(B) so

(C) much

(D) a lot

(E) far

(F) such

110. The outstanding performance of the athlete ------- that the newcomer will be a great addition to the team, which has been struggling throughout the season.

(A) convinced

(B) proved

(C) established

(D) acknowledged

(E) discovered

(F) indicated

111. Visiting professionals granted a full amount of the fellowship during their stay at this institute ------- a proof of household income every year from now on.

(A) submit

(B) submits

(C) submitted

(D) submitting

(E) to submit

(F) to be submitted

112. The new president who was assigned to the current position after the resignation of the former president is ------- changing the work environment.

(A) not

(B) yet

(C) before

(D) already

(E) however

(F) now

107. Everyone agrees that this ------- milder and more comfortable climate on the west coast attracts a lot of visitors, especially during the winter season.

西海岸のこの著しく穏やかで快適な気候は、特に冬のシーズンに多くの訪問者を引き付けることに誰もが同意します。

正解 D

(A) noticed	(A) 気づかれた
(B) noticing	(B) 気づいている
(C) noticeable	(C) 顕著な
(D) noticeably	**(D) 顕著に**
(E) to notice	(E) 気づくこと
(F) noticeability	(F) 視認性

解説　この空欄にはmilder and more comfortable「穏やかで快適な」という表現を修飾する副詞が当てはまります。よって、正解は(D)となります。(A)、(B)、(C)は形容詞、(E)は不定詞、(F)は名詞なので不正解です。直前のthisを単体で主語として捉えてしまうと、混乱してしまうかもしれませんので、ここの主語は this noticeably milder and more comfortable climate on the west coastであることも要チェックです。

108. Anyone who fails to turn in the assigned paperwork ------- the end of tomorrow will be required to work overtime.

明日の終わりまでに必要書類を提出できなかった人は、残業する必要があります。

正解 A, D

(A) by	**(A) 〜までに**
(B) when	(B) 〜のとき
(C) while	(C) 〜の間に
(D) before	**(D) 〜の前に**
(E) during	(E) 〜の間に
(F) prior	(F) 前

解説　この文ではthe end of tomorrow「明日の終わり」の前に来るのに自然な単語を見つけ出すことが重要です。(A)は「〜までに」、(D)は「〜の前に」という意味で、自然なので正解です。the end of tomorrowはある時点を指しているので、ある期間の前につける「〜の間に」という意味を持つ(C)や(E)は不自然なので不正解です。(B)は「明日の終わりぴったりに」というニュアンスになるので不自然で不正解です。(F)はprior toでbeforeと同じ意味になりますが、toがないので文法上使えません。

109. The application produced by Prop Tech is ------- more user-friendly than any other products, which accounts for its skyrocketing sales.

プロップ・テックによって作成されたアプリケーションは、他のどの製品よりもさらにユーザーにやさしく、それが急増している売上を説明しています。

正解 A, C, D, E

(A) even	**(A) さらに**
(B) so	(B) そのように
(C) much	**(C) はるかに**
(D) a lot	**(D) かなり**
(E) far	**(E) ずっと**
(F) such	(F) そのような

解説 比較級の more の前にきて「さらに〜だ」という表現を作る選択肢を選びます。この形で可能なのは選択肢の中では even, much, a lot, far です。a lot more user-friendly は lots more user friendly という形でも使えます（この方が若干くだけた印象になります）。この空欄に入る他の語句は幾つかあります。a bit, a little, slightly, still, considerably, significantly などです。

110. The outstanding performance of the athlete ------- that the newcomer will be a great addition to the team, which has been struggling throughout the season.

アスリートの卓越したパフォーマンスは、シーズンを通して苦労しているチームへ新人が素晴らしい貢献になることを証明しました。

正解 B, C, F

(A) convinced	(A) 説得した
(B) proved	**(B) 証明した**
(C) established	**(C) 立証した**
(D) acknowledged	(D) 認知した
(E) discovered	(E) 発見した
(F) indicated	**(F) 示唆した**

解説 文法的に、意味的に、語順的にどれが通るかと考えます。素晴らしい貢献になると「示した」という類いの意味であれば通るので、(B)、(C)、(F)がこれに近い意味で正解扱いとなります。establishは設立するという意味もありますが、established that SV で「〜ということを立証する」という意味になり、テストにも出題されたことがあります。(A)の convinced は convinced us that と人が入っていれば可能でした。(D)、(E)は made us acknowledge/discoverのように、使役動詞のmade 人という形であれば可能でした。今回の空欄では、confirmed, demonstrated, showed, ensured, verified, implied, revealed, meant, signified, substantiatedなども可能です。

111. Visiting professionals granted a full amount of the fellowship during their stay at this institute ------- a proof of household income every year from now on.

この研究所に滞在中に全額の奨学金を授与された訪問している専門家は、今後毎年世帯収入の証明を提出します。

正解 A

(A) submit   (A) 提出する

(B) submits   (B) 提出する

(C) submitted   (C) 提出した

(D) submitting   (D) 提出している

(E) to submit   (E) 提出するために

(F) to be submitted   (F) 提出されるべき

解説　この文では主語がどこまでかを判断することが重要です。この文の主語は Visiting professionals granted a full amount of the fellowship during their stay at this institute「この研究所に滞在中に全額の奨学金を授与された訪問している専門家」です。なので、この文で欠けているのは動詞であることがわかります。なので、(D)、(E)、(F)は文法上間違いです。(C)の過去形は、from now on「今後」という表現と一致しないのでこれも間違いです。(B)は三単現のsがついていますが、この文の主語はprofessionalsと複数なので、間違いです。よって、正解は(A)となります。

112. The new president who was assigned to the current position after the resignation of the former president is ------- changing the work environment.

前社長の辞任後、現職に就任した新社長は、職場環境を変えていません。

正解 A, D, F

(A) not   (A) していない

(B) yet   (B) まだ

(C) before   (C) 前に

(D) already   (D) すでに

(E) however   (E) しかしながら／どのように〜しても

(F) now   (F) 今

解説　まず、単語が挿入される場所を見てみましょう。ここに(C)や(E)が入るのは不自然なので間違いです。また、(B)は「まだ」というニュアンスなので、現在進行形に挿入されるには不自然なので間違いです。(A)はシンプルな現在進行形の否定形の文になり自然で正解です。(D)は「もうすでに」という意味なので、「もうすでに職場環境を変えている」という自然な文になります。よって、(D)は正解です。(F)も「今」という意味で、現在進行形にふさわしい副詞なので正解です。

SET 3

次の穴埋め問題を解け。ただし、複数回答は可能で、正解の数は0個から6個の範囲で可能とする。（正解がない場合もあるし、1個だけ、2個だけ…6個全部のいずれもありえる）

113. ------- the circumstance where no profit can be expected, the leader concluded it is wiser to suspend the project.

    (A) Given

    (B) Owing to

    (C) Considering

    (D) Provided

    (E) Providing

    (F) Under

114. Our research indicates that the ------- of the material we brought here today to show you is unquestionable.

    (A) durability

    (B) profitability

    (C) patentability

    (D) availability

    (E) stability

    (F) marketability

115. The board made a unanimous decision and declared that it has ------- the establishment of the union intended to resolve existing problems.

    (A) accepted

    (B) discharged

    (C) rejected

    (D) evaluated

    (E) approved

    (F) negotiated

116. The new regulation applies to ------- registered as a full-timer member regardless of their titles and roles in the firm.

    (A) who

    (B) whom

    (C) them

    (D) anyone

    (E) these

    (F) whoever

117. The result of the campaign was quite optimistic, but -------, the management sought further reinforcement of the undertaking.

    (A) yet

    (B) rather

    (C) then

    (D) still

    (E) so

    (F) again

118. ------- all those intense oppositions, they initiated the construction of the new factory.

    (A) However

    (B) Although

    (C) Despite

    (D) In spite of

    (E) Nevertheless

    (F) Notwithstanding

正解と解説

113. ------- the circumstance where no profit can be expected, the leader concluded it is wiser to suspend the project.

利益が期待できない状況を考えると、リーダーはプロジェクトを中断する方が賢明であると結論付けました。

正解 A, B, C, F

(A) Given	**(A) ～ということを受け**
(B) Owing to	**(B) ～により**
(C) Considering	**(C) ～ということを考慮すると**
(D) Provided	(D) ～だとすると
(E) Providing	(E) ～だとすると
(F) Under	**(F) ～という状況下で**

解説　(A)や(C)の場合、「～という状況を考えると」という表現になり、自然なので正解です。(B)は「～という状況により」という表現になり、これも自然で正解です。(F)は「～という状況下では」という意味になるので、これも正解です。provideはgiveの類義語なので、(D)や(E)も正解のように見えますが、that S V と続く接続詞の扱いとなるので誤りです。

114. Our research indicates that the ------- of the material we brought here today to show you is unquestionable.

私たちの調査によると紹介するために、今日ここに持ち込んだ素材の耐久性は疑いの余地がありません。

正解 A, B, C, D, E, F

(A) durability	**(A) 耐久性**
(B) profitability	**(B) 利益性**
(C) patentability	**(C) 特許取得可能性**
(D) availability	**(D) 入手可能性**
(E) stability	**(E) 安定性**
(F) marketability	**(F) 市場性**

解説　(A)の「耐久性」をはじめ、選択肢全てが文章として意味を成しますので、全ての選択肢が正解となります。(C)以外はTOEICの問題でよく出る単語です。

115. The board made a unanimous decision and declared that it has ------- the establishment of the union intended to resolve existing problems.

理事会は満場一致の決定を下し、既存の問題の解決を目的とした組合の設立を受け入れたと宣言しました。

正解	A, C, E

(A) accepted	**(A) 受け入れた**
(B) discharged	(B) 排出した
(C) rejected	**(C) 拒否した**
(D) evaluated	(D) 査定した
(E) approved	**(E) 許可した**
(F) negotiated	(F) 交渉した

> 解説　この文ではunanimous「満場一致の」という単語が重要になります。この単語にふさわしい動詞を選択すると自然と正解は(A)「受け入れた」、(C)「拒否した」、(E)「許可した」になります。(B)「外された」や(D)「評価された」や(F)「交渉された」という表現はunanimousと合わせると不自然なので間違いです。

116. The new regulation applies to ------- registered as a full-timer member regardless of their titles and roles in the firm.

新しい規制は会社での役職や役割に関係なく、正社員として登録されている[人たち]に適用されます。

正解	なし

(A) who	(A) 〜の人
(B) whom	(B) 〜の人
(C) them	(C) 彼ら・彼女ら
(D) anyone	(D) 誰か
(E) these	(E) これらの
(F) whoever	(F) 誰でも

> 解説　those があれば正解ですが、今回はないので正解なしとなります。他に文法的、意味的、語順的に適するものはありません。anyone は一見入るように見えるかもしれませんが、単数扱いの単語を後の their で受けることはできません。

117. The result of the campaign was quite optimistic, but -------, the management sought further reinforcement of the undertaking.

キャンペーンの結果は非常に楽観的でしたが、それでも経営陣は事業のさらなる強化を求めました。

正解	D, F

(A) yet	(A) まだ
(B) rather	(B) むしろ
(C) also	(C) 〜も

(D) still

(E) so

(F) again

(D) まだ

(E) だから

(F) また、さらに

解説 stillやagainはbutによく続く単語で、「それでもまだ」「それでもまた」という意味になり、(D)と(F)が正解です。他の選択肢は、意味的に明確な文を作ることができず、この空欄に入れるには適切ではありません。

118. ------- all those intense oppositions, they initiated the construction of the new factory.

そのような激しい反対があるにもかかわらず、彼らは新しい工場の建設を開始しました。

正解 C, D, F

(A) However

(B) Although

(C) Despite

(D) In spite of

(E) Nevertheless

(F) Notwithstanding

(A) しかしながら

(B) 〜だが

(C) 〜にもかかわらず

(D) 〜にもかかわらず

(E) それにもかかわらず

(F) 〜にもかかわらず

解説 Notwithstandingについては、All those intense oppositions notwithstandingという後ろに置く形も可能です。今回の問題では、他にもEven withも可能ですし、分詞構文にして、Neglecting, Disregarding, Suppressingなどを入れることも手段の一つです。この次元で能動的に考える習慣があると、文構造がわからず取りこぼすということもなくなります。

Part6 長文穴埋め問題

英語脳 徹底 トレーニング法⑥
正答数無制限の6択問題

Goal 》語彙力・文法力の漏れをなくす

> Part 6がPart 5と異なる点が2つあります。1点目に、パッセージ全体の流れから判断する問題があること、2点目に文挿入の問題があることです。どちらも、英文全体の流れがきちんとつかめていれば解ける問題です。

例題

次の穴埋め問題を解け。ただし、複数回答は可能で、正解の数は0個から6個の範囲で可能とする。（正解がない場合もあるし、1個だけ、2個だけ…6個全部のいずれもありえる）

Increasing Need for Male Nurses

In the past, women dominated the field of nursing in America. -------, however, more men have become interested in the nursing profession.

In a recent study of American universities, 29 percent of the students ------- nursing programs last year were males, which is a great increase from 15 percent 10 years ago. The Macon Hospital, a large public hospital in Georgia, employs ------- sixty male nurses, and they are all working happily.

One ------- nurse is Mark Biggs. He is now in charge of all hospital

---

nurses on the night shift. "The proportion of male to female employees has changed drastically in the last ------- ," says Mr. Biggs. He considers it an honor to be able to take this responsibility.
_{5.}

One in three nursing students in our country are expected to be males this year. ------- .
_{6.}

Q1 (A) Previously
   (B) Largely
   (C) Currently
   (D) Technically
   (E) Recently
   (F) Initially

Q2 (A) enrolled in
   (B) consisting of
   (C) commuting from
   (D) registered for
   (E) accepted to
   (F) studying in

Q3 (A) over
   (B) excessively
   (C) as many
   (D) more than
   (E) at least
   (F) for

Q4 (A) even
   (B) such
   (C) of
   (D) like
   (E) among
   (F) notable

Q5 (A) chance
   (B) moment
   (C) time
   (D) decade
   (E) quarter
   (F) second

Q6 (A) This trend is expected to continue.
   (B) Mr. Biggs is surprised at this news.
   (C) They want to talk with patients.
   (D) More hospitals are needed.
   (E) Many consider this as a good change.
   (F) They have to pass some exams.

Increasing Need for Male Nurses

In the past, women dominated the field of nursing in America. ---·----, however, more men have become interested in the nursing profession.

In a recent study of American universities, 29 percent of the students ---·---- nursing programs last year were males, which is a great increase from 15 percent 10 years ago. The Macon Hospital, a large public hospital in Georgia, employs ---·---- sixty male nurses, and they are all working happily.

One ---·---- nurse is Mark Biggs. He is now in charge of all hospital nurses on the night shift. "The proportion of male to female employees has changed drastically in the last ---·----," says Mr. Biggs. He considers it an honor to be able to take this responsibility.

One in three nursing students in our country are expected to be males this year. ---·----.

男性看護スタッフの需要増加

昔はアメリカの看護業界は女性が多くを占めていました。しかしながら最近では、より多くの男性が看護の職に興味を持っています。

アメリカの大学の最近の研究では、看護プログラムに去年登録した29パーセントの生徒が男性で、これは10年前の15パーセントからは大きな上昇です。ジョージア州の大規模病院であるマコン病院は、60名以上の男性看護師を雇用しており、みんな喜んで働いています。

そのような看護師の1人がマーク・ビグスです。今や彼は病院で夜間勤務に就く全看護師への責任者となっています。「男性と女性の看護師の比率はここ10年で大きく変わった」とビグス氏は言います。彼はこの責任を負うことができることを光栄に思っています。

今年の看護学生の3人に1人は男性になると見込まれています。このトレンドは続いていくでしょう。

Q1　正解　C, E

(A) Previously	(A) 以前は
(B) Largely	(B) 大きくは
(C) Currently	**(C) 現在は**
(D) Technically	(D) 厳密には、技術的には
(E) Recently	**(E) 最近では**
(F) Initially	(F) 当初は

解説　文法的に、意味的に、語順的に考えてどれが入りうるか、と考えます。品詞や配置的にはすべての選択肢が可能です。意味上はどうでしょうか。以前は女性がほとんどだったが、昨今では男性も増えてきている、という意味で(C)と(E)は意味が通り、これらが正解となります。

Q2　正解　A, D, E, F

(A) enrolled in	**(A) に登録した**
(B) consisting of	(B) を構成する
(C) commuting from	(C) から通う
(D) registered for	**(D) に登録した**
(E) accepted to	**(E) に合格した**
(F) studying in	**(F) で学ぶ**

解説　この選択肢も、文法的に、語順的には全て可能となります。ingで続くのか、edで続くのかというのは、それぞれの選択肢の単語の意味を考えてみても、いずれも間違いはありません。前後の流れも含めて自然な流れになっているかという観点で見極めます。Part 5にはなくPart 6にある要素はこれです。(B)と(C)以外は正解です。(B)のconsistは The program consists of dozens of male students. という形で使うことはできますが、今回はmale studentsが先に来ているので不可です。(C)はcommuting toであれば正解となります。

Q3　正解　A, D, E

(A) over	**(A) 超えの**
(B) excessively	(B) 過度に
(C) as many	(C) ほど多くの
(D) more than	**(D) より多い**
(E) at least	**(E) 少なくとも**
(F) for	(F) の

解説　以上、より多い、という類の意味を成す適切な語句が入れば正解となりえます。(A)、(D)、(E)がそれぞれ可能です。(B)は「過度に」という意味で程度が行き過ぎている様を表します。(C)は as many as であれば正解でした。employ はこの用法では他動詞で、forをこの位置に持ってきても意味を成す文は作れません。

Q4　正解 B, F

(A) even	(A) さえ
(B) such	**(B) そのような**
(C) of	(C) の
(D) like	(D) のような
(E) among	(E) の中の
(F) notable	**(F) 注目に値する**

解説　そのような1人の生徒がビグス氏である、という意味でsuchを使うことができます。よくOne such example is N.などという形で使われます。notableは注目に値する、という形容詞で、1人の注目に値する生徒はビグス氏である、とすることができます。distinguished, remarkable, outstanding などの形容詞も同じように使うことができます。

Q5　正解 D

(A) chance	(A) チャンス
(B) moment	(B) 瞬間
(C) time	(C) 時間
(D) decade	**(D) 10年**
(E) quarter	(E) 四半期
(F) second	(F) 秒

解説　これはある意味では難しい問題です。近年男性の割合が増えてきているとはいえ、統計によると10年単位で見たときに変化がある、という情報が出されています。ここ四半期、数秒、この瞬間でここまでの大きな変化があった、とするのは無理があるでしょう。decade（10年）というのは、ビグス氏が調べた期間の長さではありませんが、記事内に10年とあり、割合の変化はこのくらいのスパンで起こっていること、ビグス氏が全体を責任者としてまとめるに至っているので、そこまでに一定以上の期間を要したと想定されることを総合的に考え、(D)が正解となります。こうした、全体を見渡して最適な答えを選ぶ、という視点をPart 6では持つ必要があります。＊テスト本番ではもう少しはっきりした正解があります。

Q6 **正解** A, E

(A) This trend is expected to continue.

(A) この傾向は続くと思われる。

(B) Mr. Biggs is surprised at this news.

(B) ビグス氏はこのニュースに驚いている。

(C) They want to talk with patients.

(C) 彼らは患者と話したい。

(D) More hospitals are needed.

(D) もっと多くの病院が必要とされている。

(E) Many consider this as a good change.

(E) 多くの人がこれを良い変化と捉えている。

(F) They have to pass some exams.

(F) 彼らは試験に合格しなければいけない。

解説 この男性の増加傾向は続く、という(A)は全体の流れを引き継いで coherent につながります。(E)は、直接的な coherence というよりも、全体を最後に俯瞰して1文足した印象です。これら以外は、文脈、パッセージ全体の内容から判断してここに入るべき文とは考えられません。

トレーニングを実践！

1 次の穴埋め問題を解け。ただし、複数回答は可能で、正解の数は0個から6個の範囲で可能とする。（正解がない場合もあるし、1個だけ、2個だけ…6個全部のいずれもありえる）

June 22 2021
1268 Conaway Street
Green Park
New York

Dear Mr. Kilby,

We will be putting on the 7th NY Summer festival on August 14th, 2021. Participation is free of charge and those who are interested, ------- they are from outside the city, are welcome. -------, feel free to bring your friends and family with you.
_{131.}　_{132.}

There will be plenty of food stalls and shows. There will also be a main stage for live performance and we are planning to invite many special guests. The lineup will be announced about two weeks ------- the event, so stay tuned.
_{133.}

If you would like to perform at the stage or open some stalls, please fill in the form attached with this letter and send it to ------- by the 31st of July. We will be holding a rehearsal a day before the festival, and we would also like you to participate in the rehearsal as well.
_{134.}

Since the annual event preceding this one ------- canceled, we are planning this event to be more special and exciting than ever. -------.
_{135.}　_{136.}

King regards,

The Events Committee

---

131. (A) although
     (B) if
     (C) regardless of
     (D) irrespective
     (E) even if
     (F) either

132. (A) Therefore
     (B) However
     (C) On the other hand
     (D) Otherwise
     (E) As a result
     (F) Thus

133. (A) before
     (B) earlier
     (C) prior to
     (D) during
     (E) past
     (F) after

134. (A) me
     (B) you
     (C) us
     (D) them
     (E) one
     (F) it

135. (A) is
     (B) will be
     (C) will have been
     (D) was
     (E) has been
     (F) had been

136. (A) Hope to see you on the day of the event!
     (B) Will you really open a food stall this year?
     (C) Please do let us know if you have any concerns.
     (D) We hope the event will be a memorable one for all participants.
     (E) We are very much looking forward to your participation.
     (F) No one knows the reason for the cancellation.

June 22 2021
1268 Conaway Street
Green Park
New York

Dear Mr. Kilby,

We will be putting on the 7th NY Summer festival on August 14th, 2021. Participation is free of charge and those who are interested, ------- they are from outside the city, are welcome. -------, feel free to bring your friends and family with you.
_{131.}
_{132.}

There will be plenty of food stalls and shows. There will also be a main stage for live performance and we are planning to invite many special guests. The lineup will be announced about two weeks ------- the event, so stay tuned.
_{133.}

If you would like to perform at the stage or open some stalls, please fill in the form attached with this letter and send it to ------- by the 31st of July. We will be holding a rehearsal a day before the festival, and we would also like you to participate in the rehearsal as well.
_{134.}

Since the annual event preceding this one ------- canceled, we are planning this event to be more special and exciting than ever. -------.
_{135.}
_{136.}

King regards,

The Events Committee

Vocabulary
☐ **stall** 店、屋台　☐ **precede** 先行する

カービー様、

第7回ニューヨークサマーフェスティバルを2021年8月14日に開催いたします。参加

は無料で、市外の方も含め興味のある方はどなたでも参加大歓迎です。ぜひお友達やご家族もご一緒にお越しください。

たくさんの屋台やショーが行われます。ライブパフォーマンス用のメインステージを用意し、スペシャルゲストもお招きしています。ラインナップはイベントの約2週間前に発表されますので、引き続きご注目ください。

ステージでの公演や屋台の開店をご希望の場合は同封の申込書にご記入の上、7月31日までにお送りください。イベント前日にリハーサルを行いますので、リハーサルの参加もご協力お願いいたします。

昨年、イベントが中止になりましたので、今回は今まで以上に特別でエキサイティングなイベントを予定しております。イベント当日お会いできることを楽しみにしています！

よろしくお願いいたします。

イベント委員会

---

131. **正解 E**

(A) although	(A) だが
(B) if	(B) もし
(C) regardless of	(C) にかかわらず
(D) irrespective	(D) 関係ない
(E) even if	**(E) もし〜でも**
(F) either	(F) いずれかの

解説　even if they are from outside the city「市外から来る方でも」という意味になるので(E)が自然です。(A) althoughは実際に起こったことに対して使われる「〜でも」という表現なので、このような仮定の状況では不適切です。(C)や(D)も一見意味が「〜にかかわらず」なので、正解に感じますが、これらに続くのは名詞または名詞節なので間違いです。(F)はorと一緒に使い、2つの条件を提示するのがセオリーなので間違いです。

---

132. **正解 A, F**

(A) Therefore	**(A) ですので**
(B) However	(B) しかしながら

(C) On the other hand	(C) 一方で
(D) Otherwise	(D) さもなくば
(E) As a result	(E) その結果として
(F) Thus	**(F) ですので**

> 解説　前の文に「参加は無料で、興味のある方は大歓迎です」と書いてあり、続く文には「お友達やご家族をお気軽にお連れください」と書いてあるので、この2つの文を自然につなげられる接続副詞が正解になります。(A) Therefore と (F) Thus はどちらも「なので」という意味を持つので、これらを入れると自然に2つの文がつながります。よって、正解は(A)と(F)です。

133.　正解 A, C

(A) before	**(A) 前に**
(B) earlier	(B) 早く
(C) prior to	**(C) 前に**
(D) during	(D) 間に
(E) past	(E) 過ぎて
(F) after	(F) 後で

> 解説　この文では、ラインナップがいつ発表されるかを述べています。イベント後やイベント中に発表というのは文脈上筋が通らないので、(D)、(E)、(F)は間違いです。正解は「前に」という意味を持つ(A)と(C)になります。

134.　正解 C

(A) me	(A) 私に
(B) you	(B) あなたに
(C) us	**(C) 私たちに**
(D) them	(D) 彼ら・彼女らに
(E) one	(E) 1つ、人
(F) it	(F) それに

> 解説　この空欄にはフォームの送り先が入りますので、(B)、(E)、(F)はまず不自然であることがわかります。(D)も前後の文脈で明らかではないので、不自然です。この手紙の送り主が Events Committee であることから、複数人のグループであることがわかります。なので、この場合は複数形の(C) us が正解となります。

135. 正解 D

(A) is

(B) will be

(C) will have been

(D) was

(E) has been

(F) had been

(A) される

(B) されるだろう

(C) そのときまでにされていることだろう

(D) された

(E) すでにされている

(F) そのときまでにされていた

解説 この文では、いつのイベントがキャンセルされたのかが重要になります。the annual event preceding this one「これの前の年次イベント」と書かれているので、過去のイベントであることがわかります。なので、過去形でない(A)、(B)、(C)、(E)は間違いです。(D) was が正解になります。(F)の過去完了は、過去のあるポイントを起点に、「そのときまでにすでに〜していた」という意味を作る時制です。今回は、そのような過去の1点を基準にという構造にも意味にもなっておらず、過去完了形は適切ではありません。

136. 正解 A, C, D, E

(A) Hope to see you on the day of the event!

(B) Will you really open a food stall this year?

(C) Please do let us know if you have any concerns.

(D) We hope the event will be a memorable one for all participants.

(E) We are very much looking forward to your participation.

(F) No one knows the reason for the cancellation.

(A) イベントの日に会えるのを楽しみにしています！

(B) 本当に今年に屋台を開きますか。

(C) 何か心配な点があればお知らせください。

(D) イベントが参加者様に思い出深いものになりますように。

(E) あなたのご参加を心よりお待ちしております。

(F) キャンセルの理由は誰にもわかりません。

解説 結びの言葉として適切なものを選ぶ問題です。(B)は「今年は本当に屋台を開きますか」と質問しているので不適格です。(F)も「キャンセルの理由は誰にもわかりません」とキャンセルについて話しているので不自然です。よって、正解は(A)、(C)、(D)、(E)になります。いずれも結びの言葉としてよく使われるフレーズなので押さえておきましょう。

第1章 英語脳徹底トレーニング

第2章 高難度問題の徹底攻略

第3章 正答ハイテクレッスン

第4章 ハイレベル完全模試

2 次の穴埋め問題を解け。ただし、複数回答は可能で、正解の数は0個から6個の範囲で可能とする。（正解がない場合もあるし、1個だけ、2個だけ…6個全部のいずれもありえる）

Letter of recommendation

To Whom It May Concern:

-------. Daniel has been a long-standing member of Stable Trading Corp.
_{137.} for ------- nine years. ------- his supervisor, I have seen many examples
_{138.} _{139.} of his outstanding performance in the marketing department. I have also
been ------- by his cheerful character, diligence and strong work ethics.
_{140.}

This young man has been -------, not only by the marketing department
_{141.} but also by our employees from other departments. Even in difficult
circumstances, with his relentless motivation, he has continued to
challenge and overcome all obstacles.

-------, I would like to reiterate my strong recommendation for Daniel
_{142.} Smith. If you have further questions regarding Daniel's ability or this
recommendation, please do not hesitate to contact me.

Yours faithfullly,

Dylan

---

137. (A) It has been a while since we talked last time in London.

    (B) I was not expecting to read this letter when I met him.

    (C) I am delighted to be able to recommend Daniel Smith to a new position.

    (D) This is the first time I have talked to Daniel in this department.

    (E) Thank you very much for this opportunity to write this letter.

    (F) I can be reached by phone if you have any questions.

138. (A) about
    (B) almost
    (C) around
    (D) over
    (E) approximately
    (F) closely

139. (A) For
    (B) Upon
    (C) As
    (D) Within
    (E) Except
    (F) With

140. (A) notified
    (B) impressed
    (C) amazed
    (D) depressed
    (E) confused
    (F) astonished

141. (A) respects
    (B) respected
    (C) respecting
    (D) respectable
    (E) respective
    (F) respectively

142. (A) Finally
    (B) Completely
    (C) Firstly
    (D) Honesty
    (E) Lastly
    (F) Clearly

正解と解説

Letter of recommendation

To Whom It May Concern:

------. Daniel has been a long-standing member of Stable Trading Corp.
   137.
for ------- nine years. ------- his supervisor, I have seen many examples
     138.   139.
of his outstanding performance in the marketing department. I have also
been ------- by his cheerful character, diligence and strong work ethics.
     140.

This young man has been -------, not only by the marketing department but also by our employees from other departments. Even in difficult circumstances, with his relentless motivation, he has continued to challenge and overcome all obstacles.

141.

-------, I would like to reiterate my strong recommendation for Daniel Smith. If you have further questions regarding Daniel's ability or this recommendation, please do not hesitate to contact me.

142.

Yours faithfullly,

Dylan

推薦状

ご担当者様：

ダニエル・スミスを新しいポジションに推薦できることは私にとって喜びです。ダニエルはStable Trading Corp.の長年のメンバーで、勤務を始めて9年ほどになります。彼の上司として、私はマーケティング部門での彼の卓越した業績の多くの例を見てきました。彼の明るい性格、勤勉さ、しっかりとした労働倫理にも感銘を受けました。

この若者は、マーケティング部門だけでなく、他の部門の社員からも尊敬されてきました。困難な状況でも、尽きることのない意欲を持って、彼はすべての障害に挑戦し乗り越え続けてきました。

最後に、ダニエル・スミスに対する私の強い推薦を再度述べます。ダニエルの能力やこの推薦状について質問がある場合は、遠慮することなく私に連絡をください。

敬具

ディラン

137. 正解 C, E

(A) It has been a while since we talked last time in London.

(A) 前回ロンドンでお話ししてしばらくになります。

(B) I was not expecting to read this letter when I met him.

(B) 彼に逢ったときにこの手紙を読むとは思っていませんでした。

(C) I am delighted to be able to recommend Daniel Smith to a new position.

(C) ダニエル・スミスを新しいポジションに推薦できることをうれしく思います。

(D) This is the first time I talk with Daniel in this department.

(D) ダニエルとこの部署で話すのは初めてになります。

(E) Thank you very much for this opportunity to write this letter.

(E) この手紙を書く機会をいただき、誠にありがとうございます。

(F) I can be reached by phone if you have any questions.

(F) もしご質問があれば電話でご連絡いただけます。

解説 最初にLetter of recommendationと書いてあるので、これが推薦状であることがわかります。なので、推薦状に書く最初の文としてふさわしい文を選ぶことがポイントです。(C)は「ダニエル・スミスを新しいポジションに推薦できることをうれしく思います」という意味で、(E)も「この手紙を書く機会をいただき、誠にありがとうございます」という意味で、どちらも自然なので正解です。他の選択肢は、推薦状の最初の文としては不自然でしょう。

138. 正解 A, B, C, D, E

(A) about

(A) およそ

(B) almost

(B) ほぼ

(C) around

(C) くらい

(D) over

(D) より

(E) approximately

(E) およそ

(F) closely

(F) 近く

解説 for nine yearsで「9年間」という意味になります。(A)、(B)、(C)、(E)は全て「約、だいたい」という意味で、期間を表すときによく使われる副詞なので、正解です。(D)は「以上」という意味で、「9年以上の間」と自然な表現になるので、こちらも正解です。(F)は「ぴったりと、親しく」などの意味で、期間の表現と併せて使うには不自然な副詞なので、間違いです。

139. **正解** C, F

(A) For	(A) ために
(B) Upon	(B) にあたり
(C) As	**(C) として**
(D) Within	(D) 以内に
(E) Except	(E) 除いて
(F) With	**(F) 一緒に**

解説　I have seen many examples of his outstanding performance in the marketing department「マーケティング部門での彼の卓越したパフォーマンスの例をたくさん見てきました」と続きます。As his supervisor「彼の上司として」という意味になるので(C)は自然で正解です。With his supervisor「彼の上司とともに」という意味になる(F)も自然で正解です。他の前置詞は続く文を考慮すると不自然な表現になってしまいます。

140. **正解** B, C, F

(A) notified	(A) 知らせを受けて
(B) impressed	**(B) 感心して**
(C) amazed	**(C) 驚いて**
(D) depressed	(D) 落ち込んで
(E) confused	(E) 混乱して
(F) astonished	**(F) 驚いて**

解説　この文では、his cheerful character「明るい性格」やdiligence「勤勉さ」など褒め言葉が使われています。なので、ポジティブな単語を選ぶことが重要です。(B)、(C)、(F)は「感動する」や「驚く」など良い意味なので、正解になります。(A)は「知らされた」という意味で不自然ですし、(D)は「落ち込む」、(E)は「混乱する」と、ネガティブな意味を持つので、ここにはふさわしくありません。

141. **正解** B

(A) respects	(A) 尊敬する
(B) respected	**(B) 尊敬される**
(C) respecting	(C) 尊敬している
(D) respectable	(D) 見苦しくない
(E) respective	(E) それぞれの
(F) respectively	(F) それぞれ

解説　have been 過去分詞 by ～で、「～に過去分詞されている」という受動態と完了形を掛け合わせた文になります。よって、正解は(B)になります。「彼はマーケティング部だけでなく他の部の社員にも尊敬されている」という意味になります。(A)はrespectに三単現のsが付いた形（通常 respect は可算名詞の複数形の形はとらない）、(F)は副詞なので当てはまりません。他の選択肢は形容詞または形容詞扱いの単語なので文法上当てはめることはできますが、byに続く受動態であることに気づければ正解を導き出せるでしょう。

142.　正解　A, E

(A) Finally	(A) 最後に
(B) Completely	(B) 完全に
(C) Firstly	(C) 最初に
(D) Honesty	(D) 正直に
(E) Lastly	(E) 最後に
(F) Clearly	(F) はっきり

解説　結びの文に入るので、ここは「最後に」という意味を持つ(A)と(E)が正解です。(B)は「完全に」、(C)は「初めに」、(D)は「正直に」、(F)は「はっきり」という意味になり、ここで出てくるのは不自然なので間違いです。

Point

不自然さが感知できるかどうかは差を生むことがあります。その部分局所的に見ての判断ではなく、「全体の流れや脈絡を見たときに、無理がない単語選択になっているか」という視点で考えます。例えば、この最後の段落になってFirstly（最初に）というのは明らかに場所がおかしいです。この最後になってHonestly（正直に言うと）とこれまでと異なる内容を切り出すのは脈絡がありません。また、日本語に訳したらうまく聞こえるが、英語では単語の相性が合わない、もともとそういう言い方はしない、という観点もあります。

Part7 読解問題

英語脳 徹底 トレーニング法⑦
速読

Goal 》語彙力・文法力の漏れをなくす

> Part 7で必要となるスキルは、速読スキルです。1分間に少なくとも160単語、可能であれば180単語、理想的には200単語読めるレベルに到達しましょう。
>
> ※今後は1分間に読む単語数をwpm [= words per minute]で記述します

例 題

時間を計って、以下の長文を読め。9割の理解度は保つこと。読み終わるまでにかかった時間を記録し、自分の速読力を数値化せよ。

[注意]メール差出人、受取人、件名、日付など全て飛ばさずに読むこと

UNIVERSITY TIMES
March 12

The University Entertainment Club (UEC) is now taking applications for new committee members for the upcoming school year.

As part of our activities, the UEC plans movie programs for the Taylor Theater, which is located on North Campus. Committee responsibilities include selecting movies and selling tickets at the ticket gate of the theater. Members are recommended to have a wide range of knowledge of movies, but this is not an absolute requirement. Any movie lover is

---

suitable for this position.

*note: All members must attend club meetings once a week.

We also participate in various film festivals. The UEC has received several awards for movie festivals, including an award for the best collegiate film festival in the state for 2022.

There is currently a need for 3 new members for the upcoming school year. If you have any questions, please feel free to contact the UEC president, Wally Canter, at 309-233-4439.

パッセージの長さ：155単語

120 wpm	→ 78秒
140 wpm	→ 66秒
160 wpm	→ 58秒
180 wpm	→ 52秒
200 wpm	→ 46秒
220 wpm	→ 42秒

＊所要時間 ＿＿(例)＿＿＿＿ 秒（書き入れてください）

》訳で確認！

大学通信
3月12日

大学エンターテインメントクラブ（UEC）は次年度の委員会メンバーへの申請を受け付けています。

活動の一環として、UECは北キャンパスにあるテイラー・シアターでの映画上演会を企画しています。委員の役割は映画を選定することと、シアターのチケットゲートでチケットを販売することです。委員は映画への幅広い知識を持っていることが推奨されますが、これが絶対的な必須事項ではありません。映画愛好家であればどなたでもこのポジションにぴったりです。
＊メモ：全ての委員は週1回のミーティングに参加しなければいけません。

私たちはさまざまな映画祭にも参加しています。UECは2022年の州のベスト・カレッジ映画祭受賞を含め、映画祭の賞を幾つか受賞しています。

現在次年度に向けて3名の新メンバーをお迎えしたいと思っています。もし質問がある場合は、電話309-233-4439番で、UEC代表のワリー・キャンターまでご連絡ください。

トレーニングを実践！

時間を計って、以下の長文を読め。9割の理解度は保つこと。読み終わるまでにかかった時間を記録し、自分の速読力を数値化せよ。
[注意]メール差出人、受取人、件名、日付など全て飛ばさずに読むこと

速読用セット1

Orange Technology welcomes you to their annual Think Tank Meeting, to be held on Friday, the 16th of May 2021.

The primary topic of discussion will be the advancement of social media and how it influences the everyday choices we make in our lives. The speaker will be Dr. Josh Grehan, who is a professor of behavioral psychology at William Central University.

Mr. Grehan will be taking a closer look at how we make subconscious decisions based on what we see on social media apps. He will also help us understand how vision of an ideal life is shaped by the kind of media we consume daily.

パッセージの長さ：110単語

＊所要時間 _____ 秒（書き入れてください）

120 wpm → 56秒
140 wpm → 48秒
160 wpm → 42秒 ＊最低目標
180 wpm → 37秒 ＊通常目標
200 wpm → 33秒 ＊理想
220 wpm → 30秒

》 **訳で確認！** ―9割以上の理解度があるか確認しよう

オレンジ・テクノロジーは、2021年5月16日金曜日に開催される毎年恒例のシンクタンク会議にあなたを歓迎します。

議論の主なトピックは、ソーシャルメディアの進歩と、それが私たちの生活の中でする日常の選択にどのように影響するかについてです。講演者は、ウィリアム・セントラル大学の行動心理学教授、ジョシュ・グレハン氏です。

グレハン氏は、私たちがソーシャルメディアアプリで見たものに基づいて、潜在意識の決定をどのように行うかを詳述していきます。彼はまた、理想的な生活の未来像が、私たちが毎日使用するメディアの種類によってどのように形成されるかということの理解を促してくれます。

速読用セット2

From: Theo Gardner
To: Customer Service
Subject: Incorrect order received
Date: 19 August 2021, 7:15 P.M.

Hello there,

I am writing to you about an order I placed on your website last week. My order number is X317867. I received my order in the mail today but noticed that one of the jackets sent to me was not the correct size.

I ordered a Black Woolen Sherpa Jacket in a medium size but was instead sent an extra large. I can return the incorrect size to your warehouse via post and was wondering if you could please send out the correct size to me as soon as possible.

I have always appreciated your amazing customer service and have no doubt that this will be sorted in no time.

Thank you.

Kind regards,

Theo

パッセージの長さ：132単語

120 wpm → 66秒
140 wpm → 57秒
160 wpm → 50秒 *最低目標
180 wpm → 44秒 *通常目標
200 wpm → 40秒 *理想
220 wpm → 36秒

＊所要時間 _____ 秒(書き入れてください)

差出人：テオ・ガードナー
宛先：顧客サービス
件名：間違った品物を受け取りました
日付：2021年8月19日19:15

こんにちは。

先週貴社のウェブサイトで注文したことについてメールを書いています。私の注文番号は X317867 です。今日郵送で品物を受け取りましたが、送られてきたジャケットの1つが正しいサイズではないことに気づきました。

ブラックウールシェルパジャケットをミディアムサイズで注文しましたが、代わりにエクストララージが送られてきました。間違ったサイズを郵送で倉庫に返送しますので、できるだけ早く正しいサイズを送っていただくようお願いします。

私はいつも貴社の素晴らしい顧客サービスに感謝しており、即対応いただけるものと思っています。

ありがとうございます。

敬具

テオ

速読用セット3

Mother's Day is fast approaching and if you're looking for that perfect gift for your gorgeous mom, look no further than our beautiful Himalayan Pink Salt candles. These candles are available in a variety of fragrances and sizes. Here's a little about our best-selling ones.

Lily: This one is probably our favorite! With scents of cedar and vanilla, this candle has a light woody smell that is perfect for those winter nights, sitting next to the fire. The candle is topped with real lavender and rose petals, along with Himalayan pink salt.

Bessy from Texas says this about her Lily candle: "I love Candle Creations because they come up with the most innovative scents. Their customer service is fantastic too!"

Honey: Our Honey candle is made with pure Manuka honey oil and smells of lightly roasted pears, honey, and cinnamon. This one is perfect if your mother likes sweet scents. The candle also has a real vanilla pod in it, so that fragrance lasts longer.

Jasmine from Minnesota says, "The Honey candle is my favorite. I have bought three of them already! The scent is very relaxing and helps me calm down."

Flower Blast: If your mother likes floral scents, give her this candle! The fragrance is a mix of various wildflowers, orchids, roses, and jasmine. The candle also has real rose buds and rosemary on the surface, so it is really beautiful when you light it.

Kaya from Georgia wrote to us and said, "Please don't ever stop making the Flower Blast candle. The fragrance is stunning, and it feels like I'm standing in a meadow of flowers. Thank you for creating this!"

Drop into our store on Gotham St. or shop online at candlecreations. com.

パッセージの長さ：294 単語

＊所要時間 _____ 秒（書き入れてください）

120 wpm → 147秒
140 wpm → 126秒
160 wpm → 110秒 ＊最低目標
180 wpm → 98秒 ＊通常目標
200 wpm → 88秒 ＊理想
220 wpm → 80秒

母の日が近づいています。すてきなママへの完璧な贈り物をお探しの場合は、美しいヒマラヤピンクソルトキャンドルをお薦めします。これらのキャンドルは、さまざまな香りとサイズでご利用いただけます。以下は私たちのベストセラーのものについてです。

リリー：これは私たちのお気に入りです！　杉とバニラの香りがするこのキャンドルは、暖炉のそばに座って過ごす冬の夜にぴったりの、軽い木の香りがします。キャンドルは、ヒマラヤピンクソルトと一緒に、本物のラベンダーとバラの花びらでトッピングされています。

テキサスのベシーは、彼女のリリーキャンドルについて次のように述べています。「最も革新的な香りのこの商品が大好きです。彼らの顧客サービスも素晴らしいです！」

ハニー：私たちのハニーキャンドルは、純粋なマヌカハニーオイルと軽くローストした洋梨、はちみつ、シナモンの香りで作られています。お母さんが甘い香りが好きなら、これは完璧です。キャンドルには本物のバニラのさやも入っているので、香りが長持ちします。

ミネソタ州のジャスミンは、次のように述べています。「ハニーキャンドルは私のお気に入りです。すでに３つ購入しました！　香りはとてもリラックスできて、落ち着くのに役立ちます」

フラワーブラスト：お母さんが花の香りが好きなら、このキャンドルをあげてください！香りは、さまざまな野花、蘭、バラ、ジャスミンのミックスです。キャンドルの表面には本物のバラのつぼみとローズマリーが付いているので、火をつけたときとても美しくなります。

ジョージア州のカヤは私たちにメールを書き、こう伝えています。「フラワーブラストキャンドルの製作をやめないでください。香りは素晴らしく、花の牧草地に立っているような気分です。これを作成していただきありがとうございます！」

ゴッサムストーリートの当店に立ち寄るか、candlecreations.com でオンラインショッピングをお楽しみください。

速読用セット4

From: Yuma Geller
To: All Continental Express contractors and employees
Date: 30th September 2020

Subject: In recognition of services rendered

As part of Continental Express' endeavor to continuously recognize employees who have gone above and beyond what is expected of them, I would like to congratulate Ria Khan on the superb job she has done as head of our Events Management team.

Ria joined Continental Express in 2009 and has been an integral part of the Events Management team. While she joined as a member of the support staff, she has worked her way to the top through her sheer determination and hard work. In the past few years, she has ensured that every event is organized in a thoroughly professional manner.

Her most notable contribution to the Events Management team was the organization of the Continental Express Conference 2019, where she managed to pull off an event that brought the company numerous accolades. Her talent and eye for detail are unmatched throughout the company.

In recognition of the services rendered, I would like to award her the Employee of the Year award, which also comes with a gift of $10,000, pre-loaded on a Continental Express card. I hope everyone will join me in congratulating her on this achievement. I wish her many more successful years with Continental Express Pvt Ltd.

Sincerely,

Yuma Geller,
CEO, Continental Express Pvt Ltd

CONTINENTAL EXPRESS PVT LTD
EMPLOYEE OF THE YEAR AWARD 2020
to
Ria Khan

Congratulations on being recognized as Continental Express'

Employee of the Year, for the year 2019-2020. We are truly honored that you are a part of Continental Express Pvt Ltd. In recognition and appreciation of all that you do for the company, please find attached a gift card of $10,000.

We thank you for all your hard work and support!

Yuma Geller

Yuma Geller, CEO Continental Express Pvt Ltd

パッセージの長さ：310単語

＊所要時間 ＿＿＿＿＿＿ 秒（書き入れてください）

120 wpm → 155秒
140 wpm → 133秒
160 wpm → 116秒 ＊最低目標
180 wpm → 103秒 ＊通常目標
200 wpm → 93秒 ＊理想
220 wpm → 85秒

差出人：ユマ・ゲラー
宛先：全てのコンチネンタル・エキスプレスの請負業者と従業員
日付：2020年9月30日
件名：提供されたサービスをたたえて

コンチネンタル・エキスプレスは期待以上の成果を上げている従業員を継続的に表彰する試みの一環として、リア・カーンがイベント管理チームの責任者として素晴らしい仕事をしてくれたことをお祝いいたします。

リアは2009年にコンチネンタル・エキスプレスに加入し、イベント管理チームの不可欠な部分を担ってきました。彼女はサポートスタッフの一員として参加しましたが、彼女の真摯な決意と勤勉によってトップに上り詰めました。過去数年間、彼女は全てのイベントが問題なく開催されることに尽力してきました。

イベント管理チームへの彼女の最も注目すべき貢献は、コンチネンタル・エキスプレス・カンファレンス2019の統率であり、そこで彼女は会社に多くの称賛をもたらしたイベントをうまく成功させました。彼女の才能と細部まで行き届く目は、会社全体で無比のものです。

功績をたたえて、コンチネンタル・エキスプレスのカードにプリロードされた1万ドルのギフトとともに年間最優秀従業員賞を彼女に授与したいと思います。この功績を祝福する

ために、皆さんが私に賛同してくれることを願っています。彼女がコンチネンタル・エキスプレスでより多くの成功を収めることを願っています。

敬具

ユマ・ゲラー
CEO コンチネンタル・エキスプレス

コンチネンタル・エキスプレス
2020年の最優秀従業員賞
リア・カーンへ

2019～2020年のコンチネンタル・エキスプレスの年間最優秀従業員として認められたことを祝福します。あなたがコンチネンタル・エキスプレスの一員であることを心から光栄に思います。会社のために行った全てのことを評価し、感謝するために、同封された1万ドルのギフトカードをお受け取りください。

あなたのご尽力とご支援に感謝申し上げます！

ユマ・ゲラー
コンチネンタル・エキスプレス、ユマ・ゲラー

速読用セット5

CLOSING DOWN SALE
Richmond, 5th August 2021:

After 35 years of serving the Richmond community and helping customers with all their grocery needs, we are sad to announce that Richmond Grocers will be closing their store from the 15th of August 2021.

After the death of the store owner, Mr. Bob Creek, the family is unable to manage the operations of the store. As many in the Richmond community might already know, Bob lost his wife, Anne, a few years ago. Their son and daughter live overseas and have had to make this difficult decision of closing the business.

Due to these recent events, the entire inventory of the store is on sale, with at least a fifty percent discount on their marked price. The sale lasts from 7th August to 12th August.

To: Dominic Cron
From: Daniel Stone
Date: 6th August 2021
Subject: Recent Richmond Grocers article

Dear Mr. Cron,

I am writing to you about your article on Richmond Grocers closing. I believe the article was in yesterday's newspaper.

I was wondering if you have a contact phone number or an e-mail address for Mr. Creek's son or daughter. I would like to put in an offer to buy the store off so that the store does not have to close permanently or be taken in by some real estate from the city.

I have very fond childhood memories of going to Richmond Grocers with my mother. Bob was always very kind to me and would always slip me a lolly or two when my mother wasn't looking. I would hate to see the store closed, or worse being demolished.

Please let me know if there is any way you could help me get in touch with the family.

Kind regards,

Daniel

To: Daniel Stone
From: Dominic Cron
Date: 6th August 2021
Subject: Re: Recent Richmond Grocers article

Dear Mr. Stone,

Thank you for getting in touch. I think it is a wonderful idea and will do my best to put you in touch with Harry or Elizabeth, Bob's children. Richmond Grocers was always a favorite haunt of mine when I was growing up too!

I remember talking to Harry a few months ago and asking him if he had any prospective buyers for the business. Unfortunately, because Richmond is such a small town, not many people showed any interest in buying or leasing the store. I think the entire community would rally behind you if you were to take over the store and restore it to how it was when Bob owned it.

Harry can be reached at harrycreek21@gmail.com and Elizabeth can be reached at elizabethcreek198@gmail.com. I have also e-mailed them, and they are looking forward to hearing from you.

Kind regards,

Dominic

パッセージの長さ：459単語

＊所要時間 ＿＿＿＿＿ 秒(書き入れてください)

120 wpm → 230秒
140 wpm → 198秒
160 wpm → 173秒 ＊最低目標
180 wpm → 154秒 ＊通常目標
200 wpm → 138秒 ＊理想
220 wpm → 128秒

第1章 英語脳徹底トレーニング

第2章 高難度問題の徹底攻略

第3章 正答ハイテクレッスン

第4章 ハイレベル完全模試

閉店セール
リッチモンド、2021年8月5日：

リッチモンドコミュニティに35年間サービスを提供し、全ての食料雑貨のニーズに対応してきた後、リッチモンドグローサーズが2021年8月15日から店舗を閉鎖することを残念ながら発表いたします。

店主のボブ・クリーク氏の死後、家族は店の運営を管理することが不可能になりました。リッチモンドコミュニティの多くの人がすでにご存じでしょうが、ボブは数年前に妻のアンを亡くしました。彼らの息子と娘は海外に住んでいて、事業を閉鎖するというこの難しい決断をしなければなりませんでした。

これらの最近の出来事により、店の全ての在庫が特売されており、表示価格から少なくとも50パーセント割引されています。セールは8月7日から8月12日まで続きます。

宛先：ドミニク・クロン
差出人：ダニエル・ストーン
日付：2021年8月6日
件名：最近のリッチモンドグローサーズの記事

親愛なるクロン様、

リッチモンドグローサーズの閉店に関するあなたの記事についてメールを書いています。その記事は昨日の新聞に載っていたと思います。

クリーク氏の息子または娘の連絡先の電話番号またはメールアドレスをお持ちでしょうか。閉店したり、市内の不動産に持ち込まれたりすることがないように、店を買い取る提案をしたいと思います。

リッチモンドグローサーズに母と行った子供の頃の思い出が私はとても好きです。ボブはいつも私にとても親切で、母が見ていなかったときはいつも私にキャンディーを1つか2つくれていました。私は店が閉まったり、ましてや解体されているところを見たくありません。

ご家族と連絡を取るのを手伝ってくれる方法があればお知らせください。

敬具

ダニエル

宛先：ダニエル・ストーン
差出人：ドミニク・クロン
日付：2021年8月6日
件名：Re：最近のリッチモンドグローサーズの記事

親愛なるストーンさん、

ご連絡ありがとうございます。それは素晴らしいお考えだと思います。ボブの子供である
ハリーやエリザベスと連絡を取るために最善を尽くします。リッチモンドグローサーズは、
私も子どもの頃にいつも私のお気に入りの場所でした！

私は数カ月前にハリーと話をし、彼にその事業の見込みのある買い手がいるかどうか尋ね
たのを覚えています。残念ながら、リッチモンドはとても小さな町なので、店の購入や賃
貸借に興味を示した人はあまりいませんでした。あなたが店を引き継いで、ボブがそれを
所有していたときの状態に回復するとしたら、コミュニティ全体があなたの後ろにつくと
思います。

ハリーは harrycreek21@gmail.com で、エリザベスは elizabethcreek198@gmail.
com で連絡が取れます。私からも2人にメールを送りました、そして彼らはあなたから
の連絡を期待しています。

敬具

ドミニク

**990点
満点
への道**

Part 6・Part 7の速読で
求められる理解度は9割

　Part 7の速読において必要とされる理解度は9割です。速読ですから、熟読して完全理解するわけではありません。一部細かい曖昧な点や、知らない単語、読み取れない文構造があったとしても、長時間そこに足止めされることなく、読み進めていきます。情報の羅列や箇条書きの類のものは、速読時に必ずしも細部まで読み込んで行く必要はありません。もちろん知らない単語や取れない文構造がなくなるように日ごろの学習は積んでおくべきです。

　この9割の理解度で、目標の速度で一定の単語数を読めるようになることが目標となります。問題を先に見ておいて、部分的に長文を読んで行く方法でも正解できる問題も一定数ありますが、満点を取るなら、全文速読が必須と考えましょう。

　ただ、一部例外もあります。イベントの予定表でのタイムテーブル、領収書や請求書に載っている住所、電話番号などは、時々問題で聞かれる可能性があります。その場合は、該当部分に戻って読み込むことで時間を短縮しつつ、正解を重ねましょう。

単語力トレーニング

Goal ≫ 1問も落とさない語彙力を身につける

単純な語彙力が満点をめざす上では特に重要です。特に
TOEICで頻出し、そして900点以上のスコア保持者が間
違えやすい単語を覚えましょう。

Part 1　頻出単語100

appliance	器具	名詞
audience	観客	名詞
brick	レンガ	名詞
bulletin board	掲示板	名詞
cabinet	キャビネット（収納用の棚や箱）	名詞
cardboard box	段ボール	名詞
cargo	貨物	名詞
compartment	仕切り	名詞
container	容器	名詞
crate	木箱	名詞
cubicle	（仕切られた）個人用スペース	名詞
curb	縁石	名詞
dish	皿、料理	名詞
file	ファイル	名詞
folder	フォルダー	名詞
fountain	噴水	名詞
instrument	楽器	名詞
intersection	交差点	名詞

ladder	はしご	名詞
lamppost	街灯	名詞
lawn	芝生	名詞
lawn mower	芝刈り機	名詞
market	市場、店	名詞
merchandise	商品	名詞
office supply	事務用品	名詞
path	小道	名詞
patio	中庭	名詞
pedestrian	歩行者	名詞
pier	埠頭、桟橋	名詞
plate	(名前などが書いてある)プレート	名詞
post	柱、くい、郵便ポスト	名詞
pot	壺	名詞
potted plants	鉢植え	名詞
pottery	陶器	名詞
produce	農作物	名詞
railing	手すり	名詞
rug	じゅうたん	名詞
shelf	棚	名詞
shore	岸	名詞
spectator	観客	名詞
staircase	階段(=stairway, stairs)	名詞
structure	建物	名詞
traffic	交通	名詞
utensil	台所用品	名詞
vehicle	乗り物	名詞
vendor	売り子	名詞
walkway	歩道	名詞
wheelbarrow	手押し車	名詞
wood	材木	名詞

be arranged	配置されてる	動詞
be covered with	覆われている	動詞
be lined up	並んでいる	動詞
be mounted	持ち上げられている	動詞
be parked	停車されている	動詞
be piled up	積まれている	動詞
be placed	置かれている	動詞
be propped up against	立てかけてある	動詞
be put	置かれている	動詞
be scattered	散らかっている	動詞
be set up	並べられている	動詞
be spread	広げられている	動詞
be stacked	積まれている	動詞
bend over	前かがみになる	動詞
cast a shadow	影を落とす	動詞
display	展示する、[名詞]展示	動詞
face	面する	動詞
gaze at	じっと見つめる	動詞
glance at	ちらっと見る	動詞
hang	つるす	動詞
hover	空中浮遊する	動詞
kneel down	ひざをつく	動詞
lead to	つながっている	動詞
lean (on/against)	寄りかかっている	動詞
lift	持ち上げる	動詞
load	荷物を積む	動詞
look into	のぞき込む	動詞
overlook	見下ろす	動詞
pack	荷造りする	動詞
pave	舗装する	動詞
rake	かき集める	動詞

reach	手を伸ばす	動詞
repair	修理する	動詞
sort	分ける	動詞
stroll	ぶらつく	動詞
sweep	掃く	動詞
trim	刈り込む	動詞
unfold	開く	動詞
water	水をやる、[名詞]湖、海	動詞
against	～に対して(e.g. against the wall)	前置詞
along	～に沿って	前置詞
alongside	～のそばに、横側に	前置詞
beside	～の横に	前置詞
beneath	～の下に	前置詞
on top of	～の上に	前置詞
face to face	向かい合って	副詞
in a line	列に並んで(輪の場合は in a circle)	副詞
partially	部分的に	副詞
side by side	隣同士で	副詞
slanted	傾いている	形容詞

第2章

990点満点を取るためだけの
高難度問題の徹底攻略

TOEIC高得点者でも間違えてしまう「高難度問題」を徹底的に対策することで、990点取得の実現にグッと近づくことができます。
難しい問題に対しても正解が重ねる力を身につけるために、Part別に実戦形式で高難易度の問題に取り組みましょう。

Part1 写真描写問題

絶対に押さえたい満点ポイント①
受け身の英文を瞬時に理解する

> Part 1 で特に気をつけたい問題は、「現在進行形受け身」と
> 「現在完了形受け身」が使われている英文です。このような
> Part 1 に独特な文法を徹底的にマスターしましょう。

◆ 現在進行形受け身・現在完了形受け身の問題

TOEIC Part 1 では、「現在進行形受け身」や「現在完了形受け身」が使われている選択肢もあります。こうした表現にはTOEIC独特なものもあり、日常生活でよく使う表現・文ではないものもあるのですが、実際にテストで出る表現なので、理解した上で慣れておかなければいけません。

例えば、この写真では、以下のような選択肢も正解として扱われています。

例題 W

The structure **is being displayed**.

（構造物が展示されている）

→ 現在行われている動作が
受け身で表現されている！

The model **has been set up** on the foundation.

（土台の上にモデルがセットされた）

→ 完了した動作が受け身で
表現されている！

➡ 意味が理解しづらい<u>受け身の表現</u>に慣れる必要があり！

絶対に押さえたい満点ポイント②
クセのある頻出語をマスターする

> 次にPart 1で上級者が点を落としやすいのが、TOEICの
> Part 1特有ともいえる単語・フレーズです。クセのある語
> 句をきちんとマスターしましょう。

◆ Part 1になぜかよく出る単語を問う問題

なぜ「手すり（railing）」という単語が大事なのかはわかりませんが、TOEICでは
とにかくrailingという単語を極めて頻繁に登場させます。特にPart 1では、「芝
生（lawn）」、「噴水（fountain）」、「棚（shelf）」といった、頻出単語グループがあ
ります。

これらの単語の幾つかは、（少なくとも出題頻度が暗示するほどに）私たちの生
活において重要なものとは思えませんが、とにかくTOEICでは出ます。

例題 **🇬🇧 W**

(A) **Some textiles are tightly stacked on the shelves.**

(B) The items are being washed.

(C) Some products are being put into a metal cabinet.

(D) Some products are hanging on the wall.

be stacked on
(重ねられている)は
頻出のフレーズ。

➡ 頻出語句を暗記す
ることがPart 1全
6問正解への近道!

(A) **幾つかの織物は棚にタイトに積み重ねられている。**

(B) アイテムは洗われている。

(C) 幾つかの製品は金属製キャビネットの中に置かれている。

(D) 幾つかの製品は壁にかかっている。

高難度問題にトライ！

本番と同じ問題数、6問を用意しました。全問正解してください！

 M

練習問題 1

Ⓐ Ⓑ Ⓒ Ⓓ

練習問題 2

Ⓐ Ⓑ Ⓒ Ⓓ

練習問題3

Ⓐ Ⓑ Ⓒ Ⓓ

練習問題4

Ⓐ Ⓑ Ⓒ Ⓓ

練習問題5

Ⓐ Ⓑ Ⓒ Ⓓ

練習問題6

Ⓐ Ⓑ Ⓒ Ⓓ

正解と解説

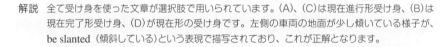

練習問題1　正解 D

(A) The trees are being cut down.

(B) Water has been pumped out.

(C) The vehicles are being washed.

(D) Part of the ground is slanted.

(A) 木が切り落とされている。

(B) 水はポンプで吸い出された。

(C) 車両が洗浄されている。

(D) 地面の一部が傾斜している。

> 解説　全て受け身を使った文章が選択肢で用いられています。(A)、(C)は現在進行形受け身、(B)は現在完了形受け身、(D)が現在形の受け身です。左側の車両の地面が少し傾いている様子が、be slanted（傾斜している）という表現で描写されており、これが正解となります。

練習問題2　正解 C

(A) The man is putting away a microscope.

(B) The man has separated the specimen.

(C) Some stones have been placed on the scale.

(D) A microscope is being displayed for examination.

(A) 男性は顕微鏡を片付けている。

(B) 男性は標本を分けた。

(C) 幾つかの石がはかりに載せられている。

(D) 顕微鏡は検査のために展示されている。

> 解説　写真右手に、2つの石がはかりに乗せられているため(C)が正解。写真の全体の中ではマイナーな箇所ではありますが、一瞬でくまなく写真を捉えて反応できるようにしておくことが肝要。

練習問題3　正解 C

(A) The woman is clearing up dishes.

(B) The woman has is holding a dish above some bread.

(C) Some glasses are positioned next to each other.

(D) The silverware is being washed by the woman.

(A) 女性は皿を片付けている。

(B) 女性はパンの上でお皿を持っている。

(C) 幾つかのグラスが隣同士に置かれている。

(D) 銀食器は女性によって洗われている。

解説　一番目に留まる女性の動作ではなく、後ろにあるグラスについての描写が正解となります。next to each other で隣同士という意味になります。

練習問題4　正解 D

(A) The man is lifting cargo by hand.

(B) The vehicle has been left unattended.

(C) Metal frames are being assembled.

(D) Boxes are piled up against the wall.

(A) 男性は貨物を手で持ち上げている。

(B) 乗り物は無人で放置されている。

(C) 金属のフレームは組み立てられている。

(D) 箱は壁沿いに積み上げられている。

解説　多くの箱が、写真奥の壁に向かって積み上げられているため(D)が正解。男性が箱を持ち上げている写真ですが、厳密には男性(の手)ではなく、機械が持ち上げているので、(A)は誤りです。

練習問題5　正解 B

(A) People are facing away from each other.

(B) Their seats are arranged in a circle.

(C) They are passing down some dishes.

(D) Diners have just finished eating the meal.

(A) 人々はお互いから顔をそむけている。

(B) 彼らの席は円形に配置されている。

(C) 彼らは幾つかの皿を手渡している。

(D) 彼らは食事を食べ終えた。

解説　seats(席)の配置について正しく描写している(B)が正解。夕食を食べ終えた様子は写っていないため、(D)を選ぶことはできません。(A)、(C)は写真に全く描かれていないので不正解です。

練習問題6　正解 C

(A) The boats are being mounted to the shore.

(B) The boats are fastened to one another.

(C) The mountains overlook the water.

(D) Some of the boats are being repaired.

(A) ボートは岸に上げられている。

(B) ボートは互いに固定されている。

(C) 山は水[海・湖]を見下ろしている。

(D) 幾つかのボートは修理されている。

解説　TOEICでは、ocean, sea, river, lake, pondなどを表す単語としてwaterを使用することがよくあります。今回は、写真奥にある山々が、その海・湖を見下ろしている、という(C)が正解となります。

Part 2 | 応答問題

絶対に押さえたい満点ポイント②
間接的な返答が正解となる問題をマスターする

> Part 2で気をつけたい問題は、「空気を読む必要がある」問題です。直接的な返答になっていなくても、相手の意図に合わせた返答を選べるかどうかが鍵となります。

◆ 間接的な返答を選ぶ必要のある問題

リスニング・セクションの問題を解くのにリスニングだけしていたら、Part 2では全問正解はできません。

上司：○○君、また飲みいこうよ、今度は2人で。
部下：ぜひ同行させてください！

© 2019 businesssozai

こんな会話があったとして、部下は本当に上司と飲みに行きたいと考えている可能性はどのくらいあるでしょうか。この部下の発言は単なる社交辞令や建前で、奥底の心情は別にある可能性は低くないでしょう。仮に上司は部下の発言を正しく聞けていても（リスニング）、発言が部下の真意に迫っているかはわからないのです。

上記の会話の続きをしましょう。部下の「ぜひ同行させてください！」の発言に対して正解となる上司の発言はどれでしょうか。

> 部下：I'm extremely honored to be able to drink with you, sir.
> 上司：(A) Then, let's go out for a drink after work tomorrow.
> 　　　(B) I was in an honor's program at college.
> 　　　(C) Well, thank you for saying that, but you must be busy.

(B)は意味不明ですから除外され、(A)は一見正解のようにも見えます。ただ、部下の発言の意図が「社交辞令」であることが見抜ければ、正解は(C)となるわけです。

このような文化的要素を考慮しなくてはいけない問題がTOEICには出ません。しかしながら、聞いた英語の意味を理解する(Listening)だけでなく、話し手の意図を考え理解できるか(Thinking)が重要となります。

例 題

Where will we have a meeting tonight?
（今晩どこで会議をするの？）

(A) Be there before 5 P.M.
　　（午後5時前にそこにいてください）
(B) I live near the Central Park.
　　（私は中央公園の近くに住んでいます）
(C) You didn't know the meeting was canceled?
　　（会議は中止になったと知らなかったの？）

「会議が中止になったことを示す」選択肢が正解になっている！

➡ 「今晩会議をする場所」ではなくても、正解になることがある！

144

高難度問題にトライ！

Part 2の実践型問題をやってみましょう。難易度をあえて上げています。より上級を目指す方は、一字一句しっかり聞き取った上で、話し手の発言の意図を考えつつ、確実に正解できているかを確認しましょう。

英文とその応答文を聞き、英文に正しく応答しているものを選べ。

SET 1

Mark your answers on your answer sheet.

1. Ⓐ Ⓑ Ⓒ   6. Ⓐ Ⓑ Ⓒ
2. Ⓐ Ⓑ Ⓒ   7. Ⓐ Ⓑ Ⓒ
3. Ⓐ Ⓑ Ⓒ   8. Ⓐ Ⓑ Ⓒ
4. Ⓐ Ⓑ Ⓒ   9. Ⓐ Ⓑ Ⓒ
5. Ⓐ Ⓑ Ⓒ   10. Ⓐ Ⓑ Ⓒ

SET 2

Mark your answers on your answer sheet.

11. Ⓐ Ⓑ Ⓒ   16. Ⓐ Ⓑ Ⓒ
12. Ⓐ Ⓑ Ⓒ   17. Ⓐ Ⓑ Ⓒ
13. Ⓐ Ⓑ Ⓒ   18. Ⓐ Ⓑ Ⓒ
14. Ⓐ Ⓑ Ⓒ   19. Ⓐ Ⓑ Ⓒ
15. Ⓐ Ⓑ Ⓒ   20. Ⓐ Ⓑ Ⓒ

SET 1 正解と解説

1. Excuse me, I'm trying to find the seminar on marketing.
   すみません、マーケティングについてのセミナーを探しているのですが。

   正解 B

   (A) I'm not familiar with marketing.   (A) マーケティングには精通していません。

   (B) You have to come back tomorrow.   **(B) 明日戻ってきてください。**

   (C) Dr. Ming is presenting.   (C) ミン博士が講演されています。

   > 解説 「マーケティングについてのセミナーを探している」という発言に対して、「明日戻ってきてください」と返すことによって、今日そのようなセミナーはないということを示唆しています。直接的な返答ではありませんが、(B)が正解となります。

2. When were the monthly assignments due?
   月次の課題の締め切りはいつでしたか。

   正解 B

   (A) I will think about the due date.   (A) 締切日について考えておきます。

   (B) You still have a few more hours.   **(B) もう何時間かありますよ。**

   (C) No, that's not the deadline.   (C) いいえ、それは締め切りではありません。

   > 解説 When 〜 ？で締め切りはいつだったかという質問に対して、「もう何時間かありますよ」と締め切りはまだ過ぎておらず、数時間後であることを伝えています。よって、正解は(B)となります。「月次課題の締め切りを今から考える」のは不自然なので、(A)は不正解です。

3. What was she conducting a study on?
   彼女は何について研究していたのでしょうか。

   正解 A

   (A) Risk management.   **(A) リスク管理です。**

   (B) She studied very hard.   (B) 彼女はとても熱心に勉強しました。

   (C) On the desk over there.   (C) あそこの机の上です。

   > 解説 She was conducting a study on risk management.という返答になります。時々出ている文の形、フレーズですので、そのまま慣れて覚えましょう。

4. Who will summarize the research results?
   研究結果のまとめは誰がしますか。

   正解 B

   (A) John was not a project member.
   (B) **I'll have my subordinate do that.**
   (C) The research ended up a great success.

   (A) ジョンはプロジェクトメンバーではありません。
   (B) **それは私の部下にやらせます。**
   (C) 研究は大成功に終わりました。

   > 解説 使役動詞 have を使って、部下にやらせる、と返答している(B)が正解です。get, help, make, have などは使役動詞で使われても即座に反応できるようにしておきましょう。

5. Do you want me to do the rest of the dishes?
   私が残りの皿洗いをしましょうか。

   正解 C

   (A) I will rest on the sofa.
   (B) I haven't prepared any dishes for you.
   (C) **Oh, thank you so much.**

   (A) 私はソファで休みます。
   (B) 私はあなたのために料理を用意していません。
   (C) **ありがとうございます。**

   > 解説 皿洗いの手伝いを申し出ているのに対して、「ありがとうございます」と返事することで、申し出を受け入れています。正解は(C)になります。(A)は Then I will take a break. (でしたら、休憩を取ります)くらいであれば自然ですが、あまりに唐突すぎます。(B)は dishesという単語を違う意味で使ったひっかけ問題です。

6. Do you want me to turn it on?
   (スイッチを)オンにしましょうか。

   正解 B

   (A) Turn up the volume.
   (B) **Is it off?**
   (C) Turn around slowly.

   (A) 音量を上げてください。
   (B) **今オフになっていますか。**
   (C) ゆっくり回ってみてください。

   > 解説 スイッチか何かをオンにしましょうか、と聞かれ、既にオンになっていると思ったので、(B)今オフになっていますか、という返答となったわけです。TOEIC テストでも同様のパターンが時々見られています。turnにつられて(C)を選ばないようにしましょう。

7. Did your house experience a power shortage this morning?
   あなたの家は今朝停電になりましたか。

   正解 C

   (A) No, I haven't been there before.
   (A) いいえ、そこに行ったことはありません。

   (B) Actually, the problem has been fixed.
   (B) 実は、問題は解決されました。

   (C) Yes, it was unusually stormy, wasn't it?
   (C) はい、今朝は異常なまでの嵐でしたね。

   解説　「今朝停電になったか」を尋ねているのに対して、「はい、今朝は異常なまでの嵐でしたね」と返答することで、嵐について言及しながら停電になったことを示唆しています。よって、正解は(C)となります。wasn't it?と付け加えて、「〜でしたね」と相手に問いかけている付加疑問文の文で、TOEIC頻出です。

8. Should I ask for permission from the CEO or the accounting manager?
   最高経営責任者と経理部長のどちらから最初に許可を取る必要がありますか。

   正解 C

   (A) He will be here soon.
   (A) 彼はすぐにここに来ます。

   (B) OK, call me around 10 P.M.
   (B) わかりました、午後10時頃私に電話してください。

   (C) I will arrange a meeting with both of them.
   (C) お2人とのミーティングを手配します。

   解説　「許可をどちらに取る必要があるか」を質問しているのに対し、「お2人のミーティングを手配します」という返事で、2人に確認が必要ということを示唆しています。正解は(C)です。長い文ですが、実際のテストでも同程度の英文が出題されます。

9. Who is credited for this work?
   この作品の功績は誰にありますか。

   正解 B

   (A) I don't have a credit card.
   (A) 私はクレジットカードを持っていません。

   (B) I'll have to ask my supervisor.
   (B) 上司に聞く必要があります。

   (C) The work was completed a few weeks ago.
   (C) 作業は数週間前に完了しました。

   解説　「功績は誰にあるか」と聞かれている一方、「上司に聞く必要があります」との返答で「自分はわからないから確認が必要だ」と伝えています。正解は(B)です。(A)はcreditという単語が違う意味で使われている例で、ひっかけ問題です。

10. All the players are in the locker room, aren't they?

選手たちは全員更衣室にいますよね？

正解 B

(A) No, they are not locked in a room.

(B) **You should hurry if you want to talk with them.**

(C) There is nothing to play with.

(A) いいえ、彼らは部屋に閉じ込められていません。

(B) **彼らと話したいなら急いだ方がいいよ。**

(C) 遊ぶものは何もありません。

解説 「選手たちは全員更衣室にいるか」を確認しているのに対して、「彼らと話したいなら急いだほうがいいよ」と返し、彼らはまだ更衣室にいるがもうすぐ離れることを示唆しています。よって、正解は(B)です。彼らと話したいから確認しているという意図をくみ取った選択肢かどうか、がポイントです。

SET 2 正解と解説 M W

11. Let me introduce my friend Paul. He is an architect.

友人のポールを紹介させてください、彼は建築家です。

正解 A

(A) **Have we met somewhere before?**

(B) OK, I was there.

(C) I have not finished my design.

(A) **以前どこかでお会いしたことはありますか。**

(B) わかりました、私はそこにいました。

(C) 私はデザインを終えていません。

解説 紹介された人に対し、「あれっ、以前どこかでお会いしたことありませんでしたっけ…」というドラマに出てきそうなワンシーンです。正解は(A)です。(B)や(C)は脈絡的にも不自然ですし、友人紹介の場でする発言としてもふさわしくはないでしょう。

12. I have ordered a birthday cake, so we need to pick it up this evening.

バースデーケーキを注文しました、夕方には受け取りに行かないといけません。

正解 C

(A) Actually, it's not my birthday.

(B) I don't know how to make a cake.

(C) **Could you go get it by yourself?**

(A) 実は私の誕生日ではありません。

(B) 私にはケーキの作り方はわかりません。

(C) **1人で行ってもらえますか。**

解説 「1人で行ってもらえますか」と返すことで、自分は取りに行けないということを伝えています。直接的な返答ではありませんが、正解は(C)です。「バースデーケーキを受け取りに行きたいから話している」という意図をくみ取ればもっとも自然な答えになります。誰

の誕生日か、と質問されているわけでもないので、(A)の「私の誕生日ではありません」と
いうのは不自然です。

13. Our wedding anniversary is coming up.
    私たちの結婚記念日が近づいています。

正解 C

(A) We are going to get married.　　(A) 私たちは結婚します。

(B) I will be on my way.　　(B) 今向かいます。

(C) Time flies, doesn't it?　　**(C) 時間がたつのは速いね。**

解説　「結婚記念日が近づいている」という発言に対して、「時間がたつのは速いね」と返すことで、
会話を続けています。正解は(C)です。結婚記念日ということは、すでに結婚しているので、
(A)は不自然です。考えられるこの問いかけへのほかの返答としては、I won't buy
diamond. やIs there anything you want to eat? などもあるでしょう。

14. Which of the paintings on the shelf is yours?
    棚にある絵のうち、どれがあなたのですか。

正解 A

(A) The one with the butterflies.　　**(A) チョウチョがあるものです。**

(B) My father made the shelf.　　(B) 私の父が棚を作りました。

(C) That one on the top is not mine.　　(C) 一番上のものは私のものではありま
　　　　　　　　　　　　　　　　　　せん。

解説　Which 〜 ? で「どの絵があなたのか」を質問しているのに対して、「チョウチョがあるもの
です」と、絵を特定しています。よって、正解は(A)です。どれかを尋ねられているので、
特定のものを否定している(C)より、(A)がより直接的で自然です。

15. How many of these do I need to order?
    これらを幾つ注文する必要がありますか。

正解 A

(A) At Least 200 cartons.　　**(A) 少なくとも200カートンです。**

(B) Our inventory is empty.　　(B) 在庫が空です。

(C) All the way from Alaska.　　(C) はるばるアラスカからです。

解説　注文する量を質問しているので、量を直接的に返答している(A)が正解です。TOEICでは、
直接的に適切な返答がある場合は、他に間接的に返答している選択肢があったとしても、
直接返答の方が正解となります。よって、在庫がなく、発注が難しいことを示唆している
(B)ではなく、(A)を選びます。

16. What are you reading?

何を読んでいるんですか。

正解 B

(A) In the library.

(B) What the president announced.

(C) It's not so difficult.

(A) 図書館で。

(B) 社長が発言したこと。

(C) それほど難しくはありません。

解説 「何を読んでいるのか」を尋ねているので、「社長が発言したこと」とシンプルに返答している(B)が正解となります。What S Vで、「～すること」という表現は頻出なので押さえておきましょう。(A)は場所について、(C)は難しさについて答えているので、読んでいる内容についての質問に対して適切ではありません。

17. Please estimate the cost it takes to refurbish this house.

この家の改装にかかる費用の見積もりをお願いします。

正解 B

(A) This house was quite expensive when I bought it.

(B) A thorough inspection is needed first.

(C) It could have taken about a week or so.

(A) この家は私が買ったときはかなり高かった。

(B) まずは詳細な検査が必要とされます。

(C) 1週間ほどかかったはずです。

解説 改装費用の見積もりをお願いしているのに対して、「まずは詳細な検査が必要とされます」と返し、見積もりはすぐには用意できないことを示唆しています。よって、正解は(B)となります。(A)はrefurbish「改装する」という単語を知っていないとひっかかる可能性があるので要注意です。

18. The match was canceled because of heavy rain.

大雨のため、試合は中止になりました。

正解 C

(A) I am fully prepared for the match.

(B) Yes, it will rain tomorrow.

(C) Oh, that's a shame.

(A) 私は試合の準備ができています。

(B) はい、明日雨が降ります。

(C) ああ、それは残念ですね。

解説 「試合は中止になりました」という発言に対して、「それは残念ですね」と思いをそのまま言葉にしている(C)が正解になります。That's a shameで「それは残念ですね」という表現を押さえておきましょう。(A)は中止の報告の後にする発言として的確ではありません。明日については尋ねられていないので、(B)も不正解です。

19. Our company is facing a financial crisis.

当社は金融危機に直面しています。

正解 C

(A) The firm is in a dangerous situation.

(B) The finance department is on the 4th floor.

(C) We need to do something about it.

(A) その会社は危機的な状況です。

(B) 財務部は4階にあります。

(C) 私たちがどうにかする必要があります。

解説 「金融危機に直面している」という発言に対して、「私たちがどうにかする必要がある」と返し、解決しようとする姿勢が表れている(C)が正解になります。最後のitはa financial crisisのことです。自社の危機の話をしているので、(A)は同じことをリピートしているだけなので、(C)を凌ぐ適切な返答とは言えません。

20. When will the next episode get released?

次のエピソードはいつ公開されますか。

正解 B

(A) I have watched the last episode.

(B) I know, I can't wait, either.

(C) The series is still airing.

(A) 私はもう最後のエピソードを見ました。

(B) わかります、私も待てません。

(C) シリーズはまだ放送中です。

解説 「いつ次のエピソードが公開されるか」を尋ねていますが、これは早く次のエピソードを見たいということを示唆しています。なので、「わかります、私も待てません」と答えている(B)が正解になります。I can't waitは「(早く〜したくて)待てない」というニュアンスが強い表現です。

どの選択肢が可能？

Part 2の間接的な応答文への対策として、実際の試験形式と同じ問題を解くことを提案しましたが、「正解となりうる答えを選ぶ」というトレーニング方法も効果的です。試しにやってみましょう。

練習問題1

次の問いかけ文に対して、間接的な応答文として可能なものを<u>全て</u>選択せよ。

<u>Who is in charge of the reception tonight?</u>

   A. We will receive lots of requests.

   B. My name is Jane, not Juan.

   C. You should ask your supervisor.

   D. You can refer to the handout.

   E. At about 7PM, Mike said.

   F. Why are you asking me?

   G. Peter won't come, Dianna said.

   H. How many times do you have to ask?

   I. Mr. Tanaka knows better.

   J. You were lucky, weren't you?

   K. Wasn't the event canceled?

   L. I'll confirm and let you know.

   M. Terry is charging the device now.

練習問題 1 正解と解説

正解 C, D, F, H, I, K, L

Who is in charge of the reception tonight?（今夜の歓迎会は誰が担当しますか？）

A. We will receive lots of requests.（私たちは多くの要望を受け付けます。）
reception-receiveの単語レベルでリンクにつられないように留意。誰が担当するのかへの何らの回答になっておらず不適格。

B. My name is Jane, not Juan.（私の名前はジュアンではなくジェーンです。）
Whoに対して名前は出ているが、担当する人の名前ではないので不適格。

C. You should ask your supervisor.（あなたは上司に尋ねるべきです。）
誰が担当するか、私ではなくあなたの上司が知っているから聞いてみて、という間接回答で成立。

D. You can refer to the handout.（あなたは配布物を参照することができます。）
誰が担当するかその紙に書いてあるよ、という意図で間接回答として成立。

E. At about 7PM, Mike said.（午後7時頃にとマイクは言いました。）
マイクという名前は出ているが、発言内容は担当者に関わることではなく不可。

F. Why are you asking me?（なぜあなたは私に尋ねるのですか？）
なぜ私に聞いているの？（他の人に聞いてよ。私が知るわけないじゃない）という意図が読み取れる回答で可能。

G. Peter won't come, Dianna said.（ピーターは来ないとダイアナは言いました。）
二人の名前が出ているが、発言内容は担当者に関わることではなく不可。

H. How many times do you have to ask?（何回あなたは尋ねる必要がありますか？）
同じことを何度も聞かないでね、という気持ちが垣間見える間接的な回答として可能。

I. Mr. Tanaka knows better.（田中さんがより知っています。）
田中さんの方がよく知っているので誰が担当者かは彼に聞いてみて、という意図の回答なので成立。

J. You were lucky, weren't you?（あなたは幸運です、そうでしょう？）
何が幸運だったのか、それがどう担当者の特定に関係するのかは不明で、不適格。

K. Wasn't the event cancelled?（そのイベントはキャンセルされませんでしたか？）
担当者云々の前に、イベントがないから担当者も何もない、という意図で成立。

L. I'll confirm and let you know.（確認してお知らせします。）
誰が担当者なのか確認して後で知らせる、という自然な流れで的確な間接回答。

M. Terry is charging the device now.（テリーは今デバイスを充電しています。）
in charge-chargingの単語レベルでのリンクにつられないように留意。機器の充電と担当者の特定には関連性が認められず不適格。

練習問題2

次の問いかけ文に対して、間接的な応答文として可能なものを<u>全て</u>選択せよ。

<u>Has your manager approved the marketing plan you submitted last week?</u>

  A. Actually, I did not hand in the document.

  B. I expect another two weeks for the decision.

  C. He has managed the new campaign surprisingly well.

  D. Marketing is definitely the most important aspect.

  E. Could you elaborate on that before you leave?

  F. Oh, has it been a week already?

  G. I'm revising it on the basis of his feedback.

  H. Which part of the plan is not well written?

  I. It seems I've received the appraisal just now.

  J. Why do you know that I'm involved in this?

  K. Maybe he hasn't, but I am not too concerned about that.

  L. My boss approved my participation at the workshop.

  M. More precise estimates were needed, it appears.

練習問題 2 正解と解説

正解 A, B, F, G, I, J, K, M

Has your manager approved the marketing plan you submitted last week?
（あなたの上司は先週提出したマーケティング計画を承認しましたか？）

A. Actually, I did not hand in the document.
（実は、その書類を提出しませんでした。）
承認されるも何も提出していない（ので判定も何も下らない）という流れで成立する間接回答。

B. I expect another two weeks for the decision.
（決定にはさらに二週間かかると思います。）
承認されるかどうかはまだ分からず、あと2週間はかかりそうという流れの回答で可能。

C. He has managed the new campaign surprisingly well.
（彼は新しいキャンペーンを驚くほどうまく管理しました。）
manage-manager、He has-Has he と単語レベルでは共通項が見られるが、計画が承認されたかに関する情報ではなく不適格。

D. Marketing is definitely the most important aspect.
（マーケティングは間違いなく最も重要な側面です。）
それは事実なのかもしれないが、承認されたか否かの直接的回答にも間接的回答にもなっておらず成立しない。

E. Could you elaborate on that before you leave?
（出る前にそれについて説明してもらえますか？）
もっと詳しく説明してくれないか？という脈絡上自然に会話が流れないセリフであるため不成立。どういうこと？状況が分からないから教えて、という推測ができなくはないが、TOEICの設定からは遠すぎる推測で、TOEICの正解にはやはりなり得ない。

F. Oh, has it been a week already?
（ああ、もう一週間ですか？）
一件関連性がないように見えるが、レポートを提出してもう一週間たったの？という意図で取れる回答として成立しうる。

G. I'm revising it on the basis of his feedback.
（私は彼のフィードバックに基づいて改善しています。）
この回答から、既に上司から改善の指摘を受け、その反映を進めている様子がうかがえ、よって先週提出した計画は承認されなかった、と推測できるため可能。

H. Which part of the plan is not well written?
（計画のどの部分がうまく書かれていませんか？）
上司に聞く質問としてはありえるが、問いかけを行った人物にする質問としては唐突過ぎるもので、自然な流れを形成できておらず不適格。

I. It seems I've received the appraisal just now.
（今しがた評価を受け取ったようです。）
提出した計画書についてたった今（メールなどで）判定の通知を受け取った、という状況なので、間接的な受け答えとして十分成立する回答。

J. Why do you know that I'm involved in this?
（なぜあなたは私がこれに関与していることを知っているのですか？）
そもそも、なぜ私が本案件に関わっているのをしっているのか？という状況を想定できる回答として可能。

K. Maybe he hasn't, but I am not too concerned about that.
（多分彼はまだ判定していませんが、私はそれについてあまり心配していません。）
承認されたか？との問いに、おそらくまだなのだが、結果について心配していない、という回答として成立。

L. My boss approved my participation at the workshop.
（私の上司は私のワークショップへの参加を承認しました。）
approved したというセリフが含まれるが、計画書への承認ではなく、別案件への承認であるため、問いかけへの関連性がなく不適格。

M. More precise estimates were needed, it appears.
（より正確な見積もりが必要だったようです。）
内容から、承認されず、されなかった理由として、より正確な見積もりが必要だったことがうかがえるため、問いかけへの間接的な回答として可能。

Part3 会話問題

絶対に押さえたい満点ポイント③
ヒントのタイミングにまどわされない

> 会話問題でまず失点しやすいのが、「正答のヒントが出てくるタイミングがおかしい問題」です。会話文が短かったり、正答のヒントとなる情報の出題タイミングが偏っていても集中力を切らさないことが重要です。

◆ 音声が短すぎる問題

会話文が短すぎると、立て続けに正解のヒントとなる情報が流れるため、塗りつぶしながら聞いていたり、同時に選択肢を読みながら聞いていると、次の問題のヒント部分を聞き逃してしまうことがあります。

例題

M: Did you listen to the song I sent you last night?
W: I loved it. I can't believe you wrote the lyrics and composed the tune yourself.
M: It was **inspired by all my experiences** and the love I have received and lost in my life.
W: **You should send it to the local radio station** for them to play!

正解がわかる箇所が集中している！

➡ 正解のヒントは続くこともある！

◆ ヒントの出題タイミングが偏った問題

最初の方に早々に最初の2問のヒントとなる情報が流れ、しばらく解答には直接関係ない間が長く続いて、突然3問目へのヒントが最後流れて終わり、という偏った構造をした問題も、答えにくいと感じる人が多いようです。

例 題

W: Hey, Henry. Did you watch **the documentary program that aired last night on Channel 1**?

M: No, I didn't! I was out playing baseball.

・
・
・

W: I'm sure you will love it. It is probably available online. I think it's on Channel 1 On-demand. And you can watch it **if you are a paid subscriber**.

M: **I'll check my membership status**.

問題文の冒頭と末尾にヒントが固まっている！

➡ 聞き逃しや集中力切れをなくそう！

絶対に押さえたい満点ポイント④

同性のナレーターが続けて話すパターンを攻略する

> 次にPart 3で気をつけたい問題は、同性のナレーターが続けて話す会話文です。男性の低い声が連続したり、女性の高い声が連続したときにも聞き取れるよう練習しましょう。

◆ 同性が登場する問題

同じ会話に男性が2人出てくる、女性が2人出てくる、という会話文では、誰が何を言っているのか混乱してしまうことがあります。特に、声色やアクセントの判別がしにくい、という人は、この手の問題に苦戦することがあるようです。

例題

M1: ·····················Today, we are in conversation with Todd Mullins and John Skater, who are both digital artists. **Welcome, Todd and Mary!**

M2: **Thank you, Andrew.**

W: ·····················

M1: **How long have you been digital artists and what prompted you to start this?**

M2: **I have been a digital artist for the last 9 years** and ·····················

W: ·····················.

男性の音声の後に男性の音声が来ている！

➡ 同性の音声でも聞き取れるよう練習しよう！

高難度問題にトライ！

Questions 32 through 34 refer to the following conversation.

32. Who most likely is the man?

(A) A musician

(B) A radio personality

(C) A pianist

(D) A poet

33. What does the man say about the song?

(A) It was composed for the woman.

(B) He referred to his own experiences.

(C) It is based mostly on fictional stories.

(D) It has already sold well.

34. What does the woman suggest the man do?

(A) Write another song

(B) Sing on the radio station

(C) Send a copy

(D) Change some lyrics

Questions 35 through 37 refer to the following conversation.

35. What are the speakers mostly discussing?

(A) Wars in Sudan

(B) A girl who grew up during the war time

(C) Fashion designers in Paris

(D) A program available on TV and online

36. According to the woman, what is required to watch the program online?

(A) A special coupon for the program

(B) A monthly subscription payment

(C) Wide knowledge of wars in Sudan

(D) Upgrading to the highest rank of membership

37. What does the man say he will do?

(A) Become a paid member

(B) Watch the documentary now

(C) Confirm his status

(D) Continue playing baseball

Questions 38 through 40 refer to the following conversation.

38. Why is the man calling the woman?

(A) To change the hotel he will stay at

(B) To try extending his trip duration

(C) To adjust the reservation he made

(D) To talk with a hotel manager

39. What is mentioned about the hotel?

(A) It rarely responds to a request for a schedule change.

(B) It hosts special events on Thanksgiving.

(C) It is one of the highest-ranked hotels in the city.

(D) It may be less busy now compared to on holiday seasons.

40. What will the woman do next?

(A) Call the hotel

(B) Upgrade the man's room

(C) Call the man back

(D) Extend the man's stay

Questions 41 through 43 refer to the following conversation with three speakers.

41. Where most likely does the conversation take place?

(A) At a computer lab

(B) At a television station

(C) At a performance theater

(D) At Andrew's house

42. Why does the woman say, "Wow, I can't believe I'm here"?

(A) She is honored to be able to attend.

(B) She is excited about drawing some pictures here.

(C) She thought she should have been invited sooner.

(D) She is happy about talking with other artists.

43. According to one of the interviewees, what motivated him to start pursuing digital art?

(A) Curiosity to inquire about local artists' motivation

(B) An interest in anime

(C) A sense of freedom obtained through artistic activities

(D) Availability of a wide range of technology

正解と解説

Questions 32 through 34 refer to the following conversation .

M: Did you listen to the song I sent you last night? Did you like it?

W: I loved it. **I can't believe you wrote the lyrics and composed the tune yourself.**

M: **It was inspired by all my experiences** and the love I have received and lost in my life.

W: **You should send it to the local radio station for them to play!**

M: 昨日の夜、僕が送った音楽は聴いた？　気に入ったかな？

W: とても気に入ったよ。あなたが曲も歌詞も作っただなんて信じられない！

M: これまでの僕のすべての経験や僕の人生の中でたくさんの人からもらったりなくしたりした愛から考え付いたんだ。

W: この曲を地元のラジオ局に送って流してもらったほうがいいよ！

Vocabulary
☐ **lyrics** 歌詞　☐ **compose the tune** 作曲する

32. Who most likely is the man?
　　男性は何である可能性が高いですか。

　　正解 A

　　(A) A musician　　　　　　　　**(A) 音楽家**
　　(B) A radio personality　　　　　(B) ラジオパーソナリティー
　　(C) A pianist　　　　　　　　　　(C) ピアニスト
　　(D) A poet　　　　　　　　　　　(D) 詩人

　　解説　I can't believe you wrote the lyrics and composed the tune yourself 「あなたが曲も歌詞も作っただなんて信じられない」と女性が述べているので、音楽関係の仕事である（A）または（C）に絞ることができます。ピアノの話は出ていないので、（A）が正解となります。女性は曲をラジオ局に送った方がいいと言っており、男性がラジオパーソナリティーではないので、単語ベースで惑わされないように気をつけましょう。

33. What does the man say about the song?
　　男性はその歌について何と言っていますか。

　　正解 B

(A) It was composed for the woman.

(B) He referred to his own experiences.

(C) It is based mostly on fictional stories.

(D) It has already sold well.

(A) 女性のために作曲された。

(B) 彼は自身の経験に言及した。

(C) それは主に架空の物語に基づいている。

(D) すでにかなり売れている。

> 解説　It was inspired by all my experiences「僕のすべての経験から考え付いたんだ」と述べているので、正解は(B)となります。be inspired by ～「～から考え付く」が、選択肢では、refer to ～「～に言及する」と言い換えられているので要注意です。

34. What does the woman suggest the man do?
女性は男性に何を提案していますか。

正解 C

(A) Write another song

(B) Sing on the radio station

(C) Send a copy

(D) Change some lyrics

(A) 別の曲を作る

(B) ラジオ局で歌う

(C) コピーを送る

(D) 歌詞を一部変更する

> 解説　You should send it to the local radio station for them to play「この曲を地元のラジオ局に送って流してもらったほうがいいよ」と、女性はshouldを使って男性に提案しています。sendは言い換えられていませんので、itが何を指すかがポイントになります。これは、女性が聴いた歌なので、(C)が正解となります。

Questions 35 through 37 refer to the following conversation .

W: Hey, Henry. Did you watch the documentary program that aired last night on Channel 1?

M: No, I didn't! I was out playing baseball.

W: It was about a young girl who grew up in war-torn Sudan but wanted to become a fashion designer in Paris.

M: Oh, was it yesterday? You had told me about it, but I was thinking the program will be aired sometime next week. Well, I'll try to watch it online.

W: I'm sure you will love it. It is probably available online. I think it's on Channel 1 On-demand. And y**ou can watch it if you are a paid subscriber.**

M: **I'll check my membership status.**

W: ヘンリー、昨日の夜チャンネル1で放送されていたドキュメンタリーは見た？

M: いや、見ていないよ！ 野球をしていたんだ。

W: 戦争で引き裂かれたスーダンで生まれ育った女の子がパリでファッションデザイナーになることを夢見ている話だったよ。

M: え、昨日だったの？ それについてはすでに聞いてたけど、そのプログラムは来週のどこかで放送されるんだと思ってたよ。もしかしたらオンラインで見てみるかもしれない。

W: きっと気に入ると思う！ 多分オンラインで公開されている。チャンネル1・オンデマンドかな。もしあなたが有料会員なら見られるよ。

M: 自分の会員ステータスを調べてみるよ。

Vocabulary

□ **air** 放送・放映する　□ **paid subscriber** 有料会員

---

35. What are the speakers mostly discussing?

話し手は何について主に話し合っていますか。

正解 D

(A) Wars in Sudan

(B) A girl who grew up during the war time

(C) Fashion designers in Paris

(D) A program available on TV and online

(A) スーダンでの戦争

(B) 戦時中に生まれ育った少女

(C) パリのファッションデザイナー

(D) テレビまたはオンラインで視聴可能の番組

解説　主に話し合っているという点では(D)が正解になります。(A)や(B)はSudanやwarなどの単語でひっかからないよう気をつけましょう。正確には言及されていない内容です。(C)は確かに言及されていますが、番組内容の一部であることから、問題のmostly discussing「主に話し合っている」という部分と合いません。

---

36. According to the woman, what is required to watch the program online?

女性によると、オンラインで番組を視聴するには何が必要ですか。

正解 B

(A) A special coupon for the program

(B) A monthly subscription payment

(C) Wide knowledge of wars in Sudan

(D) Upgrading to the highest rank of membership

(A) プログラムの特別クーポン

(B) 毎月のサブスクリプションの支払い

(C) スーダンの戦争に関する幅広い知識

(D) メンバーシップの最高ランクへのアップグレード

解説　you can watch it if you are a paid subscriber「あなたが有料会員なら見られる」という部分から正解は(B)であることがわかります。a paid subscriberからmonthly subscription paymentと言い換えられていますので、単語を聞き取るだけでなく、意味を理解することがとても重要になります。(A)、(C)、(D)に関しては言及されていないので、消去法でも答えを導き出せるでしょう。

37. What does the man say he will do?
男性は何をすると言っていますか。

正解 C

(A) Become a paid member
(B) Watch the documentary now
(C) Confirm his status
(D) Continue playing baseball

(A) 有料会員になる
(B) 今すぐドキュメンタリーを見る
(C) 彼のステータスを確認する
(D) 野球を続ける

解説　I'll check my membership status「自分の会員ステータスを調べてみるよ」と、最後に述べているので、正解は(C)になります。(D)は全く言及されていないので間違いです。また、(A)はステータスを確認した後の対応で、(B)はステータスを確認する手段なので、答えとして不適切になります。

Questions 38 through 40 refer to the following conversation .

M: Hi. **I am calling about my hotel booking** at the Miraton that I made through your travel agency. My booking number is AD863502. I would like to add another two nights to my stay, making it 5 nights in total.

W: Yes, of course, Mr. Shaun. Let me check the hotel, the Miraton, for availability. So, this would make your stay from the 2nd of December to the 6th of December. Is that correct?

M: Yes, that is correct. I had originally booked till the 4th, which I believe is Friday, but my trip has been extended.

W: This shouldn't most likely be a problem. **It's off-peak now after Thanksgiving. I will call the Miraton Hotel** and update your dates. Let me call you back when I have a confirmation from them.

M: そちらの旅行会社を通して予約したミラトンの予約についてお電話しております。私の予約番号はAD863502です。追加で2日間宿泊を延ばして合計5日の滞在に変更したいのですが。

W: はい、もちろんです、ミスター、シャウン。ミラトンホテルの空き状況を確認させていた

だきます。宿泊は12月の2日から6日までで合っていますでしょうか。

M: はい、それで合っています。もともとは4日まで、多分その日は金曜日だと思うのですが、旅行が延びることになりました。

W: おそらく宿泊の延長は問題ありません。感謝祭後のオフシーズンですので。ミラトンホテルに電話をして最新の情報を伝えておきます。ホテルの方からも確認が取れ次第、また私の方からお電話させていただきます。

38. Why is the man calling the woman?

男性は何のために女性に電話していますか。

正解 C

(A) To change the hotel he will stay at (A) 滞在するホテルを変更するため

(B) To try extending his trip duration (B) 彼の旅行期間を延長するため

(C) To adjust the reservation he made **(C) 彼が入れた予約を調整するため**

(D) To talk with a hotel manager (D) ホテルの支配人と話すため

解説　I am calling about my hotel booking「予約についてお電話しております」と最初に述べられているので、正解は(C)になります。また、I would like to add another two nights to my stay「追加で2日間宿泊を伸ばしたい」と述べられていますが、この電話で延長したいのは宿泊日数であり、旅行期間ではないので、(B)はひっかけです。本文では add another two nights ですが、選択肢では adjust the reservation と言い換えられているので注意しましょう。

39. What is mentioned about the hotel?

ホテルについて何が言及されていますか。

正解 D

(A) It rarely responds to a request for a schedule change. (A) スケジュール変更の要望に応答することがめったにない。

(B) It hosts special events on Thanksgiving. (B) 感謝祭の日に特別なイベントを主催する。

(C) It is one of the highest-ranked hotels in the city. (C) 市内で最もランクの高いホテルの1つである。

(D) It may be less busy now compared to on holiday seasons. **(D) ホリデーシーズンに比べると今はそこまで忙しくないかもしれない。**

解説　It's off-peak now after the Thanksgiving.「感謝祭後のオフシーズンです」というところがヒントになります。off-peak でそんなに混んでいないことがわかりますし、after the Thanksgiving でホリデーシーズン後であることがわかります。よって、正解は(D)になります。(A)、(B)、(C)はすべて本文での言及がありませんが、(A)に関しては rarely ～「めったに～ない」という否定的な表現に注意しましょう。否定表現であることに気づけない

と、ひっかかる可能性のある選択肢です。

40. What will the woman do next?
女性は次に何をしますか。

正解 A

(A) **Call the hotel**
(B) Upgrade the man's room
(C) Call back the man
(D) Extend the man's stay

(A) **ホテルに電話をする**
(B) 男性の部屋をアップグレードする
(C) 男性に電話をかけ直す
(D) 男性の滞在を延長する

解説　I will call the Miraton Hotel「ミラトンホテルに電話をする」と話しているので正解は(A)です。(C)や(D)に関しては、その電話で確認する内容なので、next「次に」を尋ねられているこの問題の答えとしては不適切になります。(B)は本文のupdateと似た発音であるupgradeをひっかけた選択肢なので惑わされないようにしましょう。

Questions 41 through 43 refer to the following conversation with three speakers.

M1: **I would like to welcome you to the *Andrew Garcia Show***, where we interview local artists and find out what motivates them to create such interesting pieces. Today, we are in conversation with Todd Mullins and Mary Skater, who are both digital artists. Welcome, Todd and Mary!

M2: Thank you, Andrew.

W: Thank you, Andrew. **Wow, I can't believe I'm here.**

M1: How long have you been digital artists and what got you into it?

M2: I have been a digital artist for the last 9 years and **I got into it because of the wide range of technology available** to express myself. Creating new pieces of work makes me feel free.

W: I decided to become a digital artist when I was 17, which means that I've been making art for the last 13 years! I love anime, and that's what first attracted me to it.

M1: 本日のイベント参加へのご関心ありがとうございます。アンドリュー・ガルシア・ショーに歓迎します。このショーでは地元のアーティストにインタビューをしてどんな動機でさまざまな作品を作っているのかを聞いていきます。本日はデジタルアーティストのトッド・ムリンズさんとマリー・スケーターさんにお話を伺っていきます。トッド・ムリンさん、マリー・スケイターさんどうぞ！

M2: ありがとう、アンドリュー。

W: ありがとう、アンドリュー。わあ、ここにいるなんて信じられません。

M1: これまでどのくらいの期間デジタルアートをしてきましたか。また、これを始めるきっかけは何でしたか。

M2: 僕はデジタルアートを始めて9年になります。始めたきっかけは自分を表現するのに幅広いテクノロジーがあったためです。新しい作品を作ることでとても自由に感じます。

W: 私がデジタルアーティストになろうと思ったのは17歳のときでした。つまり私は13年間芸術に携わっていることになります。アニメがとても好きだったことが、初めに私が芸術に引かれた理由です。

---

41. Where most likely does the conversation take place?

会話はどこで行われている可能性が高いですか。

正解 B

(A) At a computer lab	(A) パソコン室で
(B) At a television station	**(B) テレビ局で**
(C) At a performance theater	(C) 劇場で
(D) At Andrew's house	(D) アンドリューの家で

解説　I would like to welcome you to the *Andrew Garcia Show*「アンドリュー・ガルシア・ショーに歓迎します」という部分のshowという単語に注目しましょう。showが使われているということは、(A)や(D)ということはないことが考えられます。(C)は主題がデジタルアートのインタビューであるという点で不自然な場所と考えられます。よって、正解は(B)となります。

---

42. Why does the woman say, "Wow, I can't believe I'm here"?

なぜ女性は「わあ、ここにいるなんて信じられません」と言ったのですか。

正解 A

(A) She is honored to be able to attend.	**(A) 彼女は(プログラム)に参加できることを光栄に思っています。**
(B) She is excited about drawing some pictures.	(B) 彼女は絵を描くことに興奮しています。
(C) She thought she should have been invited sooner.	(C) 彼女はもっと早く招待されると思っていました。
(D) She is happy about talking with other artists.	(D) 彼女は他のアーティストと話すことに満足しています。

解説　彼女が紹介された直後に話す言葉として最も自然なので、正解は(A)です。WowやI can't believeは感嘆の表現なので、光栄に思っていることがわかります。(C)は招待された身として失礼な発言なので間違いです。ここで絵を描くということは全く言及されてい

ないので(B)も間違いです。(D)はどちらかというと、このインタビューの後の感想のような文言ですので、不適切となります。

43. According to one of the interviewees, what motivated him to start pursuing digital art?

インタビュー対象者の1人によれば、彼がデジタルアートを追究し始めた動機は何でしたか。

正解 D

(A) Curiosity to inquire about local artists' motivation

(B) An interest in anime

(C) A sense of freedom obtained through artistic activities

(D) The availability of a wide range of technology

(A) 地元のアーティストのモチベーションを尋ねる好奇心

(B) アニメへの関心

(C) 芸術活動を通じて得られる自由の感覚

(D) 幅広いテクノロジーの可用性

解説　I got into it because of the wide range of technology「始めたきっかけは幅広いテクノロジーがあったため」と本文で述べられているので、正解は(D)となります。Creating new pieces of work makes me feel free「新しい作品を作ることでとても自由に感じます」とも話しているので、(C)が答えかと思うかもしれませんが、あくまで動機は何かを尋ねられているので、これは答えになりません。

Part4 説明文問題

絶対に押さえたい満点ポイント⑤

短すぎる音声にまどわされない

> Part 4 でも、短い音声には要注意です。正解のヒントとなる情報を聞き逃さないよう、集中力を切らさないようトレーニングが必要です。

◆ 音声が短すぎる問題

流れる音声が短すぎると、立て続けに正解のヒントとなる情報が流れる可能性が高くなります。そのため、塗りつぶしながら聞いていると、すぐさま次の問題のヒント部分が来て、そこを聞き逃してしまうことがあります。

例題

Hi, Jennifer. My name is Trevor and I'm calling from Mitchell and King. **I am calling about the recent online inquiry you sent us concerning a potential lawsuit.** I understand you are facing an issue with the City Council regarding your residence, which is planned to be demolished to make room for a road. Mr. King has read through the documents you have sent us and would like to handle your case. Mr. King thinks that what happened to you was terribly unfair and that you have a strong reason to sue the City Council. He is also willing to **waive any initial fees**. So you do not need to pay a deposit. If you are free to meet him this week, **I can set up an appointment** for tomorrow at 2 P.M.

正解がわかる箇所が集中している！

➡ 正解のヒントは続くこともある！

絶対に押さえたい満点ポイント⑥

難解な語句にも落ち着いて対処する

> Part 3とは違う、失点しやすいポイントがPart 4では固有名詞や専門用語が多く登場する点です。難解な語句を描写している部分をきちんと聞き取り、あせらず対処することを覚えましょう。

◆ 固有名詞が多く使われている問題

Part 4では、何かの「案内」、「説明」、「お知らせ」が多く含まれるため、必然的に固有名詞が英文中にあれこれ入ってきます。この固有名詞を聞き取れなかったり、意味が取れなかったりすることが上級者でも多くあります。

例題

Smile and Shine invite you to their annual stock clearance sale, where you will find deals on products that are almost too good to be true! Our bestselling bed, the Povalis is now on sale with a 60 percent discount on its retail price. The Povalis can also...

固有名詞が多く含まれている！

➡ 「Our bestselling bed」など、固有名詞を描写している部分を聞き取ろう

スマイル・アンド・シャインは現在1年に1回の在庫売り尽くしセールをしています。本当にありえるのかわからないほどのお値段でのセール品が見つかります！ 私たちのベストセラーのベッドである、ポバリスが60パーセントオフです。ポバリスは…

◆ 専門用語が出てくる問題

Part 4の一部では、植樹の仕方、脳の機能について、行動心理学的な話、環境についての話など、日常英語や一般ビジネス英語の範囲を超えたスピーチも幾つか出されています。Part 4は一方的なコミュニケーションである「スピーチ」の形式をとっているので、シチュエーションを即座に想像できなければ、話全体の理解度が著しく下がることがあります。

例 題

The Association of Nutrition Sciences released today a study on the physiological effects of multi-vitamin tablets. The result of the study is quite astonishing. The group that had a habit of regular intake of multi-vitamins showed a significantly lower prevalence of having serious illnesses such as cancer, metabolic diseases, heart disease, and so on compared to the group that did not have such a habit.

専門性の高い語句が頻出している！

➡ ビジネス英語以外のジャンルの用語が出題されることもある

高難度問題にトライ！

Questions 71 through 73 refer to the following telephone message.

 M

71. Where does the speaker most likely work?

(A) At the City Council

(B) At a construction company

(C) At a law firm

(D) At a telephone company

72. According to the speaker, what will King offer to do?

(A) Call the City Council

(B) Tear down Jenifer's house

(C) Make a larger room for his convenience

(D) Provide the service with no initial fee

73. What does the speaker offer to do?

(A) See if Mr. King is available for a talk

(B) Arrange a meeting

(C) Meet Jenifer at 2 P.M.

(D) Refund a deposit

Questions 74 through 76 refer to the following talk.

 M

74. Where is the speaker originally from?

(A) Brazil

(B) Holland

(C) France

(D) England

75. What is mentioned about Van Gogh's self-portraits?

(A) They were portrayed in England.

(B) They are collectively called Sunflowers.

(C) They are displayed throughout the season.

(D) They are also available in digital formats.

76. What does the speaker say the listeners can do?

(A) Take pictures

(B) Smoke

(C) Eat and drink

(D) Touch exhibitions

Questions 77 through 79 refer to the following telephone message.

77. What kind of business does the speaker work for?

(A) A restaurant chain

(B) Medicine and healthcare

(C) Wholesalers

(D) A local farm

78. Why does the speaker mention butternut squash?

(A) It is widely produced in Canterbury.

(B) It is available in large quantity.

(C) It tastes better than ordinary pumpkins.

(D) It can be purchased directly from local suppliers.

79. What will Chris receive if he sends no additional request by 11 A.M.?

(A) Butternut squash as well as pumpkins

(B) Meat and vegetables except pumpkins

(C) Only meat

(D) All items except butternut squash

Questions 80 through 82 refer to the following talk.

80. What is the main focus of the talk?

(A) Human's life in the Stone Age

(B) Ancient humans and modern humans

(C) The importance of changing how we think

(D) Turning positive thinking into negative thinking

81. Why did the speaker mention the Stone Age?

(A) To describe how human looked like

(B) To explain why our brain behaves in a certain way

(C) To illustrate how we can change our thinking patterns

(D) To deny the possibility of changing ourselves

82. What does the speaker recommend the listeners do?

(A) Make a conscious effort to think positively

(B) Neglect something negative

(C) Try to behave as ancient humans did

(D) Think about why we think negatively

正解と解説

Questions 71 through 73 refer to the following telephone message.

Hi, Jennifer. My name is Trevor and I'm calling from Mitchell and King. **I am calling about the recent online inquiry you sent us concerning a potential lawsuit.** I understand you are facing an issue with the City Council regarding your residence, which is planned to be demolished to make room for a road. Mr. King has read through the documents you have sent us and would like to handle your case. Mr. King thinks that what happened to you was terribly unfair and that you have a strong reason to sue the City Council. He is also willing to **waive any initial fees**. So you do not need to pay a deposit. If you are free to meet him this week, **I can**

set up an appointment for tomorrow at 2 P.M.

ジェニファーさん。私の名前はトレバーです。ミッチェル＆キングからお電話をかけています。最近私どもにオンラインでお送りいただいた、訴訟関係のお問い合わせについてお電話しています。新しく道を建設するためにご自宅が取り壊されてしまいかねない、という市議会との問題について理解しました。送ってくださった資料をキングが読んだ上で、こちらの件を担当することになりました。キングはあなたに起こったことはとても不条理だということで、市議会を告訴することができると思っております。彼は、最初の費用は無料で対応すると言っております。ですので、手付金を支払う必要はありません。もし今週彼と会うお時間があれば、私の方から明日の午後2時にアポイントメントを取らせていただこうと思います。

Vocabulary

☐ **lawsuit** 訴訟　☐ **tear down** 取り壊す　☐ **sue** 訴える　☐ **waive** 権利などを放棄する
☐ **deposit** 頭金

71. Where does the speaker most likely work?
    話し手はどこで仕事をしていると思われますか。

    正解 C

    (A) At the City Council　　　　　(A) 市議会で
    (B) At a construction company　　(B) 建設会社で
    (C) At a law firm　　　　　　**(C) 法律事務所で**
    (D) At a telephone company　　　(D) 電話会社で

    解説　I am calling about the recent online inquiry you sent us concerning potential lawsuit「最近私どもにオンラインでお送りいただいた、訴訟関係のお問い合わせについてお電話しています」という部分で、正解は(C)となることがわかります。また、私どもに送られたという部分で、(B)や(D)が間違いであることもわかります。(A)に関しては、you are facing an issue with the City Councilで、話し手は市議会の人間ではないことに気づけるでしょう。

72. According to the speaker, what will King offer to do?
    話し手によると、キングは何をすることを申し出ますか。

    正解 D

    (A) Call the City Council　　　　(A) 市議会に電話する
    (B) Tear down Jenifer's house　　(B) ジェニファーの家を取り壊す
    (C) Make a larger room for his　　(C) 彼のためにより広い部屋を造る
        convenience

(D) Provide the service with no initial fee　**(D) 初期費用なしでサービスを提供する**

解説　waive any initial fees「最初の費用は無料で対応する」と述べられているので、正解は(D)となります。initial feeは言い換えられていませんが、waive ～「～を免除する」という表現を聞き取れるかが重要になります。頻出単語なので、慣れておく必要があります。また、このような否定形を使わなくても否定的な意味を持つ単語の言い換え問題も頻出なので注意していきましょう。

73. What does the speaker offer to do?
話し手は何をすることを提案しますか。

正解 B

(A) See if Mr. King is available for a talk　(A) キングが対談に参加可能かを確認する

(B) Arrange a meeting　**(B) 面談を手配する**

(C) Meet Jenifer at 2 P.M.　(C) 午後2時にジェニファーに会う

(D) Refund a deposit　(D) 手付金を返金する

解説　最後のI can set up an appointmentで「アポを取ります」と述べられています。よって、正解は(B)になります。set up an appointmentがarrange a conversationと言い換えられていますが、set up an appointmentの本質をしっかりとらえることができれば答えを導き出せるでしょう。(A)がひっかかりやすいですが、話し手はキングのスケジュールを把握しているということも先ほどの文でわかるので間違いです。

Questions 74 through 76 refer to the following talk.

Welcome to the Van Gogh Museum Tour. For those of you touring the museum for the first time, my name is Aram, and I am one of the tour guides here at the VG Museum. **I am originally from Salvador, Brazil**, but moved to Amsterdam to study Van Gogh and his incredible art. He was born in a city named Zundert in Holland. He lived in many places including France and England. Well, our exhibitions show his life. We will start with his very popular collection of Sunflower paintings and then move on to his self-portraits. **These are part of the museum's permanent collection**. Later in the tour, I will also take you to one of our current digital immersive exhibitions that will show you a completely different facet of Van Gogh's work. **You can take pictures** in some sections, but not in all areas. Please make sure that you don't touch any of the exhibited items. No smoking or eating is allowed. I appreciate your understanding.

第1章 英語脳徹底トレーニング　第2章 高難度問題の徹底攻略　第3章 正答ハイテクレッスン　第4章 ハイレベル完全模試

ヴァン・ゴッホ美術館ツアーへようこそ。初めてこの美術館を回る方へ、私の名前はアラムです。このVG美術館のツアーガイドの1人です。私はもともとブラジルのサルヴァドールに住んでいましたが、ヴァン・ゴッホとその素晴らしいアートを学ぶためにアムステルダムに学びに来ました。彼はオランダのズンデルトという場所で生まれ、フランスやイングランドを含むさまざまな場所で過ごしました。展示物が彼の生活を説明してくれるでしょう。では、彼のとても有名なコレクション、「ひまわり」の絵から始め、次に彼の自画像に移ります。これらはこの美術館の常設展の一部です。ツアーの後の方には、魅力的なヴァン・ゴッホの全く違う側面が見える最新デジタル没入型エキシビションにお連れします。幾つかの場所では写真を撮っても構いませんが全ての場所ではありません。展示されているものには触らないようにお願いします。喫煙、飲食は禁止です。ご理解に感謝いたします。

74. Where is the speaker originally from?

話し手の出身はどこですか。

正解 A

(A) Brazil   (A) ブラジル
(B) Holland   (B) オランダ
(C) France   (C) フランス
(D) England   (D) イングランド

解説 I am originally from Salvador, Brazil 「私はもともとブラジルのサルヴァドールに住んでいました」と述べられているので、正解は(A)となります。自己紹介の後すぐにヴァン・ゴッホについての説明でいろいろな国名が出てくるので、混乱しないように気をつけましょう。それぞれの国名が何の説明で出てきていたかしっかりキャッチできるようにすることが重要になります。

75. What is mentioned about Van Gogh's self-portraits?

ヴァン・ゴッホの自画像について述べられているのはどれですか。

正解 C

(A) They were portrayed in England.   (A) イングランドで描かれた。
(B) They are collectively called Sunflowers.   (B) 総称して「ひまわり」と呼ばれている。
(C) **They are displayed throughout the season.**   (C) **シーズンを通して展示されている。**
(D) They are also available in digital formats.   (D) デジタル形式でも用意されている。

解説　自画像について紹介した直後の文に、These are part of the museum's permanent collection「これらはこの美術館の中に永久的にある作品の一部です」と述べられています。よって正解は(C)になります。シーズンを通して展示されているという直接的な言及はありませんが、permanent「永久的な」という単語がわかれば、シーズンを通して展示されていることは当たり前だと気づけるでしょう。

76. What does the speaker say the listeners can do?
話し手は、参加者は何ができると言っていますか。

正解 A

(A) Take pictures
(B) Smoke
(C) Eat and drink
(D) Touch exhibitions

(A) 写真を撮る
(B) たばこを吸う
(C) 飲食する
(D) 展示物に触れる

解説　最後の方で、You can take pictures「写真を撮ることができる」と話しているので、正解は(A)になります。その後、but not in all areasと否定形が続きますが、「すべての場所ではない」と、写真撮影自体を否定しているわけではないので、混乱しないように要注意です。(B)、(C)、(D)に関しては、続く2つの文で全て禁止されているので、消去法でも答えを導き出せるでしょう。

Questions 77 through 79 refer to the following telephone message.

Good morning, Chris. This is Julie calling from Med-Herb Foods about **your restaurant's recent order**. Unfortunately, **we are out of pumpkins** and will not be able to supply the requested 8 kilograms. I apologize for the inconvenience caused. Because of the recent floods in Canterbury, **our supplier has not been able to deliver** his produce to Nelson. We do not know how long this shortage may last. However, if you are willing, I can send you butternut squash instead **since we have plenty in stock**. If you are happy with this, please send me an e-mail confirming this, so that I can get your order sent out to you this afternoon. If I do not receive an e-mail by 11 A.M., **I will send out the rest of your order without the butternut squash.** Thank you for your time.

おはようございます、クリス。メッド・ハーブ・フードのジュリーです。あなたのレストランの最近の注文についてお電話させていただきました。残念ながら、カボチャが品切れとなっており、ご注文いただいた8キロのご用意ができませんでした。ご不便をおかけし申し訳ありません。最近のカンタベリーでの洪水の影響で供給者の方がネルソンまで注文品を運搬できなか

ったようです。この不足についてはいつまで長引くかわかりません。しかし、もしよければ、バターナッツスクワッシュ（つるになるカボチャの一種）の在庫がたくさんあるので、それを代わりに送ることはできます。もしこちらでよければ、私の方に確認のためのメールを送ってください。そうすれば今日の午後品物を送ることができます。もし午前11時までにお返事が頂けなかった場合は、バターナッツスクワッシュ以外の残りの注文を送らせていただきます。ありがとうございます。

Vocabulary

☐ **produce** 品物

77. What kind of business does the speaker work for?
    話し手はどのようなビジネスに従事していますか。

    正解 C

    (A) A restaurant chain | (A) レストランチェーン
    (B) Medicine and healthcare | (B) 医療・健康分野
    (C) Wholesalers | **(C) 卸売り**
    (D) A local farm | (D) 地方農家

    解説 最初のyour restaurant's orderの部分で、電話相手がレストランスタッフであることがわかります。また、our supplier has not been able to deliverの部分で、供給者も別に存在し、話し手はその間を取り持っていることがわかります。つまり、正解は(C)になります。(B)は関係ありませんし、(A)や(D)は別に存在していることがわかるので、消去法でも正解を導き出すことができるでしょう。

78. Why does the speaker mention butternut squash?
    話し手がバターナッツスクワッシュに言及したのはなぜですか。

    正解 B

    (A) It is widely produced in Canterbury. | (A) カンタベリーで広く生産されているから。
    (B) It is available in a large quantity. | **(B) 大量に用意があるから。**
    (C) It tastes better than pumpkins. | (C) カボチャより味が良いから。
    (D) It can be purchased directly from local suppliers. | (D) 地方供給者から直接購入できるから。

    解説 Why ～?で理由を問う問題です。本文にsince we have plenty in stock「在庫がたくさんあるので」と述べられているので、正解は(B)となります。have plenty in stockからavailable in large quantityと言い換えられているので要注意です。このような理由を尋ねる問題では、sinceのような理由を述べる表現にいち早く気づくことがポイントになります。

79. What will Chris receive if he sends no additional request by 11 A.M.?

午前11時までに追加リクエストを送らなければクリスは何を受け取ることになりますか。

正解 D

(A) Butternut squash as well as pumpkins

(B) Meat and pumpkins

(C) Only meat

(D) All items except butternut squash and pumpkins

(A) バターナッツスクワッシュとカボチャ

(B) 肉製品とカボチャ

(C) 肉製品のみ

(D) バターナッツスクワッシュとカボチャ以外の全ての品物

解説　カボチャが品切れであることは分かっています。代替として提案されたスクワッシュも届けられないので(D)が正解です。

Questions 80 through 82 refer to the following talk.

Welcome to another session of "How to Change the Way You Think." In today's session, we will focus on the importance of conscious effort in turning negative thoughts into positive ones. On many occasions, you will notice that the human brain is still stuck in the so-called Caveman Mentality. Imagine the Paleolithic eras or Stone Age. Humans had to protect themselves from predators. Their mind always wanted to protect themselves from harm. **This is why, even now, our brain always thinks of a negative thought before thinking of a positive one. Therefore, you need to make a conscious effort to turn those thoughts into positive ones.** Change how you think! It might just lead to brilliant new experiences and learning.

「どのようにして考え方を変えるか」の続きのセッションにようこそ。本日のセッションではマイナスな思考をプラスの思考に変えることの重要さについてお話ししていきます。ほとんどの場合、人間の脳はいまだ、いわゆる穴居時代の人と精神的に変わりありません。石器時代を想像してみましょう。人類は捕食者から自らを守らねばなりませんでした。脳は危害から自らを守ろうとしました。これが今でも、われわれの脳というのは、いつもプラスのことを考えるより前に、マイナスなことを考えてしまう理由です。だからこそ、意識的にそれらの思考をプラスにひっくり返す必要があります。考え方を変えましょう！そうすることでもしかしたらとても良い経験や学びにつながるかもしれません。

Vocabulary
☐ **conscious** 意識的な　☐ **Paleolithic era** 石器時代

80. What is the main focus of the talk?

話の主な焦点は何ですか。

正解 C

(A) Human's life in the Stone Age

(A) 石器時代の人間の生活

(B) Ancient humans and modern humans

(B) 古代人と現代人

(C) The importance of changing how we think

(C) 私たちの考え方を変えることの重要性

(D) Turning positive thinking into negative thinking

(D) ポジティブ思考をネガティブ思考に変える

解説 Thereforeの後に注目してみましょう。Thereforeの後には結論が来るので、何に焦点が当てられているのかが明確です。you need to make a conscious effort to turn those thoughts into positive ones「意識的にそれらの思考をプラスにひっくり返す必要がある」と思考に関して述べられているので、(C)か(D)に絞られます。(D)は単語単位で見ると的を射ているように見えますが、文で意味を取ると真逆のことを言っているので要注意です。よって正解は(C)となります。

81. Why did the speaker mention the Stone Age?

話し手はなぜ石器時代について言及したのですか。

正解 B

(A) To describe how humans looked

(A) 人間がどのような見た目をしていたかを説明するため

(B) To explain why our brain behaves in a certain way

(B) 私たちの脳がなぜ特定の方法で動作するかを説明するため

(C) To illustrate how we can change our thinking patterns

(C) 思考パターンをどのように変えることができるかを説明するため

(D) To deny the possibility of changing ourselves

(D) 私たち自身を変える可能性を否定するため

解説 Why 〜?で理由を問う問題なので、本文のThis is why 〜に注目しましょう。「これが〜の理由だ」という意味です。our brain always thinks of a negative thought before thinking of a positive oneは、「われわれの脳というのは、いつもプラスのことを考えるより前に、マイナスなことを考えてしまう」という脳が特定の方法で動作する理由を示しています。よって、正解は(B)となります。

82. What does the speaker recommend the listeners do?

話し手は聞き手に何を勧めていますか。

正解 A

(A) Make a conscious effort to think positively

(B) Neglect something negative

(C) Try to behave as ancient humans did

(D) Think about why we think negatively

(A) 前向きに考えるように意識的に努力する

(B) ネガティブなものを無視する

(C) 古代人のように振る舞うようにする

(D) なぜネガティブに考えるかを考える

解説　What ～ ? で「何を勧めているか」を問う問題です。本文で、you need to make a conscious effort to turn those thoughts into positive ones「意識的にそれらの思考をプラスにひっくり返す必要がある」と述べられているので、正解は（A）となります。turn those thoughts into positive onesと本文の難しめの言い方から、問題ではthink positivelyとシンプルに言い換えられているので気をつけましょう。

990点満点への道

具体的なシーンをイメージできるか

　Part 4は一方的なスピーチであるため、どういうシチュエーションでのスピーチなのか即座に想像できなければ、上級者であっても話全体の理解度がいちじるしく下がることがあります。理解度が下がれば当然、3問の正答率が下がり、満点取得が遠ざかってしまいます。

　シーンの大枠を理解するためには、聞こえた英文を頭の中でイメージし、固有名詞がきた時には「あ、これは建物の名前を言っているな」と大きな枠で捉えながら、混乱しないように頭を整理して聴いていくことが必要です。

　また、単語の1つ1つを丁寧に聞き、頭の中で視覚化することがポイントでしょう。

Part5 短文穴埋め問題

絶対に押さえたい満点ポイント⑦

確信を持って正答を選ぶ「一本釣り」で解答せよ

> 語彙力、文法力を測定するPart 5では特に、あなたの実力がそのままスコアに反映されます。不正解をはじく消去法ではなく、確信を持って1つの正解をねらう「一本釣り」手法で実力を伸ばしましょう。

◆ 不正解の理由がわかることが重要

Part 5では選択肢が4つ与えられ、その中から最適なものを選ぶという問題ですが、選択肢がなかったとしても答えを想定できるレベルでの英語力を習得すれば、必ずPart 5で満点を取ることができるわけです。

惰性に任せていては私たちの脳は消極的に、消去法で思考してしまいます。正解の「一本釣り」で能動的に考えましょう。「一本釣り」とは、不正解をはじく消去法とは反対に、正解一本を釣りにいく回答法で、私が勝手に名付けたものです。

例 題

正解候補を幾つか考えた上で、問題に答えましょう。

The ------- of the training program will be designed by an experienced manager with over twenty years of experience in management accounting.

①先に考えられる正解を考えよう！

考えうる正解は…＿＿＿＿＿＿＿＿＿＿＿＿＿＿＿＿

(A) curriculum
(B) appearance
(C) location
(D) brightness

②どの選択肢が正解か「一本釣り」をしよう！

➡ 正解例を考え抜くことが、語彙力・文法力の劇的向上につながる！

トレーニングプログラムのカリキュラムは、管理会計で20年以上の経験を持つ経験豊富なマネージャーによって設計されます。

この問題の正解は(A)です。他にも以下の語句が正解例として挙げられます。

contents, detail, structure, outline, agenda, chapters, focus, schedule

高難度問題にトライ！

正解候補を幾つか考えた上で、空欄に入る英単語の選択肢を選べ。

練習問題 1

Violators who fail to complete and submit this form ------- tomorrow noon will be subject to an additional penalty.

解答例：＿＿＿＿＿＿＿＿＿

(A) for

(B) with

(C) by

(D) upon

練習問題 2

------- of the managers has the authority to make the final decision concerning the foreign marketing plans.

解答例：＿＿＿＿＿＿＿＿＿

(A) All

(B) Few

(C) Almost

(D) None

練習問題3

Unless otherwise instructed, you are not permitted to enter the main conference room until ------- 2 P.M.

解答例： _____

(A) on

(B) after

(C) by

(D) during

練習問題4

In this highly volatile market, stepwise bidding is the ------- approach even if it can reduce the leverage.

解答例： _____

(A) desirable

(B) eventful

(C) irrelevant

(D) haphazard

練習問題5

The development of new medicine is one ------- example that is often cited in media and academic journals.

解答例： _____

(A) of

(B) such

(C) another

(D) that

練習問題6

All the voters agreed that the new candidate is ------- too young to assume the role as a head.

解答例：＿＿＿＿＿＿＿＿＿

(A) more

(B) so

(C) way

(D) but

練習問題7

As many tour guides recommend, Toronto is one of the cities in North America ------- visiting.

解答例：＿＿＿＿＿＿＿＿＿

(A) worthy

(B) worth

(C) worthwhile

(D) worthless

練習問題8

------- ours is dominating the market, the best strategy to build the barrier to entry is to improve the degree of customer satisfaction.

解答例：＿＿＿＿＿＿＿＿＿

(A) So that

(B) Unless

(C) Because of

(D) Thus

練習問題9

That some of our competitors failed despite the odds won't ------- our supremacy in this niche market they are not focusing on.

解答例： _____

(A) tolerate

(B) signify

(C) heat

(D) delete

練習問題10

Among the first to ------- was no one but Face, the representative of the multinational conglomerate.

解答例： _____

(A) appear

(B) deny

(C) indicate

(D) discover

正解と解説

練習問題1　　**正解 C**　　他の正解例：before, as of など

Violators who fail to complete and submit this form ------- tomorrow noon will be subject to an additional penalty.

明日の正午までにこのフォームに記入して送信しなかった違反者には、追加のペナルティが課せられます。

(A) for　　　　　　　　　　　　　(A) ～のために
(B) with　　　　　　　　　　　　(B) ～と一緒に
(C) by　　　　　　　　　　　　**(C) ～で**
(D) upon　　　　　　　　　　　　(D) ～の上に

練習問題2　　**正解 D**　　他の正解例：Any, Either, Neither, One, Each
　　　　　　　　　　　　　　　　* Every は単数扱いだが of の前には置けないため NG。

------- of the managers has the authority to make the final decision concerning the foreign marketing plans.

外国のマーケティング計画に関する最終決定を下す権限を持っているマネージャーはいません。

(A) All　　　　　　　　　　　　　(A) すべての
(B) Few　　　　　　　　　　　　(B) ほとんど～ない
(C) Almost　　　　　　　　　　　(C) ほとんどの
(D) None　　　　　　　　　　　**(D) だれも～ない**

練習問題3　　**正解 B**　　他の正解例：around, about, Monday, at least,
　　　　　　　　　　　　　　　　　　　　　approximately

Unless otherwise instructed, you are not permitted to enter the main conference room until ------- 2 P.M.

特に指示がない限り、午後2時までメイン会議室に入室することはできません。

(A) on　　　　　　　　　　　　　(A) ～に
(B) after　　　　　　　　　　　**(B) ～の後に**
(C) by　　　　　　　　　　　　　(C) ～まで
(D) during　　　　　　　　　　　(D) ～の間

練習問題4　　**正解 A**　　他の正解例：desired, preferable, preferred, safer, ideal, recommended, orthodox, conventional, best

In this highly volatile market, stepwise bidding is the ------- approach even if it can cause to reduce the leverage.

この非常に不安定な市場では、借入資本利用の低下を引き起こす可能性がある場合でも、段階的な入札が望ましいアプローチです。

(A) desirable	**(A) 望ましい**
(B) eventful	(B) 出来事の多い
(C) irrelevant	(C) 無関係の
(D) haphazard	(D) でたらめの

練習問題5　　**正解 B**　　他の正解例：good, likely, typical, possible など

The development of new medicine is one ------- example that is often cited in media and academic journals.

新薬の開発は、メディアや学術誌でよく引用されるような事例の1つです。

(A) of	(A) 〜の
(B) such	**(B) そのような**
(C) another	(C) 別の
(D) that	(D) その

練習問題6　　**正解 C**　　他の正解例：much, far など

All the voters agreed that the new candidate is ------- too young to assume the role as a head.

すべての有権者は、新しい候補者がトップとしての役割を果たすにはかなり若すぎると意見が一致しています。

(A) more	(A) もっと
(B) so	(B) すぎる
(C) way	**(C) かなり**
(D) but	(D) しかし

練習問題7　　**正解 B**　　他の正解例：deserving など

As many tour guides recommend, Toronto is one of the cities in North America ------- visiting.

多くのツアーガイドが推薦するように、トロントは、訪問する価値がある北アメリカの都市の1つです。

(A) worthy

(B) worth

(C) worthwhile

(D) worthless

(A) 値する

(B) 〜する価値がある

(C) やりがいのある

(D) 今や〜だから

練習問題8 **正解 B** 他の正解例：because, not that, providing, although など

------- ours is dominating the market, the best strategy to build the barrier to entry is to improve the degree of customer satisfaction.

私たちのものが市場において権勢を振るっていない限り、参入障壁を構築するための最善の戦略は、顧客満足度を向上させることです。

(A) So that

(B) Unless

(C) Because of

(D) Thus

(A) 〜できるように

(B) 〜しない限り

(C) 〜なので

(D) したがって

練習問題9 **正解 B** 他の正解例：manifest, guarantee, prove など

That some of our competitors failed despite the odds won't ------- our supremacy in this niche market they are not focusing on.

見込みと違ってわれわれの競合会社が失敗したということは、それらが注力していないこのニッチ市場でのわれわれの優位性を意味するものではない。

(A) tolerate

(B) signify

(C) heat

(D) delete

(A) 耐える

(B) 意味する

(C) 温める

(D) 消す

練習問題10 **正解 A** 他の正解例：arrive, speak など

Among the first to ------- was no one but Face, the representative of the multinational conglomerate.

最初に現れた1人は、他の誰でもなく多国籍複合企業の代表であるフェイス氏でした。

(A) appear

(B) deny

(C) indicate

(D) discover

(A) 現れる

(B) 否定する

(C) 示す

(D) 発見する

Part6 長文穴埋め問題

絶対に押さえたい満点ポイント⑧
5W1Hを徹底的にとらえ、「一本釣り」で解答せよ

> Part 6で気をつけたいポイントは、「文脈」と「時系列」です。Part 5で問われた語彙力・文法力に加えて、パッセージの趣旨と流れをつかむ能力を問われます。そのためには、「だれが、だれに、何の目的で、いつ、どこで、何をしたのか」の5W1Hを一言一句違わず理解する必要があります。

◆ 5W1Hを必ず押さえる

満点を取るためのPart 6のポイントは、「文脈」と「時系列」を全問正確にとらえることです。短文穴埋め問題のPart 5とは違い、一連の流れがあるパッセージの中での穴埋めですので、パッセージ全体と通して考えたときに最適である解答を常に選ぶ必要があります。

そのために注意したいポイントは、**だれが、だれに、何の目的で、いつそのメールや伝達文を送ったのか**、の確認です。基本の5W1Hでの誤解は、誤答に直結しかねません。空欄や選択肢を観る前に、まず「だれが」（Who）、「だれに」（Whom）、「なぜ」（Why）、「いつ」（When）、「どこで」（Where）、「何を」（What）したのかという要素を押さえることが重要です。

例 題

①June 22 2021

1268 Conaway Street

Green Park

②New York

③Dear Mr. Bedford,

④We will be organizing ⑤the 7th NY Summer festival on
①August 14, 2021. Participation is free of charge and those
who are interested, ------- they are from outside the city, is
welcome. -------, feel free to bring your friends and family
with you.

There will be plenty of food stalls and shows. There will also
be the main stage for live performance and we are planning
to invite many special guests. The lineup will be announced
about two weeks ------- the event, so stay tuned.

If you would like to perform at the stage or have a stall,
please fill in the form attached with this letter and send it
to ------- by the 31st of July. We will be holding a rehearsal
the day before the festival, and we would also like you to
participate in the rehearsal as well.

Since the annual event preceding this one ------- canceled,
we are hoping this event will be more special and exciting
than ever. -------.

⑥Events Committee

①いつ
②どこで
③だれに
④何を
⑤何のために
⑥だれが

➡ 5W1Hの基礎を
押さえて、パッセ
ージ全体の流れを
正確につかむ

◆「一本釣り」の実力を身につける

Part 5と同じく、選択肢がなくとも正解（の属性を持った回答）が思いつくほどの力をつけることが重要です。990点を目指すなら、選択肢に振り回される立場での回答ではなく、選択肢を想像、創造するくらいの思考で正解していきたいものです。

高難度問題にトライ！

SET 1　どういう品詞・単語・文章が来るかまず想像してから、選択肢を読みましょう。

To: Residents of University Garden Dormitory
From: Jack Soprano, housing manager
Date: September 8
Subject: Elevator Maintenance

On Sept. 12, elevators will be out of service because of regular monthly ------- .
i.

You will be unable to use the elevators from 11:00 A.M. to approximately 3:30 P.M. Please use the stairs and ------- from pushing the elevator buttons during this time period.
ii.

------- . However, please note that we ------- to provide all residents with safe elevator service. I appreciate your understanding and cooperation.
iii. vi.

Sincerely,

Jack Soprano

---

i. (A) maintain

    (B) maintaining

    (C) maintained

    (D) maintenance

ii. (A) repair

    (B) prevent

    (C) refrain

    (D) delay

iii. (A) I really hope that all of you are having a great day.

    (B) We are sorry for any inconvenience this may cause you.

    (C) It is not your responsibility to provide the repair for this matter.

    (D) No one was allowed to use the elevator during the repair.

iv. (A) stray

    (B) strive

    (C) step up

    (D) stand

SET 2 どういう品詞・単語・文章が来るかまず想像してから、選択肢を読みましょう。

From: FSL Group
To: Richard Martin
2022/01/15
Subject: Invitation for 30th Anniversary of FSL Group

Dear Richard Martin,

FSL Group ------- to announce its 30th anniversary of providing excellent
service. To celebrate this event, everyone is invited to join us on 10th
Feb. 2022 on an RSVP basis. Please reserve a seat at your -------
convenience.

Our loyal customers, like you, are the main reason why we were able
to continue over the years. As a token of our -------, we have prepared
special gifts for everyone, so we hope you are able to attend the event.

The party will be held at Oriental Orb Resort, New Orleans.
Refreshments will be served at 6:30 P.M. and dinner will be at 8 P.M.
-------.

Best regards,

FSL Group

PS
Again, seats are limited, so we recommend prompt action!

v. (A) has pleased

(B) is pleased

(C) will have been pleased

(D) was pleased

vi. (A) nearest

(B) earliest

(C) clearest

(D) happiest

vii. (A) motivation

(B) regret

(C) excitement

(D) appreciation

viii. (A) No reservation is needed for this event.

(B) Hope to see you on the day of the event.

(C) I hope you will become a regular customer.

(D) The last event was a great success.

SET 3　どういう品詞・単語・文章が来るかまず想像してから、選択肢を読みましょう。

We are now hiring experienced building inspectors. The main duty of this position is ------- building inspections of multiple areas of construction in the City of Chestnuts. The duties include but not ------- to the inspections on the electric cables, water and gas pipes, and structural stability.

The inspectors, working as a team for two to four, evaluate all aspects of construction work. The applicants must possess a valid license granted from the State of California. Five years of experience in this field or an equivalent combination of professional training and actual experience is mandatory. -------
iii.

The City of Chestnuts will provide ------- opportunity to all job applicants and personnel, whether full time or part time, in compliance with all applicable city and state employment laws. There shall be no discrimination based on race, gender, age, gender identity, etc.

i. (A) provides

(B) provision

(C) to provide

(D) provided

ii. (A) a limit

(B) limitation

(C) limited

(D) limiting

iii. (A) You must have a driver's license for large size vehicles.

(B) The city is now hiring professionals in this field.

(C) For inquiries, visit our head office on Lincoln Avenue.

(D) The team leader will give detailed directions.

iv. (A) subjective

　(B) excellent

　(C) varying

　(D) equal

SET 1 正解と解説

To: Residents of University Garden Dormitory
From: Jack Soprano, housing manager
Date: September 8
Subject: Elevator Maintenance

On Sept. 12, elevators will be out of service because of regular monthly
------- .
　i.

You will be unable to use the elevators from 11:00 A.M. to approximately
3:30 P.M. Please use the stairs and ------- from pushing the elevator
　　　　　　　　　　　　　　　　　　　　ii.
buttons during this time period.

------- . However, please note that we ------- to provide all residents with
　iii.　　　　　　　　　　　　　　　　vi.
safe elevator service. I appreciate your understanding and cooperation.

Sincerely,

Jack Soprano

宛先：ユニバーシティガーデン寮の居住者
差出人：住宅マネージャー、ジャック・ソプラノ
日付：9月8日
件名：エレベーターのメンテナンス

9月12日は、毎月の定期メンテナンスのため、エレベーターは使用できなくなります。

午前11時から午後3時30分頃までエレベーターはご利用いただけません。この間は階段

を使用し、エレベーターのボタンを押さないでください。

ご不便をおかけして申し訳ございません。すべての居住者に安全なエレベーターサービスを提供するよう努めております。何とぞご理解およびご協力をお願い申し上げます。

よろしくお願いいたします。

ジャック・ソプラノ

i.

(A) maintain
(B) maintaining
(C) maintained
(D) maintenance

(A) 点検する
(B) 点検すること
(C) 点検される
(D) 点検

> 解説　because of ～は「～のため」という表現で、～の部分には名詞が入ります。つまり、動詞である(A) maintainや、過去分詞である(C) maintainedは必然的に除外されます。(B) maintainingは動名詞で、「点検すること」という意味になりますので、(D) maintenance「点検」が自然です。よって正解は(D)となります。

ii.

(A) repair
(B) prevent
(C) refrain
(D) delay

(A) 修理する
(B) 防ぐ
(C) 控える
(D) 遅れる

> 解説　refrain from pushing the elevator buttonsで「エレベーターのボタンを押すことを控える」という意味になります。よって正解は(C)になります。refrain from ～ ingで、「～を控える」という熟語なので、押さえておきましょう。他の選択肢は、(A)「修理する」、(B)「防ぐ」、(D)「遅れる」で、不自然なので、消去法でも導き出せるはずです。

iii.

(A) I really hope that all of you are having a great day.
(B) We are sorry for any inconvenience this may cause you.
(C) It is not your responsibility to provide the repair for this matter.

(A) あなた方の全員が素敵な日を過ごされていることを心から願います。
(B) ご不便をおかけして申し訳ございません。
(C) 本件について修理を提供するのはあなたの責任ではありません。

(D) No one was allowed to use the elevator during the repair.

(D) 修理中、エレベーターのいかなる人のご利用が許されておりません。

解説　(A)は結びの言葉として一般的なフレーズなので不自然で不正解です。(D)に関しては、You will be unable to use elevators「エレベーターをご利用いただけません」と前で似たようなことが既に述べられているのと、No one was allowedと過去形になっているので不正解です。また、直後のHowever, ~がポイントとなります。逆接なので、続く文の意味と逆のことを言っている文が一番自然に当てはまります。よって、(B) We are sorry for any inconvenience this may cause you「ご不便をおかけして申し訳ございません」が正解になります。

iv.

(A) stray

(B) **strive**

(C) step up

(D) stand

(A) 離れる

(B) **努める**

(C) 進歩する

(D) 立つ

解説　provide all residents with safe elevator serviceで、「全ての居住者に安全なエレベーターサービスを提供する」という意味になります。よって空欄は「努める」という意味である(B) striveが最も自然です。他の選択肢は、(A)「離れる」、(C)「進歩する」、(D)「立つ」で、不自然なので、消去法でも導き出せるでしょう。

SET 2 正解と解説

From: FSL Group
To: Richard Martin
2022/01/15
Subject: Invitation for 30th Anniversary of FSL Group

Dear Richard Martin,

FSL Group ------- to announce its 30th anniversary of providing excellent service. To celebrate this event, everyone is invited to join us on 10th Feb. 2022 on an RSVP basis. Please reserve a seat at your ------- convenience.

Our loyal customers, like you, are the main reason why we were able to continue over the years. As a token of our -------, we have prepared special gifts for everyone, so we hope you are able to attend the event.

The party will be held at Oriental Orb Resort, New Orleans. Refreshments will be served at 6:30 P.M. and dinner will be at 8 P.M. -------.
_{viii.}

Best regards,

FSL Group

PS
Again, seats are limited, so we recommend prompt action!

差出人：FSLグループ
宛先：リチャード・マーティン
2022/01/15
件名：FSLグループ30周年記念への招待

リチャード・マーティン様

FSLグループは、優れたサービスを提供し続け30周年を迎えました。2022年2月10日、このイベントを祝うためにRSVP形式で皆様を招待いたします。可能な限り早く席を確保してください。

お客さまのようなお得意さまが、私たちが何年にもわたって継続することができた主な理由です。感謝の印として、皆様へ特別なプレゼントもご用意しておりますので、ぜひご参加ください。

パーティーはニューオーリンズのオリエンタルオーブリゾートで開催されます。軽食は午後6時30分に、夕食は午後8時に提供されます。イベント当日お会いできることを楽しみにしています。

敬具

FSLグループ

追伸
繰り返しになりますが、席には限りがありますので、迅速な行動をお勧めいたします。

Vocabulary

☐ **RSVP** お返事お願いいたします（**Répondez s'il vous plaît** の略）

v.

(A) has pleased	(A) 喜ばせた
(B) is pleased	**(B) うれしい**
(C) will have been pleased	(C) うれしくなるだろう
(D) was pleased	(D) うれしくなった

解説　be pleased to ～という受動態で「～できてうれしい」という決まり文句です。よって、能動態である(A)は除外されます。また、うれしいのは現在なので、未来形の(C)や過去形の(D)も除外されます。よって正解は(B) is pleasedになります。

vi.

(A) nearest	(A) 最も近く
(B) earliest	**(B) 最も早く**
(C) clearest	(C) 最もきれいな
(D) happiest	(D) 最も幸せな

解説　at your earliest convenienceで「可能な限り早く」という意味の決まり文句になります。よって、正解は(B) earliestです。このフレーズを知らなくても、最後のseats are limited, so I recommend prompt action「席には限りがありますので、迅速な行動をお勧めいたします」という部分から、早めの予約が必要であることがわかるので、正解の(B)が導き出せるでしょう。

vii.

(A) motivation	(A) 動機
(B) regret	(B) 後悔
(C) excitement	(C) 興奮
(D) appreciation	**(D) 感謝の念**

解説　As a token of ～で、「～の印として」という意味になります。we have prepared special gifts「特別なプレゼントもご用意しております」と続くので、「感謝の念」という意味である(D)appreciationが一番自然に当てはまります。他の選択肢は(A)「動機」、(B)「後悔」、(C)「興奮」という意味なので、プレゼントの理由として不自然です。このようにappreciationという単語がわからずとも、消去法で自然に正解が導ける問題です。

viii.

(A) No reservation is needed for this event.

(B) Hope to see you on the day of the event.

(C) I hope you will become a regular customer.

(D) The last event was a great success.

(A) 本イベントに予約は不要です。

(B) イベントの当日にお会いできるのを楽しみにしております。

(C) あなたがわれわれをごひいきにしていただけますことを願っております。

(D) 前回のイベントは大成功でした。

解説　Please reserve a seatという部分で、予約が必要ということが示されているので、(A)は間違いです。Our customers, like youという部分で、宛先の人はすでにお得意さまであることが書かれているので、(C)も間違いであることがわかります。(D)は前回のイベントの話で、この部分で出てくると文脈的に突然であることがわかります。よって、正解は(B)となります。(B)のような表現は結びの言葉として一般的なので、消去法でなくても、自然と正解だとわかるようになるといいでしょう。

SET 3 正解と解説

We are now hiring experienced building inspectors. The main duty of this position is ------- building inspections of multiple areas of construction in the City of Chestnuts. The duties include but not ------- to the inspections on the electric cables, water and gas pipes, and structural stability.

The inspectors, working as a team for two to four, evaluate all aspects of construction work. The applicants must possess a valid license granted from the State of California. Five years of experience in this field or an equivalent combination of professional training and actual experience is mandatory. -------

The City of Chestnuts will provide ------- opportunity to all job applicants and personnel, whether full time or part time, in compliance with all applicable city and state employment laws. There shall be no discrimination based on race, gender, age, gender identity, etc.

現在、経験豊富な建築検査官を採用しています。この役職の主な仕事は、チェストナッツ市の複数の建設エリアの建物検査を提供することです。業務には、電気ケーブル、水道管とガス管、および構造安定性の検査が含まれますが、これらに限りません。

検査官は、2〜4人のチームとして作業し、建設作業のすべての側面を評価します。申請者は、カリフォルニア州から付与された有効なライセンスを所有している必要があります。この分野での5年間の経験、または同等の専門的なトレーニングと実際の経験の組み合わせが必須です。大型車の運転免許証を所有していなければいけません。

チェストナッツ市は、適用されるすべての市および州の雇用法に従い、フルタイムかパートタイムかにかかわらず、すべての求職者と職員に平等な機会を提供します。人種、性別、年齢、性同一性などに基づく差別があってはなりません。

i.

(A) provides　　　　　　　　　(A) 提供する

(B) provision　　　　　　　　 (B) 提供

(C) to provide　　　　　　　**(C) 提供すること**

(D) provided　　　　　　　　　(D) 提供された

解説　isというbe動詞に続いている空欄にあてはまる語句を選びます。仕事は〜することです、という意味を作るため不定詞で「提供すること」という意味になる(C)が正解となります。(B)は名詞ですが、「提供」という意味で、動名詞ではありません。(D)はbuildingを修飾するように使える可能性はありますが、その場合aやtheなどの冠詞が必要になるので不正解です。よって、正解は(C)となります。(C)はto不定詞で、「提供すること」という意味になり自然です。

ii.

(A) a limit　　　　　　　　　 (A) 限度

(B) limitation　　　　　　　　(B) 制限

(C) limited　　　　　　　　**(C) 制限される**

(D) limiting　　　　　　　　　(D) 制限する

解説　契約書やビジネス文書でよくみられる言い回しで、The duties include but not limited to 〜 で、仕事内容は〜を含むがそれらに限定されるわけではない、という表現です。もちろんThe dutiesの部分は他の名詞や名詞句に変えていただいて構いません。The duties include but (they are) not limited to... とthey areが省略されてあると考えれば構造が理解しやすいでしょう。

iii.

(A) **You must have a driver's license for large size vehicles.**

(A) **大型車の運転免許証を持っていなければいけません。**

(B) The city is now hiring professionals in this field.

(B) 市は現在この分野の専門家を雇用しています。

(C) For inquiries, visit our head office on Lincoln Avenue.

(C) お問い合わせはリンカーン通りの本社をお訪ねください。

(D) The team leader will give detailed directions.

(D) チームリーダーが詳細な指示を出します。

解説　雇用条件に関する話が続いた後の空欄なので、雇用条件についての内容になっている(A)が最も適切であり、正解です。(B)は最初に話している前提のことなので、ここで出てくるのは不自然でしょう。(C)のようなお問い合わせについてはだいたい一番最後に来ることが多く、まだ話が続く中で出てくるのは不自然です。(D)に関しては近いですが、来るならチーム作業の話をした直後が一番自然でしょう。雇用条件の話を間に挟むので不自然です。

iv.

(A) subjective

(A) 主観的な

(B) excellent

(B) 素晴らしい

(C) varying

(C) 変化する

(D) **equal**

(D) **平等な**

解説　この空欄で、どのような機会提供するのかが変わるので、文脈を読み取り正解を導き出す必要があります。whether full time or part time「フルタイムかパートタイムかにかかわらず」という言葉や、There shall be no discrimination based on race, gender, age, gender identity, etc.「人種、性別、年齢、性同一性などに基づく差別があってはなりません」という言葉が直後にあり、等しい機会を与えることを重要視していることが取れるので、一番自然なのは、(D)でしょう。(A)、(B)、(C)は、後の文脈を考えると不自然なので不正解です。

990点満点を取る受験者は
消去法で考えない

　TOEICで満点を取る受験者は、基本的に消去法で考えません。

　消去法というのは、正解がはっきり見えない状況で不正解を外していく思考法です。上級者になればなるほど正解が正解だと判断できるので、消去法の必要はなくなります。しかしながら、私たちの思考の過程は、エントロピーの向きとは逆に、混沌から整頓の方向で矢が向いているため、どうしても消去法で考える傾向があります。気を付けましょう。

　脳に勝手にdriveさせるのではなく、脳をdriveしましょう。

Part7 読解問題

絶対に押さえたい満点ポイント⑨

「全体像」とディテールの両方を高速でつかむ

> 満点取得のためにPart 7で重要なのは、いかに高速かつ正確に、文書の概要と詳細を読めるかに尽きます。いうなれば、「木も森も見る」ことが重要で、さらに「木も森も見る」速度と正確性を高めることが重要です。

◆ 全体像と細かい情報の両方を読む

Part 7では、詳細も全体像も両方頭に入れていく、という読み方が鍵になります。まず、詳細を追うために、速読で1単語を大事に読み進める意識を持つ必要があります。この意識は例えるなら、森の中の木、一本一本を見るようなイメージです。

一方で、単語だけ頭に残っても全体像が見えないと問題は解けないので、パッセージの全体像も見えていなければいけません。これは、森全体の形を把握しているイメージです。

いわば、「木も森も見る」意識を持ちながら、いかに高速かつ正確に読めるかが重要です。そのためには、詳細から全体まで理解していなければ解けない、難易度の高めの問題を解き続けることが重要です。

Part 7の戦略として、よく「選択肢と問題文を交互に読むべきか」、また「問題文から読むべきか、それとも長文から読むべきか」が議論の的になることがあります。990点満点を狙う皆さんは、選択肢と問題文を交互に行き来する読み方ではなく、全体を読み通すやり方が適しています。問題文→長文、長文→問題文の順番については、自分に適したものを選ぶ必要があります。あらかじめ実験して、自認しておくとよいでしょう。

例題

Mother's Day is fast approaching and if you're looking for that perfect gift for your mom, look no further than ①our beautiful Himalayan Pink Salt candles. These candles are available in a variety of fragrances and sizes. Here's a little about our best-selling ones.

①大意をつかむ：
Himalayan Pink Salt candlesの広告だな

Lily: This one is probably our favorite! With scents of cedar and vanilla, ②this candle has a light woody scent that is perfect for those winter nights, sitting next to a log fire. The candle is topped with real lavender and rose petals, along with Himalayan pink salt.

②詳細を押さえる：みんなはLilyのa light woody scentがお気に入りなんだな

➡ 大意と詳細の両方を確認しながら読み進める！

Bessy from Texas says this about her Lily candle: "I love Candle Creations because they come up with the most innovative scents. Their customer service is fantastic too!"

Honey: Our Honey candle is made with pure Manuka honey oil and smells of lightly roasted pears, honey, and cinnamon. This one is perfect if your mother likes sweet scents. The candle also has a real vanilla pod in it, so that the fragrance lasts longer.

Jasmine from Minnesota says, "The Honey candle is my favorite. I have bought 3 of them already! The scent is very relaxing and helps me relax."

Flower Blast: If your mother likes floral scents, give her this candle! The fragrance is a mix of various wildflowers, orchids, roses, and jasmine. The candle also has real rose buds and rosemary on the surface, so that it is as beautiful unlit as it is when you light it.

Kaya from Georgia wrote to us and said, "Please don't ever stop making the Flower Blast candle. The fragrance is stunning, and it feels like I'm standing in a meadow of flowers. Thank you for creating this!"

Drop into our store on Gotham St. or shop online at candlecreations.com.

990点満点への道

情報は探すのではなく理解する

　990点に遠い人ほど、情報を探しているものです。試験後に受け取る「abilities measured」を見てみると、右側の上から2番目の「文書の中の具体的な情報を見つけて理解できる」というのは長けていても、1番目の「文書の中の情報をもとに推測できる」、3番目「情報を関連付けることができる」が伸び切らない人がいます。

　これは、**情報を探すことはできていても、考えて答えを選ぶことはうまくできていない**ということを示しているデータです。

　「どこに何が書いてあったか」というのは満点を取る上では当然把握できていなければいけない第一歩目で、第二歩目としては**「書いてあった情報をもとに考え、理解する」**ところまで落とし込めるかが差になります。だから、単語レベルでもパッセージ全体レベルでも集中して読み込み、理解した上で、確信を持って答えられるようになりましょう。

第1章 英語脳徹底トレーニング

第2章 高難度問題の徹底攻略

第3章 正答ハイテクレッスン

第4章 ハイレベル完全模試

高難度問題にトライ！

SET 1

Anthro-Today

This letter is being sent to all subscribers whose annual membership is terminating in four weeks. Having been published monthly for almost 30 years, *Anthro-Today* is one of the most reputable scientific journals focusing on Archaeology and Anthropology, with over three hundred thousand subscribers from all over the world. Don't let your subscription expire. We will publish all the latest discoveries on Homo sapiens that are not seen in any other magazines.

Enclosed is a memberrship extention form. Upon renewal, all continuing subscribers will receive a rebate that is worth three months. Payment can be made by card. A money order and bank check are acceptable only for those in the US and a part of Canada*, made payable to "Anthro-Today Publisher Inc." Cash payment is no longer accepted. We are very much looking forward to receiving your renewal order.

*All non-card payment options are available for group orders only
 Discount at varying rates available for longer-term contracts

Skinner Hayden

Director, Dr. Hayden
Anthro-Today Publishing, New York, Buffalo

147. What is the main purpose of this letter?

    (A) To specify the most preferred payment method

    (B) To let the readers know their status and options

    (C) To prove that *Anthro-Today* is the most reputed journal

    (D) To encourage free users to become paid subscribers

148. What is NOT indicated about *Anthro-Today*?

    (A) It has published recent findings on Homo sapiens.

    (B) It focuses on a specific scientific field.

    (C) Its subscription fees vary depending on conditions.

    (D) It is read by people in multiple countries.

149. According to the information given, how can the readers get some money back?

    (A) By using a rebate included in a promotional e-mail

    (B) By updating their status from the US or Canada

    (C) By extending their subscription of longer terms than a year

    (D) By renewing the membership within four weeks

SET 2

The Bank of Westwood, Service Center

Dear Royal Customers,

We always appreciate your patronage of our online banking service. As we noted several times via e-mail, postal mail, and press release, the Bank of Westwood has introduced a new tool against unauthorized access to our online system.

— [1] —. This is part of our continuing endeavor to respond to our customers' increasing concerns about security issues. This new two-step authentication system assures that all of your personal information and that the account itself is securely protected. — [2] —.

To properly activate this multi-layer security patch called "DoubleW Secure," you are required to install a specific program from our website, sync it to your computer with your mobile device, and set up two six-digit passcodes. Both of these codes will be required every time you log in to your account. While the process becomes complicated, this change further assures your privacy and asset.

— [3] —. The passcodes generated using your mobile device can be altered; however, resetting them requires a course of verification steps, which may take up to a week. We, therefore, advise you to memorise your passcord.

— [4] —. Extra attention is needed when you change your cell phone, because the new phone and your computer won't synchronized automatically; you must go through the necessary steps. If you have questions about this or any other issues, please visit our website at www.bank-of-WW.com.

December 20th, 2021

Online Banking Section Director,
Kim Lockard

150. What does the letter suggest about the Bank of Westwood?

(A) It has implemented several measures for information protection.

(B) It intends to release a new security step for customers.

(C) It utilizes press releases most frequently for its publicity.

(D) It specializes in developing anti-fraud software.

151. According to the letter, what is required for the activation of the security program?

(A) six sets of passwords

(B) an agreement to the privacy policy

(C) multiple devices

(D) two security programs

152. What does the letter mention regarding a potential difficulty that users may experience?

(A) They can talk to the sender of the letter to solve the problem.

(B) They are not recommended to change cell phones.

(C) A possible solution for the issue can be found online.

(D) No transfer of information won't occur even with an online guide.

153. In which of the positions marked [1], [2], [3], and [4] does the following sentence best belong?

"We also recommend that users become familiar with the least new system."

(A) [1]

(B) [2]

(C) [3]

(D) [4]

SET3

Date: October 27th, Friday, 17:25:01
From: Nguyen
To: Peterson
Subject: Business trip to Sydney

Hello Peter. I hope all is well.

As you know, I am flying to Sydney with my supervisor on a business trip, but since this is the first time to visit Sydney for both of us, we're not sure which hotel to book. I heard you used to live there, so I was wondering if you would mind helping us. In particular, we are looking at which hotel is favorable in terms of location and the time required to go to the conference center.

I came up with the following list and summarized the necessary information for each hotel. From photos on their websites, they all look excellent.

Hotel Santa Beach is a little far away from the venue but it commands a beautiful view of the Tasman Sea, so it looks particularly attractive to me. But since we are expected to go back and forth between the hotel and the conference center, there's no doubt that being within the vicinity of the conference center is more desirable.

I have to make a reservation by next Friday, so I would really appreciate it if you could let me know before then. My information is limited, so please fill me in if you have any other hotels you would like to recommend. Also I'd really appreciate it if you could recommend any good sightseeing spots in Sydney.

Many thanks,

Nguyen

	City	Distance from conference center	Time to the venue	Vacancy
Sydney Central Hotel	Sydney	0.5 miles	1-2 minutes	△
La Rocka Hotel	Sydney	0.5 miles	1-2 minutes	○
Hotel Royal Prince	Wynyard	1 mile	5 minutes	○
King's Hotel SH	Surry Hills	3 miles	15 minutes	△
Hotel Santa Beach	Dover Heights	12 miles	50 minutes	○

154. Why is Nguyen e-mailing Peterson?

  (A) Because Peterson may know a lot about local issues

  (B) Because he has to make a reservation today

  (C) Because Peterson is Nguyen's supervisor

  (D) Because Peterson can provide accommodation

155. Where can Nguyen enjoy a great view of the Tasman Sea?

  (A) Sydney

  (B) Wynyard

  (C) Surry Hills

  (D) Dover Heights

156. The phrase "in terms of" in paragraph 1, line 5, is closest in meaning to

  (A) in exchange for

  (B) from the viewpoint of

  (C) in accordance with

  (D) at the expense of

157. What will probably happen next Friday?

  (A) Nguyen will leave for Sydney.

  (B) Peterson will e-mail Nguyen.

  (C) Nguyen will finish booking the hotel.

  (D) Peterson will make a reservation.

158. What does Nguyen intend to do in addition to his business during his trip to Australia?

    (A) Hang around the city

    (B) Spend time in the Tasman Sea

    (C) Visit Sydney

    (D) Ask for some recommendations

SET 4

TO: All Staff
FROM: Steve Jones
DATE: June 15
RE: Flextime

I am sorry for my tardiness in replying. I have been terribly busy training the new receptionist after Sally suddenly resigned, and I haven't had time to meet with most of you. For the time being, it's more time efficient to talk over the phone or mail each other than to meet with everyone in person. It will take another month before Shelly, the new receptionist, can fully take over the position and duties.

Anyway, we need to discuss the changes in the work conditions. There has been an increasing demand for more flexible working hours, and we have agreed to allow flexibility with some conditions. As a branch manager, it is my responsibility to ensure that this branch is as productive as possible. As members of work teams, it will be your responsibility to meet with your section manager to adjust and arrange your work teams' work schedule. I hope that the decisions can be made in a democratic manner. In addition, the 8-hour work schedule must be sometime between the hours of 8 A.M. and 10 P.M. Please update me on this matter within a week via e-mail, and if you have any questions by then, give me a buzz at night time since I will be busy training Shelly during the day time for the next few weeks. Seriously, I'm too busy to see anyone face to face.

TO: Steve Jones
FROM: Janet O'Reilly
DATE: June 21
RE: flextime

Hi Steve. May I request some clarification concerning the plan to implement flextime in the office, which you said is the biggest concern for you and your department? I have met and talked with my section manager and other members of my work team, but we have been unable to reach a consensus on a good schedule. The starting time works, but things would be much easier if the finishing time is 8 rather than 10. Some are working as a group, and each having liberty to decide on his/her work time will threaten the productivity. Especially, Tom's group requires tremendous communication, making it practically impossible for the members to work flexibly. I suppose we have to either set restrictions for special circumstances like this or tolerate a certain degree of reduced productivity. I am terribly sorry that I could not make things work efficiently.

Janet

PS: I really hope new receptionist will be able to start operating independently from next month. I know this is important, but you are working too much. You should relegate some tasks to others as soon as possible.

Q.1 What is the most serious concern for Steve?

　　(A) Sally left her position suddenly.

　　(B) The branch has to adjust work conditions.

　　(C) He cannot find a suitable replacement.

　　(D) His current work hour is too long.

Q.2　Why is the branch trying to adopt a flexible schedule?

(A) Because it was requested from the workers

(B) Because it can increase productivity

(C) Because it is required by regulations

(D) Because there is currently no receptionist

Q.3　What is one purpose of the second mail?

(A) To summarize the tentative schedules

(B) To ask clarification of her teams' problems

(C) To extend her apology for inefficiency

(D) To request the adjustment of her working hours.

Q.4　Which requirement specified by Steve did Janet fail to meet?

(A) Converse in a democratic fashion

(B) Update the status within a week

(C) Give a phone call for a question

(D) Set the work hour from 8 A.M. to 10 P.M.

Q.5　What does Janet hope will happen next month?

(A) Sally will return to the previous position.

(B) Steve will start relegating some of his duties.

(C) Shelly will completely take over required work.

(D) Tom's team members can reach an agreement.

Anthro-Today

This letter is being sent to all subscribers whose annual membership is terminating in four weeks. Having been published monthly for almost 30 years, *Anthro-Today* is one of the most reputable scientific journals focusing on Archaeology and Anthropology, with over three hundred thousand subscribers from all over the world. Don't let your subscription expire. We will publish all the latest discoveries on Homo sapiens that are not seen in any other magazines.

Enclosed is a memberrship extention form. Upon renewal, all continuing subscribers will receive a rebate that is worth three months. Payment can be made by card. A money order and bank check are acceptable only for those in the US and a part of Canada*, made payable to "Anthro-Today Publisher Inc." Cash payment is no longer accepted. We are very much looking forward to receiving your renewal order.

*All non-card payment options are available for group orders only
 Discount at varying rates available for longer-term contracts

Skinner Hayden

Director, Dr. Hayden
Anthro-Today Publishing, New York, Buffalo

Anthro-Today

この手紙は、年間購読があと4週間で終了するすべての購読者の皆さまに送られています。30年近くにわたり毎月発刊されている *Anthro-Today* は、世界中から30万人以上の購読者がいる、最も評判の高い、考古学や人類学の焦点を当てた科学雑誌の1つです。購読の有効期限が切れないようにしてください。他の雑誌では見られない人類に関する最新の発

見を発表しています。

会員資格の延長のための用紙が同封されています。全ての継続購読者は、3カ月間有効な
リベート（払い戻し券）を受け取ることができます。お支払いは、カードで行うことができ
ます。郵便為替と小切手はアメリカと一部のカナダに居住の方にのみ可能となっており＊、
「Anthro-Today出版社」への支払いとしてください。現金での支払いはもう受け付けてお
りません。更新のご注文をお待ちしております。

＊カード以外のすべての支払い方法はグループでの注文に限定される
　　より長期間での契約においては異なる割合での割引が可能

スキナー・ヘイデン
取締役、ヘイデン博士
Anthro-Today出版社、ニューヨーク、バッファロー

Vocabulary

☐ **reputable** 評判の良い　☐ **archaeology** 考古学　☐ **anthropology** 人類学　☐ **money order** 郵便為替
☐ **payable to** ～ ～に支払い可能

147. What is the main purpose of this letter?

この手紙の主な目的は何ですか。

(A) To specify the most preferred payment method

(B) **To let the readers know their status and options**

(C) To prove that *Anthro-Today* is the most reputed journal

(D) To encourage the readers to become paid subscribers.

(A) 最も望ましい支払い方法を指定すること

(B) **読者に現在の状態と選択肢を知らせること**

(C) *Anthro-Today*が最も評判の良い雑誌と証明すること

(D) 読者に有料会員になるのを促すこと

解説　冒頭で、This letter is being sent to all subscribers whose annual membership is
terminating in four weeks「この手紙は、年間購読があと4週間で終了する購読者の皆
さまに送られています」とあり、読者の現在の状況を知らせています。さらに、Payment
can be made by card. A money order and bank check are...「お支払いは、カードで行
うことができます。郵便為替と小切手も…」と選択肢も提示しています。正解は(B)とな
ります。

148. What is NOT indicated about *Anthro-Today*?

*Anthro-Today*について示唆されていないのはどれですか。

(A) It has published recent findings on Homo sapiens.

(B) It focuses on a specific scientific field.

(C) Its subscription fees vary depending on conditions.

(D) It is read by people in multiple countries.

(A) ホモサピエンスの最近の発見について記事をすでに出している。

(B) 科学の特定の分野に焦点を当てている。

(C) 購読料金は条件により異なる。

(D) 複数の国の人によって読まれている。

解説 *Anthro-Today*は、これからホモサピエンスの最新研究結果を出していくのであって、これまでに出したことがある、という記述はないので、(A)が正解となります。Anthro-Today は、one of the most reputable scientific journals focusing on Archaeology and Anthropology「最も評判の高い、考古学や人類学に焦点を当てた科学雑誌の1つです」と述べられているので、特定の分野に特化した学術誌であるとわかるため(B)は除外されます。Discount at varying rates available for longer-term contracts「より長期間での契約においては異なる割合での割引が可能」とあるので、(C)も除外されます。over three hundred thousand subscribers from all over the world「世界中から30万人以上の購読者」がいると述べられているので、(D)も除外されます。

149. According to the information given, how can the readers get some money back?

与えられた情報によると、読者はどのように幾らかの払い戻しを受けられますか。

(A) By using a rebate included in a promotional e-mail

(B) By updating their status from the US or Canada

(C) By extending their subscription of longer terms than a year

(D) By renewing the membership within four weeks

(A) Eメールにある払い戻し券を使うことにより

(B) ステータスをアメリカまたはカナダから更新することにより

(C) 購読を1年より長い期間で延長することにより

(D) 4週間以内に会員の更新を行うことにより

解説 Upon renewal, all continuing subscribers will receive a rebate「すべての継続購読者は、リベート(払い戻し券)を受け取ることができます」とあるので、正解は(D)です。リベートとは、支払った額の一部払い戻しのことであるため、メンバーシップを期限内に更新することで、リベート(一部の money back)を受け取ることができる、という流れです。

225

The Bank of Westwood, Service Center

Dear Royal Customers,

We always appreciate your patronage of our online banking service. As we noted several times via e-mail, postal mail, and press release, the Bank of Westwood has introduced a new tool against unauthorized access to our online system.

— [1] —. This is part of our continuing endeavor to respond to our customers' increasing concerns about security issues. This new two-step authentication system assures that all of your personal information and that the account itself is securely protected. — [2] —.

To properly activate this multi-layer security patch called "DoubleW Secure," you are required to install a specific program from our website, sync it to your computer with your mobile device, and set up two six-digit passcodes. Both of these codes will be required every time you log in to your account. While the process becomes complicated, this change further assures your privacy and asset.

— [3] —. The passcodes generated using your mobile device can be altered; however, resetting them requires a course of verification steps, which may take up to a week. We, therefore, advise you to memorise your passcord.

— [4] —. Extra attention is needed when you change your cell phone, because the new phone and your computer won't synchronized automatically; you must go through the necessary steps. If you have questions about this or any other issues, please visit our website at www.bank-of-WW.com.

December 20th, 2021

Online Banking Section Director,
Kim Lockard

Westwood銀行、サービスセンター

お客さま各位

オンラインバンキングサービスをご愛顧いただき誠にありがとうございます。メール、郵便、およびプレスリリースで何度かお伝えしたとおり、Westwood銀行はオンラインシステムへの不正アクセスに対する新しいツールを導入しました。

これは、お客さまのセキュリティ問題への強まる懸念に対しての、当社の継続した取り組みの一部です。この新しい2段階認証システムが、お客さまの口座自体、および個人情報の保護を保証します。

この「ダブルW保護」と呼ばれる複数階層の安全パッチを着実に有効にするためには、まず専用のプログラムを当社のウェブサイトからインストールいただき、コンピューターを携帯機器と同期させた上で、6桁のパスコードを2つ設定いただく必要があります。これらのコードの両方ともが口座にログインする際に毎回必要とされます。手順は複雑になりますが、この変更はお客さまのプライバシーと資産をさらに強固に保護するものとなります。

携帯機器で生成されるパスコードは変更可能ですが、再設定するには一連の確認プロセスを通る必要があり、1週間かかることもありえます。ですので、パスコードは記憶しておくようお勧めいたします。

携帯電話を変更する際には特に注意が必要です。新しい携帯とあなたのパソコンが自動的に同期されるということはなく、必要なステップを踏まなければいけません。この点においても他のことについても、ご不明な点がございましたら、当社のウェブサイトwww.bank-of-WW.comをご覧ください。

2021年12月20日

オンラインバンキング課長
キム・ロッカード

Vocabulary

☐ **unauthorized** 権限のない　☐ **endeavor** 努力　☐ **multi-layer** 複数階層の　☐ **sync** 同期させる

150. What does the letter suggest about the Bank of Westwood?

この手紙でWestwood銀行について示唆されていることは何でしょうか。

(A) It has implemented several measures for information protection.

(B) It intends to release a new security step for customers.

(C) It utilizes press releases most frequently for its publicity.

(D) It specializes in developing anti-fraud software.

(A) 情報保護のために何度か手段を講じてきた。

(B) 顧客のために新しいセキュリティーの方法を出す計画である。

(C) 宣伝のためにプレスリリースを最も頻繁に使っている。

(D) 不正対応のソフトウェアを開発することに特化している。

解説　オンラインシステムへの不正アクセスに対する新しいツールを導入したことは、our continuing endeavor「当社の継続した取り組み」と述べられているので、初めての取り組み、1回のみの取り組みではなく、複数回行ってきた様子が読み取れ、正解は(A)になります。our continuing endeavorがimplement several measures「何度か手段を講じる」と言い換えられています。

151. According to the letter, what is required for the activation of the security program?

手紙によると、セキュリティープログラムの有効化のために必要なものは何ですか。

(A) six sets of passwords

(B) An agreement to the privacy policy

(C) multiple devices

(D) two security programs

(A) 6個のパスワード

(B) プライバシーポリシーへの同意

(C) 複数の機器

(D) 2つの安全プログラム

解説　you are required to install a specific program from our website, sync it to your computer with your mobile device, and set up two six-digit passcodes「専用プログラムを当社のウェブサイトからインストールいただき、パソコンと携帯機器と同期させた上で、6桁のパスワードを2つ設定いただく必要があります」という記述があるので、パソコンに加え同期する携帯機器が別に必要であることがわかります。よって、正解は(C)となります。

152. What does the letter mention regarding a potential difficulty that users may experience?

ユーザーが経験しうる想定される問題について手紙には何と書いてありますか。

(A) They can talk to the sender of the letter to solve the problem.

(B) They are not recommended to change cell phones.

(C) A possible solution for the issue can be found online.

(D) No transfer of information won't occur even with an online guide.

(A) ユーザーはその問題を解決するために手紙の送り主と話すことができる。

(B) ユーザーは携帯電話を換えることを推奨されていない。

(C) その問題に対する解決案はオンラインで見つけることができる。

(D) オンラインの案内があっても情報の移行はできない。

解説　If you have questions about this or other issues, please visit our website「この点においても他のことについても、ご不明な点がございましたら、当社のウェブサイトをご覧ください」と記述があるので、正解は(C)になります。本文と選択肢ではissueという単語が使われていますが、質問では代わりにdifficultyという単語が使われているので、注意しましょう。携帯電話を換える際に注意が必要であることは言及されていますが、携帯を換えない方がいい、とまでは言っていないので(B)は誤りです。

153. In which of the positions marked [1], [2], [3], and [4] does the following sentence best belong?

"We also recommend that users become familiar with the new system."

次の文は、[1] [2] [3] [4]のどの場所に最も適切に挿入されるでしょうか。

「当社はユーザーが新システムについて多少の知識を有していることも推奨いたします」

(A) [1]

(B) [2]

(C) [3]

(D) [4]

解説　挿入文にalsoという単語があるので、(A)はすぐ除外できます。話題の関連性としても、(B)あたりは新しいツールに関して、(C)あたりはパスコードの変更についてと、つながりがあまりないので、不自然になるでしょう。(D)では、その後のセンテンスに「特に注意が必要」とあるので、その直前に何かしら注意喚起があるとより自然な文章の流れになります。よって、正解は(D)です。

Date: October 27th, Friday, 17:25:01
From: Nguyen
To: Peterson
Subject: Business trip to Sydney

Hello Peter. I hope all is well.

As you know, I am flying to Sydney with my supervisor on a business trip, but since this is the first time to visit Sydney for both of us, we're not sure which hotel to book. I heard you used to live there, so I was wondering if you would mind helping us. In particular, we are looking at what hotel is favorable in terms of location and the time required to go to the conference center.

I came up with the following list and summarized the necessary information for each hotel. From photos on their websites, they all look excellent.

Hotel Santa Beach is a little far away from the venue but it commands a beautiful view of the Tasman Sea, so it looks particularly attractive to me. But since we are expected to go back and forth between the hotel and the conference center, there's no doubt that being within the vicinity of the conference center is more desirable.

I have to make a reservation by next Friday, so I would really appreciate it if you could let me know before then. My information is limited, so please fill me in if you have any other hotels you would like to recommend. Also I'd really appreciate it if you could recommend any good sightseeing spots in Sydney.

Many thanks,

Nguyen

	City	Distance from conference center	Time to the venue	Vacancy
Sydney Central Hotel	Sydney	0.5 miles	1-2 minutes	△
La Rocka Hotel	Sydney	0.5 miles	1-2 minutes	○
Hotel Royal Prince	Wynyard	1 mile	5 minutes	○
King's Hotel SH	Surry Hills	3 miles	15 minutes	△
Hotel Santa Beach	Dover Heights	12 miles	50 minutes	○

日付：10月27日、金曜日 17:25:01
差出人：グエン
宛先：ピーターソン
件名：シドニーへの出張

こんにちは。すべてが順調だと良いのですが。

ご存じのように、私は上司と出張でシドニーに行きますが、私たちがシドニーを訪れるのは初めてなので、どのホテルを予約すればいいかわかりません。あなたはそこに以前住んでいたと聞いたので、私たちにお力を貸していただければと思います。特に、私たちは今、会議場に行くのに必要な場所と時間に関してどのホテルがいいかを検討しています。

以下のリストを作成し、各ホテルの必要な情報をまとめました。ウェブサイトの写真では、すべて素晴らしく見えます。

ホテルサンタビーチは会場から少し離れていますが、タスマン海の美しい景色を眺めることができるので、特に魅力的です。ただ、ホテルと会議場の間を行き来することが想定されますから、会議場の近くが望ましいことは間違いありません。

来週の金曜日までに予約しなければならないので、それまでにお知らせいただけますとありがたいです。私の情報は限られているので、他にお薦めのホテルがあれば教えてください。そして、シドニーの観光に良い場所を紹介していただければ幸いです。

ありがとう。

グエン

第1章 英語脳徹底トレーニング

第2章 高難度問題の徹底攻略

第3章 正答ハイテクレッスン

第4章 ハイレベル完全模試

	所在地	会議場からの距離	会場までの時間	空室
シドニーセントラルホテル	シドニー	0.5マイル	1-2分	△
ラロッカホテル	シドニー	0.5マイル	1-2分	○
ホテルロイヤルプリンス	ウィンヤード	1マイル	5分	○
キングスホテルSH	サリーヒルズ	3マイル	15分	△
ホテルサンタビーチ	ドーバーハイツ	12マイル	50分	○

154. Why is Nguyen e-mailing Peterson?

グエンがピーターソンにメールを送るのはなぜですか。

(A) Because Peterson may know a lot about local issues

(B) Because he has to make a reservation today

(C) Because Peterson is Nguyen's supervisor

(D) Because Peterson can provide accommodation

(A) ピーターソンは地元のことについてよく知っているかもしれないので

(B) 彼は今日中に予約を入れなければいけないから

(C) ピーターソンはグエンの監督者だから

(D) ピーターソンは泊まる場所を提供できるから

解説　Why ～?で、「グエンがピーターソンにメールしているのはなぜか」が聞かれています。I heard you used to live thereから、「ピーターソンがシドニーに以前住んでいた」ということがわかるので、(A)が正解になります。メールの送信日時が金曜日で、次の金曜日までに予約が必要と言っているので、(B)は誤り。(C)、(D)は言及がありません。

155. Where can Nguyen enjoy a great view of the Tasman Sea?

グエンはどこでタスマン海の良い景色を楽しむことができますか。

(A) Sydney

(B) Wynyard

(C) Surry Hills

(D) Dover Heights

(A) シドニー

(B) ウィンヤード

(C) サリーヒルズ

(D) ドーバーハイツ

解説　Whereから始まる疑問文なので、「どこ」が聞かれています。この答えは、Hotel Santa Beach... commands a beautiful view of the Tasman Seaからわかります。Hotel Santa Beachの所在地を表で確認すれば、正解は(D)となります。また、a beautiful viewと本文では話されていますが、この問題ではa great viewと言い換えられていることもポイントです。

156. The phrase "in terms of" in paragraph 1, line 5, is closest in meaning to

第1パラグラフ、5行目の「の観点から」という句に意味が最も近いのは

(A) in exchange for	(A) と引き換えに
(B) from the viewpoint of	**(B) の観点から**
(C) in accordance with	(C) に従って
(D) at the expense of	(D) を犠牲にして

> 解説　～ is closest in meaning toで類義表現を問う問題です。in terms of ～は「～の観点から」という意味で、(B) from the viewpoint ofが類義表現となり、正解になります。他の選択肢が問題に出ることもありますので、同時に類義表現を調べて記憶しておくといいでしょう。

157. What will probably happen next Friday?

来週の金曜日は何がありますか。

(A) Nguyen will leave for Sydney.	(A) グエンはシドニーに向けて出発します。
(B) Peterson will e-mail Nguyen.	(B) ピーターソンはグエンにメールを送ります。
(C) Nguyen will finish booking the hotel.	**(C) グエンはホテルの予約を完了します。**
(D) Peterson will make a reservation.	(D) ピーターソンが予約を入れます。

> 解説　What will happen?で、「何があるか」を問う問題です。本文のI have to make a reservation by next Fridayという部分で、金曜日には予約が完了しているだろうことがわかります。よって、正解は(C)となります。make a reservationからbookと、「予約する」という表現が言い換えられていることに気をつけましょう。

158. What does Nguyen intend to do in addition to his business during his trip to Australia?

グエンはオーストラリアへの出張中、ビジネスに加えて何をするつもりですか。

(A) Hang around the city	**(A) 街をぶらぶらする**
(B) Spend time in the Tasman Sea	(B) タスマン海で時間を過ごす
(C) Visit Sydney	(C) シドニーを訪問する
(D) Ask for some recommendations	(D) お勧め情報を聞く

> 解説　What ～ ?で「シドニーで何をするつもりか」尋ねられています。intend to do ～で、「～するつもり」という意味になります。I'd really appreciate it if you could recommend any good sightseeing spots in Sydneyから、グエンが観光もする予定であることがわかります。よって正解は(A)となります。hang around ～「～をぶらつく」という表現も押さえておきましょう。

TO: All Staff
FROM: Steve Jones
DATE: June 15
RE: Flextime

I am sorry for my tardiness in replying. I have been terribly busy training the new receptionist after Sally suddenly resigned, and I haven't had time to meet with most of you. For the time being, it's more time efficient to talk over the phone or mail each other than to meet with everyone in person. It will take another month before Shelly, the new receptionist, can fully take over the position and duties.

Anyway, we need to discuss the changes in the work conditions. There has been an increasing demand for more flexible working hours, and we have agreed to allow flexibility with some conditions. As branch manager, it is my responsibility to ensure that this branch is as productive as possible. As members of work teams, it will be your responsibility to meet with your section manager to adjust and arrange your work teams' work schedule. I hope that the decisions can be made in a democratic manner. In addition, the 8-hour work schedule must be sometime between the hours of 8 A.M. and 10 P.M. Please update me on this matter within a week via e-mail, and if you have any questions by then, give me a buzz at night time since I will be busy training Shelly during the day time for the next few weeks. Seriously, I'm too busy to see anyone face to face.

TO: Steve Jones
FROM: Janet O'Reilly
DATE: June 21
RE: flextime

Hi Steve. May I request some clarification concerning the plan to implement flextime in the office, which you mentioned the biggest concern for you and your department? I have met and talked with my section manager and other members of my work team, but we have been unable to reach a consensus on a good schedule. The starting time works, but things would be much easier if the finishing time is 8 rather than 10. Some are working as a group, and each having liberty to decide on his/her work time will threaten the productivity. Especially, Tom's group requires tremendous communication, making it practically impossible for the members to work flexibly. I suppose we have to either set restrictions for special circumstances like this or tolerate a certain degree of reduced productivity. I am terribly sorry that I could not make things work efficiently.

Janet

PS: I really hope new receptionist will be able to start operating independently from next month.I know this is important, but you are working too much. You should relegate some tasks to others as soon as possible.

TO：すべてのスタッフ
FROM：スティーブ・ジョーンズ
DATE：6月15日
RE：フレックスタイム

返信が遅くなりすみません。サリーが突然辞任したあと、新しい受付係をトレーニングするのにとても忙しく、ほとんどの方と会う時間がありませんでした。今のところ、電話やメールでやり取りする方が誰かに直接会うより効率的です。新しい受付係のシェリーが完全に役割や仕事を引き継ぐことができるのにはもう1カ月はかかります。

とにかく、労働条件の変更について話し合わなければなりません。フレックスタイムへの需要が高まってきており、いくつかの条件つきでフレックス制を入れることに同意しています。支社長として、この支社ができる限り生産的であるようにするのは私の責任です。ワークチームの一員として、課長に会ってあなたのチームのワークスケジュールを調整することはあなたの責任です。私は話し合いで民主的に決定がなされることを望みます。さらに、8時間のワークスケジュールは朝8時から夜10時のどこかに入る必要があります。この件については1週間以内にメールで更新してください。そして、もしそれまでに質問があれば、シェリーをトレーニングするのに今後数週間昼は忙しいので夜間に電話を鳴らしてください。本当に忙しくて誰にも直接会う時間がありません。

TO：スティーブ・ジョーンズ
FROM：ジャネット・オライリー
DATE：6月21日
RE：フレックスタイム

あなたとあなたの部署の一番の心配ごとと言っていた案件である、オフィスでフレックス
タイムを実施することについていくつか明確にしたいのですがよろしいでしょうか。課長
や私のチームの他のメンバーとも会って話しましたが、私たちはスケジュールについて合
意に達することができませんでした。開始時間は大丈夫ですが、終了時間が10時ではな
く8時であれば物事はもっとやりやすくなります。何人かはグループで働いていて、それ
ぞれが自由に彼らの稼働時間を決められると生産性が下がる可能性があります。特にトム
のグループは多大なるコミュニケーションを必要としますので、そのメンバーたちが柔軟
に稼働することは事実上不可能です。このような特別な事情においては何か制限を設ける
か、ある程度の生産性の低下を許容しなければいけません。物事を効率的に進めることが
できず大変申し訳ございません。

ジャネット

追伸：来月から新しい受付係の方が独立して稼働できるようになることを願っています。
これは大事なことですが、あなたは働きすぎです。いくつかの仕事をできる限り早く他の
人に委任すべきです。

Q1. What is the most serious concern for Steve?
　　スティーブにとって最も深刻な悩みは何ですか。

(A) Sally left her position suddenly.　　　　(A) サリーが突然今の仕事を辞めてしまった。

**(B) The branch has to adjust work
conditions.**　　　　　　　　　　　**(B) その支社は労働条件を調整しなければい
けない。**

(C) He cannot find a suitable
replacement.　　　　　　　　　　　(C) 適切な代理の人を見つけることができな
い。

(D) His current work hour is too long.　　(D) 彼の今の稼働時間は長すぎる。

解説　1つ目のメールの文面からだけだと、いずれの選択肢も可能性があるように見えます。ダ
ブルパッセージではこのような場合、もう1つのパッセージにヒントがあることが多くあ
ります。2つ目のパッセージで、May I request some clarification concerning the plan
to implement flextime in the office, which you said is the biggest concern for you
and your department?とあり、この部分から、スティーブが最も大きな心配事としてい
るのはフレックス制についてである、ということがわかります。TOEICでは必ずどこか
に正解を特定するためのヒントがありますので、主観や感覚でこれと選ぶのではなく、ヒ
ントに基づく確証をもって正解を選びましょう。

Q2. Why is the branch trying to adopt a flexible schedule?

なぜその支社はフレックスタイム制を採用しようとしているのでしょうか。

(A) **Because it was requested from the workers**　　(A) **労働者によって要求されたから**

(B) Because it can increase productivity　　(B) 生産性が上がるから

(C) Because it is required by regulations　　(C) 決まりによって要求されているから

(D) Because there is currently no receptionist　　(D) 現在受付係がいないから

> 解説　1つ目のメールの、第2パラグラグにある、There has been an increasing demand for more flexible working hours, and we have agreed to allow flexibility with some conditions. から、労働者側からの要求があり、会社側がそれに合意した様子が読み取れます。

Q3. What is one purpose of the second mail?

2つ目のメールの目的の1つは何でしょうか。

(A) To summarize the tentative schedules　　(A) 一時的なスケジュールをまとめること

(B) To ask clarification of her teams' problems　　(B) 彼女のチームの問題を明確にしてもらうこと

(C) **To extend her apology for inefficiency**　　(C) **彼女の非効率さへのおわびの気持ちを届けるため**

(D) To request the adjustment of her working hours.　　(D) 彼女の稼働時間の調整を要求するため

> 解説　extend は、気持ちを届ける、情報を伝える、という意味でビジネスシーンでもTOEICでも使われます。(C)のおわびの気持ちを届ける、が正解ですが、メール本文の最後の、I am terribly sorry that I could not make things work efficiently. が正解への手がかりです。うまく事を運べなかったことへのおわびの気持ちを伝えようとしている様子が伺えます。一時的なスケジュールも決まっていないので(A)は不正解、明確にしたいのはフレックスタイム制の導入の諸条件についてであり、ジャネットのチームの抱える問題を明確にしてほしいといっているわけではないので(B)も誤りです。ジャネットの労働時間の変更を要求しているわけでもなく、(D)も不正解です。選択肢のいずれも一瞬見ただけではパッとしないかもしれません。そんなときは再度問題をよく読んでみると答えが見えやすくなります。What is the main purposeという問題ではなく、What is one purposeという問題ですので、主たる目的が正解になるとは限りません。

Q4. Which requirement specified by Steve did Janet fail to meet?

スティーブによって指定された要求の中でジャネットができなかったことは何でしょうか。

(A) Converse in a democratic fashion

(A) 民主的な方法で会話をすること

(B) Update the status within a week

(B) 1週間以内に状況を更新すること

(C) Give a phone call for a question

(C) 質問については電話をすること

(D) Set the work hour from 8 A.M. to 10 P.M.

(D) 仕事時間を朝8時から夜10時に設定すること

解説 課長とメンバーと話したとあるので、独裁的な決定を試みたわけではないことが伺われ、(A)は要求を満たしているので不正解となります。返信メールの日付を見ると、スティーブからのメール差出日である6月15日から1週間以内にジャネットは返信しているので、(B)についても要求は満たしています。質問があれば夜に電話でください、という指示が出ていました。これについてはこの条件を満たさず昼電話してしまった、などの指示への違反は文中からは確認できません。いったん保留とします。2番目のメールの本文に、The starting time works, but things would be much easier if the finishing time is 8 rather than 10. とあり、この内容から、始業と終業の時間設定がうまくいっていない様子が読み取れます。これをもって(D)を正解とし、保留していた(C)は切り捨てご免とします。

Q5. What does Janet hope will happen next month?

ジャネットは1カ月後に何が起きればいいと思っていますか。

(A) Sally will return to the previous position.

(A) サリーが前の仕事に戻ってくる。

(B) Steve will start relegating some of his duties.

(B) スティーブが彼の仕事を委任し始める。

(C) Shelly will completely take over required work.

(C) シェリーが要求されている仕事を完全に引き継ぐ。

(D) Tom's team members can reach an agreement.

(D) トムのチームメンバーが合意に達する。

解説 2番目のメールの追伸に、I really hope new receptionist will be able to start operating independently from next month. とあり、ここから(C)が正解だとわかります。(A)は、辞めたサリーに戻ってきてほしいと思っているとの言及はないので不可です。戻ってきてくれたらスティーブが楽になるかもしれないのでありえるのでは？という考えもあるかもしれませんが、すでに本腰入れてトレーニングしている最中にひょっこり戻ってこられても迷惑ですね。ただ、こうした主観や個人的な感想で正解を選ぶのではなく、TOEICで正解を得るためには、あくまで書かれているヒントをもとに機械的に、客観的に答えを選びます。(B)は追伸のas soon as possibleがなければ正解候補になりえます。(D)は全く言及がありません。

第3章

990点満点を取るためだけの
正答ハイテクレッスン

満点を連発するTOEIC受験者でも、集中力の途切れや勘違いは往々にして起こります。
万が一正攻法的な解答が難しい場合に使える、1問も落とさないための試験テクニックをご紹介します。

正答ハイテクレッスン①

写真に大きく写っているものが英文で流れたら、選択肢から外せ

対象 》Part 1

> 英文がうまく聞き取れなかったとき、写真にあからさまに写っているもの・人に関する英単語を含んだ選択肢を選んでしまいがちですが、その選択肢は選ばないようにしましょう。

◆ わかりやすい英単語を含んだ選択肢は ひっかけ問題の可能性が高い

例えばドアの前に人が立っている、以下のような写真があったとします。

例 題

(A) The woman is entering the room.

(B) The woman is reading the name board on the door.

(C) The woman is leaning against the door.

(D) The woman is wearing a face mask.

本来はリスニング問題ですが、スクリプトを見ながら考察していきましょう。

正解は一番下の(D)ですが、やはりこの写真で一番目に入るのは「ドア」ですから、頭の中でも、何かしらドアについての説明を想定して待っているものです。そこで、「ドア」という単語は含んでいるが正確に写真を説明していない、(B)や(C)が選択肢に出ると、そちらに釣られていってしまいます。

はっきり聞き取れているときは当然釣られないですが、何と言ったか一字一句聞き取れなかった、という場合にはどうしても引っ張られてしまうものです。人間心理とはそのようなもので、そんな人間心理を踏まえた誤答選択肢が用意されているわけです。そのため、Part 1 では、流れた英文をうまく聞き取れなかった場合で、写真にあからさまに写っている『もの』が英文で流れたら、その選択肢は選ばないようにした方が、自信がないなりにも、より高い正解率が見込めます。

正答テクニックを実践！

Part 1

Q1.

Ⓐ Ⓑ Ⓒ Ⓓ

Q2.

Ⓐ Ⓑ Ⓒ Ⓓ

Q3.

Ⓐ Ⓑ Ⓒ Ⓓ

正解と解説

Q1.

(A) The man is taking some notes.　(A) 男性は何かメモを取っている。

(B) The man is operating heavy machinery.　(B) 男性は重機を操作している。

(C) The man is taking off his helmet.　(C) 男性がヘルメットを脱いでいる。

(D) The man is working outdoors.　**(D) 男性が屋外で作業している。**

解説　文書、重機、ヘルメット、すべて目にすぐ入ってくるかもしれませんが、それぞれの英文は写真を全く正しく描写していません。抽象度は高いですが、(D)が正解です。抽象的で当たり障りのないことを言っている選択肢が正解、というパターンはPart 1に限らず全パートにおいて時々見られます。

Q2.

(A) The buildings are being demolished.　(A) 建物が取り壊されている。

(B) They are preparing some lunch at a restaurant.　(B) 彼らはレストランで昼食の準備をしている。

(C) Some awnings are supported by the props.　**(C) いくつかの日よけが支柱で支えられている。**

(D) The board menu is hanging on the wall.　(D) ボードメニューが壁に掛けられている。

解説　建物がすぐに目に入ります。demolishは「取り壊す」という意味ですが、これがさっと流れて聞き取れなかったとしても、あからさまに写っている建物に関するこの(A)の選択肢は、ひっかけ誤答選択肢である可能性が高いと考えます。「日よけが支柱で支えられている」の(C)が今回は正解です。ぱっと見では注意が向かない部分ですが、このような正解パターーンは時々見られます。awning（日よけ），supported（支えられている），prop（支柱）はいずれもPart 1の頻出単語です。

Q3.

(A) The man is piling up some documents.

(B) Some folders are arranged on the shelves.

(C) The man is pushing a wheelchair.

(D) The tree is being trimmed.

(A) 男性がいくつかの書類を積み上げている。

(B) いくつかのフォルダーが棚に並べられている。

(C) 男性が車椅子を押している。

(D) その木は刈り込まれている。

解説　露骨に書類の束が置かれています。車いすも比較的大きく映し出されており、目が行くかもしれません。しかし、それぞれ文章は写真を正しく描写していないのでやはり誤答です。さりげなく写っているフォルダーに関する描写「棚に幾つかフォルダーが並べてある」の(B)が正解です。pile up, folders, trimはPart 1の頻出単語です。

テクニックの注意点！

・Part 1で、写真があからさまに大きく表示されているものはひっかけが多い、と心得ておこう！

・聞き取れれば中身を検討して答えるべき！

正答ハイテクレッスン②

話の流れがわからなくなったら、フレーズに注目せよ！

対象 》Part 3・4

◆ 聞こえた表現がそのまま入った選択肢を選ぶ

長文のリスニングでは、上級者であっても、一部聞き取れなかったり、話の全体像が見えなくなってしまうこともあります。

話の流れがつかみ切れなくなると、自信を持って答えを選べなくなります。そのような状況では、耳に残っているフレーズを含む選択肢を選びましょう。

ここでいう「耳に残っているフレーズ」とは、流れた英文をそのまま抜き出したようなフレーズです。言い換えをした表現ではありません。

以下のPart 3の問題のスクリプトを見てみましょう。

W: Excuse me. I've been looking for my baggage for almost an hour, but I still can't find it. Am I in the right place?

M: What's your flight number? You might not be in the right place.

W: It's JS102. There were **a few flights from the same airline** that arrived at the same time, so maybe I got confused.

M: That's a possibility. You can refer to the electric bulletin board up there.

正答ハイテク!!
全く同じフレーズの入った選択肢を選ぼう！

What does the woman say could be the cause of the problem?

(A) The baggage was sent to the wrong location.

(B) There were **a few flights from the same airline**.

(C) The flight did not arrive as scheduled.

(D) The woman was lost in the airport.

正答ハイテク!!
全く同じフレーズの入った
選択肢を選ぼう！

これは、近年のTOEICの問題を参考に作られた模擬問題（すなわち、本番のテストの特徴が反映されている問題）ですが、**ハイライト部分**にある通り、流れる英文中に、正解選択肢にあるフレーズが全くそのまま述べられています。

流れた英文中に使われている表現が、そのまま正解選択肢に使用されているという事例は少なくありません。1回のテストにおいても、10問ほどはこのような性質の問題があります。

正答テクニックを実践！

Part 4

Questions 7-9 refer to the following lecture.

Q7. What will Professor Miller mainly talk about in his lecture?

(A) His university experience

(B) Writing academic journals

(C) Deep seas and benthic organisms

(D) Water pollution caused by eruptions

Q8. According to the speaker, what is one expected effect of
submarine volcanoes?

(A) They may contribute to the diversity of marine organisms.

(B) They often cause the extinction of vulnerable creatures.

(C) They help remove toxic substances in the sea.

(D) They become the natural habitat for many species.

Q9. What will the speaker do next?

(A) Ask questions to Professor Miller

(B) Continue talking about today's topic

(C) Start explaining about volcanoes

(D) Invite Professor Miller to the podium

990点満点への道

TOEICには専門性の高いトピックの英文も時々出題される

　本スクリプトはあえて難解にするために専門性の高いトピックを使用しています。ただ、最近のTOEICでは、例えば臓器移植のような専門性があるトピックも出されていますので、実際に出題されうるレベルの専門性です。

　単語レベルで、benthic organisms「海底生物」を知っていて、難なく聞き取れ理解できた、という人は少数派になるでしょう。海底火山が周りの生物の多様性への影響、と言われてもなかなかイメージはしづらいものです。しかし、だからと言って問題が解けないわけではありません。専門用語は実際のTOEICでも本文内で説明がされますから、まずは、落ち着いてほかの英文を聴き取るようにしましょう。また、「どうしても聞き取れなかったな」、と思ったら、耳にフレーズレベルで残っている選択肢を選びましょう。

正解と日本語訳

Today, we have a special lecturer, Professor Miller, who actually graduated from our university. He will have us delve deep into the realm of **deep seas and benthic organisms**. As you know, Professor Miller is one of the most renowned scholars in this field. His papers can be found in all popular academic journals. He'll first touch upon submarine volcanoes and their effects on deep seas. The heat and substances that gush up from the volcanoes stir up the living environment that surrounds many of these esoteric organisms. He'll then expound on how these stimuli **contribute to the diversity of marine organisms** that inhabit the bottom of the ocean. If you wish to talk to the professor, you will have a chance after the lecture. OK, that's enough from me. Now I'd like to welcome **Professor Miller to the podium**.

本日は特別講師として、実際に本学を卒業されたミラー先生をお招きしています。深海と海底生物の世界を深く掘り下げていただきます。ご存知のように、ミラー教授はこの分野で最も有名な学者の一人です。彼の論文は、有名な学術雑誌に掲載されているものばかりです。まず、海底火山とその深海への影響に触れていただきます。海底火山の熱と火山から噴出する物質が、これらの神秘的な生物の多くを取り囲む生活環境を活性化しているのです。そして、これらの刺激が海底に生息する生物の多様性に寄与しているかについて詳しく説明していただきます。先生とお話をされたい方は、終了後にその機会がございます。さて、私の話はこれくらいにしておきましょう。では、ミラー教授を壇上にお迎えします。

Q7.What will Professor Miller mainly talk about in his lecture?
　　ミラー教授は講義で主に何を話すでしょう。

正解 C

(A) His university experience

(B) Writing academic journals

(C) Deep seas and benthic organisms

(D) Water pollution caused by eruptions

(A) 彼の大学時代の経験

(B) 学術ジャーナルの書き方

(C) 深海と海底生物

(D) 噴火による水質汚染

Q8. According to the speaker, what is one expected effect of submarine volcanoes?

話者によると、海底火山の影響の一つは何でしょう。

正解 A

(A) They may contribute to the diversity of marine organisms.

(B) They often cause the extinction of vulnerable creatures.

(C) They help remove toxic substances in the sea.

(D) They become the natural habitat for many species.

(A) 海洋生物の多様化に寄与しえる。

(B) 脆弱な生き物をしばしば絶滅させる。

(C) 海中の有毒な物質を取り除く。

(D) 多くの種への天然の生息地となる。

Q9. What will the speaker do next?

話者は次に何をするでしょうか。

正解 D

(A) Ask questions to Professor Miller

(B) Continue talking about today's topic

(C) Start explaining about volcanoes

(D) Invite Professor Miller to the podium

(A) ミラー教授に質問する

(B) 本日の話題について話し続ける

(C) 火山について説明し始める

(D) 演壇にミラー教授を迎える

テクニックの注意点！

・Part 3&4でどうしても聞き取れなかったときに、「耳に残ったフレーズ」がそのまま入った選択肢を選ぼう！

・単語ではなく、フレーズが入った選択肢を選ぶことが重要

正答ハイテクレッスン③
発音して表現が自然かどうか判断せよ

対象 》Part5&6

> 特にPart 5とPart 6で「こっちかこっちか自信がない」という
> ときに、若干ではありますが正解率を上げる方法の1つに「発
> 音してみる」というのがあります。

◆ 今まで培ってきた英語音声のインプットを生かす

990点を目指す皆さまは、英語を読むだけではなく、リスニングする時間もか
なり蓄積されているはずです。TOEICのリスニングもそうですし、これまで中
学、高校、その後の学業において重ねてきた英語学習の中で、リスニングして
いる英語というのは実はかなりの量になっているものです。そして、その英語
音声には、TOEICで出てきている単語、文法要素がたくさん入っています。脳
には自然な英語の音声のインプットがたまっているのです。

「自然な英語の音声」に関する情報というのは意図的に取り出すことは難しいの
ですが、英文を聞いたときに、その英語が自然なものなのかそうでないのかを
感覚的に判断するヘルプになります。

試しに下の問題を、発音しながら解いてみてください。

例 題

On the escalator, watch your step and ------- on to the hand rail for your safety.

(A) get

(B) hold

(C) ride

(D) take

エスカレーターでは、足元に注意し、安全のために手すりをつかみます。

上級者の場合は、もともと上記の問題は全て解ける英語力を持っていたかもしれませんが、発音してみると「しっくりくる・こない」がより明確になるのではないかと思います。正解は(B)です。

正答テクニックを実践！

Part 5

Q10. If you find any suspicious items, please ------- our staff.

(A) amplify

(B) signify

(C) exemplify

(D) notify

Q11. We hope you ------- enjoy your shopping at our shop, and let us know if you can't find any items.

(A) thoroughly

(B) fundamentally

(C) comprehensively

(D) selectively

正解と日本語訳

Q10.If you find any suspicious items, please ------- our staff.

不審なものを見つけた場合は、スタッフにご連絡ください。

正解 D

(A) amplify	(A) 拡大する
(B) signify	(B) 表す
(C) exemplify	(C) 例示する
(D) notify	**(D) 知らせる**

Q11. We hope you ------- enjoy your shopping at our shop, and let us know if you can't find any items.

当店でのショッピングを存分にお楽しみいただけるよう願っております。商品が見つからない場合にはお知らせください。

正解 A

(A) thoroughly	**(A) 存分に**
(B) fundamentally	(B) 根本的に
(C) comprehensively	(C) 総合的に
(D) selectively	(D) 選択的に

テクニックの注意点！

・Part 5&6で、英文が自然がどうか判断するために発音してみるのは有効！

・試験本番ではうるさくならないように注意しよう！

正答ハイテクレッスン④
直感を信じるか信じないか決めておく

対象 》全part

> 最初に「直感」で選んだものがより正解率が高いか、気になった選択肢に変えた方が正解率が高いか、自分の直感力をあらかじめ判定しておくことは有用かもしれません。その判定に基づき、選択肢の選び方を最適化しましょう。

◆ 自分の直感による正答率を知る

最初に選んだ答えから別の選択肢に切り替えた場合、そういうときに自分の正解率は上がっているものなのか、あまり変わらないのか、逆に下がるのか、それを把握しておくと、迷ったときに取るべき行動をあらかじめ決めておくことができます。主に、以下の通り3パターンの人がいます。

→ 直感による正答率が<u>高い人</u>は、途中で選択肢で変えようか迷っても変えない

→ 直感による正答率が<u>通常の人</u>も、途中で選択肢で変えようか迷っても変えない　※検討する時間でほかの問題を解けるため

→ 直感による正答率が<u>低い人</u>は、選択肢で変えようか迷ったら変える

上記のように分類ができます。満点を取る上ではささいなテクニックかもしれませんが、満点を取っている人でも特にリーディングセクションは何問か間違えているものです。直感による自分の正答率を測って、事前に方針を決めておくのがよいでしょう。

正答テクニックを実践！

Part 2　直感力特性判定トライアル　特別問題編

以下に Part 2 から特別問題を用意しました。TOEIC よりは難易度を何段階か上げ、正解が分かりにくい問題になっています。全部で 10 問あります。トライしてみてください。

一定数は間違ったとしても安心してください。間違いやすくなるようにあえて設計しています。間違うにしても、どのような選択肢の選び方をすればより間違うのか、というのを判定するための特別問題です。

【ルール】
・何度も聞いたり辞書を使うのはNG。本番と同じように1回だけ解く。
・一番良いと思う選択肢を◎に書き入れる。
・◎で選んだ答えに自信がある場合は○は空欄のまま。
・◎で選んだ答えに自信がない場合は○に「こっちかも」と思う答えを記入する。
・全く分からない場合は、集中した最善の勘で◎、○を選ぶ。
・答え合わせをして、◎、○両方に記入がある問題について、◎が正解だった数と○が正解だった数をそれぞれ記入する。
・上記の説明が理解できない場合はこのセクションは飛ばして、テスト本番では迷う、という行為自体を放棄することにする。

では解いてみましょう！　ゲーム感覚でどうぞ！

特別問題 Part 2（全10問）

🎧 29 🇦🇺 M 🇬🇧 W

Mark your answers on your answer sheet.

S1. Ⓐ Ⓑ Ⓒ   S6. Ⓐ Ⓑ Ⓒ

S2. Ⓐ Ⓑ Ⓒ   S7. Ⓐ Ⓑ Ⓒ

S3. Ⓐ Ⓑ Ⓒ   S8. Ⓐ Ⓑ Ⓒ

S4. Ⓐ Ⓑ Ⓒ   S9. Ⓐ Ⓑ Ⓒ

S5. Ⓐ Ⓑ Ⓒ   S10. Ⓐ Ⓑ Ⓒ

問題番号	◎ 一番良いと思う 選択肢	○ これかもな？と 迷っている選択肢	正解は◎／○ （不正解の場合は 無記入）
S1			
S2			
S3			
S4			
S5			
S6			
S7			
S8			
S9			
S10			

◎が正解だった数 _____

○が正解だった数 _____

※正解一覧が259ページにあります

【判定方法】

＜Ａ＞直感による正答率が高い（選択肢を途中で変えないほうがよい）

1番目に良いと思った答えでの正解数＞2番目に良いと思った答えでの正解数

◎ ＞ ○

このようなバランスで、顕著な差があるのであれば、直感力が強いことが示唆されます。この場合、迷ったとしても最初に選んだ選択肢から変えない方が望ましいと言えます。

＜Ｂ＞直感による正答率が平均的（選択肢を途中で変えないほうがよい）

1番目に良いと思った答えでの正解数≒2番目に良いと思った答えでの正解数

◎ ≒ ○

2つの選択肢にそれほど差がないのであれば、直感力はそれほど高くないということが示唆されます。この場合は、最初に選んだ答えを変えても変えなくても正解数はあまり変わらないので、変える時間がもったいないことを考慮すると、最初に選んだ選択肢のままにしておくのが望ましいと言えます。

＜Ｃ＞直感による正答率が低い（選択肢を途中で変えたほうがよい）

1番目に良いと思った答えでの正解数＜2番目に良いと思った答えでの正解数

◎ ＜ ○

このようなバランスで、顕著な差があるのであれば、直感力があまのじゃく的に弱いことが示唆されます。この場合、迷ったら、最初に選んだ選択肢から変えた方が望ましいと言えます。

【摘要】

1番目に良いと思った選択肢を、自信を持ってこれと選べている場合は上記の判定にバイアスがかかるので、あえて自信を持って正解を選べないように問題および選択肢を工夫しています。とはいえ、あくまで特性理解の仕方を示したものなので、さらに詳細に自分の特性を知りたい場合は、模試を受けて、迷ったときに、その都度第2候補を記しておき、第2候補に変えていた場合正解数が増えていたであろうか、という分析をしてみることが推奨されます。

問題番号	正解
S1	A
S2	B
S3	C
S4	C
S5	A
S6	B
S7	A
S8	B
S9	C
S10	B

S1. Do you know the area code of their fax number?

(A) Can't you look it up on your own?

(B) What do you mean by the area code?

(C) Isn't it 315 that we are using for ours?

S2. Does she prefer a window seat or an aisle seat?

(A) An aisle seat is preferred for him, I guess.

(B) The former given that there's an outlet.

(C) The train won't arrive on time, will it?

S3. Where are you planning to hold the meeting?

(A) No, I didn't, John did.

(B) I heard it was put off till tonight.

(C) Oh, it'll be room A2.

S4. Who will go pick them up at the airport?

(A) What's that frown on your face?

(B) I went to the terminal yesterday.

(C) I think you said you would.

S5. Why were you absent from the meeting this morning?

(A) No kidding!

(B) I mean it!

(C) On the double!

S6. How many applications have you received so far?

(A) Slightly fewer than 15 regions.

(B) The figure is inaccessible at the moment.

(C) The registration must be completed before 11.

S7. I should have done that for you.

(A) Actually, it was no trouble.

(B) Yes, you could do it for yourself.

(C) No, I shouldn't.

S8. Aren't we going to the city center for the event?

(A) Yes, the venue was on the outskirts of the city.

(B) Yes, get your stuff ready so we can leave.

(C) It took much longer than expected, didn't it?

S9. When are they arriving?

(A) At the North Wing of the terminal.

(B) The lunch session is scheduled after their arrival.

(C) It's gonna be sometime around noon.

S10. Aren't you supposed to be working from home?

(A) My car broke down so I was late.

(B) Well, we were given the choice.

(C) I suppose working from home is more desirable.

テクニックの注意点！

・自分の直感に関する傾向性を知る上で参考にしよう！

ひっかけを意識せず、素直に答える

対象 》全part

> 小中高大の受験問題や、各種英語試験とは違い、TOEICでは
> ひねくれた問題が極端に少ないため、素直に正解を選ぶことが
> 重要です。

◆ 裏を読まない

大学受験英語、英検、IELTS、TOEFLなど、TOEIC以外の英語に触れてきた
人は多いと思います。少なくとも、高校受験、高校授業英語、大学受験におい
て英語は何かしら学んできたはずです。受験英語や、英検をはじめとしたテス
トと比較して、TOEICにはある特徴があります。

それは、ひっかけ問題が出ないということです。ひねくれた問題は以下のよう
な問題です。Part 4風の問題を見てみましょう。

例題

Conference Room A has a large capacity and good ventilation.
However, one concern is that it is far from the entrance and only
accessible by stairs. In that regard, Room B is preferable. However, it
has no windows. I think we may need to reconsider a different venue.

Q. Which room does the speaker most likely book?

(A) Conference room A

(B) Conference room B

(C) Both conference room A and B

(D) He has not made the decision.

こういう問題はひねくれています。直球的な聞き方ではありません。受験英語や英検、IELTSの一部ではこのような問題が見られます。

最初の文を聞いた時点で、Aを選びたくなります。ところがどっこい、うんたらかんたら言いながらそれを覆す、という話の展開の仕方はTOEIC以外の英語においてはよく見られるものです。だから、そういうテストにおいては、一度「Aが正解かな？」と思っても、正解と断定することができないわけです。

TOEICはその点親切です。「えっ、本当にそのまま正解でいいのかな？　明らか過ぎて、逆に裏があるのかもしれないと心配なのですが…」と感じることがあるくらい、親切に、正解が正解と露骨にわかる問題を投げてくれます。

特に上級者になればなるほど、シンプルすぎると感じる問題が増えるでしょう。そこで、シンプルすぎて深読みし、何かのひらめきで違う選択肢に変えたりしないようにしましょう。変えてしまうと、正解が不正解に変わってしまう可能性がTOEICでは高いのです。

テクニックの注意点！

・TOEICでも「ひっかけ問題」が出ないわけではありません！
・各partに沿った正しい解法で解くことが最も重要です

第4章

990点満点を取るためだけの
ハイレベル完全模試

最後に模擬テストで、満点を取るための地力を
強化していきます。本章では、別冊についてい
る問題冊子の正解と解説が収録されています。
特に難易度が高い問題で構成されている模試で
す。過去の統計上、正解率が低い問題や、難易
度が高い問題が多く盛り込まれています。
テストで難しい問題が来てもテンポよく解き進
められる力を養っていきましょう。

ハイレベル完全模試　正解一覧表

リスニングセクション

問題番号	正解	問題番号	正解	問題番号	正解	問題番号	正解	問題番号	正解
Part 1		20	C	40	B	61	A	81	B
1	A	21	B	41	A	62	C	82	B
2	D	22	A	42	D	63	A	83	D
3	A	23	B	43	C	64	D	84	C
4	C	24	A	44	A	65	C	85	B
5	C	25	B	45	C	66	B	86	D
6	B	26	B	46	D	67	B	87	B
Part 2		27	A	47	B	68	D	88	B
7	C	28	A	48	A	69	B	89	A
8	B	29	C	49	D	70	D	90	A
9	B	30	C	50	D	Part 4		91	A
10	C	31	A	51	B	71	C	92	A
11	C	Part 3		52	B	72	C	93	C
12	B	32	B	53	B	73	C	94	D
13	C	33	C	54	C	74	C	95	A
14	A	34	A	55	A	75	A	96	D
15	A	35	A	56	A	76	D	97	C
16	B	36	D	57	B	77	C	98	C
17	C	37	D	58	C	78	D	99	D
18	A	38	D	59	C	79	A	100	B
19	C	39	C	60	D	80	D		

リーディングセクション

問題番号	正解	問題番号	正解	問題番号	正解	問題番号	正解	問題番号	正解
Part 5		121	A	141	D	161	D	182	B
101	D	122	B	142	B	162	A	183	D
102	B	123	C	143	B	163	B	184	A
103	D	124	C	144	C	164	C	185	C
104	C	125	C	145	A	165	A	186	C
105	D	126	B	146	D	166	A	187	A
106	A	127	A	Part 7		167	B	188	D
107	B	128	C	147	A	168	C	189	C
108	D	129	B	148	D	169	C	190	B
109	B	130	C	149	D	170	A	191	B
110	C	Part 6		150	B	171	A	192	C
111	A	131	C	151	B	172	A	193	A
112	D	132	A	152	A	173	C	194	D
113	B	133	A	153	B	174	A	195	A
114	D	134	C	154	C	175	C	196	D
115	A	135	B	155	C	176	A	197	C
116	B	136	C	156	A	177	D	198	C
117	A	137	A	157	D	178	A	199	A
118	D	138	A	158	D	179	D	200	A
119	D	139	A	159	D	180	D		
120	B	140	B	160	C	181	C		

Part **1** 写真描写問題

1　　**正解** A

(31) 🍁 W

(A) Vehicles are coming out of a tunnel.
(B) The traffic goes in one direction.
(C) The tunnels are blocked by the trees.
(D) The trees are being trimmed.

(A) 車両がトンネルから出てきています。
(B) 交通が同一方向に向かっています
(C) トンネルは木々で塞がれています。
(D) 木々は刈り込まれています。

(A) 69.6%
(B) 21.7%
(C) 0.0%
(D) 4.3%

解説　トンネルから出てきている場合はcoming out of、入っていっている場合にはgoing into が使われます。ここでは車両が出てきていることを表す(A)が正解。

Vocabulary
□ **trim** 刈り取る

2　　**正解** D

(32) 🇺🇸 M

(A) They are watering the plant on the table.
(B) The man is sipping from the mug.
(C) They are leaning against the glass window.
(D) One of the women is holding an electric device.

(A) 彼女たちはテーブルの上の植物に水をあげています。
(B) 男性はマグカップからすすり飲んでいます。
(C) 彼女たちはガラスの窓に寄りかかっています。
(D) 女性の1人が電子機器を持っています。

(A) 8.7%
(B) 8.7%
(C) 4.3%
(D) 73.9%

解説　タブレット端末のことをan electric deviceと表現しています。日常的に聞かない表現でも、TOEICの言いかえ表現としては使われるものもあります。

Vocabulary
□ **water** 水をやる　□ **sip** すすり飲む
□ **mug** マグカップ　□ **lean against** 寄りかかる

265

3　正解 A

(A) A floor covering is placed under furniture.

(B) A few of the drawers are partially open.

(C) Some pictures are hanging on the wall.

(D) A plant is being watered.

(A) 床の敷物が家具の下に置かれています。

(B) 幾つかの引き出しが部分的に開いています。

(C) 幾つかの写真が壁にかかっています。

(D) 植物に水が与えられています。

(A) 56.5%

(B) 8.7%

(C) 17.4%

(D) 13.0%

> 解説　coveringはrugやcarpetの言い換え表現として頻繁に登場する単語です。under the furniture の under の代わりに、beneath, underneath, belowもよく使われます。

Vocabulary
☐ covering 敷物　☐ partially 部分的に

4　正解 C

(A) Some food products are on display.

(B) Pieces of cloth are stacked on top of one another.

(C) Some people have gathered around the market.

(D) Some people are lying on the bench.

(A) 幾つかの食品が展示されています。

(B) 布は互いに積み重なっています。

(C) 何人かの人々が市場の周りに集まっています。

(D) 何人かの人々がベンチに横たわっています。

(A) 0.0%

(B) 17.4%

(C) 43.5%

(D) 34.8%

> 解説　marketは今回は「売買市場」という意味で使われています。gather around the market で「売買市場に人が集まっている」が正解です。(A)の選択肢は、foodが聞き取れていれば除外できます。

Vocabulary
☐ cloth 布、生地　☐ stack 重ねる　☐ on top of 上に

5 正解 C

(A) The man is kneeling down with some equipment.

(B) The man is holding a ruler and a drill.

(C) Some timber is leaning against the wall.

(D) The man is drilling a hole in a board.

(A) 男性は幾つかの機器を持ってひざをついています。 (A) 17.4%

(B) 男性は定規とドリルを持っています。 (B) 13.0%

(C) 材木が壁に立てかけられています。 **(C) 43.5%**

(D) 男性は板に穴を開けています。 (D) 21.7%

解説 lumber, timberともに木材として使われる単語で、Part 1に時々出てきます。写真の片隅にある木材ですが、写真全体を見渡して、大きな被写体でないものにも目を配りましょう。be leaning against（立てかけられている）も頻出表現です。

Vocabulary

☐ **kneel down** ひざをつく ☐ **ruler** 定規

---

6 正解 B

(A) Each worker is operating in a cubicle.

(B) Working spaces have been divided into some compartments.

(C) People are separating documents of different types.

(D) All the chairs are positioned at an equal distance from one another.

(A) 各労働者は個人用個室で作業しています。 (A) 4.3%

(B) 作業スペースは幾つかの仕切りによって分かれています。 **(B) 69.6%**

(C) 人々は異なるタイプの文書を分けています。 (C) 4.3%

(D) すべての椅子は等間隔で配置されています。 (D) 17.4%

解説 compartments（仕切り）が聞き取れれば正解を特定できます。(A)にあるcubicleは、同じような意味で使われることもありますが、従業員が作業しているかはわからないので、(A)は最適ではありません。

Vocabulary

☐ **cubicle** 個室

Part2 応答問題

7　正解 C

When is the annual environment conference?
毎年開催される環境会議はいつですか。

(A) It is held annually.

(B) To make the people aware of global warming.

(C) It'll be announced soon.

(A) 毎年開催されています。　(A) 13.0%

(B) 人々に地球温暖化を認識させるためです。　(B) 4.3%

(C) まもなく発表されます。　**(C) 78.3%**

> **解説**　いつ、という具体的情報を含む返答ではありませんが、いつなのかは現時点では不明、ということが分かる間接回答で、(C)が正解です。(A)は How often?への回答、(B)は Why?への回答となっており、When?への回答としては直接的にも間接的にも不適切です。(B)の make は使役動詞です。一字一句聞き取れて意味が把握できていると素晴らしいです。

Vocabulary
☐ **annually** 毎年　☐ **make + 人 + 補語** 人を〜にする

8　正解 B

Where did Laura find this stone?
ローラはどこでこの石を見つけましたか。

(A) She will make an accessory out of it.

(B) Somewhere on the shore.

(C) It can be found in any shop.

(A) 彼女はこれでアクセサリーを作ります。　(A) 8.7%

(B) 海岸のどこかです。　**(B) 47.8%**

(C) どのお店でも売っていますよ。　(C) 34.8%

> **解説**　「どこで見つけたか」という問いかけに対して、「どこか」という具体性のない返答ではありますが、海岸であることは分かり、返答としては成立します。(C)でも場所についての情報は入っていますが、どこで見つけたのか、という情報にはなっていません。

Vocabulary
☐ **out of** 使って　☐ **shore** 海岸

9　正解 B

Who will represent our party?
誰が私たちの組織を代表しますか。

(A) I will bring the present.

(B) That would be Abbey Taylor.

(C) The party will be very fun.

(A) 私がプレゼントを持ってきます。　(A) 8.7%

(B) アビー・テイラーです。　**(B) 78.3%**

(C) パーティーはとても楽しくなります。　(C) 8.7%

解説　代表者はこの人ではないかとかなり直接的に答えています。(A)と(C)は、partyという言葉から(A)のpresentを連想したり、partyという単語が違う意味で含まれる(C)を選ばないようにしましょう。

Vocabulary
☐ **party** 一団、組織、政党

10　**正解** C

Why did you make Donald rewrite his essay?
なぜドナルドにエッセイを書き直させたんですか。

(A) Show him your essay.
(B) Because he went out for dinner.
(C) An entire paragraph was off topic.

(A) 彼に君のエッセイを見せてください。　(A) 13.0%
(B) なぜなら彼は夕食を取りに行ったからです。　(B) 56.5%
(C) 1つの段落が丸々テーマから外れていたからです。　(C) 26.1%

解説　off topic（話がずれている）から書き直し、と論理は通りますが、仮にこの表現を知らなかった場合でも、(A)、(B)が成立しないので(C)が正解、という選び方はできるようになっておきましょう。(B)の理由で書き直しを要求したとすると嫌がらせになりますので、理由を述べているものではありますが正解ではありません。

Vocabulary
☐ **rewrite** 書き直す　☐ **entire** 全体の

11　**正解** C

Didn't you send out the parcels yet?
まだ小包を送っていないのですか。

(A) Those parcels are mine.
(B) To one of our partners.
(C) They'll be handled shortly.

(A) それらの小包は私の物です。　(A) 4.3%
(B) パートナーの中の1人に。　(B) 17.4%
(C) まもなく処理されます。　(C) 73.9%

解説　parcels（小包）の複数形に対してtheyを使って回答しています。まだ～していないのか、という表現にはHaven't you, Didn'tyou、両方ともTOEICで使われています。まだ処理されていないけどまもなくされます、という(C)が正解です。

Vocabulary
☐ **send out** 発送する　☐ **handle** 処理する　☐ **shortly** すぐに

12　**正解** B

Excuse me, where can I find chopsticks?
すみません、箸はどこにありますか。

(A) Spoon and fork, please.
(B) Right next to the counter.
(C) No thanks.

(A) スプーンとフォークをお願いします。　(A) 4.3%
(B) カウンターのすぐ隣です。　(B) 87.0%
(C) いいえ結構です。　(C) 0.0%

解説　箸がどこにあるか、という質問ですので、場所を示している(B)が最も自然な答えです。counterがどのようなものかイメージしづらい、果たしてカウンターの横に箸が置いてあるか、という思いが出てくる場合もありますが、では(A)、(C)が(B)よりも適切なのかとなるとそうはならず、一定の疑念があっても(B)がベストです。

13　　正解 C

I heard that William will be promoted to a regional manager.
ウィリアムは地域マネージャーに昇進すると聞きました。

(44) 🎧 🇺🇸 M 🇨🇦 W

(A) He is from a small town in Texas.	(A) 彼はテキサスの小さな町の出身です。	(A) 17.4%
(B) He wasn't able to manage the project.	(B) 彼はそのプロジェクトを管理することができませんでした。	(B) 26.1%
(C) Well, everybody knows about that.	**(C) あれ、それについては皆知っていますよ。**	(C) 52.2%

解説　よくある問題パターンです。知らなかったの？　すでにアナウンスメント出てたよ、という間接的な返答が正解となるパターンです。(B)は昇進するという事実とは逆方向に向かう情報ですので、内容的に不可となります。

Vocabulary
☐ **be promoted to ~** ～に昇進する

14　　正解 A

Who ordered the waterproof earphones?
防水イヤホンを注文したのは誰ですか。

(45) 🎧 🇨🇦 W 🇬🇧 W

(A) Didn't you say you did?	**(A) あなたが買ったと言っていませんでしたか。**	(A) 60.9%
(B) It has been in the water for a long time.	(B) それは長い間水の中にありました。	(B) 21.7%
(C) To listen to his music.	(C) 彼の曲を聴くためです。	(C) 8.7%

解説　誰が注文したのか→自分で注文したと言っていなかった？という質問に質問で返すパターンですが、自然な返答です。you did=you orderedとなり、このdidの意味が瞬時に取れれば正解が見えるはずです。他にもdo, does, is, are, was, were, can, will, have, hasなどで置き換わっても反応しましょう。

Vocabulary
☐ **waterproof** 防水の

15　　正解 A

Would you help me distribute these handouts?
このプリントを配るのを手伝ってくれませんか。

(46) 🎧 🇬🇧 M 🇬🇧 M

(A) How much more time do we have?	**(A) あとどれくらい時間がありますか。**	(A) 34.8%
(B) To the new distributor.	(B) 新しい配給会社に。	(B) 21.7%
(C) Yes, I can print them out.	(C) はい、印刷できます。	(C) 39.1%

解説　間接的に、手伝ってもいいけど、あとどれくらい時間があるのか確認したい、という気持ちから出た返答で、(A)が正解となります。distributeという言葉につられて(B)を選ばないように。handouts から連想して(C)を選ばないように注意です。

Vocabulary

☐ **distribute** 配る　☐ **handout** プリント

16　正解 B

That was a waste of time, wasn't it?
全くの時間の無駄でしたね、そうは思いませんか。

(A) Yes, it definitely will.
(B) I couldn't agree more.
(C) It's on the east side, not the west.

(A) 必ずそうなります。
(B) 本当にそう思います。
(C) 東側です、西側ではありません。

(A) 39.1%
(B) 47.8%
(C) 4.3%

解説　正解の文を文字通り訳すと、「私にはもっと賛成することはできません」となります。これ以上は賛成できない（ほどに完全に賛成している）という意味になります。他にも、It can't be better.（丁度いい）という表現がありますが、同じ理屈です。

Vocabulary

☐ **waste of time** 時間の無駄

17　正解 C

How often do you visit the branch office?
支店にはどれくらいの頻度で行っているのですか。

(A)Five to six P.M. would work well
(B)I attend seminars frequently.
(C)Whenever I am needed.

(A)午後5～6時なら大丈夫です。
(B)セミナーによく参加します。
(C)必要なときにいつでも行きます。

(A) 21.7%
(B) 39.1%
(C) 34.8%

解説　頻度を問われているのに対して、「必要なときにいつでも」と答えている(C)が正解。

Vocabulary

☐ **branch office** 支店

18　正解 A

Karen is complaining about something.
カレンが何か不満を言っています。

(A) Oh, again?
(B) Sounds good.
(C) Not for her.

(A) ああ、またですか。
(B) いい感じですね。
(C) 彼女のためではありません。

(A) 60.9%
(B) 26.1%
(C) 8.7%

解説　この問題は半ばジョークのようですね。いつも不満を言っている人がいて、また？という呆れたムードの返答です。ちなみに、自分本位で怒りっぽい人の代名詞として「カレン」という言葉がよく使われます。

19　正解 C

My essay contains 75 pages in total.
私のエッセイは全部で75ページあります。

50 🇺🇸 M 🇨🇦 W

(A) It's due tomorrow.

(B) It took five days,

(C) So does mine.

(A) 締め切りは明日ですよ。

(B) 5日かかりました。

(C) 私のエッセイもそうです。

(A) 30.4%

(B) 8.7%

(C) 56.5%

解説　倒置表現です。Mine does so. が倒置が起こっていない語順ですが、～もです、という意味を作る文では、So am I. So do I. So did I. So can I. のように倒置表現が使われます。私のものも75ページあります、という意味の(C)が正解となります。否定文の際は、Neither am I. Neither do I. とneitherが使われます。

Vocabulary
☐ **contain** ある、含む

20　正解 C

How did you get here?
どうやってここに来たのですか。

51 🇨🇦 W 🇺🇸 M

(A) The flight was canceled.

(B) I'm coming now.

(C) Oh, I actually live nearby.

フライトはキャンセルされました。

今向かっています。

その辺に住んでいるんです。

(A) 17.4%

(B) 17.4%

(C) 56.5%

解説　どうやってここに来たのですか、と聞かれた場合、バスや電車、車などという返答が想定されますが、「実は近くに住んでいるんです(だから歩いてきました)」という返答もありえます。

Vocabulary
☐ **nearby** 近くの、近くに

21　正解 B

Please can you give a price estimate for the refurbishment?
改装にかかる費用の見積もりをお願いできますでしょうか。

52 🇦🇺 M 🇨🇦 W

(A) This house was quite expensive when I bought it.

(B) A thorough inspection is needed first.

(C) It should take about a year.

(A) この家は私が買ったときはかなり高かったです。

(B) まずは詳細な検査が必要とされます。

(C) 1年ほどかかります。

(A) 34.8%

(B) 30.4%

(C) 30.4%

解説　見積もりの前に、詳細な検査が必要であるという趣旨の(B)が正解となります。(C)は不可能ではなく、(B)が的外れであれば正解として扱うことは状況によりありえます。ただ、今回は、いつまでに見積もりが出るか、というニュアンスが問いかけになく、(B)を差し置いて最適ということはできません。

Vocabulary
☐ **thorough** 徹底的な、詳しい　☐ **inspection** 検査

22　正解 A

Oh no, I cannot remember the combination for my storage box.
まずいです。収納ボックスの暗証番号が思い出せません。

 53 W M

(A) Why don't you try your birthday?　(A) 誕生日を試してみてはどうでしょう。　(A) 13.0%

(B) I've already combined the numbers.　(B) 私はもう数字を組み合わせました。　(B) 26.1%

(C) I'll keep it for you just for now.　(C) 今だけお預かりしておきます。　(C) 56.5%

解説　combinationは、暗証番号という意味があり、TOEICで再頻出ではないまでも、時々出てきます。数字の組み合わせでできている暗証番号、ということです。暗証番号が思い出せないと言っている人に対し、誕生日（の数字の組み合わせ）をまず試してみたら？という回答で(A)が正解です。現場のイメージができていなければ、なぜbirthdayが関係するのか全く関連性が見えない超難問になります。

Vocabulary

☐ **combination** 暗証番号

23　正解 B

What should we name the new delivery service we launched?
新しく始めた宅配サービスの名前は何にしましょうか。

 54 M W

(A) The estimated cost for delivery is 35 dollars.　(A) 配達にかかる費用の目安は35ドルです。　(A) 13.0%

(B) Something dissimilar to existing ones is nice.　(B) 既存のものと似ていない名前がいいですね。　(B) 60.9%

(C) Thanks but I have already had lunch.　(C) ありがとうございます。でももうお昼ご飯を食べました。　(C) 21.7%

解説　特定の名前を提案したわけではありませんが、今既にあるサービスの名前とは似ていないものの方が良い、という間接回答で、(B)が正解となります。delivery, launch等の単語につられて(A)や(C)を選んでしまわないように注意です。

Vocabulary

☐ **dissimilar** 似ていない

24　正解 A

Everyone seems happy about the new arrangement we proposed.
私たちが提案した新しい取り決めについて、みんな問題ないようです。

 55 W M

(A) Except for Josh, who e-mailed me this morning.　(A) ジョシュを除いては（今朝私にメールをくれていました）。　(A) 43.5%

(B) The explanation was not clear to anyone.　(B) 説明は誰にとってもわかりやすいものではありませんでした。　(B) 30.4%

(C) Can we arrange the next meeting as soon as possible?　(C) 次のミーティングをできるだけ早くアレンジして頂けますでしょうか。　(C) 17.4%

解説　Except (for) 〜で、〜を除いて、という意味なので、ジョシュを除いてみんな問題がないようだと返答している（A）が正解となります。ジョシュだけは、納得しきれていなくて何かしらの文章をメールにて送ってきている、という状況です。

Vocabulary
☐ **arrangement** 取り決め

25　正解 B

I'm ready to set up the new TV. Are you?
新しいテレビをセッティングする準備ができました。あなたはどうですか。

56 🇺🇸 M 🇨🇦 W

(A) I could.

(A) できるかもしれません。

(A) 52.2%

(B) I am.

(B) できています。

(B) 30.4%

(C) I don't.

(C) しません。

(C) 13.0%

解説　I am ready, are you?（私は準備できているけどあなたは？）、と聞かれて、I am (ready).（準備できています）と回答しています。短いがゆえに取りづらかったかもしれません。

26　正解 B

We need to get to the store as soon as possible!
私たちはできるだけ早くお店に行かないといけません！

57 🇬🇧 W 🇺🇸 M

(A) You can save time.

(A) 時間を節約できますよ。

(A) 30.4%

(B) I'll get the car key.

(B) 車の鍵を取ってきますね。

(B) 39.1%

(C) I think that is possible.

(C) それは可能だと思います。

(C) 26.1%

解説　car key が聞きなれていなくて、「車の鍵」と取れなかったかもしれません。そういう場合は、何度か発音しておけば脳になじませることができます。急いでいかなければいけないので、鍵を取ってくる（出発できる準備をしておく）という回答になります。

Vocabulary
☐ **save time** 時間を節約する

27　正解 A

Would you rather buy an umbrella or get wet in the rain?
傘を買いますか、それとも雨にぬれますか。

58 🇨🇦 W 🇺🇸 M

(A) Let's get a raincoat.

(A) レインコートを買いましょう。

(A) 56.5%

(B) It was windy.

(B) 風が強かったです。

(B) 4.3%

(C) I am not sure where that is.

(C) それはどこにあるかわかりません。

(C) 34.8%

解説　「1か2か」と聞かれて3にするというへそが曲がった印象の返答ですが、十分ありえる内容です。

28 　正解 A

I can't handle it without your help.
あなたの協力なしにはどうにもならないんです。

 59 M W

(A) You can or you can't?

(B) I helped Suzan yesterday.

(C) I think you are a good driver.

(A) can ですか、can't ですか。

(B) 私は昨日スーザンを手伝いました。

(C) あなたは運転が上手だと思います。

(A) 56.5%

(B) 21.7%

(C) 13.0%

解説　英会話あるあるです。can't の t が聞き取りづらくて、できるのかできないのかわからないので、はっきりしてほしいときに出てくる決まり文句のようなセリフです。can't の t はネイティブ間でも聞き取りに困るくらい、かすかに発音されるかされないか、くらいの微妙な音になります。

29 　正解 A

Is this the one you were talking about?
これが話していた例のやつですか。

 60 M W

(A) Can I see it?

(B) I'm talking to you.

(C) It was on the desk.

(A) 見せてもらってもいいですか。

(B) 私はあなたに話しているのです。

(C) 机の上に置いてありました。

(A) 47.8%

(B) 30.4%

(C) 17.4%

解説　「例のもの」がこれかと確認をしているのに対して、「見せて」と現物を確認しようとしている(A)が正解です。talk につられて(B)を選ばないようにしましょう。

30 　正解 C

Why did you use business class for your flight?
なぜビジネスクラスにしたのですか。

 61 W W

(A) It was better for the economy.

(B) Because the classroom was full.

(C) Lisa set up the itinerary.

(A) 経済のためには良かったです。

(B) 教室はいっぱいでしたので。

(C) 旅程を設定したのはリサですよ。

(A) 39.1%

(B) 43.5%

(C) 13.0%

解説　なぜビジネスクラスにしたかって、私が席を取ったわけではないし（このくらいで文句言わないで…）という不満を内包する返答のようです。(A)は、少しでも経済の金を循環させるという点でロジックは合っているのかもしれませんが、その路線で主張するとしても、恒常的な事象なので、現在形で行きたいところです。

Vocabulary

□ **itinerary** 旅程

31　正解 A

Can't I receive discounts using this voucher?
この引き換え券で割引を受けることはできますか。

(A) See, here. It has expired.

(B) The food was outstanding.

(C) Yes, you can use the voucher for payment.

(A) ここを見てください、有効期限が切れています。

(B) 料理は素晴らしかった。

(C) はい、引き換え券でお支払いいただけます。

(A) 39.1%

(B) 4.3%

(C) 52.2%

解説　有効期限が切れているので使えない、という（A）がストレートに正解となります。（C）には注意です。質問は「割引」に使えるのか聞いているわけであって、「支払い」に使えるか聞いているわけではないので、これは正解とはなりません。

Vocabulary
□ voucher 券　□ expired 失効している

Part3 会話問題

Questions 32 through 34 refer to the following conversation.
問題32-34は次の会話に関するものです。

W: Hi, I would like to enroll in your new program. Would you be able to help me?

M: Yes, of course! The program needs you to attend live Yoga or Zumba classes twice a week. Do you have any preferred days for these classes?

W: I think Tuesday and Saturday would work best for me. Thank you.

M: I can sign you up for those days right now. The program costs $200 for the first 6 months. Would you like to pay today?

W: Yes, please. May I read out my card number to you now?

M: Before I take your credit card information, I must read out a financial disclosure to you. This is a required step, so please bear with me.

W: こんにちは、こちらのプログラムの方に加入したいのですが、お手伝いしてもらえますでしょうか。

M: はい、もちろんです！ このプログラムでは週に2回ライブでヨガかズンバのクラスに出席することが必要となっています。ご希望の曜日などありますか。

W: 火曜日と土曜日が一番いいと思います。ありがとうございます。

M: 今私の方でその曜日で登録させていただきます。このプログラムは加入後最初の6カ月は月200ドルです。本日お支払いしていきますか。

W: はい、お願いします。ではカード番号を読み上げてよいですか。

M: クレジットカードの情報を頂く前に、金融情報の開示についてご説明させていただかなければいけません。必要なステップなのでお聞きください。

Vocabulary

☐ **enroll in** 登録する   ☐ **live** ライブの、生の   ☐ **preferred** 希望の、望ましい   ☐ **read out** 読み上げる
☐ **bear with me** 待ってください、我慢してください

32　**正解 B**

Where does the man work?
男性はどこで働いていますか。

(A) A professional dancers' club
(B) **A fitness center**
(C) A city council
(D) A training school for singers

(A) プロダンサーのクラブ
(B) **フィットネスセンター**
(C) 市議会
(D) 歌手のためのトレーニングスクール

(A) 26.1%
(B) **56.5%**
(C) 4.3%
(D) 8.7%

解説　TOEIC のPart 3とPart 4では、会話中に使われた単語がそのまま正解の選択肢に使われるというのはよくある傾向です。YogaまたはZumbaにライブで参加するということから、フィットネスセンターと推測されます。

Vocabulary
☐ **city council** 市議会

33　**正解** **C**

What is mentioned about the program that the woman is interested in?
女性が興味を持っているプログラムについて何が言及されていますか。

(A) Participants can come on any day without limits.	(A) 参加者はいつでも制限なしで参加できます。	(A) 13.0%
(B) The monthly fee is $200 for the first six months.	(B) 最初の6カ月の月額料金は200ドルです。	(B) 52.2%
(C) Participation to some classes is mandatory.	**(C) 一部のクラスへの参加は必須です。**	**(C) 30.4%**
(D) A credit card is the only accepted payment method.	(D) ご利用いただけるお支払方法はクレジットカードのみです。	(D) 0.0%

解説　The program needs you to attend live Yoga or Zumbaとあるので、参加する必要があることがわかります。needsをmandatoryで言い換えている（C）が正解です。

Vocabulary
☐ **on any day** どの日でも

34　**正解** **A**

What information does the man say he will explain?
男性はどのような情報を説明すると言っていますか。

(A) The terms and conditions concerning the financial disclosure	**(A) 財務開示に関する諸条件**	**(A) 13.0%**
(B) The required steps that all applicants have to follow	(B) すべての申請者が従わなければならない必要な手順	(B) 43.5%
(C) When and where the programs are held	(C) プログラムがいつどこで開催されるか	(C) 21.7%
(D) Information on which credit cards are acceptable for payment	(D) どのクレジットカードが支払いに使えるかに関する情報	(D) 8.7%

解説　男性の最後のセリフで、I must read out a financial disclosure to you. と言っており、これが直接の根拠となります。

Vocabulary
☐ **terms and conditions** 合意文、使用許諾などにおける諸条件

Questions 35 through 37 refer to the following conversation.
問題35-37は次の会話に関するものです。

W: I am looking for my keys. Have you seen them anywhere?	W: 鍵を探しているのだけど、どこかで見なかった？
M: I think I saw them on top of the kitchen counter.	M: キッチンのカウンターの上にあるのを見た気がするよ。
W: But they aren't on the kitchen counter.	W: でも、キッチンのカウンターの上にはないのよ。
M: That's strange. Do you want me to help you look for them?	M: おかしいねえ。私が一緒に探そうか。
W: Please. I am running very late and need to get to work.	W: お願いできる？ 今仕事に遅れそうになるべく早く出なければいけないの。
M: Let me go check in the bedroom. Is it possible that you may have dropped them on your way home from the grocery store?	M: 寝室の方を確認してくるよ。または、食料雑貨店から家に帰ってくる途中で落としたということは考えられない？
W: I think I should go check.	W: 行って確認してみなきゃいけないかも。

Vocabulary
☐ **run late** 遅れている　*run はこの場合「時間を取る」という意味

35　　**正解** **A**

What is the woman's problem?
女性の問題は何ですか。

(A) Her keys are missing.	**(A)** 彼女の鍵がない。	**(A)** 65.2%
(B) The man took the woman's key.	(B) 男性が彼女の鍵を取った。	(B) 13.0%
(C) She cannot enter her room.	(C) 彼女は自分の部屋に入れない。	(C) 13.0%
(D) Her refrigerator does not open.	(D) 彼女の冷蔵庫が開かない。	(D) 4.3%

解説　最初のセリフでI am looking for my keys. と言っており、ここが根拠となります。家の中で会話している様子が伺われ、部屋に入れないという(C)は不正解となります。

Vocabulary
☐ **missing** 見つからない　* ～ **is missing** の形で頻出

279

36　正解 D

Where is the conversation taking place?
どこで会話していますか。

(A) In an office	(A) オフィス	(A) 30.4%
(B) At a grocery store	(B) 食料品店	(B) 4.3%
(C) On the street	(C) 路上	(C) 4.3%
(D) In a house	**(D) 家の中**	**(D) 56.5%**

解説　キッチンのカウンターには鍵はなかった、という女性のセリフから、すでに家の中にいることは想定されます。車の鍵を探しているのかもしれません。

37　正解 D

What does the woman say she will do?
女性は彼女が何をするだろうと言っていますか。

(A) Shop at the grocery store	(A) 食料品店で買い物をする	(A) 21.7%
(B) Check her bedroom	(B) 彼女の寝室をチェックする	(B) 43.5%
(C) Start working from home	(C) 在宅勤務を開始する	(C) 4.3%
(D) Go outside	**(D) 外に出る**	**(D) 26.1%**

解説　一つ前の男性の「食料雑貨店から家に返ってくるまでに鍵を落としたのではないか」という問いかけに対して、「行って確認してみる」という返答をしているので、その道筋に落ちていないか確認しに行くものと推察されます。

© 2020 ちょうどいいイラスト

Questions 38 through 40 refer to the following conversation with three speakers.

問題38-40は3人の話し手による次の会話に関するものです。

68 & 69 🇺🇸 M1 🇨🇦 W 🇦🇺 M2

M1: I saw an ad in the newspaper that said the hotel is recruiting new staff. I would like to apply for a job. May I get an application form, please?	M1: このホテルが新しい従業員を募集していると新聞の広告で見ました。そのお仕事に申し込みをしたいです。申し込みの申請書を頂けませんでしょうか。
W: Yes, we are currently hiring new staff. Do you know what position you would like to apply for?	W: はい、私たちは今新しい従業員を募集しています。申し込みをしたい希望のポジションはありますか。
M1: Yes, I would like to apply for the chef position. I specialize in Italian cuisine.	M1: はい、職業としてはシェフとして申し込みたいです。私はイタリアン料理を専門としています。
W: OK. Let me get the person in charge, and he can talk to you about the position. In the meantime, here's an application form for that.	W: 分かりました。担当者を呼んできますので、彼からその職業についてもっとお話が聞けると思います。では、こちらの申請書をお渡しいたします。
M2: Hi, I'm Sam. I understand you would like to apply for the sous-chef position we have advertised. How long have you been a chef?	M2: こんにちは、私はサムです。募集していたスーシェフのポジションに応募したいことは聞きました。どのくらいの間シェフとしての経験がありますか。
M1: Hi, Sam. I've been a chef for the last 8 years. To be more specific, I've worked in France and the United Kingdom.	M1: こんにちは、サム。シェフとして私は8年間経験があります。もう少し詳しくいうと、フランスとイギリスで働いてきました。
M2: I see. Do you have some time available next week for an official interview and practical test?	M2: わかりました。来週、正式な面接と実技テストのために空いている時間はありますか。

Vocabulary

☐ **ad** 広告 =advertisement　　☐ **specialize in ～** ～を専門としている　　☐ **in the meantime** その間
☐ **practical test** 実技試験

38　正解 D

What field does the woman most likely work in?
女性はどの分野で働いている可能性が高いですか。

(A) In the media industry	(A) メディア業界	(A) 4.3%
(B) In the food manufacturing industry	(B) 食品製造業	(B) 47.8%
(C) In the music industry	(C) 音楽産業	(C) 8.7%
(D) In the hospitality industry	**(D) ホテル業界**	**(D) 34.8%**

解説　... the hotel is recruiting new staff members. と最初の男性（求職者）が発言していることから、受け取り側の女性はホテル業界で働いていることが分かります。選択肢の中で該当するのは(D)のみです。

39　正解 C

Why does the man say, "To be more specific, I've worked in France and the United Kingdom"?
なぜ男性は「もう少し詳しくいうと、フランスとイギリスで働いてきました」と言ったのですか。

(A) To specify the locations he wants to work in	(A) 彼が働きたい場所を指定するため	(A) 0.0%
(B) To impress the woman about his achievements	(B) 彼の業績で女性を感心させるため	(B) 21.7%
(C) To show his candidacy and experience	**(C) 彼の資格と経験を示すため**	**(C) 34.8%**
(D) To explain what kind of cuisine he specializes in	(D) 彼が専門としている料理の種類を説明するため	(D) 39.1%

解説　経験を聞かれ、I've been a chef for the last 8 years. To be more specific, I've worked in Europe and the United Kingdom. という流れで返答しています。複数の国で一定期間の経験があることを示そうとしている様子がうかがえ、それについて言及している(C)が正解です。1問目と2問目の正解の根拠となる場所がかなり離れていますが、まどわされないようにしましょう。

Vocabulary
□ **impress** 印象を与える　□ **candidacy** 適合性、資格　□ **cuisine** 料理

40 　正解 B

What do we learn about the position?
私たちはそのポジションについて何がわかっていますか。

(A) It has only a limited number of openings.	(A) 就職口の数は限られています。	(A) 8.7%
(B) Its selection process involves a practical test.	**(B) 採用プロセスには実地試験が含まれます。**	**(B) 60.9%**
(C) It will be closed sometime soon.	(C) まもなく閉まります。	(C) 8.7%
(D) It does not require intensive experience.	(D) 集中的な経験は必要ありません。	(D) 17.4%

解説 最後に2人目の男性（採用側）が、Do you have some time available next week for an official interview and practical test? と聞いているところから、実技テストがあることが分かります。2問目の根拠となるポイントからさほど離れていませんので、そういう意味で難易度が高い問題です。

Vocabulary
□ **intensive** 徹底的な、激しい

Questions 41 through 43 refer to the following conversation.
問題41-43は次の会話に関するものです。

M: Hey, Rami. I have some good news for you!	M: ラミ。幾つか良いニュースがあるよ！
W: Hi, Sam. What's the news? I'm all ears!	W: ああサム。ニュースって何？ 教えてよ！
M: Your favorite singer Kyogo is coming to town for a concert next month! Isn't that amazing news? He is going to be playing at the Spark Arena.	M: 君が大好きな歌手のキョウゴがコンサートのためにこの町に来月来るんだ！ とても最高なニュースだと思わないか。彼はスパークアリーナでコンサートをする予定らしい。
W: Is he? Wow! I'm so thrilled. Would you like to go with me?	W: そうなの？ とてもうれしくてぞくぞくする。私と一緒に行ってくれる？
M: Yes, it sounds like a lot of fun. But that isn't the only bit of good news! Because it's your birthday next month, I got you two tickets to the concert!	M: はい、とても楽しそうだね。だけどそれだけが良いニュースじゃないんだ！ 来月は君の誕生日があるから、君のために2枚コンサートのチケットを買ったんだ！
W: That is the best birthday present ever! Thank you so much! We can both enjoy the concert now! I'm so excited.	W: それはこれまでで最高な誕生日プレゼントだね！ 本当にありがとう！ これで一緒にお互いコンサートを楽しむことができるね！ とても楽しみ。

Vocabulary
☐ thrilled ぞくぞくしている

41　　**正解** A

What does the woman imply when she says, "I'm all ears"?
女性の「教えてよ！」という言葉は何を意味していますか。

(A) She really wants to know what the news is.	(A) 彼女は本当にニュースが何であるかを知りたがっています。	(A) 60.9%
(B) She has to pay attention to what the man says.	(B) 彼女はその男性が言うことに注意を払わなければなりません。	(B) 30.4%
(C) She sometimes has a hearing problem.	(C) 彼女には時々難聴の問題があります。	(C) 0.0%
(D) She can pick up sound quite precisely.	(D) 彼女は非常に正確に音を拾うことができます。	(D) 4.3%

解説　I'm all ears.（聞かせてください）という熟語表現です。私の体はすべて耳になっている、即ち、そのくらい情報を聞く準備ができているということです。良いお知らせがあるよ！→ 何、聞かせて！という流れの会話です。

Vocabulary
☐ **I'm all ears.** 聞かせてください

42　正解 D

Why is the woman thrilled?
なぜ女性はわくわくしているのですか。

(A) Because she can see Kyogo for the first time	(A) 彼女はキョウゴを初めてみることができるから	(A) 4.3%
(B) Because the man handed some tickets to the woman	(B) 男性が女性にチケットを渡したから	(B) 17.4%
(C) Because she can perform at the music show	(C) 彼女は音楽のショーでパフォーマンスできるから	(C) 17.4%
(D) Because her favorite singer will come to town	**(D) 彼女のお気に入りの歌手が町に来るから**	**(D) 56.5%**

解説　なぜわくわくしているのか、という質問に対して、お気に入りの歌手が来るから、というシンプルな回答です。Kyogoという歌手が来ると聞いて、Is he? Wow! I'm so thrilled. と答えているところが、(D)が正解と特定できます。

Vocabulary
☐ **for the first time** 初めて

43　正解 C

What will the speakers do next month?
話者は来月何をしますか。

(A) Throw a birthday party for the woman	(A) 女性の誕生日パーティーを開く	(A) 26.1%
(B) Buy some tickets as a present for the woman	(B) 女性へのプレゼントとしてチケットを購入する	(B) 34.8%
(C) Attend an event together	**(C) 一緒にイベントに参加する**	**(C) 30.4%**
(D) Sing a song at a music show	(D) 音楽のショーで歌を歌う	(D) 4.3%

解説　最後に女性が、We can both enjoy the concert now! I'm so excited. と発言しているので、ここで一緒にイベントに参加するということが分かります。なんとも素敵なプレゼントですね！

Vocabulary
☐ **throw a party** パーティーを開く

Questions 44 through 46 refer to the following conversation.
問題44-46は次の会話に関するものです。

W: Welcome to the Greenhouse Gallery. How may I help you?	W: グリーンハウスギャラリーへ、ようこそ。今日は何のご用でしょうか。
M: I am looking for Mr. Potter. I have an appointment with him at 10 A.M.	M: ポッター氏を探しています。彼との約束が午前10時からあるのですが。
W: Are you Silvia Granger?	W: あなたはシルビア・グレンジャーさんですか。
M: I am. I was invited by Mr. Potter because I deal in rare paintings and we discussed the other day that we may be able to come to some exciting and profitable arrangements.	M: はい、そうです。私は希少な絵画に精通していて、先日、エキサイティングで利益性の高いお仕事ができるかもしれないと話していたのもあり、このたびポッター氏に招かれました。
W: Yes, he did mention this to me earlier today. He said he found an art dealer who might be able to help us. He's been waiting for you. Please follow me, and I will take you to his office.	W: そうですね、彼はこのことについて今日話してしました。彼は助けになりそうなアートディーラーを見つけたと言っていました。彼はあなたを待っていました。彼のオフィスまで案内いたしますので、ついてきてください。
M: Thank you very much. Should I take off my shoes?	M: ありがとうございます。靴は脱ぐのですか。

Vocabulary
□ **deal in** 取り扱う

44　　正解 **A**

What is most likely the man's occupation?
男性の職業は何である可能性が高いですか。

(A) Buying and selling art works	(A) 芸術作品の売買	(A) 39.1%
(B) Providing consultation to galleries	(B) ギャラリーへのコンサルティング提供	(B) 8.7%
(C) Painting a rare genre of art pieces	(C) 珍しいジャンルの芸術作品の描画	(C) 30.4%
(D) Managing an art gallery	(D) アートギャラリーの管理	(D) 17.4%

解説　I deal in rare paintingsと男性が発言していることから、芸術作品の取り扱いをしていることがわかります。deal inが聞き取れなくても、芸術作品の売買で利益を生む関係を持ちたいという話の流れがあるので、(A)以外の選択肢に引っ張られないようにしましょう。

Vocabulary
□ **genre** ジャンル

45　正解 C

According to the man, why was he invited?
男性によると、なぜ男性は招待されたのですか。

(A) Because he can give detailed advice to management	(A) 経営について詳しいアドバイスができるから	(A) 30.4%
(B) Because he knows Mr. Potter personally	(B) 彼はポッターさんを個人的に知っているから	(B) 21.7%
(C) Because he might be able to discuss profitable deals	**(C) 彼は利益のある取引について話し合うことができるかもしれないから**	**(C) 17.4%**
(D) Because he can produce rare arts	(D) 彼は珍しい芸術を自分で生み出すことができるから	(D) 26.1%

解説　we may be able to come to some exciting and profitable arrangements. の部分に、招待された理由が述べられており、(C)が正解となります。(B)の「個人的に知っている」というのは事実なのかもしれませんが、それが理由で招待されたわけではなく、あくまで商取引の目的で招待されているため、(B)は不可です。

46　正解 D

What does the woman say she will do?
女性は何をすると言っていますか。

(A) Take off her shoes	(A) 靴を脱ぐ	(A) 17.4%
(B) Call Mr. Potter	(B) ポッターさんに電話する	(B) 17.4%
(C) Follow Mr. Silvia Granger	(C) シルビア・グレンジャーさんについていく	(C) 8.7%
(D) Take the man to an office	**(D) 男性を事務所に連れていく**	**(D) 52.2%**

解説　take you to his officeで、オフィスまで案内してくれることが分かります。最後の男性のセリフに靴を脱ぐべきかという質問がありますが、これは男性がしている質問であって、女性が次に何をするかではありません。聞こえた単語でなびかないよう注意です。

Questions 47 through 49 refer to the following conversation with three speakers.

問題47-49は3人の話し手による次の会話に関するものです。

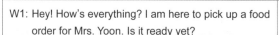 W1　 W2　 M

W1: Hey! How's everything? I am here to pick up a food order for Mrs. Yoon. Is it ready yet?	W1:調子はどうですか。ユンさんが頼んだ注文を取りに来たのですが、準備はできていますか。
W2: The order will be ready within 10 minutes. Is that OK?	W2:注文はあと10分で出来上がります。それでも大丈夫ですか。
W1: Yes, that's not a problem. I might order something to drink while I wait.	W1:はい、問題ありません。私は待っている間何か飲み物を頼むかもしれません。
W2: Certainly. I will ask one of our servers to get you a menu. Here he comes.	W2:もちろんです。他の接客係にメニューを持ってくるように言っておきます。彼が来ました。
M: Hi, my name is Adam. Fiona told me that you'd like something to drink. May I offer you some orange juice, or would you prefer a glass of apple juice?	M:こんにちは、私の名前はアダムです。フィオナからあなたが何か飲み物を注文したいと伺いました。オレンジジュースでもいかがでしょうか、それともリンゴジュースの方がお好みでしょうか。
W1: Apple juice would be lovely, thank you.	W1:リンゴジュースでお願いします。ありがとうございます。
M: My pleasure. Let me go get it for you. It won't be too long.	M:喜んで。それでは取りに行きます。長くはかからないはずです。
W1: Thank you, I appreciate it.	W1:ありがとうございます。

47　　正解 **B**

Where most likely are the speakers?

話者はどこにいる可能性が高いですか。

(A) At a supermarket	(A) スーパーマーケット	(A) 8.7%
(B) At a fast-food restaurant	**(B) ファストフード店**	**(B) 78.3%**
(C) At a cooking school	(C) 料理教室	(C) 4.3%
(D) At Mrs. Yoon's house	(D) ユンさんの家	(D) 4.3%

解説　ファストフードかを特定するセリフはないまでも、持ち帰り用の食事を注文していたことは伺え、選択肢の中で、(B)が最善となります。

48　正解 A

Who most likely is Fiona?
フィオナは誰ですか。

(A) Adam's colleague	**(A) アダムの同僚**	**(A) 39.1%**
(B) A delivery person	(B) 配達スタッフ	(B) 21.7%
(C) A culinary instructor	(C) 料理のインストラクター	(C) 13.0%
(D) Mrs. Yoon's friend	(D) ユンさんの友達	(D) 21.7%

解説　Hi, my name is Adam. Fiona told me that you'd like something to drink. このセリフから、同じ職場で働いていることがわかり、(A)の同僚が答えとなります。人物名が多いだけに、この問題は先読みができていなければ厳しいかもしれません。

Vocabulary
☐ **culinary** 料理の

49　正解 D

What will the man do next?
男性は次に何をしますか。

(A) Wait until the ordered food is ready	(A) 注文した料理ができるまで待ちます	(A) 30.4%
(B) Have a glass of apple juice	(B) リンゴジュースを1杯飲みます	(B) 39.1%
(C) Help prepare food within 10 minutes	(C) 10分以内に食事を準備するのを手伝います	(C) 13.0%
(D) Bring some beverages	**(D) 飲み物を持ってきます**	**(D) 13.0%**

解説　リンゴジュースを注文した女性に、Let me go get it for you. と言っているので、ジュースを取りに行く、の(D)が正解です。

Vocabulary
☐ **beverage** 飲み物

Questions 50 through 52 refer to the following conversation.
問題50-52は次の会話に関するものです。

W:	You are late to work again, Tony. This is becoming a habit and is completely unacceptable.	W: また仕事に遅れましたね、トニー。遅れることが習慣づいてきてしまうことは許されませんよ。
M:	I'm terribly sorry. I couldn't arrive on time because I was stuck in traffic for the last 40 minutes. It's due to the new highway they are building next to my home.	M: 大変申し訳ありません。渋滞に40分も巻き込まれていたので時間通り着けませんでした。家の近くに新しく建てられる高速道路のせいです。
W:	If you know that there are roadworks, maybe you should leave home earlier so that you can beat the early morning rush. Wouldn't you agree?	W: もし道路を造っているということを知っていたのであれば、家を早めに出て出勤ラッシュを回避できたのではないですか。そう思いませんか。
M:	Yes, I agree. Unfortunately, because we only have one car, I have to wait for my wife to drop the kids to school and come back home before I can leave for work.	M: はい、そう思います。しかし家には1台しか車がなく、私は妻が子供たちを学校に送って帰ってきてから出社することしかできません。
W:	I understand that, but surely there is an alternative route you can take to work. As per company policy, if you are late again, I will have to give you a warning letter. I do not want to do this. Hence, please ensure you are not late again.	W: それはわかりました、でも確かに違うルートもあったはずです。会社のポリシーとして、また遅れた場合、警告状を渡さなければなりません。私はそれをしたくないです。なので、これから遅れることはないようにしてください。

Vocabulary
☐ **unacceptable** 許容されない　☐ **be stuck** 足止めされる　☐ **drop** 車から降ろす　☐ **alternative** 代替の
☐ **route** ルート ＊地域によりルート、ラウトと発音が異なります。

50　　**正解 D**

What reason does the man give as to why he couldn't arrive on time?
男性は時間通りに到着できなかったのはなぜだと言っていますか。

(A) He got lost on the new highway.	(A) 彼は新しい高速道路で道に迷いました。	(A) 8.7%
(B) He was involved in a car accident.	(B) 彼は自動車事故に巻き込まれました。	(B) 13.0%
(C) He had to take care of his children.	(C) 彼は子供たちの世話をしなければなりませんでした。	(C) 13.0%
(D) He was stuck in traffic for a long time.	**(D) 彼は長い間交通渋滞に巻き込まれていました。**	**(D) 60.9%**

解説　40分間交通渋滞に巻き込まれていた、との発言があり、それをストレートに表現している(D)が正解です。渋滞にはまっている(stuck)だけで、(B)のように事故に巻き込まれたわけではありません。

51　正解 B

What possible solution does the woman propose to the man?
女性は男性にどのような解決策を提案していますか。

(A) He should let his wife see his children.	(A) 彼は彼の妻に子供たちの面倒を見させるべきです。	(A) 8.7%
(B) He could leave home earlier.	**(B) 彼はもっと早く家を出ることができました。**	**(B) 69.6%**
(C) He could take a shortcut.	(C) 彼は近道ができました。	(C) 8.7%
(D) He should never try taking alternative routes.	(D) 彼は決して別のルートを取ろうとするべきではありません。	(D) 8.7%

解説　maybe you should leave home earlierとの発言から(B)が正解であることが分かります。(A)と(C)については言及がなく、(D)については、代替のルートを考えるよう言っていたので、事実の逆となります。

Vocabulary
☐ **shortcut** 近道

52　正解 B

What does the woman mean when she says, "I do not want to do this"?
女性の「私はそれをしたくないです」という発言はどういう意味ですか。

(A) She felt lethargic about writing a warning letter.	(A) 彼女は警告の手紙を書く気がありません。	(A) 13.0%
(B) She believes a warning letter should be and can be avoided.	**(B) 彼女は、警告の手紙は避けるべきであり、避けることができると信じています。**	**(B) 26.1%**
(C) She doubts that a letter like this is effective.	(C) 彼女はこのような手紙が効果的であることを疑っています。	(C) 13.0%
(D) She predicts that the man will be late again.	(D) 彼女はその男性が再び遅れるだろうと予測しています。	(D) 43.5%

解説　I do not want to do this. を文字通り取れば「その行為をしたくない」ですが、その言葉をもって話者が何を言わんとしているか、と考えると、警告文を書く行為そのものを毛嫌いしたり無気力感を覚えているのではなく、警告文を出さなければいけない状況にならなくても済むようにしたい、という気持ちが読み取れます。(D)については、そう思っている可能性はありますが、だからこのセリフを言った、という流れは自然ではありません。

Vocabulary
☐ **lethargic** 無気力である、力が出せない

Questions 53 through 55 refer to the following conversation.
問題53-55は次の会話に関するものです。

M: Did you hear that the Minister will be visiting our company today?

W: Yes, I heard he'll stop by on his way back from a tree-planting ceremony at the Dotti Forest Reserve. He will be meeting our Vice-President, Mr. Davis, today to discuss our new environment protection policy.

M: Oh, is he planting trees at the Dotti Forest Reserve? Is it just a gimic or is he really planning to increase forest cover in the state?

W: He has announced that he would like to increase forest cover from 20 percent to at least 35 percent of the total area in the state. He has also announced a 1-million-dollar government program to ensure that these new goals are met.

M: Well, I take back what I just said. So, they are serious. Well, it is nice to see a politician care about the environment so much. Some are only concerned about increasing the number of factories and industries in the state.

M: 今日大臣が私たちの会社に訪問しに来るって聞きましたか。

W: はい、彼はドッティ森の木の植林式典の帰りに寄る予定と聞きました。彼は私たちの副社長であるデイビス氏と会って新しい環境保護のポリシーについて話し合う予定です。

M: 彼はドッティ森で植林をしているのですか。見せかけの行為なのでしょうか。それとも本当にこの州の森を増やす計画を進めているのでしょうか。

W: 彼は州の森の面積を20パーセントから少なくとも35パーセントまで増やしたいと発表していました。そして彼は100万ドルもの政府のお金を使ってこの目標を確実に達成させようとしていますね。

M: さっきの発言は撤回します。真剣なのですね。政治家がそのように環境について考えている姿を見るのはとても良いことですよね。この州で工場の数を増やしたり産業を増やすことにだけ集中してしまう人たちもいるのに。

Vocabulary
☐ **tree-planting** 植樹　☐ **reserve** 指定保護区　☐ **gimic** 策、見せかけ

53　　正解 B

According to the speakers, what will be the topic of today's meeting?
話者によると、今日の会議の議題は何でしょうか。

(A) Trees at the Dotti Forest Reserve	(A) ドッティ森林保護区の木	(A) 26.1%
(B) Policies about environmental protection	**(B) 環境保護に関する方針**	**(B) 43.5%**
(C) Projects between the company and the ministry	(C) 会社と省のプロジェクト	(C) 13.0%
(D) Upcoming regional elections	(D) 今後の地方選挙	(D) 13.0%

解説　女性が、discuss our new environment protection policyと発言していることから(B)が正解となります。(A)と(C)については協議されるかもしれませんが、会話の中で直接言及されているのはpolicyであるため、最適な議題は(B)となります。

54　正解 C

According to the woman, what is the true objective of the tree-planting activities?
女性によると、植樹活動の真の目的は何ですか。

(A) A special performance for the election	(A) 選挙のための特別なパフォーマンス	(A) 0.0%
(B) Securing governmental funding	(B) 政府資金の確保	(B) 43.5%
(C) Increasing the forest cover in the state	**(C) 州の森林被覆の増加**	**(C) 47.8%**
(D) Stopping desertification of the forest	(D) 森林の砂漠化の停止	(D) 4.3%

解説　gimic（見せかけ）なのか、との疑念が上がりましたが、本当に森林を広げようという意図で行われる、という情報があり、(C)が正解となります。(D)も可能性はありますが、問題文のAccording to the woman、という文言から、女性が言った内容からしか答えは選べないので、事実上の可能性はありながらも(D)をこの問題への正解とすることはできません。

55　正解 A

Why does the man say, "Well, I take back what I just said"?
なぜ男性は「さっきの発言を撤回します」と言ったのですか。

(A) He realized that what he just said is irrelevant.	**(A) 彼は今言ったことが不適切であったことに気づきました。**	(A) 13.0%
(B) He misunderstood the theme of the conversation.	(B) 彼は会話のテーマを誤解しました。	(B) 30.4%
(C) He felt the necessity of paraphrasing his remarks.	(C) 彼は自分の発言を言い換える必要性を感じました。	(C) 30.4%
(D) He was unhappy about the politician's behavior.	(D) 彼は政治家の行動に不満を持っていました。	(D) 21.7%

解説　この「前言を撤回する」というセリフを発した後、環境保全について真剣に考える政治家を称賛する発言をしており、見せかけなのかと一瞬疑った自分のセリフが不適切であったことを認めています。

Vocabulary
□ irrelevant 不適切な　　□ remark 発言

Questions 56 through 58 refer to the following conversation.
問題56-58は次の会話に関するものです。

W: Hello. I received a call this morning and was informed that my prescribed medicine is ready for pickup at this counter.	W: こんにちは、今朝電話を頂いて、このカウンターで私の処方薬の受け取りの準備ができていると電話をもらいました。
M: I presume you talked with another pharmacist. I will look for your folder and see if it's ready. Can I have the last four digits of your phone number?	M: おそらく別の薬剤師と話したのですね。あなたのフォルダーを探して準備できているか見てみます。電話番号の下4桁を頂けますでしょうか。
W: Sure, it's 4278. And my surname is Swart. S, W, A, R, T.	W: それなら4278のはずです。私の名字はスワートです。S, W, A, R, Tです。
M: One moment, please. So you are Julia Swart. So your medicine is... an antibiotic, antipyretic, and stomach medicine.	M: 少々お待ちください。え、ジュリア・スワートさんですね？ あなたのお薬は、抗生物質、解熱剤、胃薬になります。
W: Yes, that's right. The person said that the medicine will be ready by noon, and it's 4 P.M. now, so I suppose it's ready somewhere in the back.	W: その通りです。その方は正午までには薬は準備できていると言っていて、今は午後4時ですから、後ろのそのあたりで準備できているのではないかと思います。
M: Here is your medicine. You have three types of medicine, and their bottles look similar, so please read the labels on each bottle carefully.	M: はい、こちらが薬になります。3種類ありまして、瓶が似ているので、それぞれのラベルを注意して読んでください。

Vocabulary

☐ **prescribed** 処方された   ☐ **presume** 推測する   ☐ **pharmacist** 薬剤師   ☐ **antibiotics** 抗生物質
☐ **antipyretic** 解熱剤

56   正解 A

Who is the woman talking to?
女性は誰に話しているのですか。

(A) A pharmacist	**(A) 薬剤師**	**(A) 56.5%**
(B) A telephone operator	(B) 電話オペレーター	(B) 8.7%
(C) A doctor	(C) 医者	(C) 8.7%
(D) Julia Swart	(D) ジュリア・スワート	(D) 21.7%

解説　薬を受け取りに来ているという会話内容からも、another pharmacist（別の薬剤師）という言及からも、薬剤師と話している様子がうかがわれ、(A)が正解となります。

57　正解 B

What information did the man ask the woman for?
男性は女性にどのような情報を求めましたか。

(A) Her name	(A) 彼女の名前	(A) 13.0%
(B) Her phone number	**(B) 彼女の電話番号**	**(B) 47.8%**
(C) The time for pickup	(C) 受け取りの時間	(C) 21.7%
(D) Her symptoms	(D) 彼女の症状	(D) 13.0%

解説　電話番号の下4桁の数字を聞いており、4278との回答がありましたので、聞かれた情報は電話番号(の一部)ということが分かります。名前の確認をしていますが、名前を求めたのではなく、電話番号から名前を取り出しているので、(A)は正解ではありません。

Vocabulary
☐ **symptom** 症状

58　正解 C

What did the man tell the woman to do?
男性は女性に何をするように言いましたか。

(A) Pick up the medicine at noon	(A) 正午に薬を受け取る	(A) 13.0%
(B) Call another pharmacist	(B) 別の薬剤師に電話する	(B) 13.0%
(C) Read the labels carefully	**(C) ラベルを注意深く読む**	**(C) 65.2%**
(D) Sleep well to get better	(D) よく眠って元気になる	(D) 4.3%

解説　薬のボトルが3つあり、それぞれ似ているのでラベルをちゃんと読むように、という指示があったことから(C)が正解となります。(A)、(B)、(D)はいずれも言及がありません。

Questions 59 through 61 refer to the following telephone messages. M ◆ W

問題59-61は次の電話のメッセージに関するものです。

M: Hi, Beth. I can't type now so I'll just leave a voice message so that you can have a better understanding of what is going on and what you have to do now. We've received lots of inquiries about the new online educational service we launched last month. Though we've replied to most of them, there are still some questions that have not been answered. I flagged those messages, so you should be able to identify them instantly. A red flag was used to indicate the highest priority, yellow for the next group, and blue for the ones that are not urgent. Wait, um, it was green, I think. Yup, it's green because those are the colors for a traffic signal. There's no blue. Most of the ones with a red flag ask about our movie materials that are not working. So, tell them in the reply mails that all the necessary repairs will be made by the weekend.	M: ベス。今はタイプできないので、今の状況と何をしなければけないかを理解してもらえるように、音声メッセージを残します。先月打ち出した新規のオンライン教育サービスについて多くの問い合わせを受け取っています。大半には返答しましたが、幾つかはまだ回答されていません。すぐに見分けがつくようにそれらのメッセージにフラグ（旗）をつけておきました。赤旗は最も優先度が高いもの、黄色はその次、そして青は急ぎではないものです。待って、えーっと、緑でしたね。そう、緑です。信号の色に合わせたので。青はありませんね。赤旗のものの大半は動画で機能していないものについてです。ですので、返信で必要な修正は週末までになされるとお知らせしてください。
W: Hi, thank you very much for the message. I will let our team know what to do for which inquiries. However, I'm sure that all the technical difficulties have already been resolved. So, what they will include in the reply will be modified accordingly.	W: メッセージありがとうございました。私のチームにどの問い合わせに対してまず何をすべきか伝えます。ただ、技術的な問題はすでにすべて解決されています。ですので、チームが送るメッセージの内容はそのように変更されます。

Vocabulary

☐ **reply** 返信する　☐ **flag** フラグをつける、フラグ　☐ **technical difficulties** 技術的な問題

59　　正解 **C**

Why is the man sending the message?
なぜ男性はメッセージを送っているのですか。

(A) To explain colored flags he often uses	(A) 彼がよく使う色付きフラグの説明をするため	(A) 26.1%
(B) To launch a new service	(B) 新しいサービスを開始するため	(B) 13.0%
(C) To give instructions to the woman	**(C) 女性に指示を与えるため**	**(C) 30.4%**
(D) To inquire the current situation	(D) 現状を調査するため	(D) 26.1%

解説　重要度に応じてフラグ付けされたメールの問い合わせに返信するよう指示をしているメッセージ内容であるため(C)が正解となります。確かにフラグの色については説明がありますが、その説明をするためにメッセージを残しているわけではないので(A)は正解ではありません。

60　正解 D

According to the man, which of the following is least urgent?
男性によると、次のうちどれが最も緊急性が低いですか。

(A) Inquiries flagged in red	(A) 赤でフラグが付いた問い合わせ	(A) 30.4%
(B) Inquiries flagged in yellow	(B) 黄色でフラグが付いた問い合わせ	(B) 8.7%
(C) Inquiries flagged in blue	(C) 青色でフラグが付いた問い合わせ	(C) 8.7%
(D) Inquiries flagged in green	**(D) 緑色でフラグが付いた問い合わせ**	(D) 47.8%

解説　一度、青が緊急性が低いと発言した後、信号の色に合わせ緑だったと訂正しています。緑のフラグがついたメールが緊急性が最も低いと分かります。問題文のleastを見逃さないように気を付けましょう。

61　正解 A

What does the woman say she would do?
女性は何をすると言っていますか。

(A) Have her team start replying with slight modification	**(A) 彼女のチームに、少し変更を加えた返信を開始させる**	(A) 34.8%
(B) Change the order of priority that the man specified	(B) 男性が決めた優先順位を変更する	(B) 26.1%
(C) Confirm if the technical problems have been fixed	(C) 技術的な問題が解決したかどうかを確認する	(C) 17.4%
(D) Wait until she receives further instructions from the man	(D) 彼女が男性からさらに指示を受けるまで待つ	(D) 17.4%

解説　技術的問題はすでに解決されているため、男性のメッセージにあった指示内容から一部変更して返信をしていくとあり、それを記述している(A)が正解となります。(B)、(C)、(D)はいずれも言及がありません。

Vocabulary
☐ **modification** 変更

Questions 62 through 64 refer to the following conversation and list.

問題62-64は次の会話とリストに関するものです。

W: Good morning, Mr. Stanley. This is Ruzha. I'm calling to let you know that I have sent you a list of flight options for your flight to Auckland next month. I've finalized your hotel, but not your flight. Would you be able to look at the list?	W: おはよう、スタンレーさん。ルザです。来月の予定されているオークランドまでの飛行機のリストアップができましたので連絡させていただいております。ホテルは決定しましたが飛行機はまだです。リストをご確認いただけますでしょうか。
M: Good morning, Ruzha. Yes, if you can hold the line, I'll pull up the e-mail you sent me.	M: おはよう、ルザ。はい、もし待っていてもらえるのならメールをこれから開けます。
W: Sure, take your time.	W: もちろんです。時間はお気になさらずに。
M: OK, I'm looking at the e-mail right now. I have to attend a meeting in Auckland at 3 P.M. on the 16th. Which flight would you suggest I book?	M: オッケー、今メールを見ています。16日の午後3時からはオークランドでミーティングに行かなければならないので…どのフライトが良いかと思いますか。
W: If you have an afternoon meeting, I suggest you book the one that arrives in the morning since that gives you an ample amount of time to rest and get prepared.	W: もし午後にミーティングがあるのであれば、朝の時間に到着するものをお勧めします。そのあと休む時間と準備する時間がたくさん持てますからね。
M: That does sound good. Then, among the three options, I will go with the direct flight.	M: それは良いですね。では3つの中では、直行便を希望します。
W: Just for your information, that's the most expensive one, but would that be OK?	W: 参考までに、価格は一番高いものですが、それでよろしいでしょうか。
M: The price is not the primary concern, so no need to change my choice on the basis of price. Since our time is limited, I would appreciate it if you could proceed to the final step.	M: 価格は最優先項目ではありませんので、価格をもとに選択を変える必要はありません。時間が限られていますので、最後のステップに進んでいただければ幸いです。

Vocabulary

☐ **hold the line** 電話を保留にする　☐ **pull up** 引っ張り出す　☐ **ample** 十分な

☐ **proceed to** 〜　〜に進む

Airline	Arrives	Stopovers/Direct
Singapore Central	9 A.M.	Direct
EU High Air	1 P.M.	Direct
Qantics Airline	10:00 A.M.	1 stop
Jet Streamer	10:15 A.M.	2 stops

航空会社	到着	途中降機/直行
シンガポールセントラル	9 A.M.	直行
EUハイエア	1 P.M.	直行
クアンティックス航空	10:00 A.M.	1回
ジェットストリーマー	10:15 A.M.	2回

62 　正解 C

Where does the woman most likely work?
女性はどこで働いている可能性が高いですか。

(A) At an airline company (A) 航空会社で (A) 26.1%
(B) At a hotel in Auckland (B) オークランドのホテルで (B) 13.0%
(C) At a travel agency **(C) 旅行代理店で** **(C) 47.8%**
(D) At an international airport (D) 国際空港で (D) 8.7%

解説　flight optionという言葉を出して旅行の計画についての確認を電話で行っていることから、(C)が正解であると特定できます。電話で顧客に確認を取っているので、同じ会社で働いている同僚との解釈は自然ではなく、(C)以外の選択肢を肯定する材料が会話中にはありません。

63 　正解 A

Look at the graphic. Which airline will the man choose for his flight?
表を見てください。男性はどの航空会社のフライトを選びますか。

(A) Singapore Central **(A) シンガポールセントラル**
(B) EU High Air (B) EUハイエア
(C) Qantics Airline (C) クアンティックス航空
(D) Jet Streamer (D) ジェットストリーマー

解説　direct flight（直行便）で行くという条件と、昼の会議にゆとりをもって参加するために午前の便が推奨されている内容から、(A)が最適な選択肢とわかります。

64　正解 D

What does the man ask the woman to do?
男性は女性に何をするように頼んでいますか。

(A) Change his flight	(A) フライトを変更する	(A) 17.4%
(B) Spend some time on confirmation	(B) 確認に時間をかける	(B) 17.4%
(C) Give the price list	(C) 価格表を渡す	(C) 21.7%
(D) Move on to the final step	**(D) 最後のステップに進む**	**(D) 39.1%**

解説　最後のセリフでI appreciate it if you could proceed to the final step. と発言しており、これ
をそのまま記述している(D)が正解となります。proceed to を同義語の move on to で言い換
えています。

Questions 65 through 67 refer to the following conversation and floor plan.

問題65-67は次の会話とフロアプランに関するものです。

W: Mr. Akita, I'm calling because I've just sent through an e-mail with the floor plan that I drew for your new home. I was wondering if you could please take a look at it. I need your approval before I can send the plan to the construction company and its crew.

M: OK, I have the floor plan in front of me. Well, if I remember our last conversation correctly, I had requested skylights in the master bedroom and entrance. I don't see them on the master plan.

W: Oh! My apologies. I will incorporate skylights as requested and will send you a new draft.

M: Thank you. I would also like you to put a division between the living room and the kitchen. I tried to explain this last time but maybe it was not clear. Um, so, how much time do you think it will take for you to draw up the new floor plan?

W: I will try and send you the new plans by the end of this week.

W: 秋田さん、先ほどメールにて、私の方で作成したあなたの新居のフロアプランを送らせていただきましたのでお電話いたしました。確認をお願いしたいと思いまして。建設会社とそのクルーに渡す前に、あなたからの承認が必要になっています。

M: フロアプランを見ています。私が前の話を正確に覚えていれば、天窓をマスターベッドルームと入り口につけてくださいとリクエストしたはずです。それがこのプランには見えません。

W: 申し訳ございません。リクエストいただいた天窓を追加して、新しい草案を私の方で送らせていただきます。

M: ありがとうございます。それから、リビングと台所の間に仕切りをつけてくださいますか。説明はしていたのですが、分かりにくかったかもしれません。それで、新しいフロアプランを作るのにどのくらい時間がかかりそうでしょうか。

W: 新しいフロアプランは今週終わりまでに送らせていただきたいと思います。

Vocabulary

☐ **skylight** 天窓   ☐ **division** 仕切り

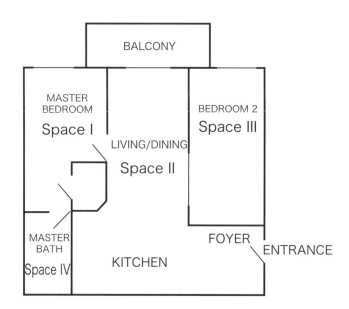

BALCONY

MASTER
BEDROOM
Space I

LIVING/DINING
Space II

BEDROOM 2
Space III

MASTER
BATH
Space IV

KITCHEN

FOYER
ENTRANCE

65 正解 C

What most likely is the woman's occupation?
女性の職業は何である可能性が高いですか。

(A) A real estate appraiser
(B) A furniture manufacturer
(C) An architectural designer
(D) A construction manager

(A) 不動産鑑定士
(B) 家具メーカー
(C) 建築デザイナー
(D) 建設マネージャー

(A) 21.7%
(B) 13.0%
(C) 34.8%
(D) 26.1%

解説 私の方で作成したあなたの新居のフロアプランについてのお話、と切り出していることから、
デザイナーであることが推測されます。自分でデザインを作成しているという情報がなければ、
(D)の建設マネージャーも可能性はありますが、今回は話し手自身がデザインしていることか
ら(C)が正解となります。

Vocabulary
□ **real estate appraiser** 不動産鑑定士

66　　正解 B

Why is a change requested?
変更はなぜ要求されましたか。

(A) The draft was not clear enough.

(B) The plan does not match the man's instruction.

(C) There were too many dividers but too few windows.

(D) The dimension is not specified in the blueprint.

(A) 草案が十分に明確ではありませんでした。

(B) プランが男性の指示と一致していません。

(C) 仕切りが多すぎて窓が少なすぎました。

(D) 寸法が設計図に明記されていません。

(A) 21.7%

(B) 56.5%

(C) 13.0%

(D) 4.3%

> 解説　天窓についての要望が反映されておらず、それが理由で変更が依頼されていることから(B)が正解となります。他の選択肢については記述がありません。

Vocabulary

☐ **match** 適合する　　☐ **divider** 仕切り　　☐ **dimension** 寸法　　☐ **blueprint** 設計図

67　　正解 B

Look at the graphic. Which part of the layout will be changed?
図を見てください。レイアウトのどの部分が変更されますか。

(A) Space I

(B) Space II

(C) Space III

(D) Space IV

(A) スペース I

(B) スペース II

(C) スペース III

(D) スペース IV

> 解説　男性のセリフで、I would also like you to put a division between the living room and the kitchen. という説明があることから、この場所に当たる II が変更されるものと特定できます。

303

Questions 68 through 70 refer to the following conversation and agenda.

問題68-70は次の会話と進行表に関するものです。

M:	I'm relieved that many competent candidates applied for the marketing manager's position.	M: 多くの有能な候補者が最初のマーケティングマネージャーのポジションに応募したので安心しました。

M: I'm relieved that many competent candidates applied for the marketing manager's position.

W: Mr. Ronalds seems particularly promising, doesn't he? His past achievements and experience will be a bonus for this position.

M: I agree. Among the four candidates who moved on to the final interview, Mr. Ronalds does seem outstanding. And, the... the final interview will be next Monday, right?

W: That's right, from 10 A.M. Here is the agenda.

M: Well, do we really have to ask all these questions? You know, we all know their past achievements from the first and second round of the interviews, so I think we can just skip this part.

W: I agree. We don't want to make them feel that we are having them answer the same questions.

M: So, that makes the total interview time for the four candidates a bit more than two hours.

W: Without a break.

M: 多くの有能な候補者が最初のマーケティングマネージャーのポジションに応募したので安心しました。

W: ロナルズさんは特に有望ですね。彼の過去の業績、および彼のすべての経験は、このポジションに適していてプラスとなるでしょう。

M: そうですね。最終面接に進んだ4人の候補者の中でも、ロナルズさんは秀でているようです。そして…最終面接は来週の月曜日でしたよね？

W: そうです、午前10時からです。これがアジェンダです。

M: 本当にこれらの質問を全部する必要がありますか。私たちは、インタビューの第1ラウンドと第2ラウンドで彼らの過去の業績は知っているので、この部分はスキップできると思います。

W: そうですよね。同じ質問に答えているように感じさせたくありません。

M: だから4人の候補者の合計面接時間が2時間強になってしまいます。

W: 休憩なしですしね。

Question Set	What to ask	Duration
1st set	Why us	5 min
2nd set	Past achievements	10 min
3rd set	Strength/Weakness	15 min
4th set	Career ambition	10 min

質問順	何を尋ねるか	時間
1st set	志望動機	5分
2nd set	過去の業績	10分
3rd set	長所と短所	15分
4th set	仕事に関する抱負	10分

Vocabulary

☐ **competent** 有能な　☐ **promising** 有望な

68 　正解 D

Who most likely are the speakers?
話者はどんな人ですか。

(A) Candidates for a manager's position	(A) マネージャーの候補者	(A) 26.1%
(B) Marketing managers	(B) マーケティングマネージャー	(B) 26.1%
(C) Mr. Ronalds' supervisors	(C) ロナルズ氏の監督者	(C) 8.7%
(D) Human resources executives	**(D) 人事部幹部**	**(D) 34.8%**

解説　最終面接に進んだ候補者の中で誰が有望かという話をしていることから、人事に関する仕事の範囲であり、選択肢の中では(D)が最も適していると判断されます。(B)のマーケティングマネージャーも可能性としてゼロではありませんが、(D)の人事部幹部に勝る特段の要素がなく、最善の選択肢とは言えません。

69 　正解 B

Look at the agenda. Which part of the interview will be omitted?
アジェンダを見てください。面接のどの部分が省略されますか。

(A) The 1st set	(A) 1セット目	(A) 21.7%
(B) The 2nd set	**(B) 2セット目**	**(B) 47.8%**
(C) The 3rd set	(C) 3セット目	(C) 13.0%
(D) The 4th set	(D) 4セット目	(D) 13.0%

解説　男性のセリフで、過去の実績については1回目と2回目の面接で聞いているから飛ばしてもいいのでは、とあり女性もそれに賛成していくことで、(B)の2nd setは省略されるとわかります。

Vocabulary
□ omit 省略する

70 　正解 A

What does the woman mean when she says, "Without a break"?
彼女の「休憩なしですしね」という言葉はどういう意味ですか。

(A) The interview could take longer depending on how they proceed.	**(A) 面接の進め方によっては、面接により時間がかかる場合があります。**	**(A) 34.8%**
(B) It is possible to make the duration even shorter.	(B) 時間をさらに短くすることが可能です。	(B) 13.0%
(C) Each candidate would feel better if he/she could take a break.	(C) 休憩が取れれば、各候補者の気分が良くなるでしょう。	(C) 4.3%
(D) She agrees with the idea that some questions should be omitted.	(D) 彼女はいくつかの質問を省くべきであるという考えに同意しています。	(D) 43.5%

解説　休憩がなければ4人の面接で2時間強かかるかと男性が発言した直後に、「休憩がなければ（その通り）」すなわち、休憩を挟むならもっと時間がかかる、ということを示唆しており、(A)が最適な答えとなります。

Vocabulary
□ **eliminate** 削除する

Part4 説明文問題

Questions 71 through 73 refer to the following recruiting information.
問題71-73は次の求人情報に関するものです。

Are you looking for part-time work that you can do in your spare time? Are you in need of an extra source of income that will help you pay your bills on time? Do you need something flexible that can work around your current schedule? If you've answered 'yes' to any of these questions, we have a solution to your problem! ALT Supermarket is looking for warehouse assistants to pack orders received online. We have a variety of shifts that need to be covered. Whether you are looking for a morning, day, evening or late-night shift, we can offer you flexibility, a fair wage and employee discounts on groceries.Call us now on 233-233-2328 for inquiries. To get an application form, e-mail us at hiring@ALT-supermarket.com.

空き時間にできるバイトをお探しですか。請求書を期限までに払うのに、新しい収入源が必要ですか。すでにある予定を崩さず融通の利く仕事をお求めですか。もしあなたが以上の質問のうち1つに「はい」と答えたのであれば、その問題の解決法はここにあります！ ALTスーパーマーケットは現在倉庫でオンライン注文を受けて荷造りをするスタッフを探しています。たくさんの空白のシフトがあります。朝、昼、夜、深夜、どの時間帯でも時間に融通の利くシフトを、それに合ったお給料と、食料雑貨に使える社員割引も含め提供させていただきます。お問い合わせは233-233-2328までお電話ください。また、申込書を入手するにはhiring@ALT-supermarket.comまでメールをお願いいたします。

Vocabulary
☐ **in need of** 〜 〜が必要　☐ **pack** 梱包する

71　正解 C

What is the main purpose of the talk?
話の主な目的は何ですか。

(A) To construct a warehouse	(A) 倉庫を建設するため	(A) 8.7%
(B) To publicize commodities	(B) 商品を宣伝するため	(B) 13.0%
(C) To recruit some staff	**(C) スタッフを雇うため**	**(C) 60.9%**
(D) To ask some questions	(D) いくつかの質問をするため	(D) 13.0%

解説　スピーチ全体を通して、スーパーマーケットでの仕事の案内をしており、作業スタッフを募集している内容であるため(C)が正解となります。

Vocabulary
☐ **publicize** 宣伝する

72　正解 C

What solution does the speaker say ALT can provide?
話者はALTには何が提供できると言っていますか。

(A) An assistance for warehouse operations
(B) High-quality, low-priced groceries
(C) **An income source that can be flexibly arranged**
(D) Shift management systems for a supermarket

(A) 倉庫業務の支援
(B) 高品質で低価格の食料品
(C) **柔軟に調整可能な収入源**
(D) スーパーマーケットのシフト管理システム

(A) 21.7%
(B) 8.7%
(C) **34.8%**
(D) 30.4%

解説　Whether you are looking for a morning, day, evening or late-night shift, we can offer you flexibilityの部分から(C)が正解となります。仕事は倉庫での業務ですが、これは仕事の内容であって、聞き手に提供されるsolutionではないので、(A)は不正解となります。(B)と(D)については言及がありません。

73　正解 C

What does the speaker suggest the listeners do if they have questions?
質問がある場合、話者は聴者に何をするように提案していますか。

(A) Send an e-mail
(B) Stop by at the supermarket
(C) **Call the office**
(D) Leave a voice message

(A) メールを送る
(B) スーパーに寄る
(C) **オフィスに電話する**
(D) ボイスメッセージを残す

(A) 43.5%
(B) 8.7%
(C) **34.8%**
(D) 8.7%

解説　質問がある場合は電話、申請書を入手する場合にはメール、と最後に案内があったので、(C)が正解となります。このようなトリッキーさはTOEICでは頻繁には見られませんが、高難度模試ということで、最後の細部まで聞き逃さないレベルのリスニングを目指します。

Vocabulary
□ **stop by** 立ち寄る

Questions 74 through 76 refer to the following announcement.
問題74-76は次のお知らせに関するものです。

M

Attention, all employees of Tera Pocket Mobile! It's been over 20 years since our establishment. The board of directors has decided to celebrate September as Employee Appreciation Month. Throughout this month, multiple employee engagement events such as Employee of the Year, Food Feast, Game Nights, etc. will be held to show the company's appreciation for all the hard work that each employee has put in throughout the year. On the last day of September, the Employee of the Year will be announced in a grand ceremony, where a chosen employee will be awarded $10,000 and an all-expenses-paid trip to New York to visit our head office. You cannot nominate yourself but if you do have someone you would like to nominate for this honor, please speak to the director of your department by the end of August as they have the relevant forms.

テラ・ポケット・モバイルの従業員へのご案内！　設立から20年がたちました。重役会が9月を従業員感謝の月として祝うことを決めました。この月には今年の従業員賞や、宴会、ゲームナイトのような従業員を交えた幾つかのイベントがあり、これらは会社の従業員へのこれまでの1年の頑張りに対する感謝です。9月の最終日にはグランドセレモニーがあり、1万ドルおよび本社を訪れるための旅費をすべて会社が負担するニューヨーク旅行を勝ち取る従業員が発表されます。自分で自分をノミネートすることはできませんが、もしノミネートしたい従業員がいましたら、8月末までにあなたの部の部長に連絡をしてください。用紙を持っていますので。

Vocabulary
☐ **all-expenses paid trip** 会社持ちの旅行　☐ **nominate** 推薦する、指名する

74　**正解** C

What is the Employee Appreciation Month held for?
従業員感謝月間は何のために開催されますか。

(A) To celebrate the 20th anniversary of the company
(B) To enjoy a variety of food served in the firm
(C) **To show gratitude toward members' hard work**
(D) To recruit a larger number of employees

(A) 会社の20周年を祝うため
(B) 会社で提供されるさまざまな料理を楽しむため
(C) 従業員の努力に感謝の意を表すため
(D) より多くの従業員を採用するため

(A) 60.9%
(B) 4.3%
(C) 17.4%
(D) 13.0%

解説　なぜこのイベントが開催されるかということについては、held to show the company's appreciation for all the hard work that each employee has put inとあり、会社からの従業員への感謝を伝えるためのイベントだということが分かります。それを表す(C)が正解です。スピーチが始まってしばらく解答の根拠となる部分が出てきませんが、こうした変化球にも落ち着いて対応していきましょう。

Vocabulary
☐ **gratitude** 感謝の気持ち

75 　正解 A

What do we learn about Tera Pocket Mobile?
テラ・ポケット・モバイルについて何がわかりますか。

(A) It has a head office in New York.	**(A) ニューヨークに本社があります。**	**(A) 34.8%**
(B) It offers $10,000-bonus each year.	(B) 毎年1万ドルのボーナスがあります。	(B) 26.1%
(C) It elected new board members recently.	(C) 最近新しい取締役が選ばれました。	(C) 17.4%
(D) Its fiscal year begins in September.	(D) 会計年度は9月に始まります。	(D) 17.4%

解説　費用は会社持ちの旅行でニューヨークに行けるそうですが、そこには本社があると説明されています。もしかすると、これは自由に楽しめる旅行ではないのかもしれません。headquarters は常に複数形で用いられますが、head office は単数、複数ともに可能です。

Vocabulary
☐ **elect** 人を選挙などで選ぶ　☐ **fiscal year** 会計年度

76 　正解 D

What will happen at the end of August?
8月末に何がありますか。

(A) The Employee of the Year will be announced.	(A) 年間最優秀従業員が発表されます。	(A) 0.0%
(B) Employees will join and enjoy special events.	(B) 従業員は特別なイベントに参加して楽しむことができます。	(B) 34.8%
(C) The prize winner will go to New York.	(C) 受賞者はニューヨークに行きます。	(C) 26.1%
(D) The candidate nomination will be closed.	**(D) 候補者の推薦は締め切られます。**	**(D) 34.8%**

解説　直接的な言及はないまでも、8月末までに部長に（受賞者を推薦するための）用紙を入手するために連絡するよう言っているので、このタイミングで締め切るものと推測できます。(A)、(B)、(C)はすべて受賞者の推薦が終わってからの話なので、(D)を飛ばして(A)、(B)、(C)が先に起こることは想定できません（候補者の決定もなくイベントが開催される、勝者が決定しその人がニューヨークに行く、ということはありえません）。

Vocabulary
☐ **prize winner** 受賞者

Questions 77 through 79 refer to the following telephone message.

問題77-79は次の電話のメッセージに関するものです。

Good morning, Mr. Patton. This is Louisa Lorenz from the Lookout Dental Clinic. I'm calling to inform you that Dr. Scholl has had to cancel all appointments today due to her child, being unwell. We expect Dr. Scholl to be out of the office until next week, but we have arranged for a dentist, Dr. Heward, to work this week starting tomorrow. She, too, has tremendous experience and knowledge in periodontal diseases, she can provide all the treatment you need. We can either reschedule your appointment with Dr. Scholl next week, or you can make an appointment with the substitute dentist this week. We apologize for any inconvenience caused, so we would like to offer you a 10 percent discount for your next appointment. Please call us soon, so we can reschedule.

パットンさん、おはようございます。ルックアウト歯科クリニックのルイザ・ロレンツです。スコール先生が、彼女のお子さまの体調が良くなく、本日の予定をすべてキャンセルしなければいけなくなったので電話しております。スコール先生は来週までオフィスには来られない状況ですが、別のヒュアード先生が今週明日から稼動できるよう手配させていただいております。彼女も歯周病における多くの経験と知識がありますので、彼女もあなたが必要とする処置を提供できます。スコール先生と来週の予定をリスケジュールすることもできますし、代理の先生と今週予約を入れることもできます。ご不便をおかけして申し訳ありませんので、次回の予約で使える10パーセント割引を提供いたします。リスケジュールのために早めに折り返しお願いできましたら幸いです。

Vocabulary

☐ **periodontal disease** 歯周病　　☐ **substitute** 代わりの

77　　**正解 C**

Why is the appointment being rescheduled?

なぜ予約が変更されるのですか。

(A) The dentist is not feeling well.	(A) 歯科医の体調が悪いです。	(A) 21.7%
(B) Dr. Scholl is out of the office for a meeting.	(B) スコール先生は会議のために不在です。	(B) 8.7%
(C) Dr. Scholl's child is ill.	**(C) スコール先生の子供の体調がよくありません。**	**(C) 60.9%**
(D) The doctors are out of town.	(D) 医者たちは町の外にいます。	(D) 4.3%

解説　Dr. Scholl本人ではなく、お子さまが調子が思わしくない旨の説明があるので、(C)が正解となります。ハイレベル模試ということで、通常では出てこないような専門用語が複数入ってきていますが、それでも全体の理解度を落とさず聞けるように、前後の流れから意味を推測しながら読んでいくスキルも990点を取るためには重要になります。

78　正解 D

What does the speaker say about Dr. Heward?
話者はヒュアード先生について何と言っていますか。

(A) She is more experienced than Dr. Scholl.	(A) 彼女はスコール先生よりも経験豊富です。	(A) 17.4%
(B) She is from a prestigious university.	(B) 彼女は一流大学出身です。	(B) 13.0%
(C) She is a permanent doctor in the clinic.	(C) 彼女はクリニックの常駐医師です。	(C) 21.7%
(D) She can provide treatment to Mr. Patton.	**(D) 彼女はパットンさんを治療することができます。**	**(D) 43.5%**

解説　代理の歯科医として Dr. Heward が対応可能である旨説明されているので、聞き手側である Mr. Patton に対しても治療可能であることがわかります。(A)、(B)、(C)いずれに対しても言及はありません。

Vocabulary
☐ prestigious 一流の　　☐ permanent 常駐の

79　正解 A

What is the listener expected to do next?
聴者は次に何をするようですか。

(A) Call back the clinic	**(A) クリニックに折り返し電話をする**	**(A) 13.0%**
(B) Use the 10 percent discount	(B) 10パーセントの割引を利用する	(B) 60.9%
(C) Go to the clinic to reschedule	(C) リスケジュールのためにクリニックに行く	(C) 21.7%
(D) Talk to Dr. Heward	(D) ヒュアード先生と話す	(D) 0.0%

解説　最後に Please call us soon, so we can reschedule. とあり、電話が求められているので、(A) が正解となります。(B)の割引は受けられると想定されますが、次に何をするよう言われているか、という問いに対しては適切な答えにはなっていません。

Questions 80 through 82 refer to the following speech.
問題80-82は次のスピーチに関するものです。

Welcome to Pine Technology Limited. We are so glad you chose us to be your professional technology partner. To give you a brief idea of what we do, we invite you to join us on a virtual tour of our head office in Oakland, California. It is here that we bring to life most of our advanced ideas concerning a wide range of applications as well as digital devices. The Oakland facility currently houses approximately 200 employees, working in multiple departments such as Product Development, Information Systems, Cloud Infrastructure, etc. We also have several smaller facilities spread across the United States, Canada, and Europe. These facilities usually house a specialized team focused on a single project, and all the members report to a manager based in Oakland. This comprehensive virtual tour may take up to 30 minutes. It may sound long, but we are certain that you will love the fully-automated, highly interactive guide. Just follow the guide and discover what we, as partners, can achieve! We would love to answer any additional questions that you may have about us after going through this 30-minute journey. E-mail is the preferred method for this. Enjoy!

パイン・テクノロジー社にようこそ。あなたのプロテクノロジーパートナーとして選んでいただけたことをとても光栄に思います。私たちがどのようなことをするのか概要を説明するのに、カリフォルニアのオークランドにある当社へのバーチャルツアーにご招待いたします。私たちはこのメインオフィスで、幅広いアプリや電子機器に関する高度なアイデアに命を吹き込んでいます。オークランドの設備は現在約200名の従業員がおり、商品部門、インフォメーションシステム、クラウドインフラ部門など幾つかのデパートメントに分かれています。それだけに限らず、その他にも幾つか小さな部門がアメリカとカナダ、ヨーロッパまでにわたって全域にあります。このような設備は基本的に特別なチームを持っていて、彼らは1つのプロジェクトを担い、オークランドにいるマネージャーの直属となります。このバーチャルツアーは30分ほどあります。長いと思われたかもしれませんが、この全自動かつインタラクティブなガイドをきっと楽しんでいただけるでしょう。案内に沿って進み、われわれがパートナーとして達成できることを想像してみてください。この30分の旅の後で追加で出てくるご質問にお答えさせていただきます。メールが望ましいです。ではお楽しみください。

Vocabulary
□ **bring to life** 実現させる、命を与える　　□ **house** 含む、抱えている
□ **report to ~** ~の直属となる　　□ **fully-automated** 完全自動化された

80 正解 D

Who is this speech intended for?
このスピーチは誰を対象としていますか。

(A) Employees of Pine Technology	(A) パイン・テクノロジーの従業員
(B) The managers of Pine Technology	(B) パイン・テクノロジーのマネージャー
(C) Customers of Pine Technology	(C) パイン・テクノロジーのお客さま
(D) Business partners of Pine Technology	**(D) パイン・テクノロジーのビジネスパートナー**

(A) 13.0%
(B) 17.4%
(C) 26.1%
(D) 39.1%

解説 冒頭から、テクノロジーパートナーになってくれて光栄に思う、という言葉を使って案内を続けていることから、パートナーに対して送っている案内であることがわかります。

81 正解 B

What does the speaker mention about the structure of the company?
話者は会社の構造について何を言っていますか。

(A) The largest number of the employees work in Oakland.	(A) オークランドで働いている従業員が一番多いです。
(B) All employees across the world report to managers in Oakland.	**(B) 世界中の従業員は全員オークランドのマネージャーの直属です。**
(C) Facilities in Europe are as big as the head office in Oakland.	(C) ヨーロッパの施設は、オークランドの本社と同じくらい大きいです。
(D) All the executives appear in the virtual office tour.	(D) 幹部は全員バーチャルオフィスツアーに参加します。

(A) 43.5%
(B) 8.7%
(C) 39.1%
(D) 4.3%

解説 all the members report to a manager based in Oaklandとの明確かつ直接的な言及があるため(B)が正解となります。report toで「直属となる」という意味でTOEICで時々出る表現です。レポートを送る、という文字通りの意味ではありませんので注意。

82 正解 B

What are the listeners expected to do before asking questions?
質問をする前に聴者は何をするようですか。

(A) Send e-mails directly	(A) メールを直接送信する
(B) Visit the head office virtually	**(B) バーチャルで本社を訪問する**
(C) Call the office in Oakland	(C) オークランドのオフィスに電話する
(D) Wait for 30 minutes at the headquarters	(D) 本社で30分待つ

(A) 52.2%
(B) 13.0%
(C) 17.4%
(D) 13.0%

解説 We would love to answer any additional questions that you may have about us after going through this 30-minute journey. の部分から、まずツアーに参加しその後に質問を受ける(その場合はメールが望ましい)ということがわかります。

Questions 83 through 85 refer to the following talk.
問題83-85は次の話に関するものです。

Thank you for getting in touch with Bay Stylish Printing for your corporate apparel needs. With over 60 years of experience, we understand design printing better than anyone else in the San Francisco Bay area. We are proud to have worked with various companies, providing them with high-quality merchandise. Making or changing a corporate uniform? We can provide the perfect solution. Upon request, we will send you our catalog and sample textiles on which we can print your company logo and slogan. Please note, all styles can be dyed in any color, to suit your company's color palette. After we receive a final approval from you, we will ship your order within 2-3 weeks. Please let us know via e-mail if you would like any of these options or if you have something specific you require. We can do more than is printed in our catalog. Bay Stylish Printing is waiting for your order!

企業用衣類についてベイ・スタイリッシュ・プリンティングへのお問い合わせいただきありがとうございます。私たちはサンフランシスコのベイエリアの中でも、60年以上の経験を持って、デザインプリンティングについて他の誰よりも理解しています。高品質な製品をこれまでさまざまな企業に提供してきたことを誇りに思います。会社のユニフォームを作る、変えるなどお考えですか。私たちの製品が解決します！　ご要望がありましたら、カタログと、会社のロゴやスローガンをプリントできる素材のサンプルをお送りいたします。どのスタイルでも御社の色の好みに合わせてどんな色にでも変更可能です。最終的なご確認を頂いた後、2、3週間以内にお品物を送らせていただきます。このオプションの中でお好みのものがありましたら、もしくは、それ以外でお求めのものがありましたら、メールにてご連絡いただければ幸いです。カタログにあるサービスを上回るものを提供できます。ベイ・スタイリッシュ・プリンティングはあなたの注文を待っています！

Vocabulary
☐ **get in touch with** ～ ～に問い合わせる　☐ **apparel** 衣類、アパレル　☐ **textile** 生地、素材

83 正解 D

What achievement is the speaker proud of?
話者はどのような成果を誇りに思っていますか。

(A) That they are based in the bay area
(B) That they have 60-year experience
(C) That they fully understand design printing
(D) That they have worked with many companies

(A) ベイエリアに拠点を置いていること
(B) 彼らが60年の経験を持っていること
(C) デザインプリンティングを十分に理解していること
(D) 彼らが多くの企業と協力してきたこと

(A) 13.0%
(B) 30.4%
(C) 34.8%
(D) 17.4%

解説　We are proud to have worked with various companiesとの説明があり、その意味をストレートに記述している(D)が正解。冒頭で前置きが長いが、集中力を切らすことなく聞き続けるスキルも990点取得には必要になります。

84 正解 C

According to the speaker, what will Bay Stylish Printing send upon request?
話者によると、ベイ・スタイリッシュ・プリンティングは要求に応じて何を送りますか。

(A) Sample liquid dyes
(B) Company logos
(C) Sample textiles
(D) Printed uniforms

(A) サンプルの液体染料
(B) 会社のロゴ
(C) サンプルの生地
(D) 印刷済みのユニフォーム

(A) 4.3%
(B) 30.4%
(C) 26.1%
(D) 34.8%

解説　(A)～(D)のすべての選択肢にある単語はスピーチにも入っていたが、事実関係として(C)を送ると言っているので、これが正解となります。

85 正解 B

What does the speaker mean when he says, "We can do more than is printed in our catalog"?
話者はどういう意味で「カタログにあるサービスを上回るものを提供できます」と言っていますか。

(A) The company is making the greatest effort possible.
(B) The catalog does not explain everything.
(C) Delivery can be made faster than two weeks.
(D) The catalog lists things that the company actually can't do.

(A) 会社は可能な限りの努力をしています。
(B) カタログですべてが説明されているわけではありません。
(C) 配達は2週間より速くすることができます。
(D) カタログには、会社が実際にはできないことがリストされています。

(A) 26.1%
(B) 30.4%
(C) 30.4%
(D) 8.7%

解説　カタログに載っていないことでもあれこれできる（カタログにすべて書かれているわけではない）のでまずはお問い合わせを、というのが該当部分の意図なので、(B)が正解となります。

Questions 86 through 88 refer to the following podcast talk.
問題86-88は次のポッドキャストに関するものです。

Welcome to yet another episode of the Thinking with Uncle Sam podcast. In today's podcast, we will focus on the emergence of social media and why today's generation is so attached to their phones. Before we begin, I would like to introduce our special guest for this episode. Welcome, Professor Chen. Professor Chen is a preeminent psychologist, who focuses on the explosive role social media plays in our society today, and why so many of us are so addicted to it. Most of us are blind to its role, but he isn't. His famous bestseller on how social media influences our daily perceptions of events is now a part of the compulsory reading list at several high schools and universities here in Florida. Now, let's get started on our first question! How did social media emerge and how did it grow so rapidly?

サムおじさんと考えてみようのポッドキャストにようこそ。本日のポッドキャストではソーシャルメディアの出現となぜ現代の人が携帯電話に取りつかれているのかということについて考えてみようと思います。議論を始める前に、今回のスペシャルゲストをご紹介いたします。チェン教授、ようこそ。チェン教授は著名な心理学者であり、爆発的な勢いで拡大するソーシャルメディアの、現在の社会に対する役割を中心に研究しておられます。なぜこれほど多くの人が依存しているのでしょうか。われわれの多くは盲目的ですが、彼はそうではありません。どのようにソーシャルメディアが私たちの日常に影響するのか、ということについて書かれた彼のベストセラーはここフロリダの幾つかの高校や大学で必須の読み物となっています。では、最初の質問に入りましょう！　どのようにソーシャルメディアは出現し、そしてどのようにして成長を加速していったのでしょう？

Vocabulary
☐ **yet another** さらに別の　☐ **emergence** 出現　☐ **preeminent** 著名な、卓越した　☐ **perception** 認識

86　正解 D

What is the topic of the podcast talk?
ポッドキャストの議題は何ですか。

(A) The emergence of the Internet
(B) Adolescent psychology
(C) The life of Uncle Sam
(D) **Why youth are attached to their phones**

(A) インターネットの出現
(B) 青年期の心理学
(C) サムおじさんの人生
(D) **なぜ若者は携帯電話に取りつかれているのか**

(A) 26.1%
(B) 8.7%
(C) 13.0%
(D) 47.8%

解説　we will focus on ... why today's generation is so attached to their phones. とあり、なぜ若者が携帯電話に執着しているか、という話がメインであることがわかります。実際にはWe will focus on A and Bとなっているので、メイントピックは2つあり、…の部分にも長めの句が入っています。そのため文全体の意味を捉えづらいかもしれませんが、長い文でも要点を常に捉えられる耳を養っていきましょう。

Vocabulary
☐ **the youth** 若者 ☐ **adolescent** 青年期の

87　　正解 B

What does the speaker mean when she says, "Most of us are blind to its role, but he isn't"?
「われわれの多くは盲目的ですが、彼はそうではありません」という彼女の発言はどういう意味ですか。

(A) He has better eyesight than average.　(A) 彼は平均よりも視力が良いです。　(A) 17.4%

(B) His insight may give us clearer ideas.　**(B) 彼の洞察は私たちにより明確な考えを与えるかもしれません。**　**(B) 39.1%**

(C) His book can be read by blind people.　(C) 彼の本は視覚障害者が読むことができます。　(C) 21.7%

(D) He can predict the future precisely.　(D) 彼は未来を正確に予測することができます。　(D) 17.4%

解説　われわれの多くは盲目的(に物事が見えていない)が、彼には見えている、ということが言いたいわけで、実際の視力うんぬんを言おうとしているわけではありません。(A)、(C)はその意図を反映しておらず、表面的にblindという言葉を誤って解釈しています。(D)は「未来を正確に予想する」というのが言い過ぎです。正確に予想できるかまではわかりません。

Vocabulary
☐ **eyesight** 視力

88　　正解 B

What will Professor Chen talk about first?
チェン教授は何について初めに話しますか。

(A) Why many people become dependent on social media　(A) なぜ多くの人がソーシャルメディアに依存するようになるのか　(A) 21.7%

(B) How social media started and gained popularity　**(B) ソーシャルメディアがどのように始まり、人気を博したか**　**(B) 30.4%**

(C) What social media is and its effects on society　(C) ソーシャルメディアとは何か、そしてそれが社会に与える影響　(C) 34.8%

(D) How often people use social media　(D) 人々がどのくらいの頻度でソーシャルメディアを使用しているか　(D) 8.7%

解説　スピーチの最後でHow did social media emerge and how did it grow so rapidly? とあり、これをうまく言い換えている(B)が正解となります。選択肢の文が長いため、聞きながらの解答が難しいかもしれません。先読みの速読が求められます。リスニングセクションでの点数アップのために、実は速読力が必要、というのは実はよくあるケースです。

Vocabulary
☐ **popularity** 人気

Questions 89 through 91 refer to the following lecture.
問題89-91は次の講義に関するものです。

So, not only our body but also our mind is affected by stress. Let's dig deep. Have you ever noticed that your overall physical health improves when you are happier? Stress is a major influence when it comes to both your physical and mental wellbeing. Constant stress can manifest in several ways including depression, trouble sleeping, heart problems, and high blood pressure, to name just a few. In my case, it was depression that affected my everyday life. I've overcome it now, but it hasn't been easy. So, what is the best solution to combat stress in our daily lives? The answer may surprise you, but one of the easiest ways to deal with stress is exercise. When we exercise regularly, our body produces hormones that improve our mood. These hormones, called endorphins, help to reduce the stress hormone cortisol. Regular exercise can also help you get a good night's sleep, which in turn reduces stress. A good night's sleep can better equip you for the day ahead. Conversely, it won't be so if you are always stressed out.

私たちの身体だけではなく精神もストレスに影響を受けます。もっと掘り下げましょう。幸福を感じているとき全体的に身体の状態が良いと気づいたことはありませんか。ストレスは身体的、そしてメンタルの健康を犯す根本的な理由です。幾つか例を挙げるとすれば、持続的なストレスは鬱や睡眠障害、心臓病や高血圧などに明確に現れます。私の場合、日々の生活を狂わせたのは鬱症状でした。今は大丈夫ですが、軽いことではありませんでした。では、何が日常生活においてストレスと戦う上で一番良い対処法なのでしょうか。その答えは驚きを伴うかもしれませんが、一番簡単な方法は運動をすることです。定期的に運動をすることで私たちの体は私たちの気持ちをよくしてくれるホルモンを作り出します。これらのホルモンはエンドルフィンと呼ばれ、コルチゾールのようなストレスホルモンを減らしてくれます。規則的な運動は夜の睡眠の質も向上し、そしてそれはストレスを減らすことにもつながります。良い睡眠は翌日の活動を向上させてくれます。逆に、ストレスにさいなまれているとそうはならないでしょう。

Vocabulary
- ☐ when it comes to ～ ～については、～の話になると　☐ wellbeing 健康　☐ depression 鬱
- ☐ combat 戦う　☐ endorphin エンドルフィン　☐ cortisol コルチゾール　☐ in turn 続いて
- ☐ better 改善する　☐ conversely 逆に

89　正解 A

What is the topic of the lecture?
講義のテーマは何ですか。

(A) How stress affects our body and mind	**(A) ストレスが私たちの体と心にどのように影響するか**	**(A) 56.5%**
(B) What causes stress	(B) 何がストレスを引き起こすか	(B) 17.4%
(C) Why we cannot eliminate stress	(C) なぜストレスを取り除けないのか	(C) 4.3%
(D) How stress changes one's entire life	(D) ストレスが人生全体をどのように変えるか	(D) 17.4%

> 解説　冒頭のセリフから、体と心がストレスに影響を受けるというテーマであることがわかります。dig deep（深く掘り下げる）というセリフから、このテーマについて話を展開していくということが示されています。(A)以外の他の選択肢についてももしかすると部分的に言及があるかもしれませんが、トークの主たるトピックにはならないので正解とはなりません。

90　正解 A

What does the speaker say she suffered from in the past?
話者は彼女が過去何に苦しんだと言っていますか。

(A) Depression	**(A) うつ病**	**(A) 43.5%**
(B) Trouble sleeping	(B) 睡眠障害	(B) 43.5%
(C) Heart problems	(C) 心臓の問題	(C) 4.3%
(D) High blood pressure	(D) 高血圧	(D) 4.3%

> 解説　In my case, it was depression that affected my everyday life. このセリフが直接的に正解につながります。今回は専門用語も出てくるので、通常より難易度が高い部分がありますが、先読みができていると、専門性が高い単語が使われたとしてもより素早く正確に反応しやすくなります。選択肢にある単語はスピーチの中に出てきてはいますが、話し手の個人のケースとなると、(A)がやはり正解です。in my case が聞き取れているかが分かれ目になります。

91 **正解** **A**

According to the speaker, how does exercising help us stay healthier?
話者によると、運動はどのように私たちの健康を維持するのに役立ちますか。

(A) By maintaining a good balance of hormones	**(A) ホルモンのバランスを保つことによって**	**(A) 34.8%**
(B) By increasing the level of cortisol	(B) コルチゾールのレベルを上げることによって	(B) 17.4%
(C) By making us sleep less at night	(C) 私たちを夜より短く眠らせることによって	(C) 21.7%
(D) By reducing the amount of endorphins	(D) エンドルフィンの量を減らすことによって	(D) 21.7%

解説 エンドルフィンとコルチゾールというホルモンの名前を持ち出し、ホルモンのバランス改善による健康増進の話をしていました。このホルモンの名前が仮にわからなくても、前後で「ホルモン」という単語は使われており、相当強く焼き肉を想像しない限りは、文脈上の流れと意味で正解にたどり着ける問題と言えます。

Questions 92 through 94 refer to the following advertisement.
問題92-94は次の広告に関するものです。

Smile and Shine invites you to our annual stock clearance sale, where you will find deals on household commodities that are almost too good to be true! Our bestselling bed, the Povalis is now on sale with a 60 percent discount on its retail price. The Povalis can also be bought together with our new memory foam mattress, in a combo deal, where you will save almost 1,000 dollars off the usual price! We are offering massive discounts since we have to clear space for our new collection that will be launched in January next year! And only for this week, we provide a special corner for foreign sofa brands. This once-a-year sale is on till the 17th of December only. These deals are only available at our Stranton warehouse. Please visit our website for a complete table of what is available for this special sale. On the website, you can also find all the available delivery options. Believe it or not, you will be able to have a great discount on the shipping costs as well!

スマイル・アンド・シャインは現在1年に1回の在庫売り尽くしセールをしています。本当にありえるのかわからないほどのお値段でのセール家庭用品が見つかります！ 私たちのベストセラーのベッドである、ボバリスが60パーセントオフです。ボバリスは私たちの新しい低反発マットレスと一緒に購入が可能で、こちらのセットですともとのお値段より約1000ドルもお安くなります！ 私たちは来年の1月に発売予定の新しいコレクションを入荷するのにスペースを確保する必要があるため、大量のセールをしています！ また、今週に限り、海外ブランドのソファコーナーを設けています。この年1回のセールは12月の17日までのみとなっております。このようなお値段でのご購入は、私たちのストラントン倉庫でのみ行っております。私たちのウェブサイトでこの特別セールで購入できる商品の全リストを見ることができます。ウェブサイトでは、可能な配送手段についても参照できます。信じられないかもしれませんが、配送においても大幅割引を受けることができます！

Vocabulary
☐ **stock clearance** 在庫処理 ☐ **retail price** 小売価格
☐ **memory foam** ポリウレタンフォーム*枕などによく使われる素材 ☐ **combo deal** セット割引
☐ **massive** 巨大な、大きな ☐ **believe it or not** 信じようとそうでなかろうと

92 　正解 A

What is being advertised?
何が宣伝されていますか。

(A) House furnishing	(A) 家具	(A) 78.3%
(B) Kitchen equipment	(B) 調理器具	(B) 4.3%
(C) Second-hand clothing	(C) 古着	(C) 4.3%
(D) Cleaning tools	(D) 掃除道具	(D) 8.7%

解説　ベッド、マットレスなどが冒頭から紹介されているので、選択肢の中では(A)がこれに最適となります。他の選択肢の商品も売られている可能性はありますが、このスピーチの中では宣伝はされていません。ちなみに、正解にあるfurnishing(s)は、家具に加え家庭用品、雑貨品も含めて家庭用製品全般を指します。furniture（集合名詞でsはつけられない）は家具のみを指すのが一般的です。

Vocabulary
☐ **second-hand** 中古の

93　正解 C

According to the speaker, what will happen in January next year?
話者によると、来年の1月に何がありますか。

(A) The annual clearance sale will end.	(A) 年間クリアランスセールが終了します。	(A) 39.1%
(B) The warehouse's space will be empty.	(B) 倉庫のスペースが片付けられます。	(B) 4.3%
(C) The new collection will be launched.	**(C) 新しいコレクションが発表されます。**	**(C) 34.8%**
(D) Foreign sofa brands will become available.	(D) 外国のソファブランドが利用可能になります。	(D) 17.4%

解説　今回のセールは、次のシーズンのコレクション用のスペースを確保するための在庫処分セールと説明があり、we have to clear space for our new collection that will be launched in January next yearと予定が明記されていることから、(C)が正解とわかります。

94　正解 D

What can the listeners obtain from the company's website?
聴者は会社のウェブサイトで何ができますか。

(A) Tables and desks that are unavailable in stores	(A) 利用できないテーブルとデスク	(A) 17.4%
(B) A discount ticket for delivery	(B) 配達の割引チケット	(B) 34.8%
(C) A coupon for an additional discount	(C) 追加割引のクーポン	(C) 17.4%
(D) The list of available items	**(D) 利用可能なアイテムのリスト**	**(D) 26.1%**

解説　アナウンスメントの後半でPlease visit our website for a complete table of what is available for this special sale. とあり、これを直接的に示している(D)が正解となります。配達のオプションが掲載されていると発言していますが、そのための割引『チケット』が掲載されているとは言っていないので、(B)は誤りとなります。

Questions 95 through 97 refer to the following telephone message and list.
問題95-97は次の電話のメッセージと表に関するものです。

This message is for Jenny. Thank you very much for the price list. Our studio is rather big and it has a lot of windows, so it's quite helpful that you can respond to a high-volume order of curtains in such a short duration of time. When I visited one of your stores, I examined the available samples and had some ideas of what we would order, and the additional information you gave us helped me make a decision. Since we are always playing music in our studio at a loud volume, the noise-reducing ones are ideal. I know it does not block all the noise, but at least we can reduce the sound going out of the room. As for the thickness, we'll go with the thicker one for better noise reduction. And for the shipping, we prefer a morning arrival. I would appreciate it if you could call us at least an hour before the delivery so that our staff can get ready.

このメッセージはジェニー宛てです。価格表をありがとうございました。私たちのスタジオはかなり大きく、窓もたくさんあるので、カーテンの大量注文に対してこんなに短い時間で対応していただけてとても助かりました。私が店舗の1つに伺ったとき、私は使用可能なサンプルを調べて、注文するものについていくつかアイデアを持っており、そしてジェニーが私たちに教えてくださった追加の情報は私が決断するのに役に立ちました。私たちはいつもスタジオでかなり大きな音量で音楽を演奏しているので騒音を低減できるものが理想的です。すべての騒音を遮断するわけではないということはわかっていますが、少なくとも部屋から出る音を減らすことはできます。厚みについては、騒音を低減するために厚みのあるものを取り入れます。そして、配達について、私たちは朝の到着だとありがたいです。スタッフが準備できるように、少なくとも配達の1時間前には電話していただければ幸いです。

Curtain Type	Noise reduction property	Thickness
Type A	X	1 mm
Type B	X	1.5 mm
Type C	O	2.5 mm
Type D	O	4 mm

カーテンの種類	騒音対策	厚み
タイプ A	X	1ミリ
タイプ B	X	1.5ミリ
タイプ C	O	2.5ミリ
タイプ D	O	4ミリ

Vocabulary
☐ **high-volume order** 大量発注　☐ **noise-reducing** 遮音性の　☐ **reduction** 低減

95　正解 A

What is the caller pleased about?
電話主は何に満足していますか。

(A) The availability of a large quantity	**(A) 大量に利用できること**	**(A) 21.7%**
(B) The price of the products	(B) 商品の価格	(B) 13.0%
(C) The variation of options	(C) オプションの種類	(C) 26.1%
(D) The size of the curtains	(D) カーテンのサイズ	(D) 34.8%

解説　何に pleased（満足している）かというと、短期間の間に大量発注に対応してくれて助かるとの発言があることから、(A)が正解であると特定できます。high-volume の volume を注文の量とその場で認識できるかがポイントです。音量のボリュームと取ると話の全体像が見えなくなってしまいます。

96　正解 D

Look at the graphic. Which type of curtain will the caller most likely buy?
表を見てください。電話主はどのタイプのカーテンを購入しそうですか。

(A) Type A	(A) タイプA	(A) 8.7%
(B) Type B	(B) タイプB	(B) 4.3%
(C) Type C	(C) タイプC	(C) 30.4%
(D) Type D	**(D) タイプD**	**(D) 52.2%**

解説　遮音性があり、より厚いものを希望するという言及があったので、それを満たす Type D が最善のチョイスとなります。なお、完全な遮音を意図する言葉としては、soundproof や sound insulation という言葉があります。sound reduction はあくまで「遮音性」があるということで、完全に音の漏れを防ぐことは意図されておらず、問題の音声の中でもそれを認識している様子が出ていました。

97　正解 C

What does the caller request to the listener?
電話主は聴者に何を要求していますか。

(A) To deliver as quickly as possible	(A) できるだけ早く配達する	(A) 56.5%
(B) To call back before noon	(B) 正午までに折り返し電話する	(B) 13.0%
(C) To give a call well in advance	**(C) 事前に電話をかける**	**(C) 13.0%**
(D) To bring in the products quietly	(D) 製品を静かに持ち込む	(D) 13.0%

解説　メッセージの最後に、到着1時間前に電話が欲しいと告げているため、(C)が正解となります。

Vocabulary
☐ **in advance** 事前に

Questions 98 through 100 refer to the following telephone message and schedule.

問題98-100は次の電話のメッセージと予定表に関するものです。

Hi, Hiroki. Thank you very much for giving me the summary for the welcome ceremony for our new staff members next month. We will all welcome them and let them know that we are happy to have them here. As a president, I will make a brief speech, but the rest will be handled under your direction. One thing regarding the agenda, could you lengthen the last part? I'm sure the remarks need to be longer. We need to make sure the speaker maximumly motivates the new members. A motivational speech requires more time. So, this part must be adjusted. Lunch can start anytime after that. As for the tour, since they'll be visiting all of our departments, make sure to communicate with the department managers for any necessary help. Without proper coordination, things won't work as planned. Plan your work and work your plan.

こんにちは、ヒロキさん。来月の新入社員歓迎式典をまとめてくださりありがとうございました。私たちは彼らを歓迎し、ここに彼らを迎えることができてうれしいことを伝えます。社長として簡単なスピーチをしますが、他はあなたの指示で動きます。アジェンダについての1つ。アジェンダの最後の部分を長くしてください。コメントはもっと長い必要があると思います。演説者が新しいメンバーのモチベーションを最大化できるようにしてください。やる気を起こさせるスピーチをするにはもっと時間が必要です。したがって、この部分を調整する必要があります。その後はいつでも昼食を取れます。ツアーの部分は、すべての部署を訪問するので、必ず部長と連絡を取り、手助けが必要なら伝えてください。適切な調整がなければ、物事は計画どおりに進みません。仕事を計画し、計画を実行してください。

	Time	Agenda
I	10:00 - 10:20	Introductory speech
II	10:20 - 10:30	Company tour
III	11:15 - 11:30	President speech
IV	11:30 - 11:40	Concluding remarks

*An optional lunch session will follow
（Participation not mandatory）

	時間	アジェンダ
I	10:00 - 10:20	はじめに
II	10:20 - 10:30	社内ツアー
III	11:15 - 11:30	社長のごあいさつ
IV	11:30 - 11:40	結びの言葉

*オプションのランチセッションが続きます
（参加は必須ではありません）

98 **正解** C

What will the speaker's employees do next month?
話者の従業員は来月何をしますか。

(A) Start preparing for a welcome ceremony
(B) Attend a ceremony outside the company
(C) Welcome newly recruited staff members
(D) Receive feedback from the president

(A) 歓迎式典の準備を始める
(B) 社外の式典に出席する
(C) 採用されたスタッフを歓迎する
(D) 社長からのフィードバックをもらう

(A) 21.7%
(B) 21.7%
(C) 34.8%
(D) 17.4%

解説 冒頭の the welcome ceremony for our new staff members next month の部分から、歓迎式典が来月にあり、そのために準備を今進めていることがわかります。(C)が正解となります。

99 **正解** D

Look at the graphic. Which part of the schedule should be adjusted?
表を見てください。 スケジュールのどの部分を調整する必要がありますか。

(A) I
(B) II
(C) III
(D) IV

(A) I
(B) II
(C) III
(D) IV

(A) 4.3%
(B) 17.4%
(C) 43.5%
(D) 30.4%

解説 指示で、could you lengthen the last part? とあり、テーブルを参照すると、最後は結びの言葉であることが分かります。これは(D)に該当し、そのまま答えとなります。社長がモチベーショナルなスピーチをしても良さそうですが、今回は部下に託したようです。

100　正解 B

What does the speaker say the listener should do?
話者は聴者に何をすべきだと言っていますか。

(A) Let department managers lead the tour	(A) 部門マネージャーにツアーを主導させる	(A) 8.7%
(B) Ask for help when necessary	**(B) 必要に応じて助けを求める**	**(B) 47.8%**
(C) Make the lunch session mandatory	(C) ランチセッションを必須にする	(C) 17.4%
(D) Work harder in making a plan	(D) 計画を立てるのにもっと熱心に取り組む	(D) 21.7%

解説　coordination（調整）を連携してうまく図るように、との言葉があったので、この内容を最もうまく言い表している(B)が正解となります。(D)は、そのように思っている可能性はありますが、メッセージの中で言及はしていません。なお、最後のPlan your work and work your plan. というのは、英語のいわゆる格言です。出典は不明とされていますが、アメリカの軍隊の指揮官が言ったのではないかという説が有力です。すべきことをしっかり計画し、計画したならあとはそれを実行せよ、という言葉ですね。TOEICの990点への道にも通じるものがあるかもしれません。

Part5 短文穴埋め問題

101　正解 D　問題ジャンル　品詞

Commentators who specialize in the food service industry were asked to name restaurants that they come back to -------.

外食産業を専門とするコメンテーターたちは定期的に訪れるレストランの名前を挙げることを求められました。

(A) regulation	規制	(A) 43.5%	(C) regular	定期的な	(C) 17.4%
(B) regulate	規制する	(B) 17.4%	**(D) regularly**	**定期的に**	**(D) 17.4%**

解説　come back to the restaurants regularlyで定期的に訪れる（戻ってくる）レストランとなります。空欄の前のtoに局所的に注目しすぎて、to不定詞、to+名詞ではないか、と早とちりしないように、文全体の意味を捉えましょう。come back to以外にも、refer to、talk toもこの形で出てきます。

Vocabulary
□ **specialize in ~** ~を専門とする　□ **name** 名前を挙げる

102　正解 B　問題ジャンル　副詞

So as not to make the same error, all the users must read the written manual including the supplemental guide, and ------- decide which functions to use.

同じエラーを起こさないように、すべてのユーザーは補足ガイドを含むマニュアルを読んで、それから使用する機能を決める必要があります。

(A) thus	それがゆえ	(A) 0.0%	(C) so	だから	(C) 8.7%
(B) then	**そして**	**(B) 52.2%**	(D) to	ために	(D) 34.8%

解説　thenは何かプロセスを説明するときによく使います。「こうして、そして次はこうして」というときの「そして」がthenにあたります。文頭のSo as not to Vも空欄にされて出題されることがある表現です。

Vocabulary
□ **so as not to ~** ~しないように

103　正解 D　問題ジャンル　品詞

Upon the launch of the new service, Joshua Text Service announced that its primary goal is to maximize customer satisfaction even at the sacrifice of -------.

ジョシュア・テキスト・サービスは新しいサービス開始時に、収益性を犠牲にしてでも顧客満足度を最大化させることを主な目標としていると発表しました。

| (A) profiting | 収益を得ること | (A) 26.1% | (C) profitable | 収益性がある | (C) 13.0% |
| (B) profited | 収益を得た | (B) 4.3% | **(D) profitability** | **収益性** | **(D) 52.2%** |

解説 収益性（profitability）を犠牲にしてでも顧客満足度を上げる、という意味でしか意味的に、文法的に成立しません。profit（収益）という選択肢があったならば正解になり得ます。profits と可算名詞としても使えますが、読み手が具体的にどういう収益か想像できる場合に可算名詞として扱います。

Vocabulary
□ **at the sacrifice of** ～ ～を犠牲にして

104 　正解 C 　問題ジャンル 品詞

All employees of Mc MacManus Painting will receive ------- financial support for their residence.

マック・マクマナス・ペインティングのすべての従業員は住居のための広範囲な経済支援を受けます。

| (A) extend | 広げる | (A) 8.7% | **(C) extensive** | **広範囲にわたる** | **(C) 43.5%** |
| (B) extending | 広がっている | (B) 30.4% | (D) extent | 程度 | (D) 13.0% |

解説 extensiveで「広範囲にわたる」という形容詞です。extensive financial supportで「さまざまな手厚い経済支援」という意味で捉えましょう。つづりが一部似ているintensiveという単語がありますが、こちらは（程度が）強い、激しい、というニュアンスです。extensiveはextend（広げる）から派生しているだけあって、範囲の広さを言うときによく使います。

105 　正解 D 　問題ジャンル 品詞

Audience was obviously getting tired of the ------- discussions among the panelists.

聴講者は明らかにその長引いたパネリスト間の討論に疲れてきていました。

| (A) prolong | 長引く | (A) 13.0% | (C) prolongs | 長引く | (C) 0.0% |
| (B) prolonging | 長引かせる[形] | (B) 26.1% | **(D) prolonged** | **長引いた** | **(D) 56.5%** |

解説 discussion（討論）は、長引かされてるのであって、何かを長引かせているわけではないので、過去分詞のprolonged discussions（長引いた討論）が正解となります。

106　正解 A　問題ジャンル 副詞

If you listen to foreign songs, the words ------- seep into unconsciousness and help you remember new words.

外国の歌を聞くと、その言葉は徐々に無意識に浸透し、新しい言葉を覚えるのに役立ちます。

(A) gradually	次第に	**(A) 60.9%**	(C) approximately	おおよそ	(C) 13.0%
(B) correctly	正確に	(B) 13.0%	(D) routinely	ルーティン的に	(D) 8.7%

解説　andはseepとhelpを並列する役割を果たしています。だんだん浸透していくという意味でgraduallyを選ぶのが正解です。聞くのはルーティーンかもしれませんが、浸透するのはルーティーンではありませんので、routinelyは適切ではありません。

Vocabulary

☐ unconsciousness 無意識

107　正解 B　問題ジャンル 接続詞

We thank you for your order, but it may be two weeks ------- we can send the books to you.

ご注文に感謝いたしますが、本をお送りするまでに2週間ほどかかる場合があります。

(A) if	もしも	(A) 4.3%	(C) however	しかしながら	(C) 13.0%
(B) before	までに	**(B) 43.5%**	(D) while	間	(D) 34.8%

解説　本を送ることができる前におよそ2週間程度だろう、という解釈でbeforeが入ります。ifでは意味が通りませんが、even if（〜だったとしても）であれば可能でした。howeverは、「しかしながら」以外にも「いかに〜しようとも」という意味があります。

108　正解 D　問題ジャンル 副詞

If the secretaries work too -------, we might discover later that they made many filing errors.

秘書の仕事が速すぎると、私たちは後で彼らが多くのファイリングミスをしたことに気づくかもしれません。

(A) hardly	ほとんど〜でない	(A) 34.8%	(C) efficiently	効率的に	(C) 4.3%
(B) greatly	素晴らしく	(B) 4.3%	**(D) quickly**	**速く**	**(D) 52.2%**

解説　意味上どれが最も自然かと考えます。仕事が速いこと自体は良いのですが、「速すぎる」と、エラーが出てきそうだという意味で自然な流れができています。greatly, efficientlyも可能性は感じられますが、「素晴らしくできすぎているとエラーが出てくる」、「効率的にできすぎるとエラーが出る」、という意味合いが、「速くしすぎるとエラーが出る」の自然さに勝るとは判定されません。

Vocabulary

☐ secretary 秘書

109　正解 B　問題ジャンル 否定

The auditors pointed out two suspicious cases, but ------- was found to be an unlawful conduct.

監査役は2つの疑わしい事件を指摘しましたが、どちらも違法行為であるとは認められませんでした。

(A) none	一つも～ない	(A) 56.5%	(C) few　少数　(C) 0.0%
(B) neither	**どちらも～ない**	**(B) 34.8%**	(D) either　いずれかが　(D) 4.3%

解説　「2つの疑わしいケースがあり、いずれも違法ではない」とするのが「2つの疑わしいケースがあり、一つも[何も]違法ではない」とするより意味上、相性の上でより自然です。

Vocabulary

☐ **auditor** 監査官　＊昔は会計監査は口頭説明の聞き取りで行われており、それを「聞く」のが監査官の仕事だったことから。**audio** 音声、**audience** 聴講者 などと語源は同じ

110　正解 C　問題ジャンル 接続詞

Technical advice, ------- given at the beginning of the session or in the middle, must be taken as an absolute order.

セッションの開始時であろうと途中であろうと、技術的なアドバイスは絶対的な指示として考えなければなりません。

(A) those	それら	(A) 39.1%	**(C) whether**	**であろうと**	**(C) 30.4%**
(B) so	そのように	(B) 13.0%	(D) since	であるから	(D) 13.0%

解説　挿入で、「～であろうと～であろうと」という情報を挟んでいます。advice が不可算なので those は続けられません。those は those people who の省略形で頻出ですので、それはそれで留意です。

111　正解 A　問題ジャンル 前置詞句

------- mileage and other relevant conditions, the one we test-drove yesterday seems to be the most favorable.

走行距離やその他の関連条件を踏まえると、昨日試乗したものが一番好ましいようです。

(A) In terms of	**～の観点から**	**(A) 30.4%**	(C) In accordance with　～に沿って　(C) 34.8%
(B) In exchange for	～と引き換えに	(B) 26.1%	(D) In response to　～に応じて　(D) 4.3%

解説　in terms of で、～の観点で、～に関しての意味となります。問題文は「走行距離や他の条件の観点から考えると」、という入りになっています。他にも Inconsideration of、Considering が選択肢にあったならば正解となり得ます。Regardless of、Irrespective of も可能です。今回は不正解となっている選択肢の表現も、それぞれが TOEIC 頻出表現です。

112　正解 D　問題ジャンル　副詞

It has been ------- fifty years since the ex-king left his country to live in exile.

元国王が国を離れて亡命生活を送ってから約50年になります。

(A) closely	厳重に	(A) 21.7%	(C) wrongly	間違った形で	(C) 0.0%
(B) highly	とても	(B) 4.3%	**(D) nearly**	**ほとんど**	**(D) 69.6%**

解説　nearly 50 years では「50年近く」となります。near=近い のニュアンスがそのまま反映されています。他にもalmostが同じような意味で使われます。ニアミスのニアもnearです。nearlyは副詞ですが、nearにも副詞の使い方があります。The anniversary is drawing near. (記念日が近づいている)となります。この場合nearlyとは言いません。

Vocabulary

☐ **be in exile** 亡命中である

113　正解 B　問題ジャンル　名詞

All complaints need to be replied in a timely -------, so as to improve the company's image in the community.

コミュニティでの会社のイメージを向上させるために、すべての苦情にはタイムリーな方法で返信する必要があります。

(A) occasion	状況	(A) 17.4%	(C) limit	限界	(C) 17.4%
(B) manner	**方法**	**(B) 56.5%**	(D) necessity	必要性	(D) 4.3%

解説　in a 形容詞 manner / in a 形容詞 way / in a 形容詞 fashionで副詞です。(例：in a nice manner ≒ nicely)　今回はtimelyが形容詞ですから、in a timely fashionで副詞句となります。

114　正解 D　問題ジャンル　前置詞

We were disappointed that the new worker was unable to perform his duties ------- the normal time period.

新入社員が通常の時間内に職務を遂行できなかったことに失望した。

(A) above	～の上に	(A) 0.0%	(C) along	～に沿って	(C) 4.3%
(B) beyond	～を越えて	(B) 8.7%	**(D) within**	**～以内に**	**(D) 82.6%**

解説　文の意味を考えてみると正解が見えます。新入社員に失望している状況です。すべき仕事を通常の時間内でできなかったから失望しているというわけです。withinは「～以内」です。within 10 daysは10日以内です。一方でin 10 daysは10日後です。

115 正解 A 問題ジャンル 前置詞

------- their successful project on LED, the gross sales of the entire company did not increase a bit.

LEDのプロジェクトの成功にもかかわらず、会社全体の総売上高は少しも増加しませんでした。

(A) Notwithstanding　～にもかかわらず　**(A) 26.1%**　(C) Nevertheless　それであっても　(C) 47.8%

(B) However　　　　　しかしながら　　(B) 17.4%　(D) In spite　　　かかわらず　　(D) 4.3%

解説　notwithstandingで1単語です。前置詞で使えばdespiteと同じく「～にもかかわらず」という意味で使われます。Notwithstanding their successでも、Their success notwithstandingでも可能です。notwithstandingは副詞としても使うことができ、howeverと同じような意味と使い方になります。

Vocabulary
☐ **LED** 発光ダイオード　*light-emitting diode の略

116 正解 B 問題ジャンル 副詞

The electrician announced that the whole system will ------- be available unless other defects are discovered.

電気技師は、他の欠陥が発見されない限り、すべてのシステムがもうすぐ利用可能になると発表しました。

(A) already　　すでに　　　　(A) 21.7%　(C) only　　　だけ　　(C) 8.7%

(B) soon　　**すぐに**　　　　**(B) 56.5%**　(D) sometimes　時々　(D) 8.7%

解説　システムがすぐに使用可能になります、という文脈でsoonが正解となります。alreadyは「すでに」の意味なので未来形にはニュアンスがありません。*The tea will have already been served by this time tomorrow. とう未来完了形で「そのときまでにはすでに」という場合は可能です。

Vocabulary
☐ **defect** 欠陥

117 正解 A 問題ジャンル 副詞

All the overdue electricity bills had been handled before the service got suspended -------.

延滞した電気料金はすべて、サービスが一時的に停止される前に処理されていました。

(A) temporarily　一時的に　　　　**(A) 60.9%**　(C) domestically　国内的に　(C) 17.4%

(B) marginally　ほんのわずかに　(B) 8.7%　(D) predictably　予想通りに　(D) 8.7%

解説　電気サービスが「一時的に」停止される前に遅延分の支払いはすべて完了したという意味で、temporarilyが最も自然な意味の文を作ります。ある過去の1点より前にすでに、という過去完了形の典型的な文章です。predictablyは、文修飾でこの文の頭に置かれていたのであれば意味を成します。

118 　正解 D 　問題ジャンル　品詞

The store will be happy to refund your money on the condition that the item still has its sales tag -------.

アイテムに販売タグが付けられているのなら、全額返金させていただきます。

(A) attaching	付けている	(A) 21.7%
(B) to be attached	付けられている	(B) 8.7%
(C) attachment	付属	(C) 13.0%
(D) attached	付けられた	(D) 52.2%

解説　使役動詞haveの後に分詞が続く形です。タグは何かを付けているのではなく、付けられている側なので、attachingとすることはできません。過去分詞のattachedが正解です。

Vocabulary

□ **on condition that** ～　～という条件で

119 　正解 D 　問題ジャンル　人称代名詞

Unlike the prototype developed by our competitors, ------- can fully recharge itself without any human commands.

競合他社が開発したプロトタイプとは異なり、当社のは人間の命令なしで完全に充電できます。

(A) we	私たち	(A) 60.9%
(B) us	私たちを	(B) 0.0%
(C) ourselves	私たち自身	(C) 8.7%
(D) ours	私たちのもの	(D) 26.1%

解説　ここには主語になるような代名詞が入る必要があります。よって目的語として使われる(B)や(C)は不自然で不正解です。Unlike the prototype developed by our competitors「競合他社が開発したプロトタイプとは異なり」とあるので、比較するのは同じくプロトタイプであると想定できます。そう考えると、we「私たち（当社）」という主語を使うのは不自然なので(A)は不正解です。ours「私たちの（当社の）もの」というのは、プロトタイプのことを指すので当てはまります。よって正解は(D)となります。

Vocabulary

□ **prototype** 原型、開発段階の模型　　□ **recharge** 充電する

120 　正解 B 　問題ジャンル　前置詞

The postcard they sent me shows that Parker's new office is located ------- 375 West Oak Street.

彼らが送ってくれたはがきは、Parkerの新しいオフィスが375西オーク通りにあることを示しています。

(A) onto	の上に	(A) 13.0%
(B) at	に(番地を含む場合)	(B) 26.1%
(C) on	に(通りの場合)	(C) 47.8%
(D) beneath	の下に	(D) 8.7%

解説 市や町レベルにはin (in Yokohama, in Kinshicho)、通りレベルにはon (on 7th Street, on Atlantic Boulevard)、番地が入った住所にはat (at 3-39-5 Supreme-ueno, Showa Street) となります。ここでは「375...」と番地を含んでいますので、(B)が正解です。

121 　正解 A 　問題ジャンル 形容詞

The accused man was judged to be innocent in the murder trial since the prosecutors could only provide ------- evidence.

検察官は状況証拠しか提供できなかったため、被告人は殺人裁判で無実であると判断されました。

(A) circumstantial	**状況的な**	**(A) 56.5%**	(C) disposable	使い捨ての	(C) 13.0%
(B) second-hand	中古の	(B) 21.7%	(D) environmental	自然環境の	(D) 4.3%

解説 evidence「証拠」の前に入るので、この問題ではどんな証拠しか提供できなかったのかを考える必要があります。circumstantial evidence「状況証拠」という表現があるので、正解は(A)です。この表現を知っていればすぐわかる問題ですが、知らなくても消去法でも答えは導き出せます。「中古の」という意味の(B)、「使い捨ての」という意味の(C)、「環境的な」という意味の(D)は、evidence「証拠」という単語と合わせると不自然です。

Vocabulary
☐ **trial** 裁判 　☐ **prosecutor** 検察官

122 　正解 B 　問題ジャンル 接続詞

A good manager must understand the temperament of his workers and understand that frustration after losing a customer can either lead to absenteeism ------- a lack of motivation.

優れたマネージャーは、労働者の人間の気質を理解し、顧客を失った後の欲求不満は、欠勤または意欲の欠如につながる可能性があることを理解しなければなりません。

(A) but	しかし	(A) 8.7%	(C) nor	また〜でもない	(C) 13.0%
(B) or	**または**	**(B) 65.2%**	(D) yet	まだ	(D) 8.7%

解説 この問題ではeitherがポイントとなります。either A or Bで、「AまたはB」という意味になる表現です。これはこの表現を知っていれば解ける問題ですが、(C)と間違いがちです。norはneither A nor Bで「AでもBでもない」という表現になります。この違いはしっかりと押さえておきましょう。

Vocabulary
☐ **temperament** 気質

123 　正解 C 　問題ジャンル　動詞

Parents should be ------- from doing their children's homework for them since children need to learn how to think for themselves.

子供たちは自分で考える方法を学ぶ必要があるので、親は子供たちの宿題をすることを思いとどまるべきです。

(A) informed	通達される	(A) 17.4%	
(B) given up	諦めさせられる	(B) 26.1%	
(C) discouraged	**思いとどまらされる**	**(C) 34.8%**	
(D) recommended	推奨される	(D) 17.4%	

解説　discourage人from ~ ingで「人が~するのを思いとどまらせる」という熟語です。このfrom ~ ingの形で「妨げる」に近い意味を持つバリエーションは幾つかあります。ban, dissuade, keep, prevent, prohibit, restrain, stopなどです。

124 　正解 C 　問題ジャンル　名詞

Online -------, many marketers say, is one of the most crucial processes that streamlines the shopping experience of all visitors.

多くのマーケターによると、オンラインカタログは、すべてのお客さまのショッピング体験を合理化する最も重要な方法の1つです。

(A) catalog	カタログ	(A) 47.8%	
(B) catalogs	カタログ（複数）	(B) 21.7%	
(C) cataloging	**一覧表を作ること**	**(C) 21.7%**	
(D) cataloged	一覧化された	(D) 4.3%	

解説　catalogは可算名詞で、単数で使うなら An online catalog is、複数形で使うなら、Online catalogs areとなりますが、問題文はその形をしていないので、(A)(B)ではないと分かります。何かを一覧化することは、作業効率を高めてくれる、という意味でcatalogingが正解となります。

Vocabulary
□ **streamline** 合理化する

125 　正解 C 　問題ジャンル　形容詞

As ------- as I can remember, Josh was always on good terms with his coworkers including Mina.

私が覚えている限り、ジョシュはミナを含む彼の同僚といつも仲が良かった。

(A) well	同様に	(A) 47.8%	
(B) early	できるだけ早く	(B) 4.3%	
(C) far	**~限り**	**(C) 26.1%**	
(D) long	~さえしてくれれば	(D) 17.4%	

解説　as far as ~で、「~な限り」という決まったフレーズです。よって正解は(C)になります。as well as ~は「~も同様に」という意味で、andのように前後に言葉が必要なので(A)は不正解です。(B)を挿入すると、as early as「早くも」という意味になり、続くI can remember「私が覚えている」という文言と合わせると文脈的に不自然です。as long as ~は「~さえしていれば」という表現なので、(D)もI can rememberと合わせると不自然です。as far asとas long asは混同しがちなので押さえておきましょう。

□ **as long as** 〜さえしてくれれば、〜限り

126　正解 B　問題ジャンル 仮定法

------- she been elected as the team leader, she could have organized the team more efficiently.

彼女がチームリーダーに選出されていれば、チームをより効率的に編成できたはずです。

(A) Has	もし〜なら	(A) 13.0%	(C) Unless	〜でない限り	(C) 26.1%
(B) Had	**もし〜だったなら**	**(B) 43.5%**	(D) Should	万が一〜なら	(D) 13.0%

解説　構文は仮定法過去完了の倒置です。問題文の後半で、could have organizedと続いているので、前半は過去完了形になることが分かります。hadを頭に持ってきてifを省略することで、仮定法過去完了の倒置を作ることができます。shouldは、Should there be any problem（万が一問題があれば）と「万が一」の意味でifとともに使われ、倒置を起こすこともよくあります。

127　正解 A　問題ジャンル 関係代名詞

The picture we want is one ------- can talk to the viewers' hearts and motivate them when they see it.

私たちが欲しいのは、見る人の心に語りかけ、見たときにやる気を起こすことができる写真です。

(A) that	**〜する（先行詞を含まない）**	**(A) 56.5%**	(C) it	それ	(C) 13.0%
(B) what	〜する（先行詞を含む）	(B) 13.0%	(D) those	それら	(D) 13.0%

解説　oneが先行詞で、これに関係代名詞thatが続いている文です。The picture we want is this one. This one can talk to viewers' heart. このthis oneがone thatとなって、2つの文がつながっています。whatを関係代名詞で使う場合は、what自体が先行詞の役割も担います。今回の文章ではoneという先行詞がすでにあるので、whatを空欄に入れることはできません。

128　正解 C　問題ジャンル 品詞

The updated rate of this VAT will be applied to an online ------- that takes place not only in Australia but also in New Zealand.

更新されたこのVATの税率は、オーストラリアだけでなくニュージーランドでのオンラインでの買い物にも適用されます。

(A) purchasing	購入すること	(A) 39.1%	**(C) purchase**	**購入（単数）**	**(C) 30.4%**
(B) purchased	購入された	(B) 13.0%	(D) purchases	購入（複数）	(D) 13.0%

解説　anという冠詞がポイントになります。この冠詞によって、空欄部分には単数の名詞が入ることがわかります。よって、過去分詞である（B）と複数形である（D）は不正解であることがわかります。（A）は動名詞ですが、このような〜 ingを名詞として使うときは、基本的に冠詞はつきませんので不自然です。よって正解は（C）の最もシンプルな名詞になります。purchaseは動詞としても使えますが、名詞としても使えることを知っていないと解けない問題なので、押さえておきましょう。

129 正解 **B** 問題ジャンル 名詞

The managers do not have infinite wisdom, but try to do the best ------- they can about the company's future.

マネージャーは無限の知恵を持っていないが、会社の未来について彼らができる最善の分析をしようとします。

(A) review　　復習・評論　　(A) 30.4%　(C) influence　影響　　(C) 13.0%
(B) analysis　**分析**　　**(B) 52.2%**　(D) interest　関心　　(D) 0.0%

解説　後ろのthey can「彼らができる」がこの空欄部分を修飾しているので、「影響」という意味の(C)や「関心」という意味の(D)は不自然で不正解です。また、about the company's future「会社の未来について」という文言から、「(過去の)見直し」という意味の(A)は不自然であることがわかります。よって正解は「分析」という意味の(B)となります。分析であれば、未来についての話題でも自然でしょう。

Vocabulary
□ **infinite** 無限の

130 正解 **C** 問題ジャンル 副詞

All newly recruited engineers are ------- dispatched to one of our subsidiary companies for training.

新たに採用されたエンジニアは全員慣例通り当社の子会社のうちの1つに研修のために派遣されます。

(A) inaccurately　不正確に　(A) 26.1%　**(C) customarily**　**慣例通りに**　**(C) 30.4%**
(B) responsibly　責任を持って　(B) 34.8%　(D) knowingly　故意に　　(D) 4.3%

解説　be dispatchedで「派遣される」という意味です。会社の派遣を不正確にすることは不自然なので(A)は不正解です。(B)や(D)は派遣される上で当たり前なので、わざわざ入れるのは不自然でしょう。customary（習慣的な、慣例的な）の形容詞も併せて覚えておきましょう。

Vocabulary
□ **dispatch** 派遣する　□ **subsidiary company** 子会社

Part6 長文穴埋め問題

Questions 131-134 refer to the following instructions.
問題131-134は次の指示書に関するものです。

Dear All, Please be aware that the policy concerning our customer service -------. _{131.} I am certain ①all of you have already been following the updated procedure, but for any request about replacement, we send a new item to the customer regardless of the reason for the request. The most ------- reasons for a replacement include ② _{132.} the wrong size or color of the shipped products, which ③account for over 90 percent of complaints. ④------- _{133.} there be any request for a refund without a receipt, let the caller know that printed proof is an absolute requirement. -------. _{134.}	すべての従業員へ カスタマーサービスに関するポリシーが変更されましたのでご注意ください。 ①すでに更新された手順に従っているかと思いますが、交換のご要望については、理由を問わず、お客さまに新しい商品をお送りします。 ③クレームの90パーセント以上を占める交換の最も頻繁な理由に、②間違ったサイズや色が出荷されたことが含まれます。④領収書なしで払い戻しのご要望がある場合は、印刷での証明が絶対条件であることをお客さまにお知らせください。これらのお客さまは状況に関係なく返金を受けることはありません。

Vocabulary
□ **replacement** 交換　□ **regardless of** 〜 〜にかかわらず　□ **account for** 〜 〜を占める

131　正解 C　問題ジャンル　時制

(A) change	(A)変える	(A) 13.0%
(B) was changing	(B)変わっていた	(B) 0.0%
(C) has changed	**(C)変わった**	**(C) 30.4%**
(D) will be changed	(D)変えられるだろう	(D) 52.2%

解説　下線①「すでに更新された手順に従っている」という部分から、ポリシーはすでに変更済みであることがわかります。よって、現在形の(A)や未来形の(D)は除外されます。(B)は過去形ですが、進行形なので、変更の最中というニュアンスがあり不自然です。よって正解は(C)となります。(C)の現在完了形は変更された状態が今も続いているという継続を表しているので最も自然です。

132　正解 A　問題ジャンル 形容詞

(A) frequent	(A) 頻繁な	(A) 26.1%
(B) serious	(B) 深刻な	(B) 43.5%
(C) evident	(C) 明らかな	(C) 8.7%
(D) fundamental	(D) 基礎的な	(D) 17.4%

解説　下線③「クレームの90パーセント以上を占める」という文言から、ここで述べられている下線②「間違ったサイズや色の出荷」という理由が一番多いことがわかります。なので、空欄に最も自然に当てはまる(A)が正解です。(B)、(C)、(D)も自然に当てはまるように感じますが、reasonsと複数形なので、もし深刻であったり、明らかであったり、基礎的なものだった場合は、他にも理由を挙げるのが自然でしょう。実際のTOEICテストでは、もう少し排除しやすい誤答選択肢となっていますが、あえて難易度を高く設定したハイレベル模試ということで、選択肢間の優劣の差を意図的に小さくしています。

133　正解 A　問題ジャンル 仮定法

(A) Should	(A) 万が一	(A) 43.5%
(B) Might	(B) 〜かもしれない	(B) 4.3%
(C) If	(C) もし〜	(C) 43.5%
(D) Unless	(D) 〜でない限り	(D) 4.3%

解説　If there should be any request（万が一要望があれば）という表現の倒置です。shouldを頭に持ってきてifを省略します。否定なら、Should you not receive any inquiry, とnotは元の場所に残しておきます。他に、Were I the decision-maker（私が意思決定者だったならば）のようにbe動詞を前に出すパターンもあります。

134　正解 C　問題ジャンル 文脈

(A) A rebate is a certain type of token that can be exchanged with cash or credits.	(A) 払い戻しは現金またはクレジットと交換できる特定の種類の引換券です。	(A) 30.4%
(B) We are trying to figure out how we can minimize errors in shipping.	(B) 配送のエラーを最小限に抑える方法を模索しています。	(B) 34.8%
(C) **These customers will not receive any money back irrespective of the circumstances.**	(C) **これらのお客さまは状況に関係なく返金を受けることはありません。**	(C) 21.7%
(D) We highly appreciate it if you could increase your working hours.	(D) 労働時間を増やしていただけるとありがたいです。	(D) 8.7%

解説　下線④「領収書なしで払い戻しのご要望がある場合は、印刷での証明が絶対条件であることをお客さまにお知らせください」という前の文から、領収書がないと払い戻し不可であることがわかります。These customers「これらのお客さま」というのは前文の領収書なしで払い戻しのご要望があるお客さまのことだと想定すると、自然に当てはまります。よって正解は(C)となります。

Vocabulary

☐ **irrespective of 〜** 〜にかかわらず

Questions 135-138 refer to the following letter.

問題135-138は次の手紙に関するものです。

Dear Returns Representative:

I am a collector of German cuckoo clocks. Two days ago, my German Timekeeper clock -------135. to slow down and keep irregular time. The clock has kept accurate time for the past four months. ①I have been very careful to follow the instructions for keeping my clock in good condition, -------136. ②I am certain that I am not responsible for any damage to the clock.

-------137. ③It clearly states that German Timekeeper will replace any clock that does not keep correct time without charge.

I am sending you the damaged clock along with my receipt. I hope that you can send me a -------138. within the next two weeks. My address is written on the receipt.

Thank you for your kind attention.

Best regards,

James Heisenberg

ジャーマン・タイムキーパー返品担当者さまへ

私はドイツの鳩時計のコレクターです。2日前、私のジャーマン・タイムキーパーの時計は遅くなり始め、不規則な時間を指すようになりました。時計は過去4カ月間正確な時刻を保っていました。①私は時計を適切な状態に保つための指示に従うように細心の注意を払っていますので、②時計の損傷については責任がないと確信しています。

保証方針を注意深く読みました。③ジャーマン・タイムキーパーは、正しい時刻を示さない時計を無料で交換することを明確に述べています。

破損した時計を領収書と一緒にお送りします。2週間以内に交換品を送っていただければ幸いです。私の住所は領収書に書かれています。

ご確認ありがとうございます。

よろしくお願いします。

ジェームズ・ハイゼンバーグ

135　正解 B　問題ジャンル 時制

(A) have begun	(A) 始まった	(A) 34.8%
(B) was beginning	(B) 始まっていた	(B) 47.8%
(C) will begin	(C) 始まるだろう	(C) 4.3%
(D) begins	(D) 始まる	(D) 8.7%

解説　この挿入問題では、Two days ago「2日前」という部分が鍵になります。ここでこの文は過去の話であることがわかりますので、(C)の未来形や(D)の現在形は入りません。(A)の完了形なら過去から始まることに使えるのではないかと思ってしまいますが、(A)も不正解です。2日前というピンポイントの時点を表しているので、継続を表す完了形は使えません。よって、正解は(B)になります。

136　正解 C　問題ジャンル 接続詞

(A) though	(A) だが	(A) 17.4%
(B) or	(B) または	(B) 13.0%
(C) so	(C) なので	(C) 39.1%
(D) but	(D) しかし	(D) 26.1%

解説　空欄部分の前後の文を分けて、前後でどのような関係性があるか考えてみましょう。下線①「私は時計を適切な状態に保つための指示に従うように細心の注意を払っている」という前の文と、下線②「時計の損傷については責任がないと確信している」という後の文の間には因果関係があります。なので、(C)が正解となります。(A)や(D)は逆接で、前後が逆のことを言っている必要があるので不正解です。

137　正解 A　問題ジャンル 文脈

(A) I have carefully read your warranty policy.	(A) 保証方針を注意深く読みました。	(A) 56.5%
(B) Do you have any concerns?	(B) 何か心配はありますか。	(B) 4.3%
(C) I am living close to one of your stores.	(C) 私はあなたのお店の近くに住んでいます。	(C) 4.3%
(D) I am deeply disappointed about this.	(D) 私はこれに深く失望しています。	(D) 30.4%

解説　この挿入問題では、次の文のItが鍵になります。このItは何かがわからないので、この空欄部分で述べる必要があります。下線③「それはジャーマン・タイムキーパーが正しい時刻を示さない時計を無料で交換することを明確に述べている」と書いてあります。つまりItは、そのような明記があるようなものを指すことになります。それは(A)にあるwarranty policy「保証方針」が適切でしょう。よって正解は(A)になります。(B)や(D)は段落の初め、つまり話が切り替わるポイントで出てくるには不自然な文なので不正解です。(C)も文脈的に唐突なので不自然で不正解です。

Vocabulary
☐ **warranty policy** 保証方針　☐ **be closed to** ～ ～に近い

138 　正解 A 　　問題ジャンル　名詞

(A) replacement	(A) 交換品	**(A) 65.2%**
(B) warranty	(B) 保証	(B) 17.4%
(C) prize	(C) 賞品	(C) 8.7%
(D) receipt	(D) 領収書	(D) 4.3%

解説　下線③「それはジャーマン・タイムキーパーが無料で正しい時刻を示さない時計を交換することを明確に述べている」という文から、故障したものと交換してくれることがわかります。なので、I hope that you can send me 〜「〜を送ってほしい」の空欄には、(A)の交換品が入るのが最も自然で正解です。(B)は交換品のように具体的でないので不自然です。(C)は文脈上突然なので間違いです。(D)は購入者側から送るものなので間違いです。

Vocabulary

□ **replacement** 交換品　□ **prize** 賞品

Questions 139-142 refer to the following report.
問題139-142は次の報告書に関するものです。

The grant proposal was finally approved last week, and we can finally start making the planned changes to our technology-driven, next generation aquarium. ①All the water tanks are finely monitored and controlled by the automated maintenance system. -------.
139.

Changes like these contribute to making the life of these creatures stable and pleasant. Our trained robot guides ------- detailed explanations about the organisms that are swimming right in front of the visitors.
140.

People can ask questions to the AI-equipped guides, and ------- ②they are simple enough, ③the intelligent guide will satisfy their curiosity.
141.

The funding will be allocated to many other technological improvements for the facility. -------, part of the grant will be the source of our future research on marine organisms.
142.

助成金の申請は先週ようやく承認されたので、技術主導型の次世代水族館へと計画した変更を加えることができるようになりました。①すべての水槽は、自動メンテナンスシステムによって細かく監視および制御されます。給餌作業でさえも完全に自動化されます。

このような変更は、生き物の生活を安定させ、快適にすることに役立ちます。訓練を受けたロボットガイドが、訪問者の前で泳いでいる生物について詳しく説明します。

人々はAIを備えたガイドに質問をすることができ、そして②質問が十分に単純であれば、③知的なガイドはあなたの好奇心を満たしてくれます。

資金は、施設の他の多くの技術的改善に割り当てられます。さらには、助成金の一部は海洋生物に関する将来の研究の源となるでしょう。

Vocabulary
☐ **grant** 助成金　☐ **technology-driven** 技術主導型の　☐ **automated** 自動化された
☐ **creature** 生き物　☐ **organism** 生き物　☐ **AI-equipped** AIを搭載した

139　正解 A　問題ジャンル　文脈

(A) Even feeding tasks are fully automated.	(A) 給餌作業でさえも完全に自動化されます。	**(A) 21.7%**
(B) Let me introduce some of the changes we are making.	(B) 私たちが行っている変更のいくつかを紹介させてください。	(B) 52.2%
(C) What we are trying to make is more stable habitats for the animals.	(C) 私たちがつくろうとしているのは、動物にとってより安定した生息地です。	(C) 17.4%
(D) It does not necessarily mean that we can accommodate more fish.	(D) 必ずしもより多くの魚を飼育できるという意味ではありません。	(D) 4.3%

解説　the planned changesという文言から変更は予定されているもので現在行われているものではないことがわかります。よって(B)は不正解です。(C)は次の段落の話と重複するので、ここで出てくるのは不自然です。(D)も特に飼育量の話が出ているわけでもないので、話の流れ的に突然です。なので、(D)も不正解です。よって正解は(A)となります。(A)は前の文の下線①に付け加えたような文なので自然です。

140　正解 B　問題ジャンル　時制

(A) for providing	(A) 与えるために	(A) 30.4%
(B) will be providing	**(B) 与えているだろう**	**(B) 47.8%**
(C) to be provided	(C) 与えられる予定の	(C) 0.0%
(D) would have provided	(D) 与えていただろう	(D) 17.4%

解説　ここには文法的に動詞が入る必要があるので、まず(A)や(C)は間違いです。(D)はwould have＋過去分詞で、「与えていただろう」という過去に関して話していますので、これも不自然です。よって正解は(B)になります。(B)はwillを使った未来形なので、自然です。Our trained robot guidesで1つの名詞「訓練を受けたわれわれのロボットガイド」として捉えられるかも重要です。Our trained robot（主語）guides（動詞）と捉えると文の構造と意味がわからなくなります。

141　正解 D　問題ジャンル　接続詞

(A) given	(A) 与えられた	(A) 17.4%
(B) although	(B) しかし	(B) 26.1%
(C) unless	(C) でない限り	(C) 21.7%
(D) as long as	**(D) である限り**	**(D) 30.4%**

解説　(A)は後ろに名詞が来る必要があるので、(A)は文法的に間違いです。次に、どんな条件下で下線③「知的なガイドはあなたの好奇心を満たしてくれる」かということを踏まえて考えてみましょう。条件は下線②「質問が十分に単純である」ことです。この文を条件として表すには(B)は不自然です。また、(C)は暗に複雑な方が答えやすいということになってしまうので不自然です。よって(D)が最も自然で正解です。

142　正解 B　問題ジャンル　接続副詞

(A) Regardless	(A) 関係なく	(A) 4.3%
(B) Moreover	**(B) さらには**	**(B) 34.8%**
(C) Otherwise	(C) さもなくば	(C) 8.7%
(D) Therefore	(D) したがって	(D) 47.8%

解説　カンマが後に来るので、接続副詞が挿入されます。この時点で(A)は、接続詞的な役割がないので、文法的に誤りです。(C)のさもなくば、も前後の流れが不自然になります。資金が技術的改善に使われるから助成金の一部は海洋生物の研究の源になるというのは文脈的に不自然なので、(D)も不正解です。この目的に加え、他にもこの目的で資金が使われる、という流れを作る(B)が正解となります。

Questions 143-146 refer to the following announcement.

問題143-146は次のお知らせに関するものです。

West Atlantic Airways made an announcement that it has decided to ------- ① the operation of one third of their flights, until at least next December. 143.	ウエストアトランティック航空は、少なくとも来年12月まで、①フライトの3分の1の運航を停止することを決定したと発表しました。
This temporary measure was due to the continuously decreasing bookings, becoming serious at the start of this year. During this time, all the ------- subject to this change will be unavailable. 144.	この一時的な措置は、今年の初めから深刻になっている予約の継続的な減少により取られました。この期間中、変更の対象となるすべての航空機が使用不可となります。
According to the spokesman, ②the company will re-start offering all flights whenever appropriate, but it is expected that, for the first few months, the operations will be carried out still at a ------- pace. 145.	広報担当者によると、②同社は必要に応じてすべてのフライトを再開する予定ですが、最初の数カ月間は、まだ頻度を少なくして運用が行われると予想されます。
Annotation: ------. Details about any modifications regarding the measure will be posted online. 146.	注釈: 状況やスケジュールは随時変更される場合があります。措置に関する変更の詳細は、オンラインで掲載されます。

Vocabulary

☐ **one third** 3分の1　☐ **temporary** 一時的な　☐ **measure** 措置

143　正解 B　問題ジャンル　動詞

(A) abandon	(A) 放棄する	(A) 30.4%
(B) suspend	**(B) 停止する**	**(B) 34.8%**
(C) advertise	(C) 宣伝する	(C) 8.7%
(D) promote	(D) 促進する	(D) 21.7%

解説　下線①「フライトの3分の1の運航」をどうするかという動詞を挿入する問題です。文脈的に、(C)や(D)のようなポジティブな印象の動詞はふさわしくありませんので、不正解です。(A)は下線②「同社はすべてのフライトを再開する予定」という文言から、再開の予定があり、完全に放棄したわけではないことがわかります。よって正解は(B)となります。suspendには「つるす」という意味もあります。ズボンにパチンとやるsuspenderは想像しやすい例です。

144　正解 C　問題ジャンル 名詞

(A) vessels	(A) 船舶	(A) 4.3%
(B) automobiles	(B) 自動車	(B) 8.7%
(C) aircraft	**(C) 航空機**	**(C) 69.6%**
(D) railways	(D) 鉄道	(D) 13.0%

解説　最初のWest Atlantic Airwaysやflightsという言葉を見逃さなければ、正解が導き出せます。craft自体は、「船」という意味も「飛行機」という意味もあります。airをつけると飛行機、spaceをつけると宇宙船となります。ほかにもたとえばcraft beer（クラフトビール）のように、「熟練した技術」という意味もあります。

145　正解 A　問題ジャンル 品詞

(A) reduced	**(A) 減らされた**	**(A) 39.1%**
(B) reduce	(B) 減らす	(B) 13.0%
(C) reduction	(C) 削減	(C) 13.0%
(D) reducing	(D) 減らしている	(D) 30.4%

解説　前に冠詞のa、後ろに名詞のpaceが続くので、ここに入るのは、名詞のpaceを修飾する形容詞です。なので、動詞である(B)と名詞である(C)は文法上当てはまりません。(A)と(D)はどちらも形容詞として使えますが、正解は(A)です。(D)の場合、「(paceが) 減らしている」という意味になり不自然です。paceは減らされた側なので、(A)が自然です。どの単語を修飾しているのかを見極めることが重要です。

146　正解 D　問題ジャンル 文脈

(A) Thank you very much for always flying with us.	(A) いつも弊社をお選びいただきありがとうございます。	(A) 21.7%
(B) A gradual increase in flights is the key to their success.	(B) フライトを徐々に増やすことが、彼らの成功の秘訣です。	(B) 13.0%
(C) The list of frequently asked questions may not be comprehensive.	(C) よくある質問のリストはわかりづらい場合があります。	(C) 8.7%
(D) The conditions and schedules are subject to change at any time.	**(D) 状況やスケジュールは随時変更される場合があります。**	**(D) 52.2%**

解説　Annotation「注釈」という言葉があるので、この部分には何か注意や備考が挿入されることがわかります。よって、(A)や(B)はふさわしくないことがわかります。(C)はAnnotationとしては自然ですが、本文でfrequently asked questions「よくある質問」について触れていないので突然出てくるのは不自然で不正解です。よって、正解は(D)となります。be subject to change「変更される場合がある」という表現は頻出ですので押さえておきましょう。

Part 7 読解問題

Questions 147-148 refer to the following instructions.
問題147-148は次の指示書に関するものです。

Attention, all visitors

Thank you for choosing to visit our Innovation and Design Hub today. Before you step into the Production Department, we would like to remind you of the following guidelines.

For security purposes, we DO NOT allow any recording devices in the Production Department. This includes any cell phones, laptops, voice recorders, video cameras, etc. If you wish to record any part of the production process, please refer to the given manual on how to get in touch with our Public Relations Department.

To avoid a fine, please leave all electronic devices at reception when you check in for your tour of our facility.

注意　ご来社された皆さまへ

本日は、イノベーションとデザインの中枢施設にお越しいただき、ありがとうございます。生産部門に入る前に、以下のガイドラインについてお知らせします。

セキュリティ上の理由から、録音デバイスを生産部門へ持ち込むことは許可されていません。これには、携帯電話、ラップトップ、レコーダー、ビデオカメラなどが含まれます。制作プロセスの一部を記録したい場合は、所定のマニュアルで広報部門への連絡方法についてご参照ください。

罰金を回避するために、当施設のツアーにチェックインする際に、フロントにすべての電子機器を預けてください。

Vocabulary
☐ **hub** ハブ、中枢　　☐ **step into ~** ~に入っていく　　☐ **electronic devices** 電子機器

147　正解 A

What is the purpose of this notification?
この通知の目的は何ですか。

(A) To specify rules for tour attendees	**(A) ツアー参加者のルールを明確にするため**	**(A) 60.9%**
(B) To collect fines for violation	(B) 違反に対する罰金を徴収するため	(B) 8.7%
(C) To make the facility open to the public	(C) 施設を一般に公開するため	(C) 8.7%
(D) To record the production process	(D) 製造工程を記録するため	(D) 17.4%

解説　生産部門に立ち入るにあたり、電子機器は持って入ってはいけないという内容で、禁止物を列挙していることから、ツアー参加者へのルールを明示する目的で出された通知（A）であることがわかります。（B）、（C）は事実なのかもしれませんが、それらの目的のためにこの通知文が出されたわけではないので誤りとなります。

148　正解 D

Which section grants permission to record?
どの部門が録音の許可を与えますか。

(A) The Innovation and Design Hub	(A) イノベーションとデザインハブ	(A) 17.4%
(B) The Production Department	(B) 生産部門	(B) 26.1%
(C) The Legal Department	(C) 法務部	(C) 4.3%
(D) The Public Relations Department	**(D) 広報部**	**(D) 47.8%**

解説　第2パラグラフの最後に、get in touch with our Public Relation Departmentとあり、この部分から（D）広報部が正解であると特定できます。

Vocabulary
□ **grant** 許可を出す

Questions 149-150 refer to the following questionnaire.
問題149-150は次のアンケートに関するものです。

Bliz Mobile invites you to take this short questionnaire to enter our annual draw to win prizes worth up to 100,000 dollars. All you need to do is complete the short form below and submit it via e-mail to annualdraw@bliz-mobile.com.

Name:
Age:
City you live in:

• What are the 3 most and least important things to you when choosing a new phone plan?
• What is the monthly budget you reserve for your mobile network plan?
• What influences this budget and what could prompt you to increase this amount?

短いアンケートに答えて、ブリッツ・モバイル社毎年恒例の抽選に参加し、最高で10万ドル相当の賞品を獲得しましょう。参加に必要な手続きは、以下の短いフォームに記入し、それをメールでannualdraw@bliz-mobile.comに送信することのみです。

名前：
年齢：
住んでいる都市：

・ 新しい電話プランを選択するときに最も重要な/重要でない3つの要素は何ですか。
・ モバイルネットワークプランのための1カ月の予算は幾らですか。
・ この予算に影響を与えるものは何ですか。また何があれば予算額は上がりえますか。

Vocabulary
□ **draw** くじ　　□ **reserve** 取っておく

149　正解　D

What can be inferred about the questionnaire?
アンケートについて何が推測されていますか。

(A) There is an age restriction.	(A) 年齢制限があります。	(A) 26.1%
(B) Winners can receive cash.	(B) 当選者は現金を受け取ることができます。	(B) 47.8%
(C) A full address is required.	(C) 住所が必要です。	(C) 4.3%
(D) It takes place periodically.	**(D) 定期的に行われます。**	**(D) 17.4%**

解説　1行目に Bliz Mobile invites you to take this short questionnaire to enter our annual draw to win prizes worth up to 100,000 dollars. とあり、annual draw（毎年恒例の抽選）とあることから、定期的に行われているイベントであることが分かります。

Vocabulary
☐ **periodically** 定期的に

150　正解　B

According to the form, what is Bliz Mobile concerned about the most?
フォームによると、ブリッツ・モバイルが最も関心を抱いていることは何ですか。

(A) Users' ratings on Bliz Mobile's devices	(A) ブリッツ・モバイルのデバイスに対するユーザーの評価	(A) 13.0%
(B) Pricing tactics	**(B) 価格戦略**	**(B) 60.9%**
(C) Average age of the users	(C) ユーザーの平均年齢	(C) 0.0%
(D) Competitors' strengths	(D) 競合他社の強さ	(D) 21.7%

解説　3つの質問がアンケートに記載されていますが、予算について、予算に影響を与えうる要因についての質問があることから、(B)の「価格戦略」について最も強く考察していると判断されます。

353

Questions 151-152 refer to the following e-mail.
問題151-152は次のEメールに関するものです。

FROM: Food Delivery <foodordersnewyork@letseat.com>
TO: Dave Wanderworth <davewanderworth@pop-mail.com>
SUBJECT: Your food is on its way!

Hi Dave!

Thank you for using Let's Eat to order dinner today. I just wanted to tell you that your food delivery from Yo Panda is now on its way to you and you should receive your meal in about 45 minutes.

As a special token of our appreciation, here's a 10 percent discount voucher on any future orders. To use, simply type THANKYOU21 while placing an order on our website or mobile app.

As always, we are taking extra care to sanitize all carrier vehicles before accepting any food to be delivered for the drivers and our customers. Our drivers are instructed to leave your delivery at your door. You will receive a call from them when they have arrived at your address. We hope you enjoy your dinner.

Yours sincerely,

Martin
Let's Eat New York

FROM：フードデリバリー <foodordersnewyork@letseat.com>
TO：デイヴ・ワンダーウォース<davewanderworth@pop-mail.com>
件名：ご注文のお食事配達中です！

デイヴ

本日は、Let's Eatをご利用いただきありがとうございます。ちょうどあなたにYoパンダから配達が向かっている途中であり、約45分でお食事を受けることができることをお伝えします。

感謝の気持ちを込めて、今後のご注文でご利用いただける10パーセント割引クーポンを差し上げます。使用するには、当社のウェブサイトまたはモバイルアプリで注文するときにTHANKYOU21と入力するだけです。

いつものように、特別な注意を持ってすべての運搬車両をお食事の配送前に運転手とお客さまのために消毒しています。また、運転手は配達物をドアに残すように指示されています。配達員があなたの住所に到着した際お電話いたします。ディナーをお楽しみください。

敬具

マーティン
Let's Eat、ニューヨーク

Vocabulary
☐ **sanitize** 衛生的にする　☐ **carrier vehicle** 配送車

151　正解 B

What can be inferred about the main service Let's Eat provides?
Let's Eatが提供する主なサービスは何だと推測できますか。

(A) It cooks meals and deliver them.	(A) 食事を作って配達します。	(A) 17.4%
(B) It delivers food from restaurants to customers.	**(B) レストランからお客さまに食事を届けます。**	**(B) 56.5%**
(C) It provides gourmet information online.	(C) グルメ情報をオンラインで提供します。	(C) 17.4%
(D) It creates apps for food suppliers.	(D) 食品供給者向けのアプリを作成します。	(D) 4.3%

解説　第1パラグラフの2文目に、現在食べ物を配送中とあるので、食べ物を配送するサービスを提供していることが分かります。別のレストラン名があることから、Let's Eatは自らがレストランというわけではなく、オンラインで注文を取って、その注文は各レストランが料理し、それをLet's Eatが配達する、という仕組みだと想像できます。

152　正解 A

What do the drivers do while providing a service?
サービスを提供している間、ドライバーは何をしますか。

(A) Call the customer	**(A) お客さまに電話する**	**(A) 34.8%**
(B) Knock the door	(B) ドアをノックする	(B) 8.7%
(C) Sanitize the carrier vehicles	(C) 配達用の乗り物を消毒する	(C) 47.8%
(D) Receive payment	(D) 支払いを受け取る	(D) 4.3%

解説　最後から2番目の文に、注文が届く前にthem(=drivers)から電話が届くとあるので、(A)が正解であると特定できます。

Questions 153-154 refer to the following online chat discussion.
問題153-154は次のオンラインチャットの話し合いに関するものです。

Roy Singh (2:30 P.M.)	Hi there. I had a quick question about my Internet services.
Troy White (2:30 P.M.)	Sure, I'd be happy to help. I need to confirm a few details for security purposes before I can access your account. Is that OK?
Roy Singh (2:32 P.M.)	Yes, go ahead.
Troy White (2:32 P.M.)	Thank you for your understanding. May I please have your registered phone number and your address?
Roy Singh (2:33 P.M.)	My phone number is 324-8794 and my address is 12, Munro Way, New York.
Troy White (2:35 P.M.)	Thank you for confirming those details. Let me look at your account and see what Internet plan you are on. Please bear with me.
Roy Singh (2:36 P.M.)	Thank you. I appreciate your help.

ロイ・シン(2:30 P.M.):	こんにちは。インターネットサービスについて簡単な質問があります。
トロイ・ホワイト(2:30 P.M.):	もちろんお手伝いさせていただきます。お客さまのアカウントにアクセスする前に、セキュリティ上の理由から幾つかの詳細を確認する必要があります。大丈夫でしょうか。
ロイ・シン(2:32 P.M.):	はい、どうぞ。
トロイ・ホワイト(2:32 P.M.):	ご理解ありがとうございます。登録した電話番号と住所を教えていただけますか。
ロイ・シン(2:33 P.M.):	私の電話番号は324-8794で、住所はニューヨークのマンローウェイ12です。
トロイ・ホワイト(2:35 P.M.):	それらの詳細を確認していただきありがとうございます。あなたのアカウントを素早く見て、あなたがどのインターネットプランを利用しているかを確認してみましょう。もうしばらくお待ちください。
ロイ・シン(2:36 P.M.):	ありがとうございます。ご対応感謝いたします。

Vocabulary
☐ **registered** 登録された

153　正解 B

Why did Troy White ask for Roy's address and phone number?
トロイ・ホワイトがロイの住所と電話番号を尋ねたのはなぜですか。

(A) To send out a bill	(A) 請求書を送るため	(A) 8.7%
(B) To confirm identification	**(B) 身元を確認するため**	**(B) 65.2%**
(C) To help Roy find his account	(C) ロイのアカウントを探すのを助けるため	(C) 21.7%
(D) To call back	(D) 折り返し電話するため	(D) 0.0%

解説　名前はチャットに記載されています。その上で、電話番号と住所を聞いていることから、身元確認を行っていることが読み取れます。

154　正解 C

At 2:35 P.M., what does Troy White most likely mean when he writes, "Please bear with me"?
午後2時35分、トロイ・ホワイトが「Please bear with me」と書いていますが、何を意味しているでしょうか。

(A) He knows Roy is already angry.	(A) 彼はロイがすでに怒っていることを知っています。	(A) 8.7%
(B) He thinks the task is easy.	(B) 彼はその仕事は簡単だと思っています。	(B) 4.3%
(C) He expects the process will take some time.	**(C) 彼は手続きに時間がかかると考えています。**	**(C) 82.6%**
(D) He wants to make sure Roy is not lost.	(D) 彼はロイが道に迷わないようにしたいです。	(D) 0.0%

解説　bear with meは訳し方としては「ご了承ください」「このままお待ちください」あたりが今回の場合適切でしょう。文字通りでは、私と一緒に辛抱してください、という意味で、しばらく時間を要するかもしれないのでこのまま待っていていただきたい、という気持ちからの発言と見受けられます。

第1章　英語脳徹底トレーニング

第2章　高難度問題の徹底攻略

第3章　正答ハイテクレッスン

第4章　ハイレベル完全模試

Questions 155-157 refer to the following e-mail.
問題155-157は次のEメールに関するものです。

HopStep Financial Services Ltd
customerservice@hopstep-accounting.com

Dear Henry,

Good morning. As your personal financial adviser, I am writing to you to inform you about certain changes to your investment portfolio and the service rates associated with supplemental assistance HopStep Financial Services Ltd will start offering to all customers.

As of last night (17 September 2021), all your investments in precious metals have suffered a loss of about 8 percent. I strongly suggest that we re-evaluate your investments. To do this, I am hoping to talk with you on any one of the following dates and times:
　　1. 22 September, at 1:15 P.M.
　　2. 22 September, at 3:30 P.M.
　　3. 25 September, at 10:15 A.M.

Please let me know which of the following times, if any, suit you the best, so that I may send you an invitation link.

As mentioned earlier, there are also certain changes to our fees structure. Primarily, we will be increasing our brokerage rate from 1.25 percent to 1.4 percent for every transaction, from the 25th of October 2021. In accordance with our policy, which was updated last month, all information is considered confidential.

I look forward to speaking with you about your investments soon.

Kind regards,

Susan Miller
Asset Manager
HopStep Financial Services Ltd

HopStep ファイナンシャルサービス株式会社
customerservice@hopstep-accounting.com

ヘンリー様

おはようございます。あなたのパーソナル投資顧問として、あなたの投資ポートフォリオへの変化と、HopStep ファイナンシャルサービス社がすべてのお客さまに提供を開始する追加サポートに関するサービス料金について知らせるためにメールをお送りしています。

昨晩（2021年9月17日）の時点で、あなたの貴金属類への投資は約8パーセントの損失を被りました。投資を再評価することを強くお勧めします。そうするために、次のいずれかの日時でお話ししたいと考えています。

1. 9月22日、午後1時15分
2. 9月22日、午後3時30分
3. 9月25日、午前10時15分

招待リンクをお送りしますので、次のどの時間が最も都合がいいかお知らせください。

前述のように、料金体系にも一定の変更があります。主に、2021年10月25日から、すべての取引の仲介率を1.25パーセントから1.4パーセントに引き上げます。先月改定されたポリシーに基づき、すべての情報が秘匿情報となります。

近いうちにあなたの投資についてお話しできることを楽しみにしています。

敬具

スーザン・ミラー
アセットマネージャー
HopStep ファイナンシャルサービス

Vocabulary
☐ **as of ～** ～の時点で　☐ **precious metals** 貴金属　☐ **brokerage** 仲買
☐ **in accordance with ～** ～に従い

155　正解 C

When did Henry receive this e-mail?
ヘンリーはいつこのメールを受け取ったでしょうか。

(A) September 16	(A) 9月16日	(A) 4.3%
(B) September 17	(B) 9月17日	(B) 13.0%
(C) September 18	(C) 9月18日	(C) 69.6%
(D) September 22	(D) 9月22日	(D) 8.7%

解説　おはよう、という文で始まり、昨夜の時点で損失が確認できた、という流れから、昨夜（9月17日）の次の日、すなわち9月18日にこのメールを書いていることが分かります。

156　正解 A

What is indicated about the intended talk between Henry and Susan?
ヘンリーとスーザン間で行われる会話について示されているのは何でしょうか。

(A) It will be conducted online.	(A) オンラインで行われる。	(A) 13.0%
(B) It will take place on September 26th.	(B) 9月26日に行われる。	(B) 8.7%
(C) It must be held immediately.	(C) 今すぐの開催が必要である。	(C) 43.5%
(D) It is exclusively about Henry's portfolio.	(D) もっぱらヘンリーのポートフォリオについてになる。	(D) 30.4%

解説　招待用リンクを送る、という説明から、この会話はオンラインで行われると推察されます。日付についてはまだこの日と決まっていないため(B)は不可。幾つか1週間先の日付までつけて話の候補日を出していることからimmediatelyとは言い難く(C)も誤り。料金についての話もなされることから、exclusively about Henry's portfolioとは言えず、(D)も正解とはなりません。

Vocabulary
☐ **exclusively** もっぱら、排他的に

157　正解 D

Why will the transaction fee increase?
なぜ手数料は上がるのでしょうか。

(A) Henry lost a significant part of his investment.	(A) ヘンリーは投資の大部分を失った。	(A) 17.4%
(B) The value of precious metals has dropped.	(B) 貴金属の価値が下落した。	(B) 26.1%
(C) The policy of HopStep has updated.	(C) HopStepのポリシーが改定された。	(C) 47.8%
(D) Additional services will be added for Henry.	(D) ヘンリーのためにサービスが追加される。	(D) 4.3%

解説　第1パラグラフで、HopStepが提供を開始する追加サービスに関しての料金についてのお話と説明した上で、第4パラグラフで料金の改定を伝えているため、料金変更の理由は、この追加サービスによるものと分かります。

Questions 158-160 refer to the following article.
問題158-160は次の記事に関するものです。

City Meeting to Discuss New Bicycle Parking Lots

The Dillard City Council will hold a special meeting on Thursday to discuss the mayor's controversial proposal to build bicycle parking lots next to all subway stations. The purpose of building new parking lots is to give cyclists a convenient place to park their bicycles. Furthermore, local businesses have recommended building bicycle parking lots as a way of getting bicycles off of city streets.

Bicycles are frequently left parked in front of stores for lengthy periods of time, and this has become an eyesore in the downtown area. If the proposal passes, the city will hire a new workforce to collect bicycles parked on the street and bring them to the city's bicycle pound where owners will have to pay 10 dollars to retrieve their illegally parked bicycles. Mayor John Charles, who instigated the proposal, said he is certain the bicycle lots "will improve the downtown area."

Not everyone agrees with the plan. James Carvelle, the president of the Dillard chapter of Green Peace, states that the city is secretly trying to dissuade people from riding bicycles. "The city should be encouraging people to get out of their cars." Local activist Johnny Leary said, "The proposed $5 parking fee for one-day parking is too high if you just want to go to the grocery store." Julia Howell said, "The land price has been rising, and we should utilize those valuable areas for something more profitable."

The City Council encourages all citizens concerned with the issue to attend Thursday's meeting before the final vote by the council committees on Friday.

新しい駐輪場についての市議会会議

ディラード市議会は木曜日に特別会議を開き、市長のすべての地下鉄駅の隣に駐輪場を建設するという物議を醸す提案について話し合います。新しい駐輪場を建設する目的は、自転車を使う人たちに便利な場所を提供することです。さらに、地元企業は路上から自転車を排除する方法として新しい駐輪場を建設することを推奨しています。

自転車は店の前に長時間駐車されることが多く、繁華街では目障りになっています。もし提案が通過した場合、市は路上に駐車された自転車を集めるための従業員を新しく雇い、所有者が法に反し駐車した自転車を回収するために10ドルを支払う必要がある市の駐輪場に運びます。提案を働きかけたジョン・チャールズ市長は、自転車置き場が「繁華街を改善する」と確信していると述べました。

誰もがその計画に同意するわけではありません。グリーンピースのディラード支部の会長であるジェームズ・カーベル氏は、市はひそかに人々が自転車に乗ることをやめさせようとしていると述べています。「市は人々に車から降りるように勧めるべきです」。地元の活動家ジョニー・リアリー氏は、「食料品店に行きたいだけの場合、提案された1日5ドルの駐輪料金は高すぎる」と述べました。 ジュリア・ハウエル氏は、「地価は上昇している。これらの貴重な場所をもっと収益性の高いものに活用すべきだ」と語りました。

市議会は、金曜日の議会委員会による最終投票の前に、この問題に関係するすべての市民が木曜日の会議に出席することを推奨しています。

Vocabulary

☐ **lengthy** 長々しい   ☐ **workforce** 労働力   ☐ **pound** 一時保管所   ☐ **retrieve** 取り戻す
☐ **instigate** けしかける   ☐ **land price** 地価

158 正解 D

What is expected to happen if the plan is approved?
計画が承認されると何が起こると期待されるでしょうか。

(A) The number of bicycle users will decrease dramatically.	自転車の数が劇的に減る。	(A) 17.4%
(B) The city can collect a large sum of fines.	市は多額の罰金を得られる。	(B) 21.7%
(C) The downtown area will be less congested with people.	市街地の人混みが減る。	(C) 8.7%
(D) Fewer bicycles will be left unattended on the streets.	**道に放置された自転車が減る。**	**(D) 47.8%**

解説 第1から第2パラグラフにかけて、通りや中心街での自転車の放置や長時間にわたる駐輪が問題で、これを解決したいという目的での提案であることが読み取れるため、(D)が正解となります。

Vocabulary

☐ **dramatically** 劇的に   ☐ **a large sum of** 多額の   ☐ **unattended** 放置された

159　正解　D

What is NOT mentioned as the basis of which some individuals are against the proposal?
何人かの人が提案に反対している根拠として掲げられていないのはどれでしょうか。

(A) The parking fee is extremely high.	(A) 駐輪料金が極めて高い。	(A) 30.4%
(B) Increased car dependence is not desirable.	(B) 車へのさらなる依存は好ましくない。	(B) 30.4%
(C) The parking space can be used differently.	(C) 駐輪場は他の目的で使われるべき。	(C) 17.4%
(D) The value of the land can be raised further.	**(D) 地価はさらに上がりうる。**	**(D) 17.4%**

解説　Julia Howell が主張しているのは、「地価が高いこの駐輪場予定地を別のもっと利益性の高い目的で使うべき」、ということで、(D)の「地価はもっと上がる」ということを主張しているわけではなく、(D)が述べられていない選択肢となります。

160　正解　D

What is true about the city council?
市議会について正しい情報はどれでしょうか。

(A) It allows all citizens to vote for this issue.	全市民に本件について投票を許可する。	(A) 21.7%
(B) It has voted to approve the bicycle parking lots.	駐輪スペースについて賛成票を投じた。	(B) 17.4%
(C) It held the final meeting last Friday.	前の金曜日に最終会議を開いた。	(C) 17.4%
(D) It wishes to hear citizens' opinions about the proposal.	**提案への市民の意見を聞きたい。**	**(D) 39.1%**

解説　最後の文で、考えがある市民は木曜日の会議に参加するようにと呼びかけているところから、市民の声を聞こうとしている様子がうかがえ、(D)が正解となります。意見がある人に対して「会議に参加して」、「メッセージを投稿して」という案内方法はTOEICでよく出てきます。

Questions 161-163 refer to the following press release.
問題161-163は次のプレスリリースに関するものです。

Be a Mountain Climbing Specialist!

Santa Ana Advisors and Experts is launching a new course for mountain climbing specialists. Participants learn various aspects of mountain climbing including: how to assist or guide beginners, how to use cutting-edge climbing gear, how to maintain this gear, knowledge pertaining to health care in case of emergencies, and so on.

Many skiers visit mountains in this state during winter, but in contrast, there are a disproportionately small number of visitors from spring to fall. Since the convention bureau of California is trying to invite visitors to the mountainous region throughout the year, they are expecting that our new program will play an important role. In fact, Arnold Lindenson, the top executive of the bureau, announced that scholarships will be available to program participants.

Our instructors include several world-famous alpinists like Tim McKinley, who leads the entire course. George Thompson, another preeminent figure, handles all administrative duties. Our main location, which is in San Jose, opened this course a year ago, and has produced dozens of graduates. Jimmy Troy is one of those graduates. Here is a comment from Jimmy:

"I'm really glad that I enrolled on this program. I liked mountain climbing, but it is even a greater pleasure that I will be able to support those who have just begun mountain climbing. I really liked your informative instruction as well as continuing encouragement."

登山スペシャリストになろう！

サンタアナ・アドバイザーズ・アンド・エキスパーツは、登山のスペシャリスト向けの新しいコースを開始します。参加者は、初心者をサポートまたはガイドする方法、最先端のクライミングギアの使用方法、このギアをメンテナンスする方法、緊急時のヘルスケアに関する知識など、登山のさまざまな側面を学びます。

冬の間、多くのスキーヤーがこの州の山を訪れますが、対照的に、春から秋にかけての訪問者は過度に少ないです。カリフォルニアの文化交流局は1年を通して山岳地帯に訪問者を招こうとしており、私たちの新しいプログラムが重要な役割を果たすことに期待しています。実際、文化交流局の最高責任者であるアーノルド・リンデンソンは、プログラム参加者が奨学金を利用できるようになると発表しました。

私たちのインストラクターには、コース全体を率いるティム・マッキンリーのような世界的に有名なアルプス登山家が何人か含まれています。もう1人の著名人であるジョージ・トンプソンは、すべての管理業務を担当しています。私たちのメインの活動場所であるサンノゼは、1年前にこのコースを開校し、数十人の卒業生を輩出してきました。ジミー・トロイは卒業生の1人です。ジミーからのコメントは次のとおりです。

「このプログラムを受講して本当に良かったです。趣味で登山をしてきました。今度は私が登山を始めたばかりの人のサポートができることをとても喜ばしく思っています。私はあなたの有益な指導と継続的な励ましに心から感謝します」

Vocabulary

☐ **pertaining to ~** ~に関する　　☐ **disproportionately** 不釣り合いに　　☐ **convention bureau** 文化交流局
☐ **alpinist** 登山家　　☐ **preeminent** 抜群の　　☐ **administrative** 管理の

161　正解 D

What kind of service is being advertised?
どのようなサービスが宣伝されていますか。

(A) Career consultation	(A) キャリアコンサルティング	(A) 13.0%
(B) Tourism	(B) 旅行	(B) 39.1%
(C) Human resources management	(C) 人事管理	(C) 8.7%
(D) Vocational training	**(D) 職業訓練**	**(D) 34.8%**

解説　登山のスペシャリストに対して、具体的な知識やスキルの習得を目的とし、さらに、登山の入門者に対してのサポートができるようになるコースを提供していることから、(D)の職業訓練が与えられた選択肢の中では最善の答えとなります。vocationは仕事という意味で、jobやoccupationと同じく可算名詞扱いです。広い意味での「仕事」という意味でも使われますが、「天職」という意味で使われることもよくあります。

162　正解 A

What is indicated about the new course?
新コースについて示されていることは何でしょうか。

(A) It is being taught in multiple places by multiple instructors.	**(A) 複数の場所で複数の先生により指導されている。**	(A) 34.8%
(B) It is headquartered in Santa Ana, Los Angeles.	(B) ロサンゼルスのサンターナに本部がある。	(B) 17.4%
(C) It has been offering a wide range of courses for years.	(C) 何年も幅広いコースを提供している。	(C) 21.7%
(D) It received a grant from the Californian organization.	(D) カリフォルニアの組織から助成金を得ている。	(D) 21.7%

解説　第3パラグラフのOur instructorsから複数の講師がいることがわかります。また、ロサンゼルスの他に、サンノゼにメインオフィスがある、という情報から、複数の場所で提供されていることが分かります。(A)が正解となります。助成金については言及がありますが、これはコース参加者向けのもので、新コースが受け取るものではなく、(D)は不正解です。

163　　正解 B

Who is the past graduate's comments intended for?
卒業生からのこのコメントは誰に宛てられたものでしょうか。

(A) Arnold Lindenson	(A) アーノルド・リンダーソン	(A) 8.7%
(B) Tim McKinley	**(B) ティム・マッキンリー**	**(B) 4.3%**
(C) George Thompson	(C) ジョージ・トンプソン	(C) 8.7%
(D) Jimmy Troy	(D) ジミー・トロイ	(D) 73.9%

解説　卒業生からのコメントの中には、情報豊富な指導と継続した励ましを評価している内容があり、感謝の言葉を述べたメッセージであることがわかります。第3パラグラフを見てみると、授業を行いリードしているのはTim McKinleyであることがわかり、(B)が正解となります。George Thompsonは運営サイドへの従事であったと書かれているので、この感謝の言葉の受取人としては最適とは考えられません。

Questions 164-167 refer to the following article.
問題 164-167 は次の記事に関するものです。

Here's why you should play badminton as a form of exercise

It is common to see people hitting the gym or going running or swimming, but how often do you hear someone saying that they play badminton as a form of exercise? — [1] —.

Badminton is such an underrated sport. While lawn tennis is popular across the world with famous tournaments like "Wimbledon," that popularity doesn't translate to badminton. However, While Asian countries do promote badminton as a sport, there's nothing stopping you from playing badminton ①to lose some of those stubborn calories!

— [2] —. Actually, the most accepted theory is that badminton was born here in England! It is said that the sport was initially played in Duke of Beaufort's residence called Badminton House. — [3] —.

Did you know that playing badminton, even a low intensity leisurely game, is akin to a full body workout? Many people get bored of the same old gym routine and often quit a few weeks or months later. That will never happen when you play badminton, ②because of the sheer amount of mental stimulation you get from the game. — [4] —. Badminton is the world's fastest racquet sport. Simply put, there's no time to get bored when you are in the middle of the game chasing the shuttle—it's that fast paced!

運動の一種として、バドミントンをすべき理由があります。

ジムに行ったり、ランニングや水泳をしたりというのはよくあることですが、運動の一種としてバドミントンをしていると言う人をどのくらいの頻度で耳にしますか。

バドミントンはそのように過小評価されているスポーツです。テニスはウィンブルドン選手権のように著名なトーナメントがあり、世界中で人気がありますが、その人気はバドミントンにはありません。アジア諸国はバドミントンをスポーツとして促進していますが、あなたがバドミントンをして、①しぶといカロリーを落とそうとすることを妨げるものは何もありません。

それは、有力な説によるとバドミントンは、ここイギリスで生まれたとされています。このスポーツは、ボーフォート公爵の邸宅であるバドミントン・ハウスで始まったと言われているのです。

バドミントンをすることは、それがたとえ軽いのんびりとしたゲームであっても、全身トレーニングに似ていることをご存じですか。多くの人々は、ジムのいつもと同じルーティーンに飽きて、しばしば数週間後、または数カ月後にやめてしまいます。バドミントンをするときには、②ゲームから得られる精神的刺激が非常に多いため、そうしたことは決して起こりません。バドミントンは世界最速のラケットスポーツです。簡単に言えば、ゲームでシャトルを追いながら、途中で退屈する時間はありません。そのくらいペースが速いのです。

Vocabulary

☐ **hit the gym** ジムに行く　☐ **underrated** 過小評価された　☐ **stubborn** 頑固な　☐ **Duke** 侯爵
☐ **leisurely** ゆっくりした　☐ **be akin to** ～ ～と同種で　☐ **sheer** 全くの、本当の

164　正解 C

For what purpose, does the writer mention lawn tennis?
筆者は何のためにテニスの話をしたのでしょうか。

(A) To indicate it requires less energy than badminton	(A) バドミントンよりエネルギー消費が少ないことを示すため	(A) 21.7%
(B) To name a sport that is not commonly played.	(B) 広く普及していないスポーツ名を挙げるため	(B) 4.3%
(C) To contrast the worldwide popularity of some sports	**(C) 幾つかのスポーツの世界的人気を対比するため**	**(C) 56.5%**
(D) To claim that a grass court is the key for its popularity	(D) 芝生が人気の秘訣であると主張するため	(D) 13.0%

解説　第2パラグラフに、テニスは世界規模で楽しまれているがバドミントンは同じ規模の人気は見られない、という説明があることから、人気の比較をするためにテニスを挙げたとわかります。(A)、(D)については言及がなく、(B)は事実と逆の内容となっており誤りです。ちなみに、テニスの世界競技人口は1億人、バドミントンは5000万人くらいだそうです。ダブルスコアですがどちらも多いですね。

165　正解 A

What is one benefit of playing badminton that the writer mentions?
筆者が挙げるバドミントンのメリットの1つは何でしょうか。

(A) You can burn calories that are otherwise difficult to do so.	**(A) 他の方法では燃やすのが難しいカロリーを燃やすことができる。**	**(A) 60.9%**
(B) You do not have to go to the gym for exercise.	(B) 運動のためにジムに行く必要がない。	(B) 8.7%
(C) You can improve your concentration skills.	(C) 集中力を高めることができる。	(C) 17.4%
(D) You will be able to make friends worldwide.	(D) 世界中に友達を作ることができる。	(D) 8.7%

Part 7 | 読解問題

解説 下線①「しぶといカロリーを落とす」という部分から、こうでもしなければ落とすのが難しいカロリーを消費できる、という(A)が、与えられた選択肢の中ではベストとなります。選択肢(A)のotherwiseは「さもなくば」「そうでもしない限り」という訳し方があります。Part 5でもこの用法で出題されるので注意。

166　正解 A

Why do badminton players never get bored?
なぜバドミントン競技者は退屈しないのでしょうか。

(A) Players keep stimulated.	(A) 刺激を受け続けるから。	(A) 39.1%
(B) The shuttle is too fast to hit back.	(B) シャトルは打ち返すには速すぎるから。	(B) 30.4%
(C) Badminton is the most intensive sport.	(C) バドミントンが強度が最も高いスポーツだから。	(C) 17.4%
(D) Players can keep losing calories.	(D) カロリーを消費し続けられるから。	(D) 8.7%

解説 下線②の部分から、刺激を受け続けるのでつまらなくならない、と読み取ることができるため、(A)が正解。シャトルの速度は初速で時速500キロメートルにも迫るそうで、新幹線の最高速度である時速320キロメートルをはるかに上回り確かに極めて速いのですが、それが理由で競技者は飽きないという説明にはなっていないので(B)は間違いです。

167　正解 B

In which of the positions marked [1], [2], [3], and [4] does the following sentence best belong?
"Do you know the origin of the sport?"
以下の文は[1] [2] [3] [4]のいずれの場所に挿入するのが最適でしょうか。
「このスポーツの起源を知っていますか」

(A) [1]	(A) [1]	(A) 13.0%
(B) [2]	(B) [2]	(B) 56.5%
(C) [3]	(C) [3]	(C) 13.0%
(D) [4]	(D) [4]	(D) 13.0%

解説 実際にバドミントンの発祥がどこからで、バドミントンという言葉が何に由来するのか、という説明が — [2] — の後に続くので、ここが最も適している場所となります。

369

Questions 168-171 refer to the following online chat discussion.
問題168-171は次のオンラインチャットの話し合いに関するものです。

Kia Neal (12:06 P.M.): Hello. Thank you for contacting Xeptel Bank. How may I help you?

David Roth (12:06 P.M.): Good afternoon. I was wondering if you could help me with logging in to my online bank account. ①I cannot locate the page.

Kia Neal (12:07 P.M.): Certainly. Do you mind if I confirm a few details before we get started?

David Roth (12:08 P.M.): No, I do not.

Kia Neal (12:08 P.M.): This is part of our required step for security purposes. I appreciate your understanding. Will you please give me your date of birth, address and phone number, Mr. Roth?

David Roth (12:10 P.M.): My date of birth is 19th of August, 1989, and my phone number is 025-372-3692. My address is 421 Queen St., Molding, Virginia.

Kia Neal (12:12 P.M.): Thank you for confirming those details. The date of birth and phone number match our records. However, the address you gave me is not the one I have on the system.

David Roth (12:13 P.M.): Is the address 126 Washington Road, Molding, Virginia? I moved to the Queen Street address in January.

Kia Neal (12:13 P.M.): Yes, that is the address I have registered. Would you like me to change it to your new address? I can then give you your Internet banking login ID and temporary password.

David Roth (12:15 P.M.): Well, I'm not sure if that makes a difference but please do send me the link that directs me to the right place.

キア・ニール（12:06 P.M.）：	こんにちは。Xeptel銀行にお問い合わせいただきありがとうございます。どのようにお手伝いいたしましょう？
デイビッド・ロス（12:06 P.M.）：	こんにちは。私のオンライン銀行口座へのログインを手伝ってくれませんか。ページが見つかりません。
キア・ニール（12:07 P.M.）：	もちろんです。始める前に詳細を幾つか確認してもよろしいでしょうか。
デイビッド・ロス（12:08 P.M.）：	問題ありません。
キア・ニール（12:08 P.M.）：	これはセキュリティーの関係で必要なステップで、ご理解に感謝いたします。ロスさん、生年月日、住所、電話番号を教えてください。
デイビッド・ロス（12:10 P.M.）：	私の生年月日は1989年8月19日で、電話番号は025-372-3692です。私の住所は、バージニア州モールディングの421クイーンストリートです。
キア・ニール（12:12 P.M.）：	詳細をご確認いただきありがとうございます。生年月日と電話番号は、我々の記録と一致しています。しかし、あなたが私に教えてくれたアドレスは、システム上にあるアドレスと異なります。
デイビッド・ロス（12:13 P.M.）：	住所はバージニア州モールディングの126ワシントンロードですか。1月にクイーンストリートの住所に引っ越しました。
キア・ニール（12:13 P.M.）：	はい、それが登録してあるアドレスです。新しい住所に変更しますか。その後、インターネットバンキングのログインIDと仮パスワードをお伝えします。
デイビッド・ロス（12:15 P.M.）：	それが何か違いを生むかは分かりませんが、とにかく正しいページに誘導してくれるリンクはお送りいただけますと幸いです。

Vocabulary
☐ **locate** 見つける、特定する

168　正解 C

What is David Roth's problem?
デイビッド・ロスの問題は何でしょうか。

(A) He forgot his password.	(A) パスワードを忘れた。	(A) 8.7%
(B) He could not open an online account.	(B) オンラインアカウントを開設できなかった。	(B) 60.9%
(C) He cannot find the right page.	**(C) 正しいページを見つけられない。**	**(C) 21.7%**
(D) He does not have a valid ID.	(D) 有効なIDを持っていない。	(D) 4.3%

解説　下線①「正しいページが見つけられない」と言っているので、IDやパスワードではなく、ログインする際のページがわからなくなっていると思われ、(C)が正解となります。(B)は正解に見えるかもしれませんが、open an accountというと、アカウントを開設することになります。入れないときはcannot log in/onという言葉が使用されます。

169 正解 D

At 12:08 P.M., what does David Roth mean when he writes, "No, I do not"?
12時08分にデイビッド・ロスは「No, I do not」と言っていますが、何を意味しているでしょうか。

(A) He wants to know why Kia needs his information.	(A) なぜキアが彼の情報が必要としているのか知りたい。	(A) 13.0%
(B) He does not want to give private information.	(B) 個人情報を渡したくない。	(B) 26.1%
(C) He does not understand what Kia is requesting.	(C) キアが何を要求しているのか理解していない。	(C) 17.4%
(D) He has no problem in sharing information.	**(D) 情報を共有することに問題を感じていない。**	**(D) 39.1%**

解説　Do you mind?「問題があると考えるか」という問いかけに、No, I do not mind.「そうは考えない」、すなわち問題があるとは考えていない、ということなので、(D)が正解となります。日本語的には、「問題ありませんか」と聞かれれば「いいえ、全然問題ありませんよ」と答えたくなりますが、英語的には、「はい、問題ありません」という答え方になります。

170 正解 A

What information was missing on the database?
データベースになかった情報は何でしょうか。

(A) David's new address	**(A) デイビッドの新しい住所**	**(A) 52.2%**
(B) David's previous address	(B) デイビッドの前の住所	(B) 34.8%
(C) David's phone number	(C) デイビッドの電話番号	(C) 8.7%
(D) David's birthday	(D) デイビッドの誕生日	(D) 0.0%

解説　12:12 P.M.および12:13 P.M.の会話で、古い住所がそのまま残っていて、引っ越し後の新しい住所が登録されていない様子が分かり、正解は(A)となります。

171 正解 A

What piece of information does David Roth need the most?
デイビッド・ロスが最も欲しがっている情報は何でしょうか。

(A) A login page	**(A) ログインページ**	**(A) 34.8%**
(B) A new login ID	(B) 新しいログインID	(B) 30.4%
(C) A temporary password	(C) 一時パスワード	(C) 21.7%
(D) The original password	(D) 最初のパスワード	(D) 8.7%

解説　どうやらキア・ニールは勘違いをしている様子で、デイビッド・ロスが求めているのは当初よりログインページであるのに、ログイン用のIDとパスワードをお送りするとデイビッド・ロスに伝えています。これに対してデイビッド・ロスは、(ID、パスワードは持っているので)それを新たにもらって意味があるのか不明だが、ログインページにつながるリンクは欲しい、と念を押しています。(A)が正解です。

Questions 172-175 refer to the following advertisement.

問題172-175は次の広告に関するものです。

Help Wanted

Headquartered in Denver, Colorado, Comp Colorado Inc. is presently seeking experienced computer experts. In this position, workers are referred to as "office designers." Our company is known throughout the state for providing companies with a wide range of diverse computer-related services, including setting up computers, arranging an office network, providing training, and installing operating systems and software. Our clients range from small to middle-sized growing companies, and our duty is to gear their work environment to a computer-equipped work space.

①All office designers should be able to work independently. You will be assigned accounts with businesses, and you will hold meetings with each company to conduct a "needs analysis." After installing the office computer network, you will be responsible for training staff. ②Excellent knowledge of office software is required. Experience in providing computer training is preferred. In the future, we plan on expanding our business to provide services for computer labs at schools, so any such experience would be valuable to us.

Comp Colorado Inc. is currently in need of five full-time office designers. We offer a competitive salary, generous benefits, and various remunerations. ③Our salary is decided in an ability-based fashion; no seniority system is adopted. Please send us your current résumé, and at least one reference letter by regular mail. A photocopy of your ID must be included as well. We will be contacting short-listed candidates by the end of July. ④Please do not contact us unless we contact you first. We are looking forward to receiving applications from a candidate with excellent manners, passion and resilience.

従業員求む

コロラド州デンバーに本社を置くコンプ・コロラド社は、現在、経験豊富なコンピューターの専門家を募集しています。この仕事では、従業員は"オフィスデザイナー"と呼ばれます。私たちの会社は企業にコンピューターの設置、オフィスネットワークの手配、トレーニングの提供やオペレーティングシステムやソフトウェアの設置を含む多種多様なコンピューター関連のサービスを提供していることで州全体に知れ渡っています。私たちのクライアントは中小企業にまで及び、そして私たちの義務は彼らの職場環境をコンピューターが備わっている職場

に調整することにあります。

すべてのオフィスデザイナーは単独で仕事ができる必要があります。あなたには企業のアカウントが割り当てられ、各社とミーティングを開いて「ニーズ分析」を行います。 オフィスのコンピュータネットワークをインストールした後、あなたはスタッフの訓練を担当します。 オフィスソフトウェアに関する優れた知識が必要です。 コンピュータトレーニングを提供した経験があれば望ましいです。 将来的には、学校のコンピューター室にサービスを提供する事業にまで拡大していく予定ですので、そのような経験はどんなものでも私たちにとって貴重なものとなるでしょう。

コンプ・コロラド社は現在、フルタイムのオフィスデザイナーを5人必要としています。 私たちは、競争ベースの給与、寛大な手当、およびさまざまな報酬を提供します。 私たちの給与は能力に基づいて決定されます。年功序列は適用されていません。 現在の履歴書と最少1通の推薦状を普通郵便で送ってください。 IDのコピーも同封する必要があります。 7月末までに候補者に連絡します。 先にこちらからご連絡しない限り、こちらへのご連絡はご遠慮ください。 優れたマナー、情熱、粘り強さがある候補者からの応募をお待ちしております。

Vocabulary

☐ **be in need of** ～ ～を必要としている　☐ **generous** 寛大な　☐ **remuneration** 報酬
☐ **seniority system** 年功序列型　☐ **reference letter** 推薦状
☐ **short-listed** 候補者名簿に名前がある　☐ **resilience** 粘り強さ

172　正解 A

What is required for this position?
このポジションに求められるものは何でしょうか。

(A) Knowledge of office software	**(A) オフィスソフトへの知識**	**(A) 52.2%**
(B) Experience in training staff	(B) スタッフ教育の経験	(B) 26.1%
(C) An outstanding academic background	(C) 卓越した学業実績	(C) 4.3%
(D) Five-year work experience	(D) 5年の職業経験	(D) 13.0%

解説　下線②から、(A)が正解であることがわかります。他はいずれも要求されるものとしての言及がなく、正解とはなりません。

173　正解 C

How do "the office designers" provide the service?
オフィスデザイナーはどのようにサービスを提供するでしょうか。

(A) They work as a member of a team.	(A) チームの一員として働く。	(A) 21.7%
(B) They lead and manage a team.	(B) チームを統率する。	(B) 0.0%
(C) Each of them works alone.	**(C) 個々で稼働する。**	**(C) 56.5%**
(D) They delegate jobs to subcontractors.	(D) 下請けに委託する。	(D) 17.4%

解説　下線①から、チームを率いたり、チームのメンバーとして稼働するのではなく、単独で独立して稼働することが示されているため、(C)が正解となります。

Vocabulary
☐ **delegate** 委託する ☐ **subcontractor** 下請け業者

174 　正解 A

What is mentioned about the salary?
給与について何が言及されていますか。

(A) Skills are the primary determinant.	(A) 能力が最大の決定要因である。	(A) 60.9%
(B) The amount won't change once determined.	(B) 一度決定されたら額は変わらない。	(B) 8.7%
(C) Workers will receive a mark-up as they age.	(C) 加齢により給与が上がる。	(C) 0.0%
(D) Staff with longer experience get paid more.	(D) 長い経験があるほど給与が上がる。	(D) 26.1%

> 解説　下線③から、能力によって給与が決まることがわかります。これに一番近い記述となっている
> (A)が正解となります。(D)は要注意です。何かしらの経験が長ければ長いほど給与が高く設
> 定されるという情報はありません。経験が長ければ能力も向上していると予想できなくはあり
> ませんが、文面には書かれておらず、あくまで能力ベースで決まるため、(A)が正解です。

Vocabulary
☐ **determinant** 決定要因 ☐ **mark-up** 賃上げ

175 　正解 C

What are the applicants instructed to do by the end of July?
申請者は7月末までに何を指示されたでしょうか。

(A) Send an inquiry if no notification has been received	(A) 通知が来なければ連絡する	(A) 8.7%
(B) Send additional documents if necessary	(B) 必要があれば追加文書を送る	(B) 17.4%
(C) Just wait for the decision to be made	(C) 決定がなされるのを待つ	(C) 47.8%
(D) Prepare another reference letter	(D) 別の推薦状を作成する	(D) 17.4%

> 解説　下線④から、申請者側から連絡はせず待つようにとの記述があるため、(C)が正解となります。
> ただ待つように、とのことです。実際に申請者が多い場合には、個々に問い合わせがあれこれ
> 来ると返信するのにも時間と労力はその分確かにかかるので、人事、採用側の立場だとこれが
> 本音なのかもしれません。

Questions 176-180 refer to the following e-mail and schedule.
問題176-180は次のEメールと予定表に関するものです。

To: Beth Harcourt <bethharcourt42@good-goods.com>
From: Jan Hans <merchandisefulfilment@zextradesigns.com>
Date: 19th June 2021
Subject: Merchandise Design Schedule

Dear Ms. Harcourt,

How are you? Since we spoke last week at your headquarters, I have been able to come up with an estimated schedule for the delivery of the merchandise finalized by your team. The sooner you can give us the go-ahead to start production, the sooner we can start shipping out the proposed merchandise to your retail stores.

Please keep in mind that the unprecedented volume of orders we have been receiving has severely impacted all production schedules and delivery timelines. Hence, the schedule mentioned below will only be applicable if approval is received before midnight on the 25th of June.

Thank you for choosing to work with Zextra Designs again. We appreciate your business.

Kind regards,

Jan Hans
Merchandise Fulfilment
Zextra Designs

Please find below the schedule for the delivery of final products, for your approval.

Merchandise Type	Date of delivery in Japan	Date of delivery in Australia	Date of delivery in USA	Date of delivery in Europe
T-shirts	31st August	2nd September	15th September	20th September
Mugs	22nd August	31st August	5th September	15th September
Stationery	15th August	20th August	1st September	10th September
Masks	20th August	30th August	5th September	15th September

* The date of delivery is to the port, NOT to the final destination
* 2-3 days expected for customs clearance after the delivery to the port
* Any unlisted products treated as the same category as T-shirts

宛先：ベス・ハーコート <bethharcourt42@good-goods.com>
差出人：ジャン・ハンズ <merchandisefulfilment@zextradesigns.com>
日付：2021年6月19日
件名：商品デザインスケジュール

ハーコート様

お元気ですか。御社の本社で先週お話を伺い、チームが最終決定した商品のお届けのスケジュールができました。生産開始の準備が早ければ早いほど、提案商品の小売店への発送を早く開始できます。

過去に前例がないほど大規模な注文を頂いており、それがすべての生産スケジュールと納期に大きな影響を与えていることをご承知おきください。したがって、下記スケジュールは、6月25日深夜までに承認が得られた場合にのみ適用されます。

再度ゼクストラデザインズをご利用くださりありがとうございます。お取引に感謝します。

敬具

ジャン・ハンズ
商品フルフィルメント
ゼクストラ・デザインズ

承認を得るために、最終製品の納品スケジュールを以下に示します。

商品の種類	日本への配達日	オーストラリアへの配達日	アメリカへの配達日	ヨーロッパへの配達日
Tシャツ	8月31日	9月2日	9月15日	9月20日
マグカップ	8月22日	8月31日	9月5日	9月15日
文房具	8月15日	8月20日	9月1日	9月10日
マスク	8月20日	8月30日	9月5日	9月15日

* 配達日は港への配達であり倉庫への配達ではない
* 港への配達後、通関手続きに2、3日見込まれる
* 載っていない商品については、Tシャツと同じカテゴリーとして扱われる

Vocabulary

☐ **the go-ahead** 許可　☐ **unprecedented** 前例のない　☐ **applicable** 適用される

176　正解 A

What is the main purpose of the e-mail?
メールの主な目的は何でしょうか。

(A) To urge an approval by June 25th	**(A) 6月25日までの承認を促す**	**(A) 26.1%**
(B) To propose a new business deal	(B) 新しい取引を提案する	(B) 21.7%
(C) To give a list of what can be manufactured	(C) 生産可能な製品を挙げる	(C) 30.4%
(D) To explain Zextra Designs' policy	(D) ゼクストラ・デザインズのポリシーを説明する	(D) 17.4%

解説　メールの内容から、すでに仕事についてはやりとりがあり、商品の配送について詳細を詰めている様子がうかがえます。6月25日深夜までに注文の確約が出れば既定の日付までに商品を届けられるので、知らせていただきたい、という趣旨のメッセージ内容となっており、これを最もよく表している(A)が正解となります。(B)は新しい取引という情報が見当たらず不正解、(C)、(D)は記載はあるものの、メールの主たる目的ではないので不正解となります。

177　正解 D

Who most likely is Beth Harcourt?
ベス・ハーコートとは誰でしょうか。

(A) An individual product designer	(A) 個人の製品デザイナー	(A) 13.0%
(B) The representative of Zextra Designs	(B) ゼクストラ・デザインズの代表者	(B) 17.4%
(C) A person in charge of a delivery company	(C) 配送会社の責任者	(C) 17.4%
(D) Personnel in Good-Goods Company	**(D) グッド・グッズ社の社員**	**(D) 47.8%**

解説　メールの宛先欄から、ベス・ハーコートはGood-Goods社の人間であることがわかり、headquartersなどの情報からも、個人ではなく法人に属する人間であると推察され、(D)が正解となります。

178　正解 A

In the e-mail, the word "unprecedented" in paragraph 2, line 1, is closest in meaning to
メールの第2パラグラフ1行目にあるunprecedentedと最も意味が近いものは

(A) extraordinary	**(A) 通常とは異なる**	**(A) 34.8%**
(B) outstanding	(B) 卓越した	(B) 26.1%
(C) rare	(C) 珍しい	(C) 21.7%
(D) commonplace	(D) ありきたりの	(D) 13.0%

解説　unprecedentedを類義語辞典で調べるとextraordinaryという単語は出てきます。一方で、前例がない＝通常とは異なる、かというと疑問符が付きます。しかしながら、同じ意味になるものは？ではなく、この特定の場所にある単語に最も意味が近いものはどれか、という問題なので、この問題においては(A)が正解になります。

179　正解　D

Which merchandise takes the longest for its delivery?
どの製品が配送に最も時間を要するでしょうか。

(A) Mugs	(A) マグカップ	(A) 34.8%
(B) Stationery	(B) 文房具	(B) 4.3%
(C) Masks	(C) マスク	(C) 21.7%
(D) Caps	**(D) 帽子**	**(D) 34.8%**

解説　最後の注釈に、この表に載っていないものはTシャツと同じ扱いとなる、とあり、日付を参照すると、このカテゴリーが最も配達に時間を要することがわかります。

180　正解　D

When can warehouses in Australia expect to receive mugs?
オーストラリアの倉庫がマグカップを受け取りを想定できるのはいつでしょうか。

(A) On August 20th	(A) 8月20日	(A) 4.3%
(B) Before August 31st	(B) 8月31日より前	(B) 17.4%
(C) On August 31st	(C) 8月31日	(C) 30.4%
(D) Sometime in September	**(D) 9月中**	**(D) 43.5%**

解説　表を参照すると、港への配達が8月31日、そこから2、3日通関手続きにかかるため、倉庫がこれらの商品を受け取れるのは9月に入ってからとなり、(D)が正解となります。

第1章　英語脳徹底トレーニング

第2章　高難度問題の徹底攻略

第3章　正答ハイテクレッスン

第4章　ハイレベル完全模試

Questions 181-185 refer to the following advertisement and letter.
問題181-185は次の広告と手紙に関するものです。

Plus Size Clothing for the Modern, Independent Woman

If you are looking for a clothing store that caters to the modern, independent woman wearing sizes 18 and above, A Little Extra is the place for you! Our founder, Kathy Statis, is a plus-size model herself and personally knows how difficult it is to find a well-tailored piece of clothing for a plus size person. This was Kathy's main motivation behind A Little Extra.

We understand that you need to look your best, whether it is for a job interview or for that special date night. Walk into our store on Hobson Street, for a free stylist-assisted makeover. Our stylists are people from the fashion industry, who have years of experience in helping clients find clothes that flatter their body type. If you don't have the time to come into the store, simply log onto our website, www.alittleextra.biz, and choose from the endless range of options we have for you!

Kathy Statis, CEO
A Little Extra

Dear Ms. Statis,

I visited your store last weekend, and I was delighted to finally see plus-sized women being offered clothes that are smart, fashionable, and most importantly, fit well. All too often, when I am out shopping for myself, the only options I see are ill-fitted and frumpy looking tunics or loose pants.

Your stylists are warm, welcoming, and non-judgmental. I would like to especially recognize the services of Janet, the lady who helped me find some spectacular clothes in the store. She obviously loves her job, and her recommendations were spot on.

Thank you for the wonderful experience. I hope more people find out about A Little Extra, because you are doing a stellar job.

Kind regards,

Sarah Jones

現代の独立した女性のためのプラスサイズの服
　サイズ18以上の自立した女性に対応したモダンな衣料品店をお探しの場合は、ア・リトル・エクストラが最適です。私たちの創設者であるキャシー・ステーティスは、自分自身がプラスサイズのモデルであり、プラスサイズの人にぴったりの服を見つけるのがいかに難しいかを個人的に知っています。これが、ア・リトル・エクストラの背景である、キャシーの主な動機でした。
　就職の面接であろうと、特別な日の夜であろうと、あなたは最高の自分に見える必要があることを私たちは理解しています。ホブソンストリートにある私たちの店に足を踏み入れ、スタイリストによる無料のイメージチェンジをお楽しみください。私たちのスタイリストはファッション業界の人々であり、クライアントが自分の体形を引き立てる服を見つけるお手伝いをしてきた長年の経験があります。来店する時間がない場合は、当社のウェブサイトalittleextra.bizにログオンして、無限のオプションから選択してください。

キャシー・ステーティス、CEO
ア・リトル・エクストラ

ステーティス様

　私は先週末あなたの店を訪れました。そして私はついに、プラスサイズの女性に、スマートでファッショナブルで、そして最も重要なよく合う服が提供されているのを見て、うれしく思いました。たいていの場合、私が買い物をするときに選べる唯一の選択肢は、体に合わず、ずんぐりとしたチュニックまたはゆったりしたズボンです。
　店のスタイリストは温かく、歓迎的で、偏った判断をしませんでした。店内で素晴らしい洋服を探すのを手伝ってくれたジャネットさんのサービスに、特に感謝します。彼女は間違いなく自分の仕事が大好きで、彼女のお薦めは的を射ていました。
　素晴らしい経験をありがとうございました。あなた方は素晴らしい仕事をしているので、もっと多くの人がア・リトル・エクストラについて知ってくれることを願っています。

敬具

サラ・ジョーンズ

Vocabulary
□ **tailored** 仕立てられた　□ **makeover** 着せ替え　□ **flatter** お世辞を言う、喜ばせる
□ **all too often** 何度も、いつも　□ **frumpy** 時代遅れの　□ **tunic** 婦人用の短い上着
□ **welcoming** 歓迎ムードの　□ **non-judgmental** 人を判断したりしない　□ **spot on** 適格である

181　正解 C

What is unique about the business?
このビジネスについてユニークな点は何でしょうか。

(A) The pricing of the clothing
(B) The durability of the clothing
(C) The size of the clothing
(D) The fabrics of the clothing

(A) 衣類の価格
(B) 衣類の耐久性
(C) 衣類のサイズ
(D) 衣類の生地

(A) 17.4%
(B) 13.0%
(C) 52.2%
(D) 8.7%

解説　パッセージの中では、サイズにおいての記述がされており、それを示す(C)が正解だと特定できます。サイズについて、他に大きいサイズを購入できる所がないわけではありませんが、(C)以外の選択肢について(C)に勝る優位性を持つものはなく、(C)が正解となります。

182　正解 B

What can we infer about A little Extra?
A Little Extra について推測できることは何でしょうか。

(A) It has shops in several countries.
(B) It accepts electronic payment.
(C) It consists of only one stylist.
(D) It has been operating for decades.

(A) 複数の国にショップがある。
(B) 電子決済に対応している。
(C) 1人のみスタイリストがいる。
(D) 数十年事業を行っている。

(A) 21.7%
(B) 17.4%
(C) 13.0%
(D) 39.1%

解説　オンラインショップでの買い物も可能ということがわかります。この情報から、オンラインで購入で必須となる電子決済に対応しているとinfer（推測）することができます。

183　正解 D

What industry was Janet in previously?
ジャネットが以前働いていた業界は何でしょうか。

(A) Consulting
(B) Logistics
(C) Cosmetics
(D) Fashion

(A) コンサルティング
(B) 物流
(C) 化粧品
(D) ファッション

(A) 17.4%
(B) 0.0%
(C) 13.0%
(D) 60.9%

解説　2つ目のパッセージでジャネットの名前が挙げられ、大変良くしてもらったと満足と感謝の気持ちが述べられています。このショップのスタッフであることがわかります。1つ目のパッセージで、スタッフは皆ファッション業界から来ていると述べているので、(D)が正解となります。

184　　正解 A

What is the purpose of the letter sent from Sarah?
サラから送られた手紙の目的は何でしょうか。

(A) To show appreciation	**(A) 感謝の意を示すため**	**(A) 56.5%**
(B) To request a refund	(B) 返金を要求するため	(B) 21.7%
(C) To buy some more clothing	(C) さらに衣類を買うため	(C) 0.0%
(D) To send an inquiry	(D) 問い合わせをするため	(D) 13.0%

解説　Thank you for the wonderful experience. という直接的な言葉をはじめ、ジャネットへの感謝の気持ちを伝える内容になっているので、(A)が正解となります。

185　　正解 C

What does Sarah say about Janet?
サラはジャネットに対して何と言っていますか。

(A) She was unknowledgeable.	(A) 知識不足だった。	(A) 30.4%
(B) She was just like other staff.	(B) 他のスタッフと同じだった。	(B) 4.3%
(C) She did a great job.	**(C) 素晴らしい仕事をした。**	**(C) 52.2%**
(D) She deserves a higher salary.	(D) 給与アップに値する。	(D) 4.3%

解説　Her recommendations were spot on. (彼女のお勧めは的確である)との褒め言葉があるなど、いい仕事をしたという印象を持っていることは容易にうかがえるため、(C)が最も適切な選択肢となります。(D)については、そう思っているかもしれませんが、文面にはそのようには書かれていません。

Vocabulary
□ **unknowledgeable** 知識がない　□ **deserve** 〜 〜に値する

383

Questions 186-190 refer to the following e-mails and schedule.
問題186-190は次の2通のEメールと予定表に関するものです。

To: Emma Thompson
From: Janice Miller
Date: 12th September
Subject: List of pre-lunch performers for Day 2

Dear Emma,

Please find attached a list of performers for the first half of Day 2 of the Great British Talent Show 2021. The performers have all been briefed on the requirements of their acts and have been told not to exceed 15 minutes in total. We have estimated that the judges will ask the performers about themselves for about 15 minutes. These 15 minutes will also include any audience interaction. The judges for Day 2 have been confirmed and are:
　• Samantha Rey—International Supermodel
　• Peter Robinson—Motivational Speaker and Singer
　• William McManus—Music Producer

Each judge will get a suite in the hotel to get ready in. ①They have been asked to report to the set one hour prior to the first performer to test their microphones and other equipment. Lunch is set at 12:30 P.M., after Mr. Dev Reddy finishes his performance. ②The judges will eat in their own suites, while the hotel has been asked to provide a buffet lunch for the rest of the crew.

We have started selling audience tickets to the general public and the numbers are trending well. At this point, we have sold more than 2,000 tickets. Assuming all tickets are sold out, we are expecting a full house by the third or fourth performances. Let me know what you think and if you have any concerns on the order of the sessions.

Kind regards,

Janice Miller
Head Co-coordinator
The Great British Talent Show

The Great British Talent Show 2021

Royal Silver Hotel
16th November

Time	Performer	Type of Performance
9:00 A.M.	Ted Barker	Dancing
9:30 A.M.	Maya Thompson	Ballet
10:00 A.M.	Ria Soni	Singing
10:30 A.M.	Nala White	Sketching
11:00 A.M.	Chris Columbus	Magic
11:30 A.M.	Kaiya Graham	Acrobatics
12:00 P.M.	Dev Reddy	Singing

To: Janice Miller
From: Emma Thompson
Date: 12th September
Subject: Re: List of pre-lunch performers for Day 2

Dear Janice,

I am very impressed with the professional and efficient way you seem to be organising everything! The sign-up numbers do seem to be trending well at this stage. Perhaps we should increase the advertising to sell out all 3,500 seats. (FYI, it was 3,000 last time.) I will speak to James in Marketing about this and will copy you in on any e-mails I send him.

₃ The only feedback I have is to perhaps swap the second and third performers, for we don't want to be doing consecutive dance acts. I would rather have a dance followed by a singer, followed by another dancer. Please let me know if this makes sense. Also, I would appreciate it if you could send me the performers list for the final day.

Other than that, I think you and your team are doing a fabulous job! Keep up the good work and let me know if I can help in any way.

Kind regards,

Emma Thompson
Vice President, Events & Marketing
The Great British Talent Show 2021

宛先：エマ・トンプソン
差出人：ジャニス・ミラー
日付：9月12日
件名：2日目のランチ前のパフォーマーのリスト

エマ様

添付のグレート・ブリティッシュ・タレント・ショー2021、2日目の前半の出演者リストをご確認ください。出演者は全員、演技の要件について説明を受け、合計15分を超えないよう伝達されています。審査員は約15分間、出演者に彼ら自身のことについて質問する予定です。この15分間には、観客とのやりとりも含まれます。2日目の審査員は決定されており、次のとおりです。
　・Samantha Rey—国際スーパーモデル
　・Peter Robinson—モチベーショナル・スピーカー、歌手
　・William McManus—音楽プロデューサー

各審査員には、準備のためにホテルのスイートルームを提供します。マイクやその他の機器をテストするために、①最初の出演者の1時間前にセットに報告するように求められています。デヴ・レディ氏がパフォーマンスを終えた後、昼食は午後12時30分に設定されています。②審査員はスイートルームで食事をしますが、ホテル側は残りのクルーにはビュッフェ式ランチを提供するように依頼しています。

チケットの一般向け販売を開始し、好調な売れ行きです。現時点で、2000枚以上のチケットを販売しました。すべてのチケットが売れたと仮定すると、3番目か4番目のパフォーマンス頃には満席になると予想されます。ご意見や、セッションの順番についてご不明な点がございましたら、お気軽にお問い合わせください。

敬具

ジャニス・ミラー
ヘッドコーディネーター
グレート・ブリティッシュ・タレント・ショー

グレート・ブリティッシュ・タレント・ショー2021
ロイヤル・シルバー・ホテル
11月16日

時間	演者	演技の種類
9:00 A.M.	テッド・バーカー	ダンス
9:30 A.M.	マヤ・トンプソン	バレエ
10:00 A.M.	リア・ソニ	歌
10:30 A.M.	ナラ・ホワイト	スケッチ
11:00 A.M.	クリス・コロンブス	マジック
11:30 A.M.	カイヤ・グラハム	アクロバット
12:00 P.M.	デヴ・レディ	歌

宛先：ジャニス・ミラー
差出人：エマ・トンプソン
日付：9月12日
件名：Re：2日目のランチ前のパフォーマーのリスト

___

ジャニス様

的確かつ効率的にすべての準備を進められているようでとても素晴らしいです！　登録者数は、この段階では順調に推移しているようです。3500席分を売り切るために宣伝を増やす必要がありそうです（参考までに前回は3000席でした）。このことについてマーケティングのジェームズと話しますが、彼にメールを送るときにはジャニスさんにもコピーを送るようにします。

③2日目についての唯一のフィードバックは、2番目と3番目のパフォーマーの順番を入れ替えることです。これは、連続してダンスアクトを行いたくないためです。それよりはむしろ、ダンスの次に歌手、次にまた別のダンサーがいるほうがいいです。これが良いと思われる場合はお知らせください。また、最終日のパフォーマーリストも送っていただければ幸いです。

それ以外については、あなたとあなたのチームは素晴らしい仕事をしていると思います！　良い仕事を続けて、何らかの形で私に手伝えることがあればお知らせください。

敬具

エマ・トンプソン
イベント＆マーケティング担当副社長
グレート・ブリティッシュ・タレント・ショー 2021

Vocabulary
- ☐ **brief** 要点を手短に伝える　☐ **suite** スイートルーム　☐ **trend** 推移する
- ☐ **sign-up numbers** 登録者数　☐ **FYI For your information** の略　☐ **consecutive** 連続した、並んだ

186　　正解 C

What is NOT indicated about the Great British Talent Show?
グレート・ブリティッシュ・タレント・ショーに関して示されていないことは何でしょうか。

(A) It spans several days.	(A) 数日間に及ぶ	(A) 26.1%
(B) Famous figures judge performers.	(B) 著名人が審査を行う	(B) 26.1%
(C) It takes place annually.	**(C) 毎年行われる**	**(C) 34.8%**
(D) It is a live performance show.	(D) ライブパフォーマンスである	(D) 4.3%

解説　3つ目のパッセージで前回開催があったことはわかるが、毎年開催を示す記述はなく、(C)が正解となります。この予定はDay 2の予定であること、Day 3があることからも、(A)には言及があります。3名の著名な審査員が挙げられているため(B)にも言及があります。オーディエンスを入れての開催であることから、(D)にも言及があることがわかります。

187　正解 A

By what time are the judges supposed to arrive at the venue?
審査員は何時に会場入りすることになっているでしょうか。

(A) 8:00 A.M.	**(A) 午前8時**	**(A) 43.5%**
(B) 8:45 A.M.	(B) 午前8時45分	(B) 17.4%
(C) 9:00 A.M.	(C) 午前9時	(C) 8.7%
(D) 12:30 P.M.	(D) 午後12時30分	(D) 17.4%

解説　下線①から、最初のパフォーマーの9:00 A.M.よりも1時間早い8:00 A.M.までに到着することが求められているので(A)が正解となります。

188　正解 D

Who do the judges have lunch with?
審査員は昼食は誰と取るでしょうか。

(A) With other crew members	(A) 他の撮影スタッフと	(A) 26.1%
(B) With performers	(B) パフォーマーと	(B) 8.7%
(C) With all the other judges	(C) 他の審査員皆と	(C) 13.0%
(D) With no one else	**(D) 誰と一緒でもない**	**(D) 43.5%**

解説　下線②から、それぞれの部屋で食事をするということが示されており、(D)が正解となります。同じく第2パラグラフにEach judge will get a suiteとあるので、部屋はそれぞれ別室であるため、3者が同じ部屋で宿泊しそこで一緒に食事をするということは示されておらず、(C)は不正解となります。(A)、(B)には言及がなく誤りとなります。

189　正解 C

What does Emma say she will do for marketing?
エマはマーケティングのために何をすると言っていますか？

(A) She will place more advertisements online.	(A) もっとオンラインで広告を出す	(A) 26.1%
(B) She will increase the number of seats by 500.	(B) 席を500席増やす	(B) 34.8%
(C) She will communicate with a person in charge.	**(C) 責任者と話す**	**(C) 21.7%**
(D) She will have James purchase as many tickets as possible.	(D) ジェームズにチケットをできる限り多く購入させる	(D) 8.7%

解説　マーケティングのジェームズと話すと書いてあるため(C)が正解となります。エマ自身が広告掲載を行うという情報はなく、またオンラインと限定することもできないため(A)は誤りです。問題は、マーケティングのために何をするか、ですので、マーケティングのために500席増やすという説明は成り立たず、(B)も不正解です。前回から500席増えたのは事実ですが、今回のマーケティングのために500席増やすわけではありません。(D)は、文章中に言及もなく誤りです。また、これをやってしまうとパワハラになりますので、人が取るべき行為としても誤りです。

190　　正解　B

Who does Emma's suggest should start performing at 10 A.M.?
エマは午前10時から演じるのは誰にすべきと提案していますか。

(A) Ted Barker	(A) テッド・バーカー	(A) 26.1%
(B) Maya Thompson	**(B) マヤ・トンプソン**	**(B) 39.1%**
(C) Ria Soni	(C) リア・ソニ	(C) 21.7%
(D) Nala White	(D) ナラ・ホワイト	(D) 4.3%

解説　下線③から、Maya Thompson と Ria Soni が入れ替わることになるので、(B)Maya Thompson が 10 A.M. から開始することになります。

Questions 191-195 refer to the following notice, article, and report.

問題191-195は次のお知らせ、記事、報告書に関するものです。

Book Lovers of Packerson, UNITE!

A new subscription offer from Bob Archer Library, Packerson

Tired of reading books on your electronic device? Do you long for the feel of a real book in your hands? If this sounds like you, come pick up one of our new subscription cards that give you access to over 7,000 books that you can hold! No more paying per book!

	Price/year	Invitation to reading events	Unlimited book checkout	Reserve & Deliver *to registered address
Platinum members for voracious readers	$300	○	○	○
Gold members for our busy patrons	$200	○	○	○
Silver members for beginners	$100	○	○	
Free members For dormant readers	free	○		

*Seminar/Meeting rooms are available for Platinum members only.

The Packerson Times

March 31, 2021 (Packerson) With the 20th Anniversary of the Bob Archer Library fast approaching, ①Theo, the head librarian, has come up with an innovative idea of returning to paper books in conjunction with a monthly payment style, which has been seen only in online formats, to increase engagement with the local community. Theo says the reserve & delivery service must be appealing to many people. Together with the room-renting options, the service can be viable, he stresses.

"The idea came from a conversation with one of our young readers, Elsa, who mentioned that she was tired of reading on her device and longed for a real hardcover to hold and read. This got me thinking that if the younger generation feels this way, imagine how older adults must feel," Theo said in a recent interview with *The Packerson Daily Times*.

It remains to be seen if this initiative will prove to be a game changer or if Packerson will continue to flock to online stores for the latest e-books.

Report on the Initial Performance of the Bob Archer Library Subscription Cards Program

This is a report on the progress and scope of the Bob Archer Library Subscription Cards Program, where we examine if the program led to an increase in the number of customers.

The program was launched on the 1st of April, 2021, and saw 1654 people signed up for cards in the first fortnight after its launch. Of these 1,654 people who were surveyed, 865 members signed up for the platinum membership. It appears Theo's vision was correct. In fact, many people find the room-renting service quite cost-efficient. 311 opted for the Gold, and the remaining 478 signed up for the Silver membership.

Total membership numbers have seen a steady increase throughout the last year and initiatives such as a discounted price for local students have also helped drive a growth in the total membership numbers. Students account for about 10%, of which Silver is dominant.

Over the last year, the library has seen an increase in profit of almost 200,000 dollars. Theo is being credited with this huge turnaround in the library's fortunes. He plans to invest half of the revenue earned on newer books and magazines for the library and the rest on updating the library's infrastructure.

バッカーソンの本の愛好家、集まれ!
バッカーソンのボブ・アーチャー図書館からの新しい購読提供

電子機器で本を読むのにうんざりしていませんか。本物の本の感触を待ち望んでいますか。あなたがそのように思っている場合は、7000冊以上の本にアクセスできる新しいサブスクリプションカードを手に入れてください!　本ごとに支払う必要はもうありません!

	年会費	読書イベントへの招待	無制限の本の貸し出し	予約と登録住所への配達
熱心な読書家のためのプラチナメンバー	300ドル	○	○	○
多忙な常連客のためのゴールドメンバー	200ドル	○	○	○
ビギナーのためのシルバーメンバー	100ドル	○	○	
読書離れしている人のための無料メンバー	無料	○		

*セミナー / 会議室はプラチナ会員のみ利用できます。

バッカーソン・タイムズ

　2021年3月31日 (バッカーソン)、20周年が間近に迫るボブ・アーチャー図書館の①テオ図書館長は、地域社会との関わりを深めるための、これまではオンラインでしか見られなかった月額ベースの課金スタイルを紙の本で行うという革新的なアイデアを思いつきました。テオは、予約&配達サービスは多くの人に魅力的だろうと言います。部屋の貸し出しオプションと合わせ、このサービスは成立すると強調しています。

　「このアイデアは、若い読者の1人であるエルサとの会話から生まれました。彼女は、自分のデバイスで読むのにうんざりしていて、本物のハードカバーを持って読むことを切望していると述べました。このことから、若い世代がこのように感じるのなら、大人がどのように感じているかを考えました」と、テオはバッカーソン・デイリー・タイムズとの最近のインタビューで述べました。

　この発案が大変革をもたらすかどうか、またはバッカーソン市民が最新の電子書籍を求めてオンラインストアに殺到し続けるかどうかはまだわかりません。

ボブ・アーチャー図書館サブスクリプションカードプログラムの初期パフォーマンスに関するレポート

これは、ボブ・アーチャー図書館サブスクリプションカードプログラムの進捗と展望に関するレポートで、プログラムが継続客の増加につながったかどうかを調べるものです。

このプログラムは2021年4月1日に開始され、開始直後の2週間で1654人がカードにサインアップしました。この調査の対象となった1654人のうち865人が、プラチナメンバーシップに登録しました。テオの構想が正しかったようです。実際多くの人は、部屋貸しサービスを極めて費用対効果が高いと認識しています。311人がゴールドを選択し、残りの478人がシルバーメンバーシップに登録しました。

総会員数は昨年を通じて着実に増加しており、地元学生向けの割引価格などといった発案も総会員数の増加を後押ししています。生徒は全体の10パーセントを占め、その中ではシルバーが大多数です。

昨年、図書館は約20万ドルの利益増加がありました。テオは、この図書館の未来への大転換において称賛されています。彼は、収入の半分を図書館の新しい本や雑誌に投資し、残りを図書館のインフラの更新に投資することを計画しています。

Vocabulary

☐ **voracious** 貪欲な　　☐ **patron** 図書館利用者、常連客　　☐ **dormant** 眠っている
☐ **in conjunction with** 〜　〜と合わせ　　☐ **game changer** 変革をもたらすもの
☐ **fortnight** 2週間　　☐ **turnaround** 転換

191　正解 B

What is the innovation that Bob Archer is trying to bring about?
ボブ・アーチャーが起こそうとしている変革は何でしょうか。

(A) The room-renting service	(A) 部屋貸しサービス	(A) 56.5%
(B) A non-online subscription model	**(B) 非オンラインのサブスクリプションモデル**	**(B) 4.3%**
(C) Availability of thousands of paper books	(C) 数千冊もの紙の本の用意	(C) 21.7%
(D) A rich variety of subscription plans	(D) 豊かなサブスクリプションプラン	(D) 8.7%

解説　下線①から、(B)がこのビジネスモデルの革新的な部分であることが読み取れます。他の選択肢についても正しい情報ではあるが、innovativeな要素は？となると(B)に勝ることはできず、この問題においては正解とはなりません。(A)は第1パッセージ、第3パッセージを参照してみると、成功への大きな要因であったと予想できますが、部屋貸しサービスの導入を「イノベーション」と考えていたわけではないので、(A)は正解にはなりません。

192　正解 C

What is NOT true about Theo?
テオについて正しくないのはどれでしょうか。

(A) He works for the Bob Archer Library.	(A) 彼はボブ・アーチャー図書館で働いている。	(A) 26.1%
(B) He came up with the new business idea.	(B) 彼が新しいビジネスアイデアを考えついた。	(B) 8.7%
(C) He himself is a subscriber to the Platinum plan.	**(C) 彼自身がプラチナプランの読者である。**	**(C) 43.5%**
(D) He intends to invest more in his business.	(D) さらに自分のビジネスに投資しようと思っている。	(D) 13.0%

解説　特に第2パッセージ、第3パッセージにおいて(A)、(B)、(D)の情報は記載があるが、(C)の情報はいずれのパッセージにも記載がないため、これが正解となります。

193　正解 A

In the second article, the word "flock to" in paragraph 3, line 2, is closest in meaning to
2番目のパッセージで、パラグラフ3、2行目にある flock to に最も意味が近いものはどれでしょうか。

(A) inundate	**(A) 殺到する**	**(A) 21.7%**
(B) utilize	(B) 活用する	(B) 43.5%
(C) neglect	(C) 無視する	(C) 21.7%
(D) acknowledge	(D) 認知する	(D) 4.3%

解説　flock toは押し寄せる、という意味なので、(A)がこれに最も近く正解となります。

194　正解 D

What can be learned about the Gold members plan?
ゴールド会員について何を読み取ることができるでしょうか。

(A) The price remains constant for students.	(A) 学生にも価格は同一である。	(A) 17.4%
(B) Its subscribers increased the most last year.	(B) その登録者数が1年で最も増加した。	(B) 17.4%
(C) It is the most cost-efficient plan.	(C) それが最も費用対効果が高いプランである。	(C) 30.4%
(D) It generated greater revenue than the Silver plan.	**(D) シルバープランよりも大きな収入を上げた。**	**(D) 26.1%**

解説　第1パッセージと第3パッセージの両方を参照してみると、Goldプランの料金はSilverプランの2倍で、登録者はさほど大きな違いはないことから、正確な計算をしなくても、論理的に考えて、Goldプランの収入の方が大きかったということが分かります。そのため(D)が正解となります。

195　正解 A

What category do the majority of the surveyed individuals fall into?
調査された人たちでどのカテゴリーに入る人が最も多いでしょうか。

(A) Voracious readers	**(A) 熱心な読書家**	**(A) 43.5%**
(B) Busy patrons	(B) 多忙な常連客	(B) 13.0%
(C) Beginners	(C) ビギナー	(C) 21.7%
(D) Dormant readers	(D) 読書離れしている人	(D) 13.0%

解説　第1パッセージと第3パッセージの両方を参照してみると、過半数の有料会員はPlatinumプランに加入していることがわかり、このプランの対象者を表現した(A)のVoracious readersが正解になります。また調査の対象となったのはこの有料会員1654人であることから、Free membersに当てはまる(D)のDormant readersはこの問題の「調査された人たち」には入らず、実際に何人いてもこの問題への正解とはなりません。

Vocabulary

☐ **fall into the category** そのカテゴリーに入る

Questions 196-200 refer to the following e-mails and list.
問題196-200は次の2通のEメールと表に関するものです。

To: Nathan Miller
From: Steve Lee
Date: 18th July 2021
Subject: Greeting. Change in Account Manager

Dear Mr. Miller,

I am writing to you to notify you of a slight change in your account with SaluteFoods. I understand that your account manager used to be Gavin Felix. Your account has now been passed onto me since Gavin has retired from the business. I assure you that there will be no change in the level of customer service you expect from us.

If you prefer, I could come down to the hotel to double-check all standing orders that you have placed with us for the next quarter. ①I could have my assistant call or e-mail you with a list of possible times. At this point, everything that you have ordered for the hotel's restaurant is in stock, except those from Culture-wide, and I see no problems procuring any of your usual ingredients.

Kind regards,

Steve Lee
Account Manager
SaluteFoods

To: Steve Lee
From: Nathan Miller
Date: 18th July 2021
Subject: Re: Greeting. Change in Account Manager

Hi Steve,

Thank you for e-mailing me. I look forward to working with you too. I'm glad to hear that supply will not be a problem when it comes to any of our usual orders. As you know, we are getting into a busy summer and the hotel earns most of its annual revenue during this time.

We are expecting to change the restaurant's menu to a more summer-based one and will be needing a few extra ingredients added to our standing order list. Please find the additional ingredients attached to this e-mail.

Should you face any issues procuring these additional ingredients, please let me know so that I can come up with some viable substitutes.

I would be happy to meet you to discuss the matter further. I would prefer to meet on a weekday when there is a delivery of the newly added ingredients for Korean food, as I will definitely be at the restaurant to check the items. I would like to meet you so that I can put a face to the name.

Kind regards,

Nathan Miller
Executive Chef
The Far-West Millennium Hotel

Ingredient Name	Quantity per Week	Brand	Delivery Day
Black Truffle Oil	20 × 250 ml bottles	Culture-wide	Tuesday
Pecan Nuts	10 × 1-kilogram bags	Sweet-Smooth	Friday
Gochujang Paste	4 × 1-kilogram bins	Korean Chilly	Monday
Black Garlic	2-kilogram bag	Stella Farmers	Tuesday
Avocado Oil	20 × 250 ml bottles	Culture-wide	Sunday

宛先:ネイサン・ミラー
差出人:スティーブ・リー
日付:2021年7月18日
件名:アカウントマネージャーの変更

ミラー様

サリュート・フーズの取引に関することで少し変更があり、それをお知らせするために、メールを書いています。あなたのアカウントマネージャーは、以前はギャビン・フェリックスでしたが、ギャビンが退職後、御社のアカウントは私のほうで引き継ぎいたしました。あなたが期待する顧客サービスのレベルに変化がないことを保証します。

ご希望があれば、ホテルに伺い、次の四半期分に頂いている全注文を再確認することもできます。①それが可能

な時間のリストを、アシスタントに、電話かメールさせることができます。現時点で、ホテルのレストラン用に注文したものは、カルチャーワイド製のもの以外はすべて在庫があり、通常の食材を調達するのに問題はないようです。

敬具

スティーブ・リー
アカウントマネージャー
サリュート・フーズ

宛先：スティーブ・リー
差出人：ネイサン・ミラー
日付：2021年7月18日
件名：Re：アカウントマネージャーの変更

スティーブさん、こんにちは

メールをお送りいただきありがとうございます。私もあなたと一緒に働けることを楽しみにしています。通常の注文に関しては、供給に問題はないと聞いて安心しました。ご存じのように、私たちは忙しい夏を迎えており、ホテルはこの期間中、年間収益の多くを得ています。

レストランのメニューを夏仕様にしたメニューに変更する予定でして、継続注文リストに幾つか食材を追加する必要があります。このメールに添付されている追加材料の確認をお願いいたします。

これらの追加材料の調達で問題が発生した場合は、可能な代替品を考えられるよう、お知らせくださいませ。

ぜひあなたにお会いして、顔と名前を一致させたいです。平日でコリアンフードのための、新しく追加した材料の配達がある日が望ましいです。それらの日は配達物の確認のために必ずレストランに来ていますので。お会いできるのを楽しみにしています。

敬具

ネイサン・ミラー
エグゼクティブシェフ
ファー・ウエスト・ミレニアムホテル

材料名	週あたりの数量	ブランド	配達日
ブラックトリュフオイル	20 × 250 ml瓶	カルチャーワイド	火曜日
ピーカンナッツ	10 × 1 kg袋	スィートスムーズ	金曜日
コチュジャンソース	4 × 1 kg瓶	コリアン・チリー	月曜日
ブラックガーリック	2 kg袋	ステラ・ファーマーズ	火曜日
アボカドオイル	20 × 250 ml本	カルチャーワイド	金曜日

Vocabulary
☐ **standing order** 継続注文、定期的に行っている通常の注文　☐ **procure** 仕入れる　☐ **viable** 可能な
☐ **substitute** 代替のもの　☐ **put a face to the name** 顔と名前を一致させる

196 　正解 D

What is the main purpose of the first e-mail?
最初のメールの目的は何でしょうか。

(A) To account for a potential problem	(A) 起こりえる問題を説明する	(A) 30.4%
(B) To assure timely delivery	(B) 迅速な配達を保証する	(B) 26.1%
(C) To receive additional orders	(C) 追加注文をもらう	(C) 17.4%
(D) To send a greeting message	**(D) あいさつ文を送る**	**(D) 17.4%**

解説　人事の変更を伝えつつ、新しく担当となったことを伝えているので、(D) が正解となります。あいさつの要素以外にも細かな情報が含まれていますが、いずれもこのメールの主たる目的と呼ぶには十分ではなく、(D) 以外の選択肢は正解とはなりません。タイトルにもGreetingとあり、このメールの目的があいさつであることが読み取れます。

197 　正解 C

In the first e-mail, what does Steve say he can do?
最初のメールで、スティーブは何ができると言っていますか。

(A) Find a replacement for missing items	(A) ない素材に対して代替品を見つける	(A) 34.8%
(B) Include more items to the standing order	(B) 継続注文リストにもっと多くの品を含める	(B) 17.4%
(C) Let his colleague contact Nathan	**(C) 彼の同僚にネイサンに連絡させる**	**(C) 21.7%**
(D) Double the order for the next quarter	(D) 次の四半期に注文を2倍にする	(D) 17.4%

解説　下線①のhaveは使役動詞で、アシスタントに電話かメールさせることができる、と書いてあるため、(C) が正解となります。

198　正解 C

What is the main purpose of the second e-mail sent to Steve Lee?
2番目のスティーブ・リーへのメールの主な目的は何でしょうか。

(A) To discuss new summer-based dishes	(A) 新しい夏向けのメニューを協議する	(A) 43.5%
(B) To show gratitude toward Gavin Felix	(B) ガービン・フェリックスに感謝の意を示す	(B) 4.3%
(C) To specify items for additional orders	**(C) 追加注文の品を指定する**	**(C) 39.1%**
(D) To clarify which ingredient is missing	(D) どの食材が足りていないか明らかにする	(D) 4.3%

解説　まずはあいさつをした上で、新メニューのための材料について添付ファイル付きで説明していることから、その新メニューのための追加材料の発注についての内容が、このメールの主な目的と言えます。よって(C)が正解となります。

199　正解 A

Which ingredient can SaluteFoods NOT deliver now?
サリュート・フーズが現在発送できない食材、原材料はどれでしょうか。

(A) Black Truffle Oil	**(A) ブラックトリュフオイル**	**(A) 43.5%**
(B) Pecan Nuts	(B) ピーカンナッツ	(B) 17.4%
(C) Gochujang Paste	(C) コチュジャンソース	(C) 26.1%
(D) Black Garlic	(D) ブラックガーリック	(D) 4.3%

解説　第1パッセージと第3パッセージの両方を参照しながら答えます。第1パッセージにカルチャーワイドの製品だけは在庫がないと書かれています。第3パッセージ（添付されている表）を見ると、選択肢にあるものの中では、(A)のブラックトリュフオイルがカルチャーワイド製のものであることがわかり、これが正解となります。

200　正解 A

On what day of the week, will Nathan and Steve most likely meet?
ネイサンとスティーブは会う可能性が最も高い日はどれでしょうか。

(A) Monday	**(A) 月曜日**	**(A) 34.8%**
(B) Wednesday	(B) 水曜日	(B) 13.0%
(C) Thursday	(C) 木曜日	(C) 21.7%
(D) Sunday	(D) 日曜日	(D) 17.4%

解説　第2パッセージと第3パッセージの両方を参照しながら答えます。第2パッセージに、配達された製品の確認のために、その配送日にはホテルのレストランに確実にいるので、平日の配達がある日が望ましい、と記載されています。第2パッセージ（添付されている表）を見ると、配送日が記載されており、選択肢の中では(A)の月曜日に配送があることがわかります。よって(A)が正解となります。

●著者

山内勇樹　Yamauchi Yuki

1980年、長崎県生まれ広島県育ち。UCLA（カルフォルニア大学ロサンゼルス校）卒。株式会社Sapiens Sapiens代表取締役・最高責任講師。

独自のTOEIC指導法には定評があり、TOEIC指導実績は延べ1000人を超える。3ヵ月で100～200点以上UPを達成する受講者も多く、TOEIC990点満点取得者も輩出。

TOEICテスト990点満点。TOEICテストSW400点満点、TOEIC IIBC Award of Excellence 総合パーフェクト（満点）受賞者。

著書に『Storyで覚える！TOEICテスト エッセンシャル英単語』、『Storyで覚える！TOEIC テスト エッセンシャル英文法』（かんき出版）など多数。

カバーデザイン	滝デザイン事務所	ナレーション
帯デザイン	花本浩一（麒麟三隻館）	Howard Colefield［米］
本文デザイン・DTP	アトリエマーブル	Nadia McKechnie［英］
英文校正	TRAアカデミー	Nadia Jaskiw［加］
編集協力	巣之内史規	Stuart O［豪］

本書へのご意見・ご感想は下記URLまでお寄せください。
https://www.jresearch.co.jp/contact

TOEIC® L&R TEST 990点徹底スピードマスター ハイレベル完全模試1回分付

令和4年（2022年）2月10日　初版第1刷発行
令和4年（2022年）6月10日　　第2刷発行

著　者	山内勇樹
発行人	福田富与
発行所	有限会社　Jリサーチ出版
	〒166-0002 東京都杉並区高円寺北2-29-14-705
	電話 03（6808）8801（代）　FAX 03（5364）5310（代）
	編集部 03（6808）8806
	URL https://www.jresearch.co.jp
印刷所	㈱シナノパブリッシングプレス

第4章 990点満点を取るためだけの
ハイレベル完全模試

問題冊子

◆**用意するもの**

☑ 音源(Track 30 ～ 111)

☑ 筆記用具

☑ 腕時計

☑ P53, 55のマークシート

◆**ココがポイント！**

① 時間を計って解こう

2時間ですべて解き終わらなくても最後まで解いて、
オーバーした時間を覚えておこう。

② 答え合わせをしよう

解説を読んで、しっかり身につけよう。間違えた問題は、
なぜ間違えたのかを考えて、同じミスをくり返さないようにしよう。

LISTENING TEST

In the Listening test, you will be asked to demonstrate how well you understand spoken English. The entire Listening test will last approximately 45 minutes. There are four parts, and directions are given for each part. You must mark your answers on the separate answer sheet. Do not write your answers in your test book.

PART 1

Directions: For each question in this part, you will hear four statements about a picture in your test book. When you hear the statements, you must select the one statement that best describes what you see in the picture. Then find the number of the question on your answer sheet and mark your answer. The statements will not be printed in your test book and will be spoken only one time.

Statement (C), "They're sitting at a table," is the best description of the picture, so you should select answer (C) and mark it on your answer sheet.

1.

2.

GO ON TO THE NEXT PAGE

3.

4.

5.

6.

GO ON TO THE NEXT PAGE ➔

Directions

PART 2

Directions: You will hear a question or statement and three responses spoken in English. They will not be printed in your test book and will be spoken only one time. Select the best response to the question or statement and mark the letter (A), (B), or (C) on your answer sheet.

7.   Mark your answer on your answer sheet.

(8.〜30.は省略)

31.   Mark your answer on your answer sheet.

Directions

PART 3

Directions: You will hear some conversations between two or more people. You will be asked to answer three questions about what the speakers say in each conversation. Select the best response to each question and mark the letter (A), (B), (C), or (D) on your answer sheet. The conversations will not be printed in your test book and will be spoken only one time.

32. Where does the man work?
   (A) A professional dancers' club
   (B) A fitness center
   (C) A city council
   (D) A training school for singers

33. What is mentioned about the program that the woman is interested in?
   (A) Participants can come on any day without limits.
   (B) The monthly fee is $200 for the first six months.
   (C) Participation to some classes is mandatory.
   (D) A credit card is the only accepted payment method.

34. What information does the man say he will explain?
    (A) The terms and conditions concerning the financial disclosure
    (B) The required steps that all applicants have to follow
    (C) When and where the programs are held
    (D) Information on which credit cards are acceptable for payment

---

35. What is the woman's problem?
    (A) Her keys are missing.
    (B) The man took the woman's key.
    (C) She cannot enter her room.
    (D) Her refrigerator does not open.

36. Where is the conversation taking place?
    (A) In an office
    (B) At a grocery store
    (C) On the street
    (D) In a house

37. What does the woman say she will do?
    (A) Shop at the grocery store
    (B) Check her bedroom
    (C) Start working from home
    (D) Go outside

---

38. What field does the woman most likely work in?
    (A) In the media industry
    (B) In the food manufacturing industry
    (C) In the music industry
    (D) In the hospitality industry

39. Why does the man say, "To be more specific, I've worked in France and the United Kingdom"?
    (A) To specify the locations he wants to work in
    (B) To impress the woman about his achievements
    (C) To show his candidacy and experience
    (D) To explain what kind of cuisine he specializes in

40. What do we learn about the position?
    (A) It has only a limited number of openings.
    (B) Its selection process involves a practical test.
    (C) It will be closed sometime soon.
    (D) It does not require intensive experience.

GO ON TO THE NEXT PAGE

41. What does the woman imply when she says, "I'm all ears"?
(A) She really wants to know what the news is.
(B) She has to pay attention to what the man says.
(C) She sometimes has a hearing problem.
(D) She can pick up sound quite precisely.

42. Why is the woman thrilled?
(A) Because she can see Kyogo for the first time
(B) Because the man handed some tickets to the woman
(C) Because she can perform at the music show
(D) Because her favorite singer will come to town

43. What will the speakers do next month?
(A) Throw a birthday party for the woman
(B) Buy some tickets as a present for the woman
(C) Attend an event together
(D) Sing a song at a music show

44. What is most likely the man's occupation?
(A) Buying and selling art works
(B) Providing consultation to galleries
(C) Painting a rare genre of art pieces
(D) Managing an art gallery

45. According to the man, why was he invited?
(A) Because he can give detailed advice to management
(B) Because he knows Mr. Potter personally
(C) Because he might be able to discuss profitable deals
(D) Because he can produce rare arts.

46. What does the woman say she will do?
(A) Take off her shoes
(B) Call Mr. Potter
(C) Follow Mr. Silvia Granger
(D) Take the man to an office

47. Where most likely are the speakers?
(A) At a supermarket
(B) At a fast-food restaurant
(C) At a cooking school
(D) At Mrs. Yoon's house

48. Who most likely is Fiona?
(A) Adam's colleague
(B) A delivery person
(C) A culinary instructor
(D) Mrs. Yoon's friend

49. What will the man do next?
(A) Wait until the ordered food is ready
(B) Have a glass of apple juice
(C) Help prepare food within 10 minutes
(D) Bring some beverages

50. What reason does the man give as to why he couldn't arrive on time?
- (A) He got lost on the new highway.
- (B) He was involved in a car accident.
- (C) He had to take care of his children.
- (D) He was stuck in traffic for a long time.

51. What possible solution does the woman propose to the man?
- (A) He should let his wife see his children.
- (B) He could leave home earlier.
- (C) He could take a shortcut.
- (D) He should never try taking alternative routes.

52. What does the woman mean when she says, "I do not want to do this"?
- (A) She felt lethargic about writing a warning letter.
- (B) She believes a warning letter should be and can be avoided.
- (C) She doubts that a letter like this is effective.
- (D) She predicts that the man will be late again.

---

53. According to the speakers, what will be the topic of today's meeting?
- (A) Trees at the Dotti Forest Reserve
- (B) Policies about environmental protection
- (C) Projects between the company and the ministry
- (D) Upcoming regional elections

54. According to the woman, what is the true objective of the tree-planting activities?
- (A) A special performance for the election
- (B) Securing governmental funding
- (C) Increasing the forest cover in the state
- (D) Stopping desertification of the forest

55. Why does the man say, "Well, I take back what I just said"?
- (A) He realized that what he just said is irrelevant.
- (B) He misunderstood the theme of the conversation.
- (C) He felt the necessity of paraphrasing his remarks.
- (D) He was unhappy about the politician's behavior.

---

56. Who is the woman talking to?
- (A) A pharmacist
- (B) A telephone operator
- (C) A doctor
- (D) Julia Swart

GO ON TO THE NEXT PAGE

57. What information did the man ask the woman for?
(A) Her name
(B) Her phone number
(C) The time for pickup
(D) Her symptoms

58. What did the man tell the woman to do?
(A) Pick up the medicine at noon
(B) Call another pharmacist
(C) Read the labels carefully
(D) Sleep well to get better

59. Why is the man sending the message?
(A) To explain colored flags he often uses
(B) To launch a new service
(C) To give instructions to the woman
(D) To inquire the current situation

60. According to the man, which of the following is least urgent?
(A) Inquiries flagged in red
(B) Inquiries flagged in yellow
(C) Inquiries flagged in blue
(D) Inquiries flagged in green

61. What does the woman say she would do?
(A) Have her team start replying with slight modification
(B) Change the order of priority that the man specified
(C) Confirm if the technical problems have been fixed
(D) Wait until she receives further instructions from the man

62. Where does the woman most likely work?
(A) At an airline company
(B) At a hotel in Auckland
(C) At a travel agency
(D) At an international airport

63. Look at the graphic. Which airline will the man choose for his flight?
(A) Singapore Central
(B) EU High Air
(C) Qantics Airline
(D) Jet Streamer

Airline	Arrives	Stopovers/Direct
Singapore Central	9 A.M.	Direct
EU High Air	1 P.M.	Direct
Qantics Airline	10:00 A.M.	1 stop
Jet Streamer	10:15 A.M.	2 stops

64. What does the man ask the woman to do?
(A) Change his flight
(B) Spend some time on confirmation
(C) Give the price list
(D) Move on to the final step

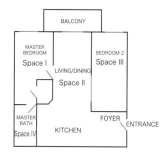

65. What most likely is the woman's occupation?
(A) A real estate appraiser
(B) A furniture manufacturer
(C) An architectural designer
(D) A construction manager

66. Why is a change requested?
(A) The draft was not clear enough.
(B) The plan does not match the man's instruction.
(C) There were too many dividers but too few windows.
(D) The dimension is not specified in the blueprint.

67. Look at the graphic. Which part of the layout will be changed?
(A) Space I
(B) Space II
(C) Space III
(D) Space IV

68. Who most likely are the speakers?
(A) Candidates for a manager's position
(B) Marketing managers
(C) Mr. Ronalds' supervisors
(D) Human resources executives

Question Set	What to ask	Duration
1st set	Why us	5 min
2nd set	Past achievements	10 min
3rd set	Strength/Weakness	15 min
4th set	Career ambition	10 min

69. Look at the agenda. Which part of the interview will be omitted?
(A) The 1st set
(B) The 2nd set
(C) The 3rd set
(D) The 4th set

70. What does the woman mean when she says, "Without a break"?
(A) The interview could take longer depending on how they proceed.
(B) It is possible to make the duration even shorter.
(C) Each candidate would feel better if he/she could take a break.
(D) She agrees with the idea that some questions should be omitted.

GO ON TO THE NEXT PAGE

PART 4

Directions: You will hear some talks given by a single speaker. You will be asked to answer three questions about what the speaker says in each talk. Select the best response to each question and mark the letter (A), (B), (C), or (D) on your answer sheet. The talks will not be printed in your test book and will be spoken only one time.

---

71. What is the main purpose of the talk?
(A) To construct a warehouse
(B) To publicize commodities
(C) To recruit some staff
(D) To ask some questions

72. What solution does the speaker say ALT can provide?
(A) An assistance for warehouse operations
(B) High-quality, low-priced groceries
(C) An income source that can be flexibly arranged
(D) Shift management systems for a supermarket

73. What does the speaker suggest the listeners do if they have questions?
(A) Send an e-mail
(B) Stop by at the supermarket
(C) Call the office
(D) Leave a voice message

74. What is the Employee Appreciation Month held for?
(A) To celebrate the 20th anniversary of the company
(B) To enjoy a variety of food served in the firm
(C) To show gratitude toward members' hard work
(D) To recruit a larger number of employees

75. What do we learn about Tera Pocket Mobile?
(A) It has a head office in New York.
(B) It offers $10,000-bonus each year.
(C) It elected new board members recently.
(D) Its fiscal year begins in September.

76. What will happen at the end of August?
- (A) The Employee of the Year will be announced.
- (B) Employees will join and enjoy special events.
- (C) The prize winner will go to New York.
- (D) The candidate nomination will be closed.

---

77. Why is the appointment being rescheduled?
- (A) The dentist is not feeling well.
- (B) Dr. Scholl is out of the office for a meeting.
- (C) Dr. Scholl's child is ill.
- (D) The doctors are out of town.

78. What does the speaker say about Dr. Heward?
- (A) She is more experienced than Dr Scholl.
- (B) She is from a prestigious university.
- (C) She is a permanent doctor in the clinic.
- (D) She can provide treatment to Mr. Patton.

79. What is the listener expected to do next?
- (A) Call back the clinic
- (B) Use the 10 percent discount
- (C) Go to the clinic to reschedule
- (D) Talk to Dr. Heward

---

80. Who is this speech intended for?
- (A) Employees of Pine Technology
- (B) The managers of Pine Technology
- (C) Customers of Pine Technology
- (D) Business partners of Pine Technology

81. What does the speaker mention about the structure of the company?
- (A) The largest number of the employees work in Oakland.
- (B) All employees across the world report to managers in Oakland.
- (C) Facilities in Europe are as big as the head office in Oakland.
- (D) All the executives appear in the virtual office tour.

GO ON TO THE NEXT PAGE

82. What are the listeners expected to do before asking questions?
(A) Send e-mails directly
(B) Visit the head office virtually
(C) Call the office in Oakland
(D) Wait for 30 minutes at the headquarters

---

83. What achievement is the speaker proud of?
(A) That they are based in the bay area
(B) That they have 60-year experience
(C) That they fully understand design printing
(D) That they have worked with many companies

84. According to the speaker, what will Bay Stylish Printing send upon request?
(A) Sample liquid dyes
(B) Company logos
(C) Sample textiles
(D) Printed uniforms

85. What does the speaker mean when he says, "We can do more than is printed in our catalog"?
(A) The company is making the greatest effort possible.
(B) The catalog does not explain everything.
(C) Delivery can be made faster than two weeks.
(D) The catalog lists things that the company actually can't do.

---

86. What is the topic of the podcast talk?
(A) The emergence of the Internet
(B) Adolescent psychology
(C) The life of Uncle Sam
(D) Why youth are attached to their phones

87. What does the speaker mean when she says, "Most of us are blind to its role, but he isn't"?
(A) He has better eyesight than average.
(B) His insight may give us clearer ideas.
(C) His book can be read by blind people.
(D) He can predict the future precisely.

88. What will Professor Chen talk about first?
   (A) Why many people become dependent on social media
   (B) How social media started and gained popularity
   (C) What social media is and its effects on society
   (D) How often people use social media

89. What is the topic of the lecture?
   (A) How stress affects our body and mind
   (B) What causes stress
   (C) Why we cannot eliminate stress
   (D) How stress changes one's entire life

90. What does the speaker say she suffered from in the past?
   (A) Depression
   (B) Trouble sleeping
   (C) Heart problems
   (D) High blood pressure

91. According to the speaker, how does exercising help us stay healthier?
   (A) By maintaining a good balance of hormones
   (B) By increasing the level of cortisol
   (C) By making us sleep less at night
   (D) By reducing the amount of endorphins

92. What is being advertised?
   (A) House furnishing
   (B) Kitchen equipment
   (C) Second-hand clothing
   (D) Cleaning tools

93. According to the speaker, what will happen in January next year?
   (A) The annual clearance sale will end.
   (B) The warehouse's space will be empty.
   (C) The new collection will be launched.
   (D) Foreign sofa brands will become available.

94. What can the listeners obtain from the company's website?
   (A) Tables and desks that are unavailable in stores
   (B) A discount ticket for delivery
   (C) A coupon for an additional discount
   (D) The list of available items

GO ON TO THENEXT PAGE

Curtain Type	Noise reduction property	Thickness
Type A	X	1 mm
Type B	X	1.5 mm
Type C	O	2.5 mm
Type D	O	4 mm

	Time	Agenda
I	10:00 - 10:20	Introductory speech
II	10:20 - 10:30	Company tour
III	11:15 - 11:30	President speech
IV	11:30 - 11:40	Concluding remarks

*An optional lunch session will follow
(Participation not mandatory)

95. What is the caller pleased about?
(A) The availability of a large quantity
(B) The price of the products
(C) The variation of options
(D) The size of the curtains

96. Look at the graphic. Which type of curtain will the caller most likely buy?
(A) Type A
(B) Type B
(C) Type C
(D) Type D

97. What does the caller request to the listener?
(A) To deliver as quickly as possible
(B) To call back before noon
(C) To give a call well in advance
(D) To bring in the products quietly

98. What will the speaker's employees do next month?
(A) Start preparing for a welcome ceremony
(B) Attend a ceremony outside the company
(C) Welcome newly recruited staff members
(D) Receive feedback from the president

99. Look at the graphic. Which part of the schedule should be adjusted?
(A) I
(B) II
(C) III
(D) IV

100. What does the speaker say the listener should do?
(A) Let department managers lead the tour
(B) Ask for help when necessary
(C) Make the lunch session mandatory
(D) Work harder in making a plan

READING TEST

In the Reading test, you will read a variety of texts and answer several different types of reading comprehension questions. The entire Reading test will last 75 minutes. There are three parts, and directions are given for each part. You are encouraged to answer as many questions as possible within the time allowed. You must mark your answers on the separate answer sheet. Do not write your answers in your test book.

PART 5

Directions: A word or phrase is missing in each of the sentences below. Four answer choices are given below each sentence. Select the best answer to complete the sentence. Then mark the letter (A), (B), (C), or (D) on your answer sheet.

---

101. Commentators who specialize in the food service industry were asked to name restaurants that they come back to -------.
(A) regulation
(B) regulate
(C) regular
(D) regularly

102. So as not to make the same error, all the users must read the written manual including the supplemental guide, and ------- decide which functions to use.
(A) thus
(B) then
(C) so
(D) to

103. Upon the launch of the new service, Joshua Text Service announced that its primary goal is to maximize customer satisfaction even at the sacrifice of -------.
(A) profiting
(B) profited
(C) profitable
(D) profitability

104. All employees of Mc MacManus Painting will receive ------- financial support for their residence.
(A) extend
(B) extending
(C) extensive
(D) extent

GO ON TO THENEXT PAGE

105. Audience was obviously getting tired of the ------- discussions among the panelists.
(A) prolong
(B) prolonging
(C) prolongs
(D) prolonged

106. If you listen to foreign songs, the words ------- seep into unconsciousness and help you remember new words.
(A) gradually
(B) correctly
(C) approximately
(D) routinely

107. We thank you for your order, but it may be two weeks ------- we can send the books to you.
(A) if
(B) before
(C) however
(D) while

108. If the secretaries work too -------, we might discover later that they made many filing errors.
(A) hardly
(B) greatly
(C) efficiently
(D) quickly

109. The auditors pointed out two suspicious cases, but ------- was found to be an unlawful conduct.
(A) none
(B) neither
(C) few
(D) either

110. Technical advice, ------- given at the beginning of the session or in the middle, must be taken as an absolute order.
(A) those
(B) so
(C) whether
(D) since

111. ------- mileage and other relevant conditions, the one we test-drove yesterday seems to be the most favorable.
(A) In terms of
(B) In exchange for
(C) In accordance with
(D) In response to

112. It has been ------- fifty years since the ex-king left his country to live in exile.
(A) closely
(B) highly
(C) wrongly
(D) nearly

113. All complaints need to be replied in a timely -------, so as to improve the company's image in the community.
(A) occasion
(B) manner
(C) limit
(D) necessity

114. We were disappointed that the new worker was unable to perform his duties ------- the normal time period.
(A) above
(B) beyond
(C) along
(D) within

115. ------- their successful project on LED, the gross sales of the entire company did not increase a bit.
(A) Notwithstanding
(B) However
(C) Nevertheless
(D) In spite

116. The electrician announced that the whole system will ------- be available unless other defects are discovered.
(A) already
(B) soon
(C) only
(D) sometimes

117. All the overdue electricity bills had been handled before the service got suspended -------.
(A) temporarily
(B) marginally
(C) domestically
(D) predictably

118. The store will be happy to refund your money on the condition that the item still has its sales tag -------.
(A) attaching
(B) to be attached
(C) attachment
(D) attached

119. Unlike the prototype developed by our competitors, ------- can fully recharge itself without any human commands.
(A) we
(B) us
(C) ourselves
(D) ours

120. The postcard they sent me shows that Parker's new office is located ------- 375 West Oak Street.
(A) onto
(B) at
(C) on
(D) beneath

GO ON TO THE NEXT PAGE

121. The accused man was judged to be innocent in the murder trial since the prosecutors could only provide ------- evidence.
(A) circumstantial
(B) second-hand
(C) disposable
(D) environmental

122. A good manager must understand the temperament of his workers and understand that frustration after losing a customer can either lead to absenteeism ------- a lack of motivation.
(A) but
(B) or
(C) nor
(D) yet

123. Parents should be ------- from doing their children's homework for them since children need to learn how to think for themselves.
(A) informed
(B) given up
(C) discouraged
(D) recommended

124. Online -------, many marketers say, is one of the most crucial processes that streamlines the shopping experience of all visitors.
(A) catalog
(B) catalogs
(C) cataloging
(D) cataloged

125. As ------- as I can remember, Josh was always on good terms with his coworkers including Mina.
(A) well
(B) early
(C) far
(D) long

126. ------- she been elected as the team leader, she could have organized the team more efficiently.
(A) Has
(B) Had
(C) Unless
(D) Should

127. The picture we want is one ------- can talk to the viewers' hearts and motivate them when they see it.
(A) that
(B) what
(C) it
(D) those

128. The updated rate of this VAT will be applied to an online ------- that takes place not only in Australia but also in New Zealand.
(A) purchasing
(B) purchased
(C) purchase
(D) purchases

129. The managers do not have infinite wisdom, but try to do the best ------- they can about the company's future.
(A) review
(B) analysis
(C) influence
(D) interest

130. All newly recruited engineers are ------- dispatched to one of our subsidiary companies for training.
(A) inaccurately
(B) responsibly
(C) customarily
(D) knowingly

GO ON TO THENEXT PAGE

PART 6

Directions: Read the texts that follow. A word, phrase, or sentence is missing in parts of each text. Four answer choices for each question are given below the text. Select the best answer to complete the text. Then mark the letter (A), (B), (C), or (D) on your answer sheet.

Questions 131-134 refer to the following instructions.

Dear All,

Please be aware that the policy concerning our customer service ----131----.

I am certain all of you have already been following the updated procedure, but for any request about replacement, we send a new item to the customer regardless of the reason for the request.

The most ----132---- reasons for a replacement include the wrong size or color of the shipped products, which account for over 90 percent of complaints. ----133---- there be any request for a refund without a receipt, let the caller know that printed proof is an absolute requirement. ----134----.

131. (A) change
   (B) was changing
   (C) has changed
   (D) will be changed

132. (A) frequent
   (B) serious
   (C) evident
   (D) fundamental

133. (A) Should
   (B) Might
   (C) If
   (D) Unless

134. (A) A rebate is a certain type of token that can be exchanged with cash or credits.
   (B) We are trying to figure out how we can minimize errors in shipping.
   (C) These customers will not receive any money back irrespective of the circumstances.
   (D) We highly appreciate it if you could increase your working hours.

Questions 135-138 refer to the following letter.

Dear Returns Representative:

I am a collector of German cuckoo clocks. Two days ago, my German Timekeeper clock ---135--- to slow down and keep irregular time. The clock has kept accurate time for the past four months. I have been very careful to follow the instructions for keeping my clock in good condition, ---136--- I am certain that I am not responsible for any damage to the clock.

---137---. It clearly states that German Timekeeper will replace any clock that does not keep correct time without charge.

I am sending you the damaged clock along with my receipt. I hope that you can send me a ---138--- within the next two weeks. My address is written on the receipt.

Thank you for your kind attention.

Best regards,

James Heisenberg

135. (A) have begun
(B) was beginning
(C) will begin
(D) begins

136. (A) though
(B) or
(C) so
(D) but

137. (A) I have carefully read your warranty policy.
(B) Do you have any concerns?
(C) I am living close to one of your stores.
(D) I am deeply disappointed about this.

138. (A) replacement
(B) warranty
(C) prize
(D) receipt

GO ON TO THE NEXT PAGE

Questions 139-142 refer to the following report.

The grant proposal was finally approved last week, and we can finally start making the planned changes to our technology-driven, next generation aquarium. All the water tanks are finely monitored and controlled by the automated maintenance system. ----139.----.

Changes like these contribute to making the life of these creatures stable and pleasant. Our trained robot guides ----140.---- detailed explanations about the organisms that are swimming right in front of the visitors.

People can ask questions to the AI-equipped guides, and ----141.---- they are simple enough, the intelligent guide will satisfy their curiosity.

The funding will be allocated to many other technological improvements for the facility. ----142.----, part of the grant will be the source of our future research on marine organisms.

139. (A) Even feeding tasks are fully automated.
    (B) Let me introduce some of the changes we are making.
    (C) What we are trying to make is more stable habitats for the animals.
    (D) It does not necessarily mean that we can accommodate more fish.

140. (A) for providing
    (B) will be providing
    (C) to be provided
    (D) would have provided

141. (A) given
    (B) although
    (C) unless
    (D) as long as

142. (A) Regardless
    (B) Moreover
    (C) Otherwise
    (D) Therefore

Questions 143-146 refer to the following announcement.

West Atlantic Airways made an announcement that it has decided to ---143.--- the operation of one third of their flights, until at least next December.

This temporary measure was due to the continuously decreasing bookings, becoming serious at the start of this year. During this time, all the ---144.--- subject to this change will be unavailable.

According to the spokesman, the company will re-start offering all flights whenever appropriate, but it is expected that, for the first few months, the operations will be carried out still at a ---145.--- pace.

Annotation:
---146.---. Details about any modifications regarding the measure will be posted online.

---

143. (A) abandon
(B) suspend
(C) advertise
(D) promote

144. (A) vessels
(B) automobiles
(C) aircraft
(D) railways

145. (A) reduced
(B) reduce
(C) reduction
(D) reducing

146. (A) Thank you very much for always flying with us.
(B) A gradual increase in flights is the key to their success.
(C) The list of frequently asked questions may not be comprehensive.
(D) The conditions and schedules are subject to change at any time.

GO ON TO THENEXT PAGE

PART 7

Directions: In this part you will read a selection of texts, such as magazine and newspaper articles, e-mails, and instant messages. Each text or set of texts is followed by several questions. Select the best answer for each question and mark the letter (A), (B), (C), or (D) on your answer sheet.

Questions 147-148 refer to the following instructions.

Attention, all visitors

Thank you for choosing to visit our Innovation and Design Hub today. Before you step into the Production Department, we would like to remind you of the following guidelines.

For security purposes, we DO NOT allow any recording devices in the Production Department. This includes any cell phones, laptops, voice recorders, video cameras, etc. If you wish to record any part of the production process, please refer to the given manual on how to get in touch with our Public Relations Department.

To avoid a fine, please leave all electronic devices at reception when you check in for your tour of our facility.

147. What is the purpose of this notification?
    (A) To specify rules for tour attendees
    (B) To collect fines for violation
    (C) To make the facility open to the public
    (D) To record the production process

148. Which section grants permission to record?
    (A) The Innovation and Design Hub
    (B) The Production Department
    (C) The Legal Department
    (D) The Public Relations Department

Questions 149-150 refer to the following questionnaire.

Bliz Mobile invites you to take this short questionnaire to enter our annual draw to win prizes worth up to 100,000 dollars. All you need to do is complete the short form below and submit it via e-mail to annualdraw@bliz-mobile.com.

Name:
Age:
City you live in:

• What are the 3 most and least important things to you when choosing a new phone plan?
• What is the monthly budget you reserve for your mobile network plan?
• What influences this budget and what could prompt you to increase this amount?

149. What can be inferred about the questionnaire?
  (A) There is an age restriction.
  (B) Winners can receive cash.
  (C) A full address is required.
  (D) It takes place periodically.

150. According to the form, what is Bliz Mobile concerned about the most?
  (A) Users' ratings on Bliz Mobile's devices
  (B) Pricing tactics
  (C) Average age of the users
  (D) Competitors' strengths

GO ON TO THENEXT PAGE

FROM: Food Delivery <foodordersnewyork@letseat.com>
TO: Dave Wanderworth <davewanderworth@pop-mail.com>
SUBJECT: Your food is on its way!

Hi Dave!

Thank you for using Let's Eat to order dinner today. I just wanted to tell you that your food delivery from Yo Panda is now on its way to you and you should receive your meal in about 45 minutes.

As a special token of our appreciation, here's a 10 percent discount voucher on any future orders. To use, simply type THANKYOU21 while placing an order on our website or mobile app.

As always, we are taking extra care to sanitize all carrier vehicles before accepting any food to be delivered for the drivers and our customers. Our drivers are instructed to leave your delivery at your door. You will receive a call from them when they have arrived at your address. We hope you enjoy your dinner.

Yours sincerely,

Martin
Let's Eat New York

---

151. What can be inferred about the main service Let's Eat provides?
   (A) It cooks meals and deliver them.
   (B) It delivers food from restaurants to customers.
   (C) It provides gourmet information online.
   (D) It creates apps for food suppliers.

152. What do the drivers do while providing a service?
   (A) Call the customer
   (B) Knock the door
   (C) Sanitize the carrier vehicles
   (D) Receive payment

Questions 153-154 refer to the following online chat discussion.

Roy Singh (2:30 P.M.)	Hi there. I had a quick question about my Internet services.
Troy White (2:30 P.M.)	Sure, I'd be happy to help. I need to confirm a few details for security purposes before I can access your account. Is that OK?
Roy Singh (2:32 P.M.)	Yes, go ahead.
Troy White (2:32 P.M.)	Thank you for your understanding. May I please have your registered phone number and your address?
Roy Singh (2:33 P.M.)	My phone number is 324-8794 and my address is 12, Munro Way, New York.
Troy White (2:35 P.M.)	Thank you for confirming those details. Let me look at your account and see what Internet plan you are on. Please bear with me.
Roy Singh (2:36 P.M.)	Thank you. I appreciate your help.

153. Why did Troy White ask for Roy's address and phone number?
(A) To send out a bill
(B) To confirm identification
(C) To help Roy find his account
(D) To call back

154. At 2:35 P.M., what does Troy White most likely mean when he writes, "Please bear with me"?
(A) He knows Roy is already angry.
(B) He thinks the task is easy.
(C) He expects the process will take some time.
(D) He wants to make sure Roy is not lost.

GO ON TO THENEXT PAGE

HopStep Financial Services Ltd
customerservice@hopstep-accounting.com

Dear Henry,

Good morning. As your personal financial adviser, I am writing to you to inform you about certain changes to your investment portfolio and the service rates associated with supplemental assistance HopStep Financial Services Ltd will start offering to all customers.

As of last night (17 September 2021), all your investments in precious metals have suffered a loss of about 8 percent. I strongly suggest that we re-evaluate your investments. To do this, I am hoping to talk with you on any one of the following dates and times:
    1. 22 September, at 1:15 P.M.
    2. 22 September, at 3:30 P.M.
    3. 25 September, at 10:15 A.M.

Please let me know which of the following times, if any, suit you the best, so that I may send you an invitation link.

As mentioned earlier, there are also certain changes to our fees structure. Primarily, we will be increasing our brokerage rate from 1.25 percent to 1.4 percent for every transaction, from the 25th of October 2021. In accordance with our policy, which was updated last month, all information is considered confidential.

I look forward to speaking with you about your investments soon.

Kind regards,

Susan Miller
Asset Manager
HopStep Financial Services Ltd

155. When did Henry receive this e-mail?
- (A) September 16
- (B) September 17
- (C) September 18
- (D) September 22

156. What is indicated about the intended talk between Henry and Susan?
- (A) It will be conducted online.
- (B) It will take place on September 26th.
- (C) It must be held immediately.
- (D) It is exclusively about Henry's portfolio.

157. Why will the transaction fee increase?
- (A) Henry lost a significant part of his investment.
- (B) The value of precious metals has dropped.
- (C) The policy of HopStep has updated.
- (D) Additional services will be added for Henry.

GO ON TO THE NEXT PAGE

City Meeting to Discuss New Bicycle Parking Lots

The Dillard City Council will hold a special meeting on Thursday to discuss the mayor's controversial proposal to build bicycle parking lots next to all subway stations. The purpose of building new parking lots is to give cyclists a convenient place to park their bicycles. Furthermore, local businesses have recommended building bicycle parking lots as a way of getting bicycles off of city streets.

Bicycles are frequently left parked in front of stores for lengthy periods of time, and this has become an eyesore in the downtown area. If the proposal passes, the city will hire a new workforce to collect bicycles parked on the street and bring them to the city's bicycle pound where owners will have to pay 10 dollars to retrieve their illegally parked bicycles. Mayor John Charles, who instigated the proposal, said he is certain the bicycle lots "will improve the downtown area."

Not everyone agrees with the plan. James Carvelle, the president of the Dillard chapter of Green Peace, states that the city is secretly trying to dissuade people from riding bicycles. "The city should be encouraging people to get out of their cars." Local activist Johnny Leary said, "The proposed $5 parking fee for one-day parking is too high if you just want to go to the grocery store." Julia Howell said, "The land price has been rising, and we should utilize those valuable areas for something more profitable."

The City Council encourages all citizens concerned with the issue to attend Thursday's meeting before the final vote by the council committees on Friday.

158. What is expected to happen if the plan is approved?
(A) The number of bicycle users will decrease dramatically.
(B) The city can collect a large sum of fines.
(C) The downtown area will be less congested with people.
(D) Fewer bicycles will be left unattended on the streets.

159. What is NOT mentioned as the basis of which some individuals are against the proposal?
(A) The parking fee is extremely high.
(B) Increased car dependence is not desirable.
(C) The parking space can be used differently.
(D) The value of the land can be raised further.

160. What is true about the city council?
(A) It allows all citizens to vote for this issue.
(B) It has voted to approve the bicycle parking lots.
(C) It held the final meeting last Friday.
(D) It wishes to hear citizens' opinions about the proposal.

Questions 161-163 refer to the following press release.

Be a Mountain Climbing Specialist!

Santa Ana Advisors and Experts is launching a new course for mountain climbing specialists. Participants learn various aspects of mountain climbing including: how to assist or guide beginners, how to use cutting-edge climbing gear, how to maintain this gear, knowledge pertaining to health care in case of emergencies, and so on.

Many skiers visit mountains in this state during winter, but in contrast, there are a disproportionately small number of visitors from spring to fall. Since the convention bureau of California is trying to invite visitors to the mountainous region throughout the year, they are expecting that our new program will play an important role. In fact, Arnold Lindenson, the top executive of the bureau, announced that scholarships will be available to program participants.

Our instructors include several world-famous alpinists like Tim McKinley, who leads the entire course. George Thompson, another preeminent figure, handles all administrative duties. Our main location, which is in San Jose, opened this course a year ago, and has produced dozens of graduates. Jimmy Troy is one of those graduates. Here is a comment from Jimmy:

"I'm really glad that I enrolled on this program. I liked mountain climbing, but it is even a greater pleasure that I will be able to support those who have just begun mountain climbing. I really liked your informative instruction as well as continuing encouragement."

161. What kind of service is being advertised?
- (A) Career consultation
- (B) Tourism
- (C) Human resources management
- (D) Vocational training

162. What is indicated about the new course?
- (A) It is being taught in multiple places by multiple instructors.
- (B) It is headquartered in Santa Ana, Los Angeles.
- (C) It has been offering a wide range of courses for years.
- (D) It received a grant from the Californian organization.

163. Who is the past graduates's comments intended for?
- (A) Arnold Lindenson
- (B) Tim McKinley
- (C) George Thompson
- (D) Jimmy Troy

GO ON TO THE NEXT PAGE

Here's why you should play badminton as a form of exercise

It is common to see people hitting the gym or going running or swimming, but how often do you hear someone saying that they play badminton as a form of exercise? — [1] —.

Badminton is such an underrated sport. While lawn tennis is popular across the world with famous tournaments like "Wimbledon", that popularity doesn't translate to badminton. However, While Asian countries do promote badminton as a sport, there's nothing stopping you from playing badminton to lose some of those stubborn calories!

— [2] —. Actually, the most accepted theory is that badminton was born here in England! It is said that the sport was initially played in Duke of Beaufort's residence called Badminton House. — [3] —.

Did you know that playing badminton, even a low intensity leisurely game, is akin to a full body workout? Many people get bored of the same old gym routine and often quit a few weeks or months later. That will never happen when you play badminton, because of the sheer amount of mental stimulation you get from the game. — [4] —. Badminton is the world's fastest racquet sport. Simply put, there's no time to get bored when you are in the middle of the game chasing the shuttle—it's that fast paced!

164. For what purpose, does the writer mention lawn tennis?
   (A) To indicate it requires less energy than badminton
   (B) To name a sport that is not commonly played.
   (C) To contrast the worldwide popularity of some sports
   (D) To claim that a grass court is the key for its popularity

165. What is one benefit of playing badminton that the writer mentions?
   (A) You can burn calories that are otherwise difficult to do so.
   (B) You do not have to go to the gym for exercise.
   (C) You can improve your concentration skills.
   (D) You will be able to make friends worldwide.

166. Why do badminton players never get bored?
   (A) Players keep stimulated.
   (B) The shuttle is too fast to hit back.
   (C) Badminton is the most intensive sport.
   (D) Players can keep losing calories.

167. In which of the positions marked [1], [2], [3], and [4] does the following sentence best belong?
   "Do you know the origin of the sport?"
   (A) [1]
   (B) [2]
   (C) [3]
   (D) [4]

GO ON TO THENEXT PAGE

Questions 168-171 refer to the following online chat discussion.

Kia Neal (12:06 P.M.):	Hello. Thank you for contacting Xeptel Bank. How may I help you?
David Roth (12:06 P.M.):	Good afternoon. I was wondering if you could help me with logging in to my online bank account. I cannot locate the page.
Kia Neal (12:07 P.M.):	Certainly. Do you mind if I confirm a few details before we get started?
David Roth (12:08 P.M.):	No, I do not.
Kia Neal (12:08 P.M.):	This is part of our required step for security purposes. I appreciate your understanding. Will you please give me your date of birth, address and phone number, Mr. Roth?
David Roth (12:10 P.M.):	My date of birth is 19th of August, 1989, and my phone number is 025-372-3692. My address is 421 Queen St., Molding, Virginia.
Kia Neal (12:12 P.M.):	Thank you for confirming those details. The date of birth and phone number match our records. However, the address you gave me is not the one I have on the system.
David Roth (12:13 P.M.):	Is the address 126 Washington Road, Molding, Virginia? I moved to the Queen Street address in January.
Kia Neal (12:13 P.M.):	Yes, that is the address I have registered. Would you like me to change it to your new address? I can then give you your Internet banking login ID and temporary password.
David Roth (12:15 P.M.):	Well, I'm not sure if that makes a difference but please do send me the link that directs me to the right place.

168. What is David Roth's problem?
- (A) He forgot his password.
- (B) He could not open an online account.
- (C) He cannot find the right page.
- (D) He does not have a valid ID.

169. At 12:08 P.M., what does David Roth mean when he writes, "No, I do not"?
- (A) He wants to know why Kia needs his information.
- (B) He does not want to give private information.
- (C) He does not understand what Kia is requesting.
- (D) He has no problem in sharing information.

170. What information was missing on the database?
- (A) David's new address
- (B) David's previous address
- (C) David's phone number
- (D) David's birthday

171. What piece of information does David Roth need the most?
- (A) A login page
- (B) A new login ID
- (C) A temporary password
- (D) The original password

GO ON TO THE NEXT PAGE

Help Wanted

Headquartered in Denver, Colorado, Comp Colorado Inc. is presently seeking experienced computer experts. In this position, workers are referred to as "office designers." Our company is known throughout the state for providing companies with a wide range of diverse computer-related services, including setting up computers, arranging an office network, providing training, and installing operating systems and software. Our clients range from small to middle-sized growing companies, and our duty is to gear their work environment to a computer-equipped work space.

All office designers should be able to work independently. You will be assigned accounts with businesses, and you will hold meetings with each company to conduct a "needs analysis." After installing the office computer network, you will be responsible for training staff. Excellent knowledge of office software is required. Experience in providing computer training is preferred. In the future, we plan on expanding our business to provide services for computer labs at schools, so any such experience would be valuable to us.

Comp Colorado Inc. is currently in need of five full-time office designers. We offer a competitive salary, generous benefits, and various remunerations. Our salary is decided in an ability-based fashion; no seniority system is adopted. Please send us your current résumé, and at least one reference letter by regular mail. A photocopy of your ID must be included as well. We will be contacting short-listed candidates by the end of July. Please do not contact us unless we contact you first. We are looking forward to receiving applications from a candidate with excellent manners, passion and resilience.

172. What is required for this position?
- (A) Knowledge of office software
- (B) Experience in training staff
- (C) An outstanding academic background
- (D) Five-year work experience

173. How do "the office designers" provide the service?
- (A) They work as a member of a team.
- (B) They lead and manage a team.
- (C) Each of them works alone.
- (D) They delegate jobs to subcontractors.

174. What is mentioned about the salary?
- (A) Skills are the primary determinant.
- (B) The amount won't change once determined.
- (C) Workers will receive a mark-up as they age.
- (D) Staff with longer experience get paid more.

175. What are the applicants instructed to do by the end of July?
- (A) Send an inquiry if no notification has been received
- (B) Send additional documents if necessary
- (C) Just wait for the decision to be made
- (D) Prepare another reference letter

GO ON TO THENEXT PAGE

Questions 176-180 refer to the following e-mail and schedule.

To: Beth Harcourt <bethharcourt42@good-goods.com>
From: Jan Hans <merchandisefulfilment@zextradesigns.com>
Date: 19th June 2021
Subject: Merchandise Design Schedule

Dear Ms. Harcourt,

How are you? Since we spoke last week at your headquarters, I have been able to come up with an estimated schedule for the delivery of the merchandise finalized by your team. The sooner you can give us the go-ahead to start production, the sooner we can start shipping out the proposed merchandise to your retail stores.

Please keep in mind that the unprecedented volume of orders we have been receiving has severely impacted all production schedules and delivery timelines. Hence, the schedule mentioned below will only be applicable if approval is received before midnight on the 25th of June.

Thank you for choosing to work with Zextra Designs again. We appreciate your business.

Kind regards,

Jan Hans
Merchandise Fulfilment
Zextra Designs

Please find below the schedule for the delivery of final products, for your approval.

Merchandise Type	Date of delivery in Japan	Date of delivery in Australia	Date of delivery in USA	Date of delivery in Europe
T-shirts	31st August	2nd September	15th September	20th September
Mugs	22nd August	31st August	5th September	15th September
Stationery	15th August	20th August	1st September	10th September
Masks	20th August	30th August	5th September	15th September

* The date of delivery is to the port, NOT to the final destination
* 2-3 days expected for customs clearance after the delivery to the port
* Any unlisted products treated as the same category as T-shirts

176. What is the main purpose of the e-mail?
- (A) To urge an approval by June 25th
- (B) To propose a new business deal
- (C) To give a list of what can be manufactured
- (D) To explain Zextra Designs' policy

177. Who most likely is Beth Harcourt?
- (A) An individual product designer
- (B) The representative of Zextra Designs
- (C) A person in charge of a delivery company
- (D) Personnel in Good-Goods Company

178. In the e-mail, the word "unprecedented" in paragraph 2, line 1, is closest in meaning to
- (A) extraordinary
- (B) outstanding
- (C) rare
- (D) commonplace

179. Which merchandise takes the longest for its delivery?
- (A) Mugs
- (B) Stationery
- (C) Masks
- (D) Caps

180. When can warehouses in Australia expect to receive mugs?
- (A) On August 20th
- (B) Before August 31st
- (C) On August 31st
- (D) Sometime in September

GO ON TO THENEXT PAGE

Plus Size Clothing for the Modern, Independent Woman

If you are looking for a clothing store that caters to the modern, independent woman wearing sizes 18 and above, A Little Extra is the place for you! Our founder, Kathy Statis, is a plus-size model herself and personally knows how difficult it is to find a well-tailored piece of clothing for a plus size person. This was Kathy's main motivation behind A Little Extra.

We understand that you need to look your best, whether it is for a job interview or for that special date night. Walk into our store on Hobson Street, for a free stylist-assisted makeover. Our stylists are people from the fashion industry, who have years of experience in helping clients find clothes that flatter their body type. If you don't have the time to come into the store, simply log onto our website, www.alittleextra.biz, and choose from the endless range of options we have for you!

Kathy Statis, CEO
A Little Extra

Dear Ms. Statis,

I visited your store last weekend, and I was delighted to finally see plus-sized women being offered clothes that are smart, fashionable, and most importantly, fit well. All too often, when I am out shopping for myself, the only options I see are ill-fitted and frumpy looking tunics or loose pants.

Your stylists are warm, welcoming, and non-judgmental. I would like to especially recognize the services of Janet, the lady who helped me find some spectacular clothes in the store. She obviously loves her job, and her recommendations were spot on.

Thank you for the wonderful experience. I hope more people find out about A Little Extra, because you are doing a stellar job.

Kind regards,

Sarah Jones

181. What is unique about the business?
- (A) The pricing of the clothing
- (B) The durability of the clothing
- (C) The size of the clothing
- (D) The fabrics of the clothing

182. What can we infer about A little Extra?
- (A) It has shops in several countries.
- (B) It accepts electronic payment.
- (C) It consists of only one stylist.
- (D) It has been operating for decades.

183. What industry was Janet in previously?
- (A) Consulting
- (B) Logistics
- (C) Cosmetics
- (D) Fashion

184. What is the purpose of the letter sent from Sarah?
- (A) To show appreciation
- (B) To request a refund
- (C) To buy some more clothing
- (D) To send an inquiry

185. What does Sarah say about Janet?
- (A) She was unknowledgeable.
- (B) She was just like other staff.
- (C) She did a great job.
- (D) She deserves a higher salary.

GO ON TO THENEXT PAGE

Questions 186-190 refer to the following e-mails and schedule.

To: Emma Thompson
From: Janice Miller
Date: 12th September
Subject: List of pre-lunch performers for Day 2

Dear Emma,

Please find attached a list of performers for the first half of Day 2 of the Great British Talent Show 2021. The performers have all been briefed on the requirements of their acts and have been told not to exceed 15 minutes in total. We have estimated that the judges will ask the performers about themselves for about 15 minutes. These 15 minutes will also include any audience interaction. The judges for Day 2 have been confirmed and are:
  • Samantha Rey—International Supermodel
  • Peter Robinson—Motivational Speaker and Singer
  • William McManus—Music Producer

Each judge will get a suite in the hotel to get ready in. They have been asked to report to the set one hour prior to the first performer to test their microphones and other equipment. Lunch is set at 12:30 P.M., after Mr. Dev Reddy finishes his performance. The judges will eat in their own suites, while the hotel has been asked to provide a buffet lunch for the rest of the crew.

We have started selling audience tickets to the general public and the numbers are trending well. At this point, we have sold more than 2,000 tickets. Assuming all tickets are sold out, we are expecting a full house by the third or fourth performances. Let me know what you think and if you have any concerns on the order of the sessions.

Kind regards,

Janice Miller
Head Co-coordinator
The Great British Talent Show

The Great British Talent Show 2021

Royal Silver Hotel
16th November

Time	Performer	Type of Performance
9:00 A.M.	Ted Barker	Dancing
9:30 A.M.	Maya Thompson	Ballet
10:00 A.M.	Ria Soni	Singing
10:30 A.M.	Nala White	Sketching
11:00 A.M.	Chris Columbus	Magic
11:30 A.M.	Kaiya Graham	Acrobatics
12:00 P.M.	Dev Reddy	Singing

To: Janice Miller
From: Emma Thompson
Date: 12th September
Subject: Re: List of pre-lunch performers for Day 2

Dear Janice,

I am very impressed with the professional and efficient way you seem to be organising everything! The sign-up numbers do seem to be trending well at this stage. Perhaps we should increase the advertising to sell out all 3,500 seats. (FYI, it was 3,000 last time.) I will speak to James in Marketing about this and will copy you in on any e-mails I send him.

The only feedback I have is to perhaps swap the second and third performers, for we don't want to be doing consecutive dance acts. I would rather have a dance followed by a singer, followed by another dancer. Please let me know if this makes sense. Also, I would appreciate it if you could send me the performers list for the final day.

Other than that, I think you and your team are doing a fabulous job! Keep up the good work and let me know if I can help in any way.

Kind regards,

Emma Thompson
Vice President, Events & Marketing
The Great British Talent Show 2021

GO ON TO THE NEXT PAGE

186. What is NOT indicated about the Great British Talent Show?
- (A) It spans several days.
- (B) Famous figures judge performers.
- (C) It takes place annually.
- (D) It is a live performance show.

187. By what time are the judges supposed to arrive at the venue?
- (A) 8:00 A.M.
- (B) 8:45 A.M.
- (C) 9:00 A.M.
- (D) 12:30 P.M.

188. Who do the judges have lunch with?
- (A) With other crew members
- (B) With performers
- (C) With all the other judges
- (D) With no one else

189. What does Emma say she will do for marketing?
- (A) She will place more advertisements online.
- (B) She will increase the number of seats by 500.
- (C) She will communicate with a person in charge.
- (D) She will have James purchase as many tickets as possible.

190. Who does Emma's suggest should start performing at 10 A.M.?
- (A) Ted Barker
- (B) Maya Thompson
- (C) Ria Soni
- (D) Nala White

Questions 191-195 refer to the following notice, article, and report.

Book Lovers of Packerson, UNITE!

A new subscription offer from Bob Archer Library, Packerson

Tired of reading books on your electronic device? Do you long for the feel of a real book in your hands? If this sounds like you, come pick up one of our new subscription cards that give you access to over 7,000 books that you can hold! No more paying per book!

	Price/year	Invitation to reading events	Unlimited book checkout	Reserve & Deliver *to registered address
Platinum members for voracious readers	$300	○	○	○
Gold members for our busy patrons	$200	○	○	○
Silver members for beginners	$100	○	○	
Free members For dormant readers	free	○		

*Seminar/Meeting rooms are available for Platinum members only.

The Packerson Times

March 31, 2021 (Packerson) With the 20th Anniversary of the Bob Archer Library fast approaching, Theo, the head librarian, has come up with an innovative idea of returning to paper books in conjunction with a monthly payment style, which has been seen only in online formats, to increase engagement with the local community. Theo says the reserve & delivery service must be appealing to many people. Together with the room-renting options, the service can be viable, he stresses.

"The idea came from a conversation with one of our young readers, Elsa, who mentioned that she was tired of reading on her device and longed for a real hardcover to hold and read. This got me thinking that if the younger generation feels this way, imagine how older adults must feel," Theo said in a recent interview with *The Packerson Daily Times*.

It remains to be seen if this initiative will prove to be a game changer or if Packerson will continue to flock to online stores for the latest e-books.

Report on the Initial Performance of the Bob Archer Library Subscription Cards Program

This is a report on the progress and scope of the Bob Archer Library Subscription Cards Program, where we examine if the program led to an increase in the number of customers.

GO ON TO THE NEXT PAGE

The program was launched on the 1st of April, 2021, and saw 1654 people signed up for cards in the first fortnight after its launch. Of these 1,654 people who were surveyed, 865 members signed up for the platinum membership. It appears Theo's vision was correct. In fact, many people find the room-renting service quite cost-efficient. 311 opted for the Gold, and the remaining 478 signed up for the Silver membership.

Total membership numbers have seen a steady increase throughout the last year and initiatives such as a discounted price for local students have also helped drive a growth in the total membership numbers. Students account for about 10%, of which Silver is dominant.

Over the last year, the library has seen an increase in profit of almost 200,000 dollars. Theo is being credited with this huge turnaround in the library's fortunes. He plans to invest half of the revenue earned on newer books and magazines for the library and the rest on updating the library's infrastructure.

191. What is the innovation that Bob Archer is trying to bring about?
(A) The room-renting service
(B) A non-online subscription model
(C) Availability of thousands of paper books
(D) A rich variety of subscription plans

192. What is NOT true about Theo?
(A) He works for the Bob Archer Library.
(B) He came up with the new business idea.
(C) He himself is a subscriber to the Platinum plan.
(D) He intends to invest more in his business.

193. In the second article, the word "flock to" in paragraph 3, line 2, is closest in meaning to
(A) inundate
(B) utilize
(C) neglect
(D) acknowledge

194. What can be learned about the Gold Members plan?
(A) The price remains constant for students.
(B) Its subscribers increased the most last year.
(C) It is the most cost-efficient plan.
(D) It generated greater revenue than the Silver plan.

195. What category do the majority of the surveyed individuals fall into?
(A) Voracious readers
(B) Busy patrons
(C) Beginners
(D) Dormant readers

To: Nathan Miller
From: Steve Lee
Date: 18th July 2021
Subject: Greeting. Change in Account Manager

Dear Mr. Miller,

I am writing to you to notify you of a slight change in your account with SaluteFoods. I understand that your account manager used to be Gavin Felix. Your account has now been passed onto me since Gavin has retired from the business. I assure you that there will be no change in the level of customer service you expect from us.

If you prefer, I could come down to the hotel to double-check all standing orders that you have placed with us for the next quarter. I could have my assistant call or e-mail you with a list of possible times. At this point, everything that you have ordered for the hotel's restaurant is in stock, except those from Culture-wide, and I see no problems procuring any of your usual ingredients.

Kind regards,

Steve Lee
Account Manager
SaluteFoods

To: Steve Lee
From: Nathan Miller
Date: 18th July 2021
Subject: Re: Greeting. Change in Account Manager

Hi Steve,

Thank you for e-mailing me. I look forward to working with you too. I'm glad to hear that supply will not be a problem when it comes to any of our usual orders. As you know, we are getting into a busy summer and the hotel earns most of its annual revenue during this time.

GO ON TO THE NEXT PAGE

We are expecting to change the restaurant's menu to a more summer-based one and will be needing a few extra ingredients added to our standing order list. Please find the additional ingredients attached to this e-mail.

Should you face any issues procuring these additional ingredients, please let me know so that I can come up with some viable substitutes.

I would be happy to meet you to discuss the matter further. I would prefer to meet on a weekday when there is a delivery of the newly added ingredients for Korean food, as I will definitely be at the restaurant to check the items. I would like to meet you so that I can put a face to the name.

Kind regards,

Nathan Miller
Executive Chef
The Far-West Millennium Hotel

Ingredient Name	Quantity per Week	Brand	Delivery Day
Black Truffle Oil	20 × 250 ml bottles	Culture-wide	Tuesday
Pecan Nuts	10 × 1-kilogram bags	Sweet-Smooth	Friday
Gochujang Paste	4 × 1-kilogram bins	Korean Chilly	Monday
Black Garlic	2-kilogram bag	Stella Farmers	Tuesday
Avocado Oil	20 × 250 ml bottles	Culture-wide	Sunday

196. What is the main purpose of the first e-mail?
  (A) To account for a potential problem
  (B) To assure timely delivery
  (C) To receive additional orders
  (D) To send a greeting message

197. In the first e-mail, what does Steve say he can do?
  (A) Find a replacement for missing items
  (B) Include more items to the standing order
  (C) Let his colleague contact Nathan
  (D) Double the order for the next quarter

198. What is the main purpose of the second e-mail sent to Steve Lee?
  (A) To discuss new summer-based dishes
  (B) To show gratitude toward Gavin Felix
  (C) To specify items for additional orders
  (D) To clarify which ingredient is missing

199. Which ingredient can SaluteFoods NOT deliver now?
  (A) Black Truffle Oil
  (B) Pecan Nuts
  (C) Gochujang Paste
  (D) Black Garlic

200. On what day of the week, will Nathan and Steve most likely meet?
  (A) Monday
  (B) Wednesday
  (C) Thursday
  (D) Sunday

Stop! This is the end of the test. If you finish before time is called, you may go back to Part 5, 6, and 7 check your work.

スコア換算表

学習の参考として、模試の結果をおおよそのスコアに換算してみましょう。

リスニングセクション	
素点（正解数）	換算点範囲
96 − 100	475 − 495
91 − 95	435 − 495
86 − 90	405 − 475
81 − 85	370 − 450
76 − 80	345 − 420
71 − 75	320 − 390
66 − 70	290 − 360
61 − 65	265 − 335
56 − 60	235 − 310
51 − 55	210 − 280
46 − 50	180 − 255
41 − 45	155 − 230
36 − 40	125 − 205
31 − 35	105 − 175
26 − 30	85 − 145
21 − 25	60 − 115
16 − 20	30 − 90
11 − 15	5 − 70
6 − 10	5 − 60
1 − 5	5 − 50
0	5 − 35

リーディングセクション	
素点（正解数）	換算点範囲
96 − 100	460 − 495
91 − 95	425 − 490
86 − 90	395 − 465
81 − 85	370 − 440
76 − 80	335 − 415
71 − 75	320 − 390
66 − 70	280 − 365
61 − 65	250 − 335
56 − 60	220 − 305
51 − 55	195 − 270
46 − 50	165 − 240
41 − 45	140 − 215
36 − 40	115 − 180
31 − 35	95 − 145
26 − 30	75 − 120
21 − 25	60 − 95
16 − 20	30 − 75
11 − 15	30 − 55
6 − 10	10 − 40
1 − 5	5 − 30
0	5 − 15

	素点（正解数）	換算点範囲	
リスニングセクション			①
リーディングセクション			②
合計の参考スコア範囲			③

※換算表は『公式 TOEIC Listening & Reading 問題集 3』をもとに作成。
　換算表はあくまで参考上のものであり、実際のテストのスコアは上下することがあります。

ハイレベル完全模試マークシート No.1

フリガナ

NAME 名前

LISTENING SECTION

PART 1

NO.	ANSWER A B C D
1	Ⓐ Ⓑ Ⓒ Ⓓ
2	Ⓐ Ⓑ Ⓒ Ⓓ
3	Ⓐ Ⓑ Ⓒ Ⓓ
4	Ⓐ Ⓑ Ⓒ Ⓓ
5	Ⓐ Ⓑ Ⓒ Ⓓ
6	Ⓐ Ⓑ Ⓒ
7	Ⓐ Ⓑ Ⓒ
8	Ⓐ Ⓑ Ⓒ
9	Ⓐ Ⓑ Ⓒ
10	Ⓐ Ⓑ Ⓒ

PART 2

NO.	ANSWER A B C
11	Ⓐ Ⓑ Ⓒ
12	Ⓐ Ⓑ Ⓒ
13	Ⓐ Ⓑ Ⓒ
14	Ⓐ Ⓑ Ⓒ
15	Ⓐ Ⓑ Ⓒ
16	Ⓐ Ⓑ Ⓒ
17	Ⓐ Ⓑ Ⓒ
18	Ⓐ Ⓑ Ⓒ
19	Ⓐ Ⓑ Ⓒ
20	Ⓐ Ⓑ Ⓒ

NO.	ANSWER A B C
21	Ⓐ Ⓑ Ⓒ
22	Ⓐ Ⓑ Ⓒ
23	Ⓐ Ⓑ Ⓒ
24	Ⓐ Ⓑ Ⓒ
25	Ⓐ Ⓑ Ⓒ
26	Ⓐ Ⓑ Ⓒ
27	Ⓐ Ⓑ Ⓒ
28	Ⓐ Ⓑ Ⓒ
29	Ⓐ Ⓑ Ⓒ
30	Ⓐ Ⓑ Ⓒ

PART 3

NO.	ANSWER A B C
31	Ⓐ Ⓑ Ⓒ
32	Ⓐ Ⓑ Ⓒ Ⓓ
33	Ⓐ Ⓑ Ⓒ Ⓓ
34	Ⓐ Ⓑ Ⓒ Ⓓ
35	Ⓐ Ⓑ Ⓒ Ⓓ
36	Ⓐ Ⓑ Ⓒ Ⓓ
37	Ⓐ Ⓑ Ⓒ Ⓓ
38	Ⓐ Ⓑ Ⓒ Ⓓ
39	Ⓐ Ⓑ Ⓒ Ⓓ
40	Ⓐ Ⓑ Ⓒ Ⓓ

NO.	ANSWER A B C D
41	Ⓐ Ⓑ Ⓒ Ⓓ
42	Ⓐ Ⓑ Ⓒ Ⓓ
43	Ⓐ Ⓑ Ⓒ Ⓓ
44	Ⓐ Ⓑ Ⓒ Ⓓ
45	Ⓐ Ⓑ Ⓒ Ⓓ
46	Ⓐ Ⓑ Ⓒ Ⓓ
47	Ⓐ Ⓑ Ⓒ Ⓓ
48	Ⓐ Ⓑ Ⓒ Ⓓ
49	Ⓐ Ⓑ Ⓒ Ⓓ
50	Ⓐ Ⓑ Ⓒ Ⓓ

NO.	ANSWER A B C D
51	Ⓐ Ⓑ Ⓒ Ⓓ
52	Ⓐ Ⓑ Ⓒ Ⓓ
53	Ⓐ Ⓑ Ⓒ Ⓓ
54	Ⓐ Ⓑ Ⓒ Ⓓ
55	Ⓐ Ⓑ Ⓒ Ⓓ
56	Ⓐ Ⓑ Ⓒ Ⓓ
57	Ⓐ Ⓑ Ⓒ Ⓓ
58	Ⓐ Ⓑ Ⓒ Ⓓ
59	Ⓐ Ⓑ Ⓒ Ⓓ
60	Ⓐ Ⓑ Ⓒ Ⓓ

NO.	ANSWER A B C D
61	Ⓐ Ⓑ Ⓒ Ⓓ
62	Ⓐ Ⓑ Ⓒ Ⓓ
63	Ⓐ Ⓑ Ⓒ Ⓓ
64	Ⓐ Ⓑ Ⓒ Ⓓ
65	Ⓐ Ⓑ Ⓒ Ⓓ
66	Ⓐ Ⓑ Ⓒ Ⓓ
67	Ⓐ Ⓑ Ⓒ Ⓓ
68	Ⓐ Ⓑ Ⓒ Ⓓ
69	Ⓐ Ⓑ Ⓒ Ⓓ
70	Ⓐ Ⓑ Ⓒ Ⓓ

PART 4

NO.	ANSWER A B C D
71	Ⓐ Ⓑ Ⓒ Ⓓ
72	Ⓐ Ⓑ Ⓒ Ⓓ
73	Ⓐ Ⓑ Ⓒ Ⓓ
74	Ⓐ Ⓑ Ⓒ Ⓓ
75	Ⓐ Ⓑ Ⓒ Ⓓ
76	Ⓐ Ⓑ Ⓒ Ⓓ
77	Ⓐ Ⓑ Ⓒ Ⓓ
78	Ⓐ Ⓑ Ⓒ Ⓓ
79	Ⓐ Ⓑ Ⓒ Ⓓ
80	Ⓐ Ⓑ Ⓒ Ⓓ

NO.	ANSWER A B C D
81	Ⓐ Ⓑ Ⓒ Ⓓ
82	Ⓐ Ⓑ Ⓒ Ⓓ
83	Ⓐ Ⓑ Ⓒ Ⓓ
84	Ⓐ Ⓑ Ⓒ Ⓓ
85	Ⓐ Ⓑ Ⓒ Ⓓ
86	Ⓐ Ⓑ Ⓒ Ⓓ
87	Ⓐ Ⓑ Ⓒ Ⓓ
88	Ⓐ Ⓑ Ⓒ Ⓓ
89	Ⓐ Ⓑ Ⓒ Ⓓ
90	Ⓐ Ⓑ Ⓒ Ⓓ

NO.	ANSWER A B C D
91	Ⓐ Ⓑ Ⓒ Ⓓ
92	Ⓐ Ⓑ Ⓒ Ⓓ
93	Ⓐ Ⓑ Ⓒ Ⓓ
94	Ⓐ Ⓑ Ⓒ Ⓓ
95	Ⓐ Ⓑ Ⓒ Ⓓ
96	Ⓐ Ⓑ Ⓒ Ⓓ
97	Ⓐ Ⓑ Ⓒ Ⓓ
98	Ⓐ Ⓑ Ⓒ Ⓓ
99	Ⓐ Ⓑ Ⓒ Ⓓ
100	Ⓐ Ⓑ Ⓒ Ⓓ

READING SECTION

PART 5

NO.	ANSWER A B C D
101	Ⓐ Ⓑ Ⓒ Ⓓ
102	Ⓐ Ⓑ Ⓒ Ⓓ
103	Ⓐ Ⓑ Ⓒ Ⓓ
104	Ⓐ Ⓑ Ⓒ Ⓓ
105	Ⓐ Ⓑ Ⓒ Ⓓ
106	Ⓐ Ⓑ Ⓒ Ⓓ
107	Ⓐ Ⓑ Ⓒ Ⓓ
108	Ⓐ Ⓑ Ⓒ Ⓓ
109	Ⓐ Ⓑ Ⓒ Ⓓ
110	Ⓐ Ⓑ Ⓒ Ⓓ

NO.	ANSWER A B C D
111	Ⓐ Ⓑ Ⓒ Ⓓ
112	Ⓐ Ⓑ Ⓒ Ⓓ
113	Ⓐ Ⓑ Ⓒ Ⓓ
114	Ⓐ Ⓑ Ⓒ Ⓓ
115	Ⓐ Ⓑ Ⓒ Ⓓ
116	Ⓐ Ⓑ Ⓒ Ⓓ
117	Ⓐ Ⓑ Ⓒ Ⓓ
118	Ⓐ Ⓑ Ⓒ Ⓓ
119	Ⓐ Ⓑ Ⓒ Ⓓ
120	Ⓐ Ⓑ Ⓒ Ⓓ

PART 6

NO.	ANSWER A B C D
121	Ⓐ Ⓑ Ⓒ Ⓓ
122	Ⓐ Ⓑ Ⓒ Ⓓ
123	Ⓐ Ⓑ Ⓒ Ⓓ
124	Ⓐ Ⓑ Ⓒ Ⓓ
125	Ⓐ Ⓑ Ⓒ Ⓓ
126	Ⓐ Ⓑ Ⓒ Ⓓ
127	Ⓐ Ⓑ Ⓒ Ⓓ
128	Ⓐ Ⓑ Ⓒ Ⓓ
129	Ⓐ Ⓑ Ⓒ Ⓓ
130	Ⓐ Ⓑ Ⓒ Ⓓ

NO.	ANSWER A B C D
131	Ⓐ Ⓑ Ⓒ Ⓓ
132	Ⓐ Ⓑ Ⓒ Ⓓ
133	Ⓐ Ⓑ Ⓒ Ⓓ
134	Ⓐ Ⓑ Ⓒ Ⓓ
135	Ⓐ Ⓑ Ⓒ Ⓓ
136	Ⓐ Ⓑ Ⓒ Ⓓ
137	Ⓐ Ⓑ Ⓒ Ⓓ
138	Ⓐ Ⓑ Ⓒ Ⓓ
139	Ⓐ Ⓑ Ⓒ Ⓓ
140	Ⓐ Ⓑ Ⓒ Ⓓ

PART 7

NO.	ANSWER A B C D
141	Ⓐ Ⓑ Ⓒ Ⓓ
142	Ⓐ Ⓑ Ⓒ Ⓓ
143	Ⓐ Ⓑ Ⓒ Ⓓ
144	Ⓐ Ⓑ Ⓒ Ⓓ
145	Ⓐ Ⓑ Ⓒ Ⓓ
146	Ⓐ Ⓑ Ⓒ Ⓓ
147	Ⓐ Ⓑ Ⓒ Ⓓ
148	Ⓐ Ⓑ Ⓒ Ⓓ
149	Ⓐ Ⓑ Ⓒ Ⓓ
150	Ⓐ Ⓑ Ⓒ Ⓓ

NO.	ANSWER A B C D
151	Ⓐ Ⓑ Ⓒ Ⓓ
152	Ⓐ Ⓑ Ⓒ Ⓓ
153	Ⓐ Ⓑ Ⓒ Ⓓ
154	Ⓐ Ⓑ Ⓒ Ⓓ
155	Ⓐ Ⓑ Ⓒ Ⓓ
156	Ⓐ Ⓑ Ⓒ Ⓓ
157	Ⓐ Ⓑ Ⓒ Ⓓ
158	Ⓐ Ⓑ Ⓒ Ⓓ
159	Ⓐ Ⓑ Ⓒ Ⓓ
160	Ⓐ Ⓑ Ⓒ Ⓓ

NO.	ANSWER A B C D
161	Ⓐ Ⓑ Ⓒ Ⓓ
162	Ⓐ Ⓑ Ⓒ Ⓓ
163	Ⓐ Ⓑ Ⓒ Ⓓ
164	Ⓐ Ⓑ Ⓒ Ⓓ
165	Ⓐ Ⓑ Ⓒ Ⓓ
166	Ⓐ Ⓑ Ⓒ Ⓓ
167	Ⓐ Ⓑ Ⓒ Ⓓ
168	Ⓐ Ⓑ Ⓒ Ⓓ
169	Ⓐ Ⓑ Ⓒ Ⓓ
170	Ⓐ Ⓑ Ⓒ Ⓓ

NO.	ANSWER A B C D
171	Ⓐ Ⓑ Ⓒ Ⓓ
172	Ⓐ Ⓑ Ⓒ Ⓓ
173	Ⓐ Ⓑ Ⓒ Ⓓ
174	Ⓐ Ⓑ Ⓒ Ⓓ
175	Ⓐ Ⓑ Ⓒ Ⓓ
176	Ⓐ Ⓑ Ⓒ Ⓓ
177	Ⓐ Ⓑ Ⓒ Ⓓ
178	Ⓐ Ⓑ Ⓒ Ⓓ
179	Ⓐ Ⓑ Ⓒ Ⓓ
180	Ⓐ Ⓑ Ⓒ Ⓓ

NO.	ANSWER A B C D
181	Ⓐ Ⓑ Ⓒ Ⓓ
182	Ⓐ Ⓑ Ⓒ Ⓓ
183	Ⓐ Ⓑ Ⓒ Ⓓ
184	Ⓐ Ⓑ Ⓒ Ⓓ
185	Ⓐ Ⓑ Ⓒ Ⓓ
186	Ⓐ Ⓑ Ⓒ Ⓓ
187	Ⓐ Ⓑ Ⓒ Ⓓ
188	Ⓐ Ⓑ Ⓒ Ⓓ
189	Ⓐ Ⓑ Ⓒ Ⓓ
190	Ⓐ Ⓑ Ⓒ Ⓓ

NO.	ANSWER A B C D
191	Ⓐ Ⓑ Ⓒ Ⓓ
192	Ⓐ Ⓑ Ⓒ Ⓓ
193	Ⓐ Ⓑ Ⓒ Ⓓ
194	Ⓐ Ⓑ Ⓒ Ⓓ
195	Ⓐ Ⓑ Ⓒ Ⓓ
196	Ⓐ Ⓑ Ⓒ Ⓓ
197	Ⓐ Ⓑ Ⓒ Ⓓ
198	Ⓐ Ⓑ Ⓒ Ⓓ
199	Ⓐ Ⓑ Ⓒ Ⓓ
200	Ⓐ Ⓑ Ⓒ Ⓓ

ハイレベル完全模試マークシート No.2

フリガナ

NAME 名前

LISTENING SECTION

PART 1

NO.	ANSWER A B C D
1	Ⓐ Ⓑ Ⓒ Ⓓ
2	Ⓐ Ⓑ Ⓒ Ⓓ
3	Ⓐ Ⓑ Ⓒ Ⓓ
4	Ⓐ Ⓑ Ⓒ Ⓓ
5	Ⓐ Ⓑ Ⓒ Ⓓ
6	Ⓐ Ⓑ Ⓒ Ⓓ
7	Ⓐ Ⓑ Ⓒ
8	Ⓐ Ⓑ Ⓒ
9	Ⓐ Ⓑ Ⓒ
10	Ⓐ Ⓑ Ⓒ

PART 2

NO.	ANSWER A B C
11	Ⓐ Ⓑ Ⓒ
12	Ⓐ Ⓑ Ⓒ
13	Ⓐ Ⓑ Ⓒ
14	Ⓐ Ⓑ Ⓒ
15	Ⓐ Ⓑ Ⓒ
16	Ⓐ Ⓑ Ⓒ
17	Ⓐ Ⓑ Ⓒ
18	Ⓐ Ⓑ Ⓒ
19	Ⓐ Ⓑ Ⓒ
20	Ⓐ Ⓑ Ⓒ

NO.	ANSWER A B C
21	Ⓐ Ⓑ Ⓒ
22	Ⓐ Ⓑ Ⓒ
23	Ⓐ Ⓑ Ⓒ
24	Ⓐ Ⓑ Ⓒ
25	Ⓐ Ⓑ Ⓒ
26	Ⓐ Ⓑ Ⓒ
27	Ⓐ Ⓑ Ⓒ
28	Ⓐ Ⓑ Ⓒ
29	Ⓐ Ⓑ Ⓒ
30	Ⓐ Ⓑ Ⓒ

PART 3

NO.	ANSWER A B C
31	Ⓐ Ⓑ Ⓒ
32	Ⓐ Ⓑ Ⓒ Ⓓ
33	Ⓐ Ⓑ Ⓒ Ⓓ
34	Ⓐ Ⓑ Ⓒ Ⓓ
35	Ⓐ Ⓑ Ⓒ Ⓓ
36	Ⓐ Ⓑ Ⓒ Ⓓ
37	Ⓐ Ⓑ Ⓒ Ⓓ
38	Ⓐ Ⓑ Ⓒ Ⓓ
39	Ⓐ Ⓑ Ⓒ Ⓓ
40	Ⓐ Ⓑ Ⓒ Ⓓ

NO.	ANSWER A B C D
41	Ⓐ Ⓑ Ⓒ Ⓓ
42	Ⓐ Ⓑ Ⓒ Ⓓ
43	Ⓐ Ⓑ Ⓒ Ⓓ
44	Ⓐ Ⓑ Ⓒ Ⓓ
45	Ⓐ Ⓑ Ⓒ Ⓓ
46	Ⓐ Ⓑ Ⓒ Ⓓ
47	Ⓐ Ⓑ Ⓒ Ⓓ
48	Ⓐ Ⓑ Ⓒ Ⓓ
49	Ⓐ Ⓑ Ⓒ Ⓓ
50	Ⓐ Ⓑ Ⓒ Ⓓ

NO.	ANSWER A B C D
51	Ⓐ Ⓑ Ⓒ Ⓓ
52	Ⓐ Ⓑ Ⓒ Ⓓ
53	Ⓐ Ⓑ Ⓒ Ⓓ
54	Ⓐ Ⓑ Ⓒ Ⓓ
55	Ⓐ Ⓑ Ⓒ Ⓓ
56	Ⓐ Ⓑ Ⓒ Ⓓ
57	Ⓐ Ⓑ Ⓒ Ⓓ
58	Ⓐ Ⓑ Ⓒ Ⓓ
59	Ⓐ Ⓑ Ⓒ Ⓓ
60	Ⓐ Ⓑ Ⓒ Ⓓ

PART 4

NO.	ANSWER A B C D
71	Ⓐ Ⓑ Ⓒ Ⓓ
72	Ⓐ Ⓑ Ⓒ Ⓓ
73	Ⓐ Ⓑ Ⓒ Ⓓ
74	Ⓐ Ⓑ Ⓒ Ⓓ
75	Ⓐ Ⓑ Ⓒ Ⓓ
76	Ⓐ Ⓑ Ⓒ Ⓓ
77	Ⓐ Ⓑ Ⓒ Ⓓ
78	Ⓐ Ⓑ Ⓒ Ⓓ
79	Ⓐ Ⓑ Ⓒ Ⓓ
80	Ⓐ Ⓑ Ⓒ Ⓓ

NO.	ANSWER A B C D
81	Ⓐ Ⓑ Ⓒ Ⓓ
82	Ⓐ Ⓑ Ⓒ Ⓓ
83	Ⓐ Ⓑ Ⓒ Ⓓ
84	Ⓐ Ⓑ Ⓒ Ⓓ
85	Ⓐ Ⓑ Ⓒ Ⓓ
86	Ⓐ Ⓑ Ⓒ Ⓓ
87	Ⓐ Ⓑ Ⓒ Ⓓ
88	Ⓐ Ⓑ Ⓒ Ⓓ
89	Ⓐ Ⓑ Ⓒ Ⓓ
90	Ⓐ Ⓑ Ⓒ Ⓓ

NO.	ANSWER A B C D
91	Ⓐ Ⓑ Ⓒ Ⓓ
92	Ⓐ Ⓑ Ⓒ Ⓓ
93	Ⓐ Ⓑ Ⓒ Ⓓ
94	Ⓐ Ⓑ Ⓒ Ⓓ
95	Ⓐ Ⓑ Ⓒ Ⓓ
96	Ⓐ Ⓑ Ⓒ Ⓓ
97	Ⓐ Ⓑ Ⓒ Ⓓ
98	Ⓐ Ⓑ Ⓒ Ⓓ
99	Ⓐ Ⓑ Ⓒ Ⓓ
100	Ⓐ Ⓑ Ⓒ Ⓓ

READING SECTION

PART 5

NO.	ANSWER A B C D
101	Ⓐ Ⓑ Ⓒ Ⓓ
102	Ⓐ Ⓑ Ⓒ Ⓓ
103	Ⓐ Ⓑ Ⓒ Ⓓ
104	Ⓐ Ⓑ Ⓒ Ⓓ
105	Ⓐ Ⓑ Ⓒ Ⓓ
106	Ⓐ Ⓑ Ⓒ Ⓓ
107	Ⓐ Ⓑ Ⓒ Ⓓ
108	Ⓐ Ⓑ Ⓒ Ⓓ
109	Ⓐ Ⓑ Ⓒ Ⓓ
110	Ⓐ Ⓑ Ⓒ Ⓓ

NO.	ANSWER A B C D
111	Ⓐ Ⓑ Ⓒ Ⓓ
112	Ⓐ Ⓑ Ⓒ Ⓓ
113	Ⓐ Ⓑ Ⓒ Ⓓ
114	Ⓐ Ⓑ Ⓒ Ⓓ
115	Ⓐ Ⓑ Ⓒ Ⓓ
116	Ⓐ Ⓑ Ⓒ Ⓓ
117	Ⓐ Ⓑ Ⓒ Ⓓ
118	Ⓐ Ⓑ Ⓒ Ⓓ
119	Ⓐ Ⓑ Ⓒ Ⓓ
120	Ⓐ Ⓑ Ⓒ Ⓓ

PART 6

NO.	ANSWER A B C D
131	Ⓐ Ⓑ Ⓒ Ⓓ
132	Ⓐ Ⓑ Ⓒ Ⓓ
133	Ⓐ Ⓑ Ⓒ Ⓓ
134	Ⓐ Ⓑ Ⓒ Ⓓ
135	Ⓐ Ⓑ Ⓒ Ⓓ
136	Ⓐ Ⓑ Ⓒ Ⓓ
137	Ⓐ Ⓑ Ⓒ Ⓓ
138	Ⓐ Ⓑ Ⓒ Ⓓ
139	Ⓐ Ⓑ Ⓒ Ⓓ
140	Ⓐ Ⓑ Ⓒ Ⓓ

NO.	ANSWER A B C D
141	Ⓐ Ⓑ Ⓒ Ⓓ
142	Ⓐ Ⓑ Ⓒ Ⓓ
143	Ⓐ Ⓑ Ⓒ Ⓓ
144	Ⓐ Ⓑ Ⓒ Ⓓ
145	Ⓐ Ⓑ Ⓒ Ⓓ
146	Ⓐ Ⓑ Ⓒ Ⓓ
147	Ⓐ Ⓑ Ⓒ Ⓓ
148	Ⓐ Ⓑ Ⓒ Ⓓ
149	Ⓐ Ⓑ Ⓒ Ⓓ
150	Ⓐ Ⓑ Ⓒ Ⓓ

PART 7

NO.	ANSWER A B C D
151	Ⓐ Ⓑ Ⓒ Ⓓ
152	Ⓐ Ⓑ Ⓒ Ⓓ
153	Ⓐ Ⓑ Ⓒ Ⓓ
154	Ⓐ Ⓑ Ⓒ Ⓓ
155	Ⓐ Ⓑ Ⓒ Ⓓ
156	Ⓐ Ⓑ Ⓒ Ⓓ
157	Ⓐ Ⓑ Ⓒ Ⓓ
158	Ⓐ Ⓑ Ⓒ Ⓓ
159	Ⓐ Ⓑ Ⓒ Ⓓ
160	Ⓐ Ⓑ Ⓒ Ⓓ

NO.	ANSWER A B C D
161	Ⓐ Ⓑ Ⓒ Ⓓ
162	Ⓐ Ⓑ Ⓒ Ⓓ
163	Ⓐ Ⓑ Ⓒ Ⓓ
164	Ⓐ Ⓑ Ⓒ Ⓓ
165	Ⓐ Ⓑ Ⓒ Ⓓ
166	Ⓐ Ⓑ Ⓒ Ⓓ
167	Ⓐ Ⓑ Ⓒ Ⓓ
168	Ⓐ Ⓑ Ⓒ Ⓓ
169	Ⓐ Ⓑ Ⓒ Ⓓ
170	Ⓐ Ⓑ Ⓒ Ⓓ

NO.	ANSWER A B C D
171	Ⓐ Ⓑ Ⓒ Ⓓ
172	Ⓐ Ⓑ Ⓒ Ⓓ
173	Ⓐ Ⓑ Ⓒ Ⓓ
174	Ⓐ Ⓑ Ⓒ Ⓓ
175	Ⓐ Ⓑ Ⓒ Ⓓ
176	Ⓐ Ⓑ Ⓒ Ⓓ
177	Ⓐ Ⓑ Ⓒ Ⓓ
178	Ⓐ Ⓑ Ⓒ Ⓓ
179	Ⓐ Ⓑ Ⓒ Ⓓ
180	Ⓐ Ⓑ Ⓒ Ⓓ

NO.	ANSWER A B C D
181	Ⓐ Ⓑ Ⓒ Ⓓ
182	Ⓐ Ⓑ Ⓒ Ⓓ
183	Ⓐ Ⓑ Ⓒ Ⓓ
184	Ⓐ Ⓑ Ⓒ Ⓓ
185	Ⓐ Ⓑ Ⓒ Ⓓ
186	Ⓐ Ⓑ Ⓒ Ⓓ
187	Ⓐ Ⓑ Ⓒ Ⓓ
188	Ⓐ Ⓑ Ⓒ Ⓓ
189	Ⓐ Ⓑ Ⓒ Ⓓ
190	Ⓐ Ⓑ Ⓒ Ⓓ

NO.	ANSWER A B C D
191	Ⓐ Ⓑ Ⓒ Ⓓ
192	Ⓐ Ⓑ Ⓒ Ⓓ
193	Ⓐ Ⓑ Ⓒ Ⓓ
194	Ⓐ Ⓑ Ⓒ Ⓓ
195	Ⓐ Ⓑ Ⓒ Ⓓ
196	Ⓐ Ⓑ Ⓒ Ⓓ
197	Ⓐ Ⓑ Ⓒ Ⓓ
198	Ⓐ Ⓑ Ⓒ Ⓓ
199	Ⓐ Ⓑ Ⓒ Ⓓ
200	Ⓐ Ⓑ Ⓒ Ⓓ